Routledge Revivals

The Polish Economy

Originally published in 1985, this study by Polish authors was the first in the English language to cover Poland's economic development from 1900 to the mid-1980s and it was published at a time when the Polish economy was in crisis and before the fall of the Iron Curtain. The book presents a detailed and penetrating analysis of the Polish economy. It charts the various stages of Poland's development from the rule of the Three Black Eagles – Russia, Austria and Prussia, to the effects of the Great Depression, through Nazi occupation to the inflation and economic decline of the late-twentieth century. For each period, besides economic and monetary factors, the authors survey aspects of the effects of economic growth on social mobility and career perception, public health education and technology, backed up with comprehensive statistical data.

The Polish Economy

In the Twentieth Century

Zbigniew Landau and Jerzy Tomaszewski.
Translated by Wojciech Roszkowski.

Routledge
Taylor & Francis Group
ROUTLEDGE REVIVALS

First published in 1985 by Croom Helm Ltd.

This edition first published in 2026 by Routledge
4 Park Square, Milton Park, Abingdon, Oxon, OX14 4RN
and by Routledge
605 Third Avenue, New York, NY 10158.

Routledge is an imprint of the Taylor & Francis Group, an informa business

ISBN 13: 978-1-041-12865-6 (hbk)
ISBN 13: 978-1-003-66700-1 (ebk)
ISBN 13: 978-1-041-12869-4 (pbk)
Book DOI 10.4324/9781003667001

THE POLISH ECONOMY In the Twentieth Century

Zbigniew Landau and Jerzy Tomaszewski

Translated by Wojciech Roszkowski

CROOM HELM
London & Sydney

Croom Helm Ltd, Provident House, Burrell Row,
Beckenham, Kent BR3 1AT

Croom Helm Australia Pty Ltd, First Floor,
139 King Street, Sydney, NSW 2001, Australia

Landau, Zbigniew
The Polish economy.–(Croom Helm series on the contemporary economic history of Europe)
1. Poland–Economic conditions–20th century
I. Title II. Tomaszewski Jerzy
330.9438'05 HC337.P7

ISBN 0-7099-1607-8

Printed and bound in Great Britain
by Billing & Sons Limited, Worcester.

CONTENTS

EDITOR'S INTRODUCTION

Derek H. Aldcroft

By comparison with the nineteenth century, the twentieth has been very much more turbulent, both economically and politically. Two world wars and a great depression are sufficient to substantiate this claim without invoking the problems of more recent times. Yet despite these setbacks Europe's economic performance in the present century has been very much better than anything recorded in the historical past, thanks largely to the super-boom conditions following the post-Second World War reconstruction period. Thus, in the period 1946-75, or 1950-73, the annual increase in total European GNP per capita was 4.8 and 4.5 per cent respectively, as against a compound rate of just under 1 per cent in the nineteenth century (1800-1913) and the same during the troubled years between 1913-50. As Bairoch points out, within a generation or so European per capita income rose slightly more than in the previous 150 years (1947-75 by 250 per cent, 1800-1948 by 225 per cent) and, on rough estimates for the half century before 1800, by about as much as in the preceding two centuries. (1)

The dynamic growth and relative stability of the 1950s and 1960s may however belie the natural order of things as the events of the later 1970s and early 1980s demonstrate. Certainly it would seem unlikely that the European economy, or the world economy for that matter, will see a lasting return to the relatively stable conditions of the nineteenth century. No doubt the experience of the present century can easily lead to an exaggerated idea about the stability of the previous one. Nevertheless, one may justifiably claim that for much of the nineteenth century there was a degree of harmony in the economic development of the major powers and between the metropolitan economies and the periphery which has been noticeably absent since 1914. Indeed, one of the reasons for the apparent success of the gold standard post-1870, despite the aura of stability it allegedly shed, was the absence of serious external disturbances and imbalance in development among the major participating powers. As Triffin writes:

> The residual harmonization of national monetary and credit policies depended far less on ex post corrective action, requiring an extreme flexibility, downward as well as upward, of national price and wage levels, than on an ex ante avoidance of substantial disparities in cost competitiveness and the monetary policies that would allow them to develop. (2)

Whatever the reasons for the absence of serious economic and political conflict, the fact remains that through to 1914 international development and political relations, though subject to strains of a minor nature from time to time, were never exposed to internal and external shocks of the magnitude experienced in the twentieth century. Not surprisingly therefore, the First World War rudely shattered the liberal tranquillity of the later nineteenth and early twentieth centuries. At the time few people realised that it was going to be a lengthy war and, even more important, fewer still had any conception of the enormous impact it would have on economic and social relationships. Moreover, there was a general feeling, readily accepted in establishment circles, that following the period of hostilities it would be possible to resume where one had left off - in short, to recreate the conditions of the pre-war era.

For obvious reasons this was clearly an impossible task, though for nearly a decade statesmen strove to get back to what they regarded as 'normalcy', or the natural order of things. In itself this was one of the profound mistakes of the first post-war decade since it should have been clear, even at that time, that the war and post-war clearing-up operations had undermined Europe's former equipoise and sapped her strength to a point where the economic system had become very sensitive to external shocks. The map of Europe had been rewritten under the political settlements following the war and this further weakened the economic viability of the Continent and left a dangerous political vacuum in its wake. Moreover, it was not only in the economic sphere that Europe's strength had been reduced; in political and social terms the European continent was seriously weakened and many countries in the early post-war years were in a state of social ferment and upheaval. (3)

Generally speaking, Europe's economic and political fragility were ignored in the 1920s, probably more out of ignorance than intent. In their efforts to resurrect the pre-war system statesmen believed they were providing a viable solution to the problems of the day, and the fact that Europe shared in the prosperity of the later 1920s seemed to vindicate their judgement. But the post-war problems - war debts, external imbalances, currency issues, structural distortions and the like - defied solutions along traditional lines. The most notable of these was the attempt to restore a semblance of the gold standard in the belief that it had been responsible for the former stability. The upshot was a set of haphazard and inconsistent currency stabilisation policies which took no account of the changes in relative costs and prices among countries since 1914. Consequently, despite the apparent prosperity of the latter half of the decade, Europe remained in a state of unstable equilibrium, and therefore vulnerable to any external shocks. The collapse of US foreign lending from the middle of 1928 and the subsequent downturn of the American economy a year later exposed the weaknesses of the European economy. The structural supports were too weak to withstand violent shocks and so the edifice disintegrated.

That the years 1929-32/3 experienced one of the worst depressions and financial crises in history is not altogether surprising given the convergence of many unfavourable forces at that point in time. Moreover, the fact that a cyclical downturn occurred against the backdrop of structural disequilibrium only served to exacerbate the problem, while the inherent weakness of certain financial institutions in Europe and the United States led to extreme instability. The intensity of the crisis varied a great deal but few countries, apart from the USSR, were unaffected. The action of governments tended to aggravate rather than ease the situation. Such policies included expenditure cuts, monetary contraction, the abandonment of the gold standard and protective measures designed to insulate domestic economies from external events.

In effect these policies, while sometimes affording temporary relief to hard-pressed countries, in the end led to income destruction rather than income creation. When recovery finally set in in the winter of 1932/3 it owed little to policy contributions, though subsequently some Western governments did attempt more ambitious programmes of stimulation, while many of the poorer Eastern European countries adopted autarchic policies in an effort to push forward industrialisation. Apart from some notable exceptions, Germany and Sweden in particular, recovery from the slump, especially in terms of employment generation, was slow and patchy and even at the peak of the upswing in 1937 many countries were still operating below their resource capacity. A combination of weak real growth forces and structural imbalances in development would no doubt have ensured a continuation of resource under-utilisation had not rearmament and the outbreak of war served to close the gap.

Thus, by the eve of the Second World War Europe as a whole was in a much weaker state economically than it had been in 1914, with her shares of world income and trade notably reduced. Worse still, she emerged from the second war in 1945 in a more prostrate condition than in 1918, with output levels well down on those of pre-war. In terms of the loss of life, physical destruction and decline in living standards Europe's position was much worse than after the First World War. On the other hand, recovery from wartime destruction was stronger and more secure than in the previous case. In part this can be attributed to the fact that in the reconstruction phase of the later 1940s some of the mistakes and blunders of the earlier experience were avoided. Inflation, for example, was contained more readily between 1939 and 1945 and the violent inflations of the early 1920s were not for the most part perpetuated after the Second World War. With the exception of Berlin, the map of Europe was divided much more cleanly and neatly than after 1918. Though it resulted in two ideological power blocks, the East and the West, it did nevertheless dispose of the power vacuum in Central/East Europe which had been a source of friction and contention in the inter-war years. Moreover, the fact that each block was dominated or backed by a wealthy and rival superpower meant that support was forthcoming for the satellite countries. The vanquished powers were not, with the exception of East Germany, burdened by unreasonable exactions which had been the cause of so much bitterness and squabbling during the 1920s. Finally, governments no longer hankered after the 'halcyon' pre-war days, not surprisingly - given the rugged conditions of the 1930s. This time it was to be planning for the future which occupied their attention, and which found expression in the commitment to maintain full employment and all that that entailed in terms of growth and stability, together with a conscious desire to build upon the earlier social welfare foundations. In wider perspective, the new initiatives found positive expression in terms of a readiness to co-operate internationally, particularly in trade and monetary matters. The liberal American aid programme for the West in the later 1940s was a concrete manifestation of this new approach.

Thus despite the enormity of the reconstruction task facing Europe at the end of the war, the recovery effort, after some initial difficulties, was both strong and sustained, and by the early 1950s Europe had reached a point where she could look to the future with some confidence. During the next two decades or so virtually every European country, in keeping with the buoyant conditions in the world economy as a whole, expanded very much more rapidly than in the past. This was the super-growth phase during which Europe regained a large part of the relative losses incurred between 1914 and 1945. The Eastern block countries forged ahead the most rapidly under their planned regimes, while the Western democracies achieved their success under mixed enterprise systems with varying degrees of market freedom. In both cases the state played a far more important role than hitherto, and neither system could be said to be without its problems. The planning mechanism in Eastern Europe never functioned as smoothly as originally anticipated by its proponents, and in due course most of the socialist countries were forced to make modifications to their systems of control. Similarly, the semi-market systems of the West did not always produce the right results so that governments were obliged to intervene to an increasing extent. One of the major problems encountered by the demand-managed economies of the West was that of trying to achieve a series of basically incompatible objectives simultaneously - namely full employment, price stability, growth and stability and external equilibrium. Given the limited policy weapons available to governments this proved an impossible task to accomplish in most cases, though West Germany managed to achieve the seemingly impossible for much of the period.

Although these incompatible objectives proved elusive *in toto*, there was, throughout most of the period to the early 1970s, little cause for serious alarm. It is true that there were minor lapses from full employment; fluctuations still occurred but they were very moderate and took the form of growth cycles; some countries experienced periodic balance of payments problems; while prices generally rose continuously though at fairly modest annual rates. But such lapses could readily be accommodated, even with the limited policy choices, within an economic system that was growing rapidly. And there was some consolation from the fact that the planned socialist economies were not immune from some of these problems, especially later on in the period. By the later 1960s, despite some warning signs that conditions might be deteriorating, it seemed that Europe had entered a phase of perpetual prosperity not dissimilar to the one the Americans had conceived in the 1920s. Unfortunately, as in the earlier case, this illusion was to be rudely shattered in the first half of the 1970s. The super-growth of the post-war period culminated in the somewhat feverish and speculative boom of 1972-3. By the following year the growth trend had been reversed, the old business cycle had reappeared and most countries were experiencing inflation at higher rates than at any time in the past half-century. From that time onwards, according to Samuel Brittan, 'Everything seems to have gone sour and we have had slower growth, rising unemployment, faster inflation, creeping trade restrictions and all the symptoms of stagflation.'(4) In fact, compared with the relatively placid and successful decades of the 1950s and 1960s, the later 1970s and early 1980s have been extremely turbulent, reminiscent in some respects of the inter-war years.

It should of course be stressed that by comparison with the inter-war years or even with the nineteenth century, economic growth has been quite respectable since the sharp boom and contraction in the first half of the 1970s. It only appears poor in relation to the rapid growth between 1950 and 1973 and the question arises as to whether this period should be regarded as somewhat abnormal with the shift to a lower growth profile in the 1970s being the inevitable consequence of long-term forces involving some reversal of the special growth promoting factors of the previous decades. In effect this would imply some weakening of real growth forces in the 1970s which was aggravated by specific factors, for example energy crises and policy variables.

The most disturbing feature of this later period

was not simply that growth slowed down but that it became more erratic, with longer recessionary periods involving absolute contractions in output, and that it was accompanied by mounting unemployment and high inflation. Traditional Keynesian demand management policies were unable to cope with these problems and, in an effort to deal with them, particularly inflation, governments resorted to ultradefensive policies and monetary control. These were not very successful either since the need for social and political compromise in policy-making meant that they were not applied rigorously enough to eradicate inflation, yet at the same time their influence was sufficiently strong to dampen the rate of growth thereby exacerbating unemployment. In other words, economic management is faced with an awkward policy dilemma in the prevailing situation of high unemployment and rapid inflation. Policy action to deal with either one tends to make the other worse, while the constraint of the political consensus produces an uneasy compromise in an effort to 'minimise macroeconomic misery'. (5) Rostow has neatly summarised the constraints involved in this context:

> Taxes, public expenditure, interest rates, and the supply of money are not determined antiseptically by men free to move economies along a Phillips curve to an optimum trade-off between the rate of unemployment and the rate of inflation. Fiscal and monetary policy are, inevitably, living parts of the democratic political process. (6)

Whether the current problems of contemporary Western capitalism or the difficulties associated with the planning mechanisms of the socialist countries of Eastern Europe are amenable to solutions remains to be seen. It is not, for the most part, the purpose of the volumes in this series to speculate about the future. The series is designed to provide clear and balanced surveys of the economic development and problems of individual European countries from the end of the First World War through to the present, against the background of the general economic and political trends of the time. Though most European countries have shared a common experience for much of the period, it is none the less true that there has been considerable variation among countries in the rate of development and the manner in which they have sought to regulate and control their economies. The problems encountered have also varied widely, in part reflecting disparities in levels of development. While most European countries had, by the end of the First World War, achieved some industrialisation and made the initial breakthrough into modern economic growth, nevertheless there existed a wide gulf between the richer and poorer nations. At the beginning of the period the most advanced region was north-west Europe including Scandinavia and as one moved east and south so the level of per capita income relative to the European average declined. In some cases, notably Bulgaria, Yugoslavia and Portugal, income levels were barely half the European average. The gap has narrowed over time but the general pattern remains basically the same. Between 1913 and 1973 most of the poorer countries in the east and south (apart from Spain) raised their real per capita income levels relative to the European average, with most of the improvement taking place after 1950. Even so, by 1973 most of them, with the exception of Czechoslovakia, still fell below the European average, ranging from 9-15 per cent in the case of the USSR, Hungary, Greece, Bulgaria and Poland, to as much as 35-45 per cent in Spain, Portugal, Romania and Yugoslavia. Italy and Ireland also recorded per capita income levels some way below the European average. (7)

The modern history of Poland is probably one of the most tragic of all European countries. Partitioned by three powers at the end of the eighteenth century Poland did not emerge reunited until after the First World War, a conflict which badly damaged the country and left it in a weak state to face the task of welding together three highly differentiated territories whose development had in the past been subordinated to the political, military and economic interests of the dominating powers. In the immediate post-war years the new Polish state was confronted with a whole host of complex problems - reconstruction,severe shortages of goods and foreign exchange, high unemployment, social unrest, border conflicts and inflation to name but a few; it is not surprising therefore that recovery from the wartime ravages was slow and painful so that even by the end of the 1920s industrial output was still only 91 per cent of the 1913 level.

Being primarily an agrarian country, Poland was badly hit by the economic depression of the early 1930s when farm prices fell dramatically. In fact the depression was longer and deeper than in almost any other country, with recovery being delayed by the orthodox financial policies of the government. It was not until the later 1930s that a burst of activity occurred, assisted in part by an increase in public investment and an extension of the state's role in economic affairs which laid the basis for the socialised economy of the post-war period. Even so, by the end of the decade industrial output had barely reached the pre-war level, while in per capita terms it was some 13-15 per cent below the 1913 base. Thus Poland had little to show economically for 20 years of independent statehood.

Poland's fate was sealed yet again during the Second World War. It can only be described as a holocaust since the Nazi occupation and administration virtually devastated the country. Some six million Poles or Polish Jews perished in the Nazi terror, equivalent to 22.2 per cent of the pre-war population. But if one also takes into account the people deported as forced labour, those who suffered resettlement or displacement and the survivors of the concentration camps, then at least 40 per cent of the population was directly affected by the Nazi regime. By comparison military casualties were very small. Population losses apart, Nazi policies caused extreme devastation and exploitation of Poland's resource base, and created severe destitution and poverty among the population. Poland probably suffered more than any other country in the Second World War, and total destruction was far greater than in the previous conflict. Between 1939 and 1945 loss or damage accounted for 38 per cent of Poland's national property as against 10 per cent in the First World War.

It speaks much for the resilience of the Polish people that the country achieved a remarkably rapid recovery in the later 1940s under the new socialist republic. This laid the foundations for a period of unprecedented growth in subsequent decades, which was accompanied by a gradual transformation of the economy towards an industrial society. This post-war success has not, however, been achieved without problems. The task of running a socialised economy has proved no easier than that of managing a capitalist one, a point borne out by the frequent debates about the nature and format of economic policy, and by the fact that Poland has not escaped some of the problems, notably inflation and more recently a decline in economic activity, experienced by her counterparts in the West. Moreover, despite the rapid economic progress made over the past 30 years, it is somewhat sad to record that the living standards of the population have not advanced commensurately. This, of course, fits in with the socialist ethos of diverting a large share of resources to investment to ensure future productive potential, but one cannot help feeling that the Polish population deserves a better deal after so many years of hardship suffered in the past.

NOTES

1. P. Bairoch; 'Europe's Gross National Product: 1800-1975', The Journal of European Economic History, 5 (Fall 1976), pp. 298-9.

2. R. Triffin, Our International Monetary System: Yesterday, Today and Tomorrow (1968, New York), p.14; see also D.H. Aldcroft, From Versailles to Wall Street, 1919-1929 (1977), pp. 162-4. Some of the costs of the gold standard system may however have been borne by the countries of the periphery, for example Latin America.

3. See P.N. Stearns, European Society in Upheaval (1967).

4. Financial Times, 14 February 1980.

5. J.O.N. Perkins, The Macroeconomic Mix to Stop Stagflation (1980).

6. W.W. Rostow, Getting From Here to There (1979).

7. See Bairoch, 'Europe's Gross National Product', pp. 297, 307.

CHAPTER ONE

POLAND UNDER THE RULE OF THREE BLACK EAGLES

In the second half of the eighteenth century there were clear signs of an economic and political revival in Poland. Growing military strength, increasingly centralised power and economic recovery posed a threat to the three powers adjacent to Poland - Austria, Prussia and Russia. As a means of neutralising this threat, the three subsequent treaties of 1772, 1793 and 1795 partitioned Poland's territories among the above-mentioned monarchies: Poland had ceased to exist as a sovereign state.

Having defeated the Prussian army in October 1806, French troops entered Poland's former territories but despite Polish hopes Napoleon did not attempt the reconstruction of an independent statehood. In 1807 he did, however, create the Duchy of Warsaw, which included at first part of the territory taken by Prussia and later, also, some lands previously incorporated by Austria. In 1815 the Congress of Vienna brought a new division of Polish territories and the frontiers established then were to survive - only slightly modified - until the First World War. Most of the liquidated Duchy of Warsaw was incorporated into the Russian Empire as an autonomous Kingdom of Poland. Its autonomy was limited after the November Uprising of 1831 and finally suppressed after the January Uprising of 1863.

The partitioning of Poland checked her economic development and restricted the reforms that had begun. Soon the three parts of the Polish territories became integrated with the political and economic systems of the partitioning powers. In the nineteenth century agrarian reforms were carried out in all the three monarchies. Serfdom was abolished and peasants were given property rights to their plots of land. This process was completed in the Austrian part of Poland in 1848, in the Prussian part in 1850 and in the Russian part of Poland in 1864. Major industrial centres developed in Upper Silesia and in some areas of the Russian partition (the Łódź region - textiles; the Dąbrowskie region - mining and heavy industry; Warsaw - engineering, food-processing and textiles, and Białystok - textiles). The least industrialised was Austrian Galicia (which also included the earliest petroleum mining region in the world).

The economy of each part of the Polish territories developed in close connection with the markets of the partitioning powers. Poland was cut by political and economic frontiers and customs barriers made it impossible to maintain economic unity. Each partition was subject to different legislation. Disparity in the laws concerning agrarian reform was especially important as it intensified the already existing regional differences in the agricultural structure. The various economic policies of the partitioning monarchies created differentiated conditions for industrial and farming activities. As a result on the eve of the twentieth century Polish industry, farming, trade, transportation and finance were considered only as components of the economic systems of Austria-Hungary, Germany and Russia. None of the partitions was a self-contained economic body. This is clearly illustrated by the trade exchange figures for the Polish territories in the years directly before the First World War, as shown in Tables 1.1 and 1.2.

Table 1.1 shows that the Kingdom of Poland exported its products almost exclusively to the Russian Empire; its textile industry in particular depended overwhelmingly on eastern markets. The figures for imported products in Table 1.1 also demonstrate a similarly close interrelationship between the Kingdom of Poland and Russia.

Protected from foreign competition by tariffs, industry in the Congress Kingdom of Poland found advantageous markets in Russia. In the course of time, due to competition from companies in other parts of the tsar's immense empire, there developed a certain division of labour. Most of the textile production from the Polish territories was exported eastwards, while raw materials and other textiles were imported from Russia. Similarly, heavy industry exported some of its products to Russia and imported iron ore. On the other hand food-processing industries (mainly sugar-mills and distilleries at first) sold their products at home.

Agricultural production in the Kingdom of Poland

Table 1.1: Trade Balance of the Kingdom of Poland before 1914

Goods	Exports			Imports		
	Total roubles (millions)	To Russia: roubles (millions)	%	Total roubles (millions)	To Russia: roubles (millions)	%
Agriculture & foodstuffs	24.4	2.1	8.6	50.0	40.6	81.2
Raw materials	13.6	1.8	13.2	175.2	72.1	41.2
Industrial goods	431.1	421.9	97.9	258.2	170.6	66.1
of which:						
Textiles	302.6	302.6	100.0	101.6	83.9	82.6
Total	469.1	425.8	90.8	483.4	283.3	58.6

Source: H. Tennenbaum, Bilans handlowy Królestwa Polskiego, (Warsaw, 1916) pp. 392-5.

faced less favourable conditions. Russia was an agricultural country and farming in the Polish territories had to contend with relatively poorer natural conditions than did competitors from other regions. Low prices diminished capital returns from investments in machinery and fertilisers. Progress in modern farming techniques was much slower than in Western Europe. At the same time large estates still had access to relatively cheap manpower. Numerous small peasant farms could not support their owners and their families. There was thus a reserve of manpower which found employment in seasonal farm works or in industry.

Farming in the Congress Kingdom was principally geared to the country's home market; even then it could not satisfy demand in all areas of production and so certain imports from Russia were necessary. These imports grew, while farming production lagged behind increases in both population and demand.

Greater Poland and Pomerania - incorporated as a result of partitions to Prussia - disposed of surplus agricultural production by exporting it to other parts of the German state or abroad. Industrial goods were imported here from Upper Silesia and from other parts of the German Reich and only occasionally from the Russian partition. Greater Poland and Pomerania also supplied the German market with some food-processing products, their sugar-refining and alcohol-distilling industries being particularly well developed.

Upper Silesia was a large mining centre where coal was mined along with zinc and lead ores. With these raw materials it supplied not only local industry but also customers in some other regions of the Reich, and Eastern Germany in particular. Products of the Silesian heavy industry were mainly sold in Germany and much less frequently exported to the Russian or Austrian partition. What is more, these exports diminished as a result of Russian and Austro-Hungarian policies of market protection.

Agriculture in Greater Poland and Pomerania found more favourable conditions within the economic system of the German Reich. The manner in which agrarian reforms were carried out here made it possible to maintain estates and to create large peasant farms. Most of the smaller peasant holdings were liquidated. Large estates and peasant farms could easily sell their products in the German industrial centres. Protective tariff policies maintained high prices which stimulated more intensive production.

It was the aim of German agricultural policy to

Table 1.2: Trade Balance of the Prussian Partition and Upper Silesia before 1914 (DM millions)

Direction	Exports in million DM	(%)	Imports in million DM	(%)
Germany (Outside Prussian partition and Upper Silesia)	1,238.2	67.7	781.9	65.9
Galicia and Kingdom of Poland	192.8	10.5	103.7	8.7
West Prussian ports	182.3	10.0	174.8	14.8
Abroad (without other partitions)	216.7	11.8	125.8	10.6
Total	1,830.0	100.0	1,186.2	100.0

Source: A. Rose, Bilans handlowy ziem b. dzielnicy pruskiej (Warsaw, 1920), pp. 664-5.

encourage German colonisation of land bought from Polish landowners. Colonists received credit aid and other facilities so that they could economically dominate their Polish neighbours. At the same time administrative regulations (such as building licences) created obstacles to the formation of new Polish farms. Under these circumstances Polish landowners and the more affluent peasants established a network of co-operative institutions to counteract the policy of Germanisation. All this led to an effective economic resistance; the German authorities therefore passed a bill which provided for the expropriation of large estates in order to parcel them out among German colonists.

In Greater Poland and Pomerania there developed rather scattered and mostly small-to medium-sized industrial plants connected with agriculture, such as food-processing factories, brickyards or workshops producing and repairing farm implements.

Trade balance figures associated with the Austrian partition of that time are not available. However, fragmentary data show beyond doubt that Galicia was closely connected with other parts of Austria-Hungary; trade with Germany was also of a certain importance. Home production attempted to satisfy the demand for foodstuffs, but even allowing for the low living standards of its population the Austrian partition was not self-sufficient in food. Apart from agriculture there was also some mining (petroleum and salt as well as certain quantities of coal). Industrial activity was limited; a few large enterprises were accompanied by numerous but technically primitive handicraft workshops, both in the country and in the towns.

From an economic point of view the Austrian partition was in many respects the least favourable *vis à vis* the other Polish territories. Agrarian reforms were conducive to maintaining the historically-formed land property distribution. Apart from a few large estates there existed a vast number of tiny peasant holdings. The splitting up of farm units was organised on a greater scale than elsewhere in the Polish territories.

All through the nineteenth and at the beginning of the twentieth century Galician agriculture experienced adverse conditions of development. The main agricultural centres of the Habsburg monarchy were situated in Hungary and Moravia, while the Austrian part of Poland was on the periphery of the state, behind mountains which separated it from the major market. Local sales were limited in view of the backward state of industry. Agricultural prices were low and failed to attract worthwhile investment. The division of peasant property and a lack of jobs outside agriculture made manpower very cheap and as a consequence checked technical progress in farming.

Galician industry had a limited home market and faced competition from Czech and Austrian goods. In the first half of the nineteenth century it also had to overcome administrative restraints. As a result it was backward and not until the beginning of the twentieth century were signs of industrial improvement evident.

All this made the Galician standard of living very low. The term 'Galician poverty' became widely used; it was even said that an average inhabitant of Galicia ate for half a man and worked for a quarter of a human being. In the second half of the nineteenth century poor country people and some of the townsfolk emigrated in search of work.

The divisions in the separate economies of the Polish territories and their increasing involvement with the partitioning powers were reflected in the network of railway lines which were built in the 1840s. Galicia had eight connections with Austria-Hungary and only two with the railway system of the Kingdom of Poland. More than 50 Austrian and German lines went up to the frontier but only ten of them extended further on to Russia. (1) The different economic structure of each partition made the density of railway networks vary; a relatively low density of railways in the Congress Kingdom was connected with Russian military policy which aimed at preventing development of connections in the border areas. Moreover, the Russian partition had - like all Russia - tracks of a wider gauge than was used in Germany, Austria-Hungary and the rest of Europe.

The economic life of the Polish territories tended to be dominated by geographical location; they were situated on the peripheries of the three partitioning powers. Main centres of decision-making were far away and this had negative consequences in terms of economic policy. The Polish territories were treated as appendices to the three imperial systems and all local initiatives faced distrust in Berlin, Petersburg and Vienna.

Under these circumstances, only in the Russian partition did independent Polish financial groups come into being. This was additionally accelerated by the fact that capital formation in the Kingdom of Poland slightly preceded other areas within the Russian Empire. Thus the Russian partition of Poland in the nineteenth century, saw a gradual development of powerful business circles which had their origins from among the bourgeoisie or aristocracy.

Social relations in other partitions where Polish capitalists played a lesser role developed in a different way. In Greater Poland and Pomerania the policy of Germanisation produced to a certain degree two independent economic environments: the Polish and the German. The latter enjoyed the support of the authorities who in turn put various obstacles in the way of Polish enterprises.

In Upper Silesia mining developed above all on the large estates belonging to the German aristocracy: there was thus no room for Polish capital and almost all the Polish population belonged to the plebeian groups - workers and peasants.

The inability to exploit and develop indigenous capital was the main reason why the predominant role in the Austrian partition was also played by foreign centres of economic decision. Home capital managed to start only small enterprises of local importance.

Although industrial expansion, albeit at varying rates, took place in all the Polish territories, together with agricultural reforms and changes, it was not enough to absorb the growing number of the population seeking work and pay. Rough data concerning demographic movements in the Polish territories are included in Table 1.3.

Comparisons of data shown in Table 1.3 with later evidence referring to the population of Poland are not easy to make due to the fact that administrative divisions before 1914 differed considerably from the political frontiers set up after the First World War. For instance Upper Silesia (the Opole Region) and Teschen Silesia were divided and certain areas found themselves within the newly constituted Poland. According to the Polish Central Statistical Office, the territory of the future Second Polish Republic was inhabited in 1870 by 16.9 million people, while in 1900 a figure of 25.1 million people is given. (2)

An excess of population unable to find employment gave rise to emigration, beginning around the middle of the nineteenth century. (3) The turn of the twentieth century saw a particularly rapid increase in emigration, mostly in Galicia.

Emigration was thus set in motion by the economic backwardness and bleak prospects of the Austrian partition. People who could not make their living in the overmanned agricultural sector or gain

Table 1.3: Population of the Polish Territories in the Years 1870 - 1910 (thousands)

Area	1870	1890	1900	1910
In Russia: Kingdom of Poland	6,079	8,258	10,000	12,129
In Austria-Hungary:				
Galicia	5,492	6,608	7,316	8,026
Teschen Silesia	233a	300	369	435
In Germany:				
Greater Poland	1,582b	1,753	1,886	2,100
Pomerania	1,312b	1,434	1,561	1,704
Opole Region	1,310b	1,578	1,868	2,208

Note: a. 1869; b. 1871.

Source: A Krzyżanowski, K.Kumaniecki, Statystyka Polski. Handbuch der polnischen Statistik. Tableau statistique de la Pologne (Cracow, 1915), pp. 6-7.

employment in industry had to seek work abroad. Permanent emigration went especially overseas, mainly to America. Roughly one million people went abroad in the years 1870-1910. In the years 1899-1910 and 1912-13 around 490,000 Poles emigrated to the United States along with 170,000 Ukrainians. A second group of emigrants included inhabitants of small towns - principally Jews. According to rough estimates 174,000 Jews emigrated from Galicia to America from 1900 to 1914.

Peasant emigration from Galicia went also towards Canada (especially Ukrainians), Brazil and Argentina. Poor peasants from western Galicia also left for Teschen Silesian factories and mines.

Still more numerous was seasonal agricultural emigration. Seasonal workers wandered from Galicia to the Kingdom of Poland, where wages were higher, and to Germany. Shortly before the First World War large numbers of seasonal emigrants went to Germany, to work mostly in farming: in 1905, for example, a total of 106,000, and in 1912, 330,000. The number of emigrants seeking work in other countries was lower.

Emigration from Galicia moderated its overpopulation. This was particularly important in the most densely populated areas. At the same time emigration supplied the country with money as seasonal emigrants brought their earnings back home. Those who left for overseas sent savings to their families; others who returned after many years could sometimes afford to buy land.

Emigration from the Russian partition was less pronounced. At the beginning of the twentieth century most of the emigrants from this part of Poland went to the United States. Some of the intelligentsia were also leaving for Russia, not being able to find work in their homeland. By the First World War the number of Poles living in Russia proper had reached 600,000.

On the other hand seasonal emigrants, coming mostly from western districts of the Congress Kingdom, went in great numbers to Germany.

Migrations in the Prussian partition were different. Overseas emigration, quite considerable in the 1870s, decreased in the first decade of the twentieth century to about 4,000 people per annum. At the same time emigration to Western Germany grew. Before 1914 the number of Poles living there probably reached about half a million people. Most of them worked in mines and factories. Around 100,000 Poles were employed in Berlin and its surroundings.

Polish emigration from the Prussian partition was only a part of the migration taking place in the eastern regions of the Reich. According to data of 1907 Berlin and Brandenburg were inhabited by 859,000 people born in eastern provinces; Westphalia and Ruhrland by 492,000. Germans moved willingly to the economically advanced regions of the Reich, whereas the emigration of Poles was checked by feelings of cultural and language alienation. The westward movement of Germans called Ostflucht could not be restrained by the German government's policies.

These migrations did not lead to any strengthening of the existing economic links between individual partitions. Yet despite the hindrance to economic ties the three parts of the Polish territories maintained or even consolidated cultural and political connections. It was essential that in the second half of the nineteenth century Poles in the Austrian partition should gain relative autonomy in educational, cultural and national matters. The Cracow and Lvov Universities became important research centres; the Lvov University also having Ukrainian departments. Schoolchildren were taught in Polish. There were Polish cultural and educational organisations and institutions as well as political parties. These liberties were of course limited, mainly by the necessity to remain loyal to the monarchy.

The outbreak of the First World War was to bring about essential changes in the Polish economy and society in general. After the initial Russian successes, mainly in the Austrian part of Poland, German and Austro-Hungarian troops managed to regain lost ground and moved eastwards. In the autumn of 1915 the front line ran across Ukrainian, Belorussian and Latvian lands. Almost the whole of the territories which were to be included in the Second Polish Republic were controlled by the central powers. Military operations affected the entire Russian partition and most of Galicia. Along with policies undertaken by the partitioning powers,these operations had very deleterious effects.

Large numbers of buildings, factories, transport facilities, as well as farms and crops were destroyed as a result of military operations. Arable land adjacent to the front lines was cut by trenches and defences or demolished by bomb explosions. Troops quartered there devastated the country. Apart from direct war damage great losses were caused by the Russian evacuation of 1915. Offices, institutions, even whole industrial plants were moved deep into Russia in order to prevent their falling into German hands. Many employees were evacuated as well. The Russians adopted a scorched earth policy; their troops destroying whatever could not be evacuated in time. Similar tactics were used during retreats by the central powers.

German and Austro-Hungarian occupation of the Polish territories did not mean the end of devastation. The German policy towards the Kingdom of Poland had two basic objectives: maximum exploitation of the productive potential and population of the occupied areas and, for German industry, liquidation of competition. In this connection the occupation authorities started looting all the economic resources in Poland. Wasteful exploitation of mines began. Mined minerals - coal, metal ores - were transported to Germany and Austria without regard to the demands of local factories and households. Reserves of raw materials and products gathered in processing plants and warehouses, which the Russians had not had time to evacuate - such as wool, cotton, metals, machinery and their components - were also taken away. Because of a non-ferrous metal shortage in Germany the occupation authorities requisitioned various objects made of copper and its alloys, like bells, pots, door handles, etc. Machine parts, made of various materials (such as leather drive-belts) were taken away from factories. This plunder was principally directed at the textile industry whose products successfully competed with German goods before the First World War.

Similar looting took place in other branches of the economy. There was large-scale felling of forests and the initially processed timber was transported to Germany. The country was charged with high levies imposed on various farming products which decreased the food consumption of the Polish population. At the same time the occupation authorities made it impossible for local industry to process food. Free trade in basic foodstuffs was prohibited under the German occupation. Surplus farm produce had to be sold to the invaders at fixed low prices and the local population received modest food rations. Under these circumstances agricultural output diminished and the black market flourished.

The preclusion of investments, suspension of production in many factories,and the plundering of machinery and facilities - all this contributed to a disparity between the technical level of Polish industry and industrial plants abroad. While industrial progress in the Kingdom of Poland was checked during the First World War, in other countries technology advanced due to the exigencies of war. In Germany, for instance, there was a boom in the chemical industry whose products were to substitute for imported materials.

A fall in production in the occupied Kingdom of Poland dramatically raised unemployment. Conversely, in Germany and Austria-Hungary, mobilisation caused a shortage of manpower. In order to make Polish workers leave for Germany the occupation authorities prohibited the paying out of unemployment benefits, advocated recruitment or even ordered the forced resettlement of workers. Altogether 'voluntary' and forced recruitment included about 250,000 industrial workers. In addition farm labourers were removed, and about 350,000 seasonal emigrants, who were working in Germany the moment the war broke out, were detained there. (4)

The position of the former Prussian partition was much better. Industry in Upper Silesia benefited from the prosperity often found in wartime. Production grew along with profits. The favourable market situation of industry in Upper Silesia was due also to its participation in the exploitation of resources which properly belonged to the Kingdom of Poland. Silesian steel mills received scrap metal and iron ore from Polish mines, as well as a plentiful supply of timber, while the shortage of manpower was supplemented by workers brought from the Kingdom by force and by prisoners of war who were getting lower wages.

War demand for raw materials and finished products also had some negative effects. For example, essential preparatory work in mines was often neglected and this consequently limited the coal output. A certain de-capitalisation in industry was also recorded.

Farming in Greater Poland and Pomerania fared reasonably well. Although agricultural production fell here also, due to a shortage of labour caused by mobilisation, and a lack of fertilisers, both regions avoided military operations. At the same time demand for food was constant and prices increased rapidly, swelling the incomes of landowners and peasants alike.

In the Austrian partition military operations caused serious damage, mainly to the petroleum industry, but also to farming: vast tracts of productive land were simply turned into battlefields. Smallholdings also suffered, as landowners usually managed to maintain good relations with both Russian and Austrian authorities; thus the burden of requisitions and levies fell mostly on peasants. At the same time Russian and, later, Austrian authorities would often support large estates by directing prisoners of war to work there.

The First World War caused very heavy losses in the Polish territories. Apart from France, Poland was one of the worst-affected countries. The total area of the Polish Republic (in the years 1922-38) amounted to 388,000 sq. km; during the First World War military operations affected 335,000 sq. km, of which about 100,000 sq. km saw long and heavy fighting. Less damage occurred in towns where most of the losses affected industrial plants. In district towns and smaller urban settlements almost 40 per cent of buildings were destroyed. In small towns where most buildings were made of wood the damage sometimes exceeded 75 per cent. Polish farmers lost 1,817,000 cattle and 987,000 horses. At the end of the war more than 4.5 million hectares, that is 30 per cent of the total arable land in the front line areas, lay fallow.

Industry in the Kingdom of Poland was so badly disrupted that in 1918 the number of employed workers fell to 15 per cent of the 1914 level. A total of 4,250 electric engines, almost 4,000 machine tools as well as 98,000 tons of industrial fittings were removed from Polish factories by foreign forces.

Rough estimates of losses suffered by the Polish economy as a result of the First World War and the occupation, prepared by the Polish delegation to the Paris Peace Conference of 1919, totalled 73,000 million French francs. (5)

Even in the course of the war there began a gradual,though limited, reconstruction of some sections of the national economy. After the Russian retreat of 1915 and the stabilisation of the front line, owners of small farms and handicraft workshops started to restore ruined buildings. Reconstruction of the farming sector was that much easier since the central powers occupying the Kingdom of Poland badly needed food supplies. Government aid was given not only to farms affected by military operations in Galicia but also to holdings and estates in the occupied Congress Kingdom. As they supplied most of the foodstuffs, this aid referred mainly to large estates.

NOTES

1. T. Bissaga, Geografia kolejowa Polski z uwzględnieniem stosunków gospodarczo-komunikacyjnych (Wyd. Ministerstwo Komunikacji, Warsaw, 1938), pp. 104-5; J. Ginsbert, Drogi żelazne Rzeczypospolitej (M. Arct, Warsaw, n.d.), p. 57.

2. Mały Rocznik Statystyczny 1938, p.19.

3. C. Bobińska and A. Pilch (eds.), Employment-seeking Emigration of the Poles World-Wide XIX and XX C. (Uniwersytet Jagielloński, Cracow, 1975), pp. 39, 43-7, 64-7, 86, 92; I. Schiper, Dzieje handlu żydowskiego na ziemiach polskich (Centrala Zwiazku Kupców, Warsaw, 1937), p. 456.

4. Polska w czasie wielkiej wojny (1914-1918), vol. 3, (Towarzystwo Badania Zagadnień Międzynarodowych, Warsaw, 1936), pp. 113, 435.

5. Zniszczenia i odbudowa Polski, (Przemysł i Handel, Warsaw, 1929), passim; W. Grabski, Wyjaśnienia dotyczące ratyfikacji Traktatu Pokojowego z Niemcami i Umowy Wielkich Mocarstw z Polską przez Delegata pełnomocnego Polski na Kongresie Pokojowym... (publishing house not given, Paris, 1919); F. Zweig, 'Stosunki gospodarcze' in Wielka ilustrowana encyklopedia powszechna, vol. 13 - Polska (Gutenberg, Cracow, 1930), p. 75.

CHAPTER TWO

INDEPENDENT POLAND

INFLATION AND RECONSTRUCTION, 1918-23

TERRITORY

A coincidence of favourable circumstances made it possible for Poland to regain independence in November 1918, after 123 years of partitions. Revolution in Russia, the breakdown of monarchies in Germany and Austria-Hungary, as well as an unceasing struggle by Polish society for its own statehood finally brought about the founding of the Second Polish Republic. The emerging new Polish state had no fixed frontiers. It was an open question as to whether Poland would be reborn with the frontiers it had before the First Partition (1772), the Second Partition (1793), before the Third Partition (1795) or in other frontiers.

The Polish-German frontier was delimited by the Treaty of Versailles, 1919. Only two sectors - in Upper Silesia and in Warmia and Mazuria (East Prussia) - were to be subject to plebiscites. The plebiscite in Warmia and Mazuria was held on 11 July 1920 and resulted in a heavy defeat for Poland. The Upper Silesian plebiscite was held on 20 March 1921 but interpretation of its results brought serious controversy. A considerable part of the industrial region was finally ceded to Poland only after the Third Silesian Uprising, which broke out in the night on 2 May 1921. The Polish population in Upper Silesia rebelled three times against the German administration and protested against the intention to cede a large part of Upper Silesia inhabited by Poles to Germany. The eastern part of Upper Silesia, however, was taken over by Poland as late as June 1922.

On the grounds of the Versailles Treaty, Gdańsk (Danzig) was separated as a 'Free City' under the supervision of the League of Nations. By the Treaty Poland was awarded a number of rights including utilisation of harbour facilities (and hence access to the Baltic Sea) and control of the railway network and waterways. Gdańsk was included in the Polish customs area but had its own currency.

The frontier with Poland's southern neighbour - Czechoslovakia - was delimited by the big powers in the summer of 1920. The major controversy referred to the Teschen Silesia claimed by both countries - in January 1919 Czech troops actually crossed the provisional frontier line and fighting broke out on a local scale. Minor controversies referred to small parts of Spisz and Orawa. The big powers decided to divide the disputed areas, not satisfying Polish postulates.

Demarcation of the Polish-Soviet frontier was preceded by almost two years of military operations. Territorial disputes developed into a Polish-Ukrainian war (Poland against the short-lived West-Ukrainian People's Republic) and, later, a Polish-Soviet war. There followed the Peace of Riga, signed on 18 March 1921. The Riga treaty included delimitation of the frontier between Poland and the Soviet Union but the southern section of the Riga frontier line was not accepted by the big powers until 1923.

The Polish-Lithuanian frontier was also settled by war. The Polish Army took the disputed Wilno region by force of arms and incorporated it into the rest of the country. Only the frontiers with Romania and Latvia were demarcated in a peaceful way.

The length of Polish frontiers then amounted to 5,534 km, of which 97.5 per cent was land frontier and 2.5 per cent (140 km) was sea frontier. The border with Germany was 1,912 km long, with the USSR, 1,412 km, with Czechoslovakia, 984 km, with Lithuania, 507 km, with Romania, 349 km, with the Free City of Gdańsk, 121 km and with Latvia, 109 km long. The area of Poland was then 388,400 sq. km, making the Second Polish Republic the sixth largest country in Europe after the USSR, France, Spain, Germany and Sweden.

Emerging after more than 100 years of dismemberment the country was highly differentiated. The level of economic development of its various parts was a result of both the general level of development of the partitioning powers and of their policies towards the Polish territories. Usually these policies were aimed at checking socio-economic advance and subordinating the Polish territories to the superior political, military and economic interests of the partitioning powers.

Germany was the most economically developed of the annexing powers and appeared to offer the possibility of enhancing the development prospects of the Prussian partition. But within the German economic system the Polish territories (with the exception of Upper Silesia) were only able to develop the agricultural sector to any great advantage. Agrarian reforms during the first half of the nineteenth century and favourable market conditions in Germany stimulated private farming in Prussian Poland. Under Russian rule, however, the degree of economic development was differentiated. Industry expanded in the Kingdom of Poland but further eastwards the level of economic development was lower. The country was dominated by small peasant holdings with what little surplus production there was being of limited value. The Austrian partition was also economically backward. It had hardly any industry, except for oil extraction and processing, and the Galician peasant holdings were extremely fragmented and of poor quality.

The level of economic development in the various territories constituting the Polish state can be illustrated by a comparison of average yields per hectare before the First World War, as in Table 2.1.

Table 2.1: Comparison of Average Yields per Hectare in Various Parts of the Second Polish Republic before the First World War (a) (in quintals).

Region	Wheat	Rye	Potatoes
Kingdom of Poland	12.6	11.3	103.5
Eastern provinces	9.8	10.5	94.4
Galicia	11.7	11.2	111.2
Prussian partition	20.8	17.2	144.3

Note: a. For the former Russian partition the 1908, 1909 and 1911-13 average; for Galicia the 1909-13 average; for the former Prussian partition the 1908-13 average.
Source: Rocznik Statystyki Rzeczypospolitej Polskiej 1920/22 (Główny Urząd Statystyczny, Warsaw, 1923), vol. 2, p.76.

Similar differences occurred in the employment of industrial workers. In Upper Silesia 169 people per 1,000 inhabitants worked in industry, compared with 72 in Greater Poland, 68 in the Kingdom of Poland, 37 in Galicia, and in the eastern parts of the former Russian partition - only about 20. (1) Though only approximate, these data illustrate the degree of differentiation that could then be found in the various parts of Poland.

The Second Republic was at first a conglomerate of economic areas. Their unification was hindered not only by divergent levels of economic development but also by war damage (which particularly affected the eastern and central regions), different legislation and separate communication networks. Railway lines in the Polish territories were usually adjusted to the military requirements of the partitioning powers. Thus several major centres in the newly formed Poland had no direct connections, and the situation of other types of transportation was hardly any better.

POPULATION

The first post-war population census of Poland was held (not including Upper Silesia and part of the Wilno region) on 30 September 1921. According to the census data and to estimates concerning the excluded areas, the population of Poland amounted to 27.2 million people, the average density being 70 people per 1 sq. km. Some 24 per cent of the population lived in towns with 76 per cent living in the country. The extent of urbanisation varied from region to region. In Central Poland the urban population accounted for 32 per cent of the total, but in the eastern provinces only for 13 per cent. (2) In terms of population size, Poland took sixth place in Europe after the USSR, Germany, Great Britain, Italy and France.

The 1921 population census also recorded ethnic composition but the results that were obtained were not very precise and underestimated the number of national minorities: Poles 69 per cent; Ukrainians 14 per cent; Jews 8 per cent; Belorussians 4 per cent; Germans 4 per cent and others 1 per cent. The geographical distribution of nationalities was rather uneven. Most of the eastern provinces were dominated by non-Polish populations. Germans tended to be concentrated in the former Prussian partition. Jews lived mainly in the towns of Central and East Poland. In some smaller towns they formed a majority of the population. The eastern provinces were inhabited mainly by Slavs (Poles, Ukrainians and Belorussians), with no clear ethnic boundaries, Ukrainians and Belorussians prevailing in the country, with Poles more frequently living in urban areas.

The nationality structure was in some measure influenced by migrations in the years between 1918 and 1923 - caused by territorial changes in post-war Europe and by emigration in search of work. Refugees and evacuees from the areas affected by military offensives returned to Poland at the same time as nationals of the former partitioning powers (mainly Germans) were leaving for their home countries. It was estimated that repatriation between 11 November 1918 and the end of 1922 involved 1,131,000 people but these data seem incomplete. Later on the rate of repatriation was much lower. At the same time about 250,000 people left the former Prussian partition for Germany. Poles coming in from other regions took the place of departing Germans.

Population movements due to the emergence of the Polish state were much greater than those caused by emigration in search of work. In the years between 1918 and 1923 about 409,000 people emigrated from Poland while an unknown number of people returned. Re-emigration from overseas accounted for almost 100,000 people. Emigration was partially organised and the Polish government signed emigration agreements with several countries. The Franco-Polish Convention, for instance, provided that 120,000 workers would leave Poland for France. The Polish government had little option but to support emigration: it dealt with the problem of high unemployment due to war damage.

Repatriation did not of course include all Poles living outside Poland. In Germany about one million Poles remained, in Czechoslovakia, more than 100,000, and in Lithuania about 200,000 Poles. A certain number of Poles lived in the Soviet Union. Most of the Poles living abroad were concentrated in the United States where they numbered about three million. A precise estimate of the number of Polish people abroad seems unlikely as in many countries authorities tended to underestimate the number of national minorities.

The 1921 census made it possible to study the social structure of Poland's society by occupation. Most of the population (65.5 per cent) depended on agriculture, forestry and the like. Of the economically active agricultural population 26 per cent were self-employed people and employers, 59 per cent

assisted members of their families and 15 per cent were agricultural workers. This last figure was a reflection of the small-scale market production prevalent in Polish agriculture. The non-agricultural, economically active population included 45 per cent workers, 26 per cent self-employed people and entrepreneurs with 4 per cent assisting family members, and 11 per cent salaried workers.
The relatively high share of self-reliant non-agricultural workers in the population is also striking; these were mainly artisans and traders working on their own. Most of these self-employed people in handicraft lived on tailoring (97,000), shoemaking (94,000) and food-processing (58,000).

The majority of industrial workers found employment in light industry. The textile and clothing industry employed 235,000 workers, mining 85,000, while engineering and electrical industries employed 25,000. (3) These data, however, refer to the occupational structure as it was before the eastern part of Upper Silesia was incorporated into Poland.

Generally speaking, the Polish economy of 1921 was dominated by small-scale producers and workers employed in factories of limited size and output. A large-scale industrial proletariat had not materialised. Such a structure reflected the country's economic backwardness due to partitions and the destruction of the First World War.

Education was in a perilous condition. In 1921 as much as 33 per cent of the population aged ten years and over were illiterate. Although the western provinces fared better, illiteracy in the eastern provinces reached 65 per cent. It was clearly essential to develop a more effective educational system. Despite the determined efforts of the government, in 1923-4 it proved impossible to include all children in the compulsory education system. There was a shortage of personnel with secondary and higher education, especially in state administration. Qualified civil servants were in short supply, as administration in the former Prussian and Russian partitions had been entirely dominated by Germans and Russians. Only in Galicia was there an adequate supply of Polish staff. Germany and Russia deliberately limited the chances of the Polish intelligentsia. In the Russian partition schools were prohibited from teaching in the Polish language until after the 1905 revolution. In Prussian Poland German schools maintained their monopoly until the liberation of 1918.

INDEPENDENT POLAND

INDUSTRY

One of the most fundamental tasks of the Polish government after regaining independence was to revitalise industrial activity. It was both an economic and a political problem. Industry supplied the growing Polish army and, no less importantly, provided work for a huge mass of workers who would otherwise have been unemployed. It was argued in government circles that reducing unemployment would probably be essential in order to neutralise communist influence. Such was the opinion of the Minister of labour and social welfare, Jerzy Iwanowski, at the government session of 6 June 1919: 'If during the forthcoming summer at least half of the unemployed cannot be given work, it may come to a disaster, as maintaining peace and quiet among such a large number of discontented people who are ready to do anything is impossible.'(4)

The first Polish cabinets directed by socialist premiers Ignacy Daszyński and Jędrzej Moraczewski suggested nationalising part of Polish industry on the grounds of a law to be passed by the Seym which at that time had not been elected. This meant shelving the problem for an indefinite period. It seems that the nationalisation programme was aimed mainly at placating the masses and preventing the spontaneous takeover of factories by workers' councils.

The first task facing the authorities was to get the undamaged factories started and keep functioning plants in operation. There was some reluctance and hesitation among private entrepreneurs who feared nationalisation, a war with Russia or Germany, revolution or a takeover of factories by discontented workers.

Under these circumstances the government was moved into a position where it had to operate its own factories and this contributed to the trend towards extension of state control of industry. The ideology of state control was given substance not as an attempt to realise theoretical concepts but as a result of passivity in the private business sector. The nationalisation programme was put forward by the socialist governments but had been dropped by January 1919. Although the government withdrew its nationalisation programme and officially emphasised the necessity to return to a free market economy, state control was maintained until the end of the Polish-Soviet war, that is until March 1921. In June 1919 the Minister of industry and trade, Kazimierz Hącia, said: 'It should be considered settled that reconstruction of industry is to be accomplished by society by means of a private initiative, the only one called for this purpose, and not by the government.' (5)

The government encouraged the private sector to reconstruct and operate its own factories. Businessmen were granted favourable credits, large government orders and the like, although the products ordered were in some instances unnecessary for the government.

Productivity was also fettered by a shortage of coal and other raw materials. It was estimated in 1919 that only 35 per cent of the industrial demand for coal in the former Kingdom of Poland was met. There were a number of reasons for this shortfall; Upper Silesia remained outside Poland, coal imports were limited by a shortage of foreign currency and coal transportation by a lack of railway freight wagons. Many lines of industry, such as textiles based on imported wool and cotton, had no raw material resources or foreign currency with which to buy them abroad. The Łódź textile industry could not operate until it had received relief credits granted by the Entente countries. Further purchases followed on the grounds of credits guaranteed by the government.

All these difficulties explain why the level of industrial production in 1919 was so low. If we compare the number of workers employed in the Kingdom of Poland in the first half of 1919 with that of 1913 it appears that the textile industry employed 3 per cent, building 4 per cent, metal-working industries 10 per cent, and the chemical industry 11 per cent. The highest level of employment was reached in mining and metallurgy (82 per cent). In view of the decrease in labour productivity, the material results of production were even lower. It was estimated that wool and cotton production amounted to only 1.5 per cent of the 1913 level, metal-processing production to only 1 per cent, timber to 10 per cent, paper to 15 per cent, mineral products to 30 per cent and coal mining to 66 per cent of the 1913 level. (6)

At the turn of 1919 and 1920 the war with Soviet Russia began to have a positive effect on Polish industry. Government orders stimulated demand for several goods and semi-finished products and this encouraged further factories to start production. Unemployment diminished also. The varied requirements of the army stimulated government interest in developing a strong industrial base. Indirect motivation of private initiative began in the shape of advancing loans, financing of some investments in private factories or construction of new plants. These inducements were designed to encourage private businessmen to increase production, some of the risks involved being underwritten by the government and by state-owned banks.

The introduction of a war economy extended state control of industry through indirect manipulation of private factories and by the construction of government factories subordinate to the military administration. Some of these factories developed afterwards into large, state-controlled armaments plants, as the military authorities were usually in favour of state-control.

Private industry, however, could not make the best use of a favourable economic situation. Coal and raw materials were still in short supply along with qualified staff since called up by the army. Coal supply depended on imports and on the transport capability of railways. When the Polish front collapsed in the east in the summer of 1920, coal supplies to factories almost ceased, even to those working for the army.

Despite many obstacles employment grew in 1920 by 62 per cent, steel output by 225 per cent, pig iron production by 80 per cent and production of rolled goods by 185 per cent. The total industrial output was still much lower than in 1913 and the very high increments were in fact due to the extremely low level of 1919. The boom in industry took place only in those regions not affected by military operations. Fighting generally took place in non-industrial areas so that Polish-Soviet war damage had little material effect on industrial production.

All in all it would seem that the Polish-Soviet war had a positive impact on industrial activity, as it prompted renewed business activity: production for military purposes increased; industrial plants employed more and more workers, and there was an increase in demand for consumer goods. Private profits grew and accelerated the reconstruction and expansion of industry.

The end of the war did not interfere with prosperity. Military orders were replaced by the requirements of the civilian population and the bids of entrepreneurs. Direct government support of private firms diminished in line with the general trend to return to a free market economy (and the growing financial problems of the Treasury).

A decrease in government support was paradoxically compensated for by a growing inflationary process. Inflation made it possible for entrepreneurs to reduce some of the costs of production (in real terms of course)and extend the market. For instance, costs of non-valorised credits diminished, the tax burden which remained non-valorised until 1923 rapidly came down, costs of transportation decreased as railway tariffs grew at a slower rate than the Polish mark was depreciating and real wages were gradually falling. At the same time a flight from currency caused a bulk-buying spree in the home market. The exportation of Polish goods was paid for by inflationary export premiums.

In a time of creeping inflation in 1921-2 many war-damaged factories were rebuilt and launched production. New investments were undertaken to create industries which had previously not existed in so far as it had been a policy of the partitioning powers to locate them outside the Polish territories. Thus the electricity industry developed alongside the armaments, locomotive, engineering, precision and optical industries. At the end of 1922 employment had reached 82 per cent of the 1913 level. A rapid recovery is illustrated by annual percentage increases in employment which grew by 75 per cent in 1921 and by a further 32 per cent in 1922.Industrial production expanded at a lower rate. Together with the construction industry it reached, in 1922, about 74 per cent of the 1913 level. (7)

In the second half of 1922 Poland's industrial potential was radically altered by the incorporation of the eastern part of Upper Silesia. If compared with the rest of Polish production, Upper Silesian production figures were as follows: coal (278 per cent), iron ore (26 per cent), zinc ore (323 per cent), pig iron (508 per cent), steel (337 per cent), rolled goods (462 per cent) and zinc (844 per cent). (8) The division of Upper Silesia nevertheless brought serious problems. The frontier separated some factories and broke already established links. Industry in Upper Silesia was mainly in German hands and Germans often consciously hampered unification of the area with the rest of Poland for political reasons. In order to lessen these problems special agreements were concluded between Poland and Germany providing a duty-free improvement trade turnover between both parts of Upper Silesia for 15 years, Polish duty-free exports of certain quotas to Germany until June 1925 and a temporary maintenance of the German currency, etc. (9)

There was some anxiety as to whether the Polish

market would absorb Upper Silesian production. But these fears proved pointless as inflation stimulated demand and production grew in the years 1922-3. The French occupation of the Ruhrland was also of some significance here as it raised the demand for Upper Silesian products in Germany. In some lines of production exports to the Reich accounted for 80 per cent of the output. Despite favourable market conditions German entrepreneurs in Upper Silesia did not invest. Indeed, there were cases where existing facilities were dismantled and removed to Germany.

Prosperity connected with creeping inflation proved to be short-lived. When hyperinflation began in 1923 production ceased to grow and signs of depression appeared. While creeping inflation extended the market, hyperinflation reversed the effect. Decreasing real wages meant a curtailment of the home market. Real budget revenues diminished and so restrained government purchases of industrial goods. Falling consumer and government demand coincided with the disappearance of the inflationary export premium in the second half of 1923. Reduced productivity meant fewer jobs and a further fall in consumer demand. It also meant a reduction of tax revenues and a further decrease of government purchases. An economic crisis began - often called a post-inflation or a stabilisation depression. It was - contrary to the Great Depression - mainly due to internal factors and not to the world market situation.

In spite of the incipient depression,production in 1923 was higher than in 1922 but still lower than before the First World War.

The early post-war years brought radical changes to the organisational structure of Polish industry. Whereas before the First World War individual or family enterprises enjoyed a dominant role (excepting Upper Silesia), in 1918 a rapid development of joint-stock companies began due to the absolute necessity of gathering enough capital for reconstruction. In the first five years of independence 1,455 joint-stock companies were established; this was a fivefold increase in their number.(10)

At the same time most of the cartels broke up and Polish industry gradually returned to the system of free competition. High profits made by individual businessmen did not accord with cartelisation but although on 1 January 1919 there were only nine monopoly agreements in Poland (not including Upper Silesia), at the end of 1923 their number had grown to 31. Monopolies were mainly concentrated in the sugar-refining and textile industries; in other areas they played only a minor role. (11)

A major part of industrial production came from handicraft workshops. Employment in this sector was even higher than the number of workers in large and medium-size industries. From the end of 1919 to December 1921 the number of handicraft workshops doubled while employment increased even more rapidly. This showed how quickly handicrafts recovered but it had to face serious competition. But inflation brought handicrafts some benefits: debts were discharged and there was a reduction in the actual tax burden but at the same time the demand for handicraft products and services gradually diminished. As a result this sector began to experience the effects of depression by the second half of 1922. (12) This caused a virtual loss of independence to many handicraftsmen who in fact became home-workers. Many of the poorest people in rural areas began to earn money as home-workers at this time too.

Despite post-war confusion and the Polish-Soviet war for the eastern frontier, the years between 1918 and 1923 were rather favourable for industrial reconstruction. Productivity and employment increased rapidly. Enterprises from various parts of new Poland established connections and co-operation agreements. Industry shifted from the previous markets of the partitioning powers to the home market. However, for many kinds of goods the loss of traditional markets proved very difficult to overcome. This mainly concerned certain industries of the former Kingdom of Poland which traditionally exported to Russia or even to the Far East. After the First World War this was no longer possible and the result was particularly dramatic for the textile and metal-processing industries. There was also a gradual integration of Upper Silesian industry with the rest of Poland, though this was checked by German entrepreneurs who wanted to prove that Poland would be incapable of making use of the Upper Silesian potential.

AGRICULTURE

Just as in industry, agriculture was also affected by war damage. Crops diminished not only in the areas where military operations had been carried out but also over large areas of farmland, the result of mobilisation of the male population, requisition of horses and a lack of necessary equipment and fertilisers, especially in the private farming sector of the former Prussian partition. The First World War reduced the area of land under cultivation, and grain yields, potato crops and livestock all diminished. One method of measuring change in Polish agriculture is to compare yields per hectare. In the years between 1911 and 1913, and between 1919 and 1920 they fell from 20.1 quintals to 12.8 quintals for wheat and from 18.0 quintals to 7.2 quintals for rye. At the same time yields of the two remaining partitions decreased but to a lesser extent. (13) The number of horses fell by 26 per cent, while pig livestock diminished by as much as 61 per cent. (14) In addition, much of the land could not be cultivated because of mines, unexploded shells, trenches or dugouts.

To redress this damage was but one of the major problems faced by Polish farmers. Another was the legacy of a disadvantageous agricultural structure. Agriculture, in all the three partitions, developed in the nineteenth century according to the so-called 'Prussian road to capitalism'. As a result Polish agriculture included a relatively small number of large, capitalist, landed estates (with feudal vestiges in the east) on the one hand and an immense number of small, not self-sufficient peasant holdings on the other. This structure is shown in Table 2.2.

Table 2.2 shows that about 61.6 per cent of farms that were not self-sufficient (below 5 ha) held only 14 per cent of the land, while a mere 0.9 per cent of farms owned more than 48 per cent of the land. Among these were latifundia as, for example the Dawidgródek tail estate of Prince Radziwiłł of 155,000 ha, the Prince von Pless-Pszczyński estate of 42,000 ha or the Prince Hohenlohe estate of 18,000 ha. Most of the smallholdings could not support owners and their families. These semi-proletarian plots were backward and their owners supplemented their earnings as hired workers or casual labourers. In view of the very small size of these plots and the numerous families living on them (the birth-rate among peasants was the highest in Poland) the Polish countryside was over-populated in relation to the economic productivity of the smallholding. A Polish economist, Zdzisław Ludkiewicz, estimated this concealed unemployment at two million people in 1921. (15) The existence of such a large number of farms that were not self-sufficient and which produced only very limited incomes frustrated industrial expansion. The home

Table 2.2: Agricultural Structure in Poland in 1921

Area of farms	Number of farms in thousands	Number of farms (%)	Total area in thousands ha	Total area (%)
0-2 ha	1,013.4	29.0	1,060.7	2.8
2-5 ha	1,138.5	32.6	4,248.3	11.2
5-10 ha	861.1	24.7	6,562.6	17.3
10-20 ha	360.0	10.3	5,201.7	13.7
20-50 ha	87.6	2.5	2,611.1	6.9
50-100 ha	11.2	0.3)		
over 100 ha	18.9	0.6)	18,241.6.	48.1
Total	3,490.7	100.0	37,926.0	100.0

Source: M. Mieszczankowski, Struktura agrarna Polski międzywojennej, (Państwowe Wydawnictwo Naukowe, Warsaw, 1960), pp. 339-40.

market was very restricted and demand for manufactured goods was limited.

Improving the agricultural structure was an essential commitment of the Polish peasant movement. Peasants had always subscribed to the parcelling out of large estates. In 1918-19 there were cases of impromptu seizure of land belonging to large landowners. The socialist governments of Daszyński and Moraczewski included agrarian reform in their programmes but postponed its realisation until the Seym had passed adequate laws. Under pressure from peasant parties and because of social unrest in the country, the Seym adopted a resolution concerning principles of land reform in the summer of 1919. The maximum holding of landed property was determined at 60-180 ha, according to local conditions; in some cases this limit could be raised to 400 ha. Owners of expropriated land were to be fully compensated. The Seym resolution, however, only settled general principles of land reform. The legal foundation for land redistribution could only be provided by a special law, and therefore the Seym resolution did not in fact change the status quo.

The Polish retreat on the eastern front made the Seym pass the Land Reform Act in July 1920.The act slightly modified the 1919 principles. Only half of the expropriated land value was to be compensated, while the expropriation procedure made it possible to prolong the distribution of land for many years. However, realisation of the Land Reform Act was blocked by the March, 1921 Constitution which guaranteed the protection of private property rights. The Supreme Court of Administration stated that the 50 per cent compensation for the expropriated land value was contrary to the Constitution. But these problems did not stop the voluntary division of land by large landowners sold at market prices. Between 1919 and 1923 more than 530,000 ha were parcelled out voluntarily. This was, however, a mere drop in the ocean vis à vis peasant requirements. Moreover, because of rather high market prices for land, due to heavy demand, the parcelled lots could be purchased only by rich peasants. Thus this kind of land redistribution did nothing to change an agricultural system that was already fundamentally unsound.

As soon as the Polish-Soviet war was over, farmers set about reconstructing buildings that had been destroyed and developing land cultivation. They had to face grave problems. During the First World War and the Polish-Soviet military operations 1.7 million buildings were destroyed (including about 75 per cent of farm buildings). The government offered facilities for reconstruction, for instance, supplying cheap building timber. By the end of 1922 about 47 per cent of buildings had been reconstructed, although in December 1923 there were still 600,000 damaged buildings. Reconstruction lagged behind in the eastern territories, which were the most seriously affected by the Polish-Ukrainian and Polish-Soviet wars. Land lying fallow was more rapidly managed. In 1918/19 their area was estimated at 4.6 million ha, in 1919/20 at 2.5 million ha, and by 1923 the figure had dropped to only 0.4 million ha. Bringing fallow land under cultivation involved a number of factors, such as the supply of agricultural equipment, the amount of horse livestock, availability of sowing seeds, seed potatoes and government aid provided for the removal of trenches, barbed wire, etc. These tasks were sometimes beyond the power of individual farmers.

The volume of crop production depended on such agents as the area under cultivation, the level of agricultural technology or weather conditions. In the first post-war years the area under cultivation gradually grew, this of course being the key to an increase in crop production. The supply of agricultural tools and artificial fertilisers did not satisfy the then existing demand, even though it was rather low. Between 1922 and 1923 (precise data do not exist for earlier dates) rye, barley, oats and potato crops exceeded the 1909-13 level, while those of wheat and sugar beet were still lower. Yields per hectare also grew, except for sugar beet. (16) These positive results were achieved mainly because of excellent weather conditions in 1923. Increasing crop production, given a relatively low peasant consumption, meant that the Polish grain deficit of 1920/1 had disappeared by 1921/2. This was mainly due to the ending of war in the eastern territories and the area under crop cultivation had almost doubled in 1921/2.

Animal husbandry was also rapidly improving. According to the 1921 livestock census the number of farm animals was similar to that before the First World War, with the exception of sheep. Thus it may be estimated that in the years 1922/3 animal breeding in Poland had reached the 1913 level. However, quantitative improvements did not mean similar qualitative effects. The destruction of pedigree livestock and a shortage of feeding stuffs had depressed the value of livestock. The milking capacity of cows had also dropped to unusually low levels.

Despite the immense damage due to war Polish agriculture began a steady recovery in the years from 1918 to 1923. A particularly important milestone was the attainment of the pre-war levels of basic crops, yields and livestock, and this provided hope for the future.

FINANCE

The necessity to create the Polish state anew, in the face of immense war damage, made large deficits appear in the budget. Immediately after regaining independence they had seemed inevitable. Government expenditure had to be much higher than under normal circumstances, whereas budget revenues remained very low. Deficits additionally increased in the course of the Polish-Soviet war due to heavy military expenditure, which absorbed as much as 62 per cent of all budget expenses between 1 July 1919 and 31 March 1920. The end of war did not improve the situation. Expenditure remained higher than revenue and actual deficits as a rule exceeded estimates. In 1921 the deficit was estimated at 35 per cent; in practice it reached as much as 61 per cent. In 1922 the estimated deficit was 22 per cent; the actual 48 per cent, while in 1923 it was, respectively, 42 per cent and 45 per cent. (17)

Whereas in 1918-20 budget deficits were mainly due to the post-war situation in Poland, later deficits can be traced to the fact that it was always easier for the Treasury to cover expenses by inflationary issues. There was also some resistance from the propertied classes who were unwilling to accept increased taxation in favour of the Treasury.

Treasury ministers announced energetic plans that, it was hoped, would balance the budget. Many proposals to combat inflation were put forward but the outcome was usually a new issue of paper money. Some ministers wanted to balance the budget by means of foreign loans, others planned domestic loans or intended to increase the tax burden. Foreign loans proved unobtainable, domestic loans would bring too little too late, while taxation failed to raise sufficient revenue until after December 1923 when taxes and charges were valorised. As inflation grew the real tax burden depreciated. According to an estimate by the Polish economist, Roman Rybarski, the per capita taxation in the Polish territories amounted in 1914 to about $7(US). In 1921 the real value of taxation was only $1.61 (23 per cent), in 1922,

$2.22 (31 per cent) and in the first half of 1923 - due to lack of valorisation - it amounted to a mere $0.71, giving $1.42 for the whole of 1923 (20 per cent). (18)

The budget deficit resulted in growing inflation. The Treasury took up credits in the state-owned issuing bank, Polska Krajowa Kasa Pożyczkowa, which constantly launched new issues. At first inflation was only creeping but soon an inflationary spiral developed. Apart from regular budget deficits inflationary issues served as financing credits for private entrepreneurs. The major source of these credits were the state-owned banks. By 1923 hyperinflation, with all its negative effects, had arrived. While more modest inflation stimulated demand in the home market and provided for favourable exports, hyperinflation totally disorganised the economic life of the country.

Table 2.3 provides a dramatic illustration of the course of inflation in Poland between 1918 and 1923.

Excessive issues led to the occurrence of the so-called 'inflationary tax' which consisted of a gradual loss of a part of the primary purchasing power of the currency by all users who delayed spending money received. The difference between the purchasing power at the moment of receiving the money and at the moment of spending it some time later was taken over by the state. Thus the longer some people had to keep their money, the more they contributed to financing the Treasury. Precise estimates of the 'inflationary tax' in Poland in 1918-23 are difficult to make and this is why various calculations can be found. They differ from $533 million to $809 million. (19) Compared with the whole of budget revenues in the years 1918-23 the 'inflationary tax' amounted to between 64 per cent and 78 per cent. (20) It was therefore of constant importance to the public finance sector.

The 'inflationary tax' benefited not only the Treasury but private entrepreneurs also; they gained from $76 million to $91 million in the shape of non-valorised government loans. These loans were in fact an indirect method of government subsidy for the reconstruction of private companies.

The moment Poland regained independence there were other financial pitfalls besides inflation. There were, for example, several legal tenders. In the former Prussian partition there was the German mark; in the former Russian partition occupied by the Germans, the Polish mark issued under their con-

Table 2.3: Inflation in Poland, 1918-23

Date	Circulation in million Polish marks	Increase %	$US price in Polish marks	Increase %
11 Nov 1918	8,000	100	8	100
31 Dec 1918	9,000	113	9	113
30 June 1919	12,150	152	18	225
31 Dec 1919	15,300	191	110	1,375
30 June 1920	21,730	272	142	1,775
31 Dec 1920	49,362	617	590	7,375
30 June 1921	102,697	1,283	2,075	25,937
31 Dec 1921	229,537	2,869	2,923	36,537
30 June 1922	300,101	3,751	4,700	58,750
31 Dec 1922	793,438	9,911	17,800	222,500
30 June 1923	3,566,649	44,582	104,000	1,300,000
31 Dec 1923	125,371,955	1,567,149	6,375,000	79,687,500

Source: J. Zdziechowski, <u>Finanse Polski w latach 1924 i 1925, (Biblioteka Polska, Warsaw, 1925)</u>, pp. 13-15.

trol; in Galicia, Austrian crowns; in the north-eastern territories, Ost-marks, Ost-roubles and roubles; and in the south-east, roubles, 'hrivnas' and Ukrainian 'karbovantsi'. Each of these currencies had a different purchasing power which was also changing, while exchange rate fluctuations resulted frequently from political reasons. Most of these currencies were issued by banks situated outside the Polish territories.

It seemed likely that the government would exchange all the currencies in circulation for a new monetary unit. But the Polish government did not have the technology to print new banknotes, neither could they authorise one of the circulating currencies, as this would merely have accentuated existing regional differences. Finally it was decided that Polish marks would continue to be issued but according to a new pattern; and unification of the currency began in 1919. At first a bi-currency system was introduced in individual regions: Polish marks continued to circulate along with formerly used currencies. On 20 November 1919 the Polish mark was introduced as the only legal tender in former Prussian Poland and likewise on 24 March 1920 in Galicia. In April 1920 roubles were deprived of the right to circulate and be exchanged into Polish marks. (21) Unification was completed in the first half of 1920. When new territories were ceded to Poland in the east and in Upper Silesia the Polish mark was to be the only legal tender. The monetary unification the eastern territories with the rest of Poland became law on 4 July 1921, and in Upper Silesia on 1 November 1923. However, some currencies continued in use, enjoying more public confidence than the inflationary Polish mark.

It was an open secret that monetary unification would not solve the problem of inflation. Subsequent Treasury ministers made preparations for the currency exchange but the technical difficulties concerning the printing of new banknotes and fears of a repeated depreciation of the new monetary unit kept the government from exchanging the currency.

The war and inflation seriously affected banks, especially in the former Russian partition. The situation of banks in Prussian Poland was relatively better. The emergence of the Polish state and the need for reconstruction also brought a need to reorganise the existing banking structure. Before very long, however, most banks neglected credit operations (which led to financial losses because of inflation) and became involved with speculative exchange operations or with intermediation in establishing industrial companies, which were frequently very short-lived. A president of the Banking Association in Poland recorded in his diary: 'More and more dubious banks are created. If you are in trouble - start a bank, that's what is frequently said and done.' (22) The number of banks increased from 16 in 1913 to 111 in 1923. But at the same time inflation diminished the role of traditional banking operations such as accepting money on deposit, long-term credits, commercial credits, etc. Currency depreciation virtually eliminated any propensity to save, as shown by the falling value of deposits. In 1913 all deposits in joint-stock banks amounted to 456 million French francs in gold, but at the beginning of 1924 this had fallen to 21 million French francs. Saving deposits in credit co-operatives and savings banks had dropped from about 2.5 billion French francs before the First World War to almost nil.

Fearing losses, the banks raised interest rates on loans. The main issuing bank increased the rate of interest from 6 per cent to 72 per cent, while private banks took up to 3,000 per cent interest on loans on open accounts and up to 5,000 per cent on discounting private bills. (23) Even such high interest rates could not prevent losses which sometimes exceeded 50 per cent of the capital employed per month during the period of hyperinflation. It was estimated in 1923 that if banks wanted to secure their capital against inflation they would have to charge an annual interest rate of 72,000 per cent. Shrinking private credit operations made the state-controlled banks grant more and more credits. In 1919 private banks granted 79 per cent of the total sum of credits, but in 1923 only 29 per cent.

The role of the state-owned banks was also increasing: large private banks which did not deal in speculative operations bore such huge losses that they could not continue to function without government aid. The capital reserves of seven major private banks of the former Kingdom of Poland and Galicia diminished by 89 per cent. The largest bank in the Kingdom of Poland - Bank Handlowy w Warszawie SA had to cover losses with its reserve fund, thereby spending all its special reserves and diminishing its stock capital. The largest bank in the former Prussian partition - Bank Związku Spółek Zarobkowych w Poznaniu SA lost about 33 per cent of its capital.

DOMESTIC TRADE

Polish domestic trade developed under complicated conditions. In view of the lack of essential goods, the Polish government maintained in force several occupation regulations concerning market control. This was aimed at providing the people with at least minimum quantities of articles of prime necessity. The market control system was based on a few specialised government offices: the exclusive right of importation and sale of necessities was given to the State Office for Purchasing Essential Goods; coal management to the State Coal Office; petroleum management to the State Petroleum Office, etc.

Essential articles could be bought either for coupons at fixed prices or on the open market. Apart from the rationed supply system many institutions organised their own supplies for employees. Trade turnover was therefore mixed - including rationing and free trade. The rationed supply system required maintenance of quotas delivered by farmers in kind. From time to time they could sell the remaining surplus products on the open market. This policy, however, was frequently changed according to the market situation and for political reasons. For instance, during the Polish-Soviet war, the system of quota deliveries at fixed prices was predominant. It must also be pointed out that rationing and quota systems were not uniform throughout Poland. Former Prussian Poland was not interested in an entire unification with other regions when it came to disposing of surplus foodstuffs. The exchange of goods between the former Prussian partition and the rest of Poland was in many respects similar to foreign trade. A customs frontier was maintained for a certain time and even after it was abolished all exports from the former Prussian partition were licensed. Grain, for example, was imported from Greater Poland in exchange for coal from the former Russian partition. Unification was completed in 1921 and this helped to bring about price equalisation throughout Poland.

Only when the Polish-Soviet war was over and the country's economic reconstruction got under way did it seem pragmatic to change domestic trade policy. In April 1921 restrictions on crop turnover were lifted, and in the second half of 1921 other restrictions relating to domestic trade turnover were gradually dropped and Poland entered into a free trade period.

Abolition of the trade control system and an economic demilitarisation resulted in a commercial crisis. Prices increased rapidly but turnover diminished. This was temporary, however, and the introduction of free trade finally proved beneficial to the economy.

Inflation meant a constant increase in prices. High costs of living attracted common interest and concern. In order to check price increases the government imposed restrictions on exports of foodstuffs from Poland, tried to stimulate market supply, or granted credits to develop processing industries. In April 1922 a special office of 'extraordinary commissioner for the reduction of high costs of living' was established. But the hoped-for effects of these steps proved to be rather elusive. An increase in the money supply inevitably led to price increases. Inflation made normal cost accounting impossible. Having added average profits to the purchasing price and distribution costs, traders obtained a selling price for which they could not buy the same quantities of goods in the wholesale trade. In 1923, when the purchasing power of the Polish mark diminished at an unprecedented rate, traders began to count into their selling prices not only regular costs and profits but also a kind of insurance against the risk of a further currency depreciation.

In the period from 1918 to 1923 Polish domestic trade was rather small-scale and non-capitalist in nature. Most traders aimed at satisfying the demand of poor customers, not only in most small country shops but also in many shops in towns. Retail dealers frequently had goods of poor quality and sold them in rooms without windows, booths, stands, etc. Only in the major cities were there modern shops offering articles of better quality but their number was rather small. Trade in the western regions was at a higher level than in the east. Inflation and the struggle for survival frequently led to regulations of one kind or another being broken. Under these circumstances many well-established firms went bankrupt and were replaced by speculative traders. A short supply of goods, market controls and price differences between regions were conducive only to the development of speculation.

FOREIGN ECONOMIC RELATIONS

It is not easy to discuss normal foreign trade in Poland in the first years of independence. The country had large import requirements (foodstuffs, medicines, industrial machinery, raw materials, coal, armaments, etc. were in short supply) but did not have any commodities to export. At first Polish foreign trade came under strict government control but ill-defined frontiers and insufficient personnel left a wide margin for contraband, estimated at about half of the total foreign trade turnover. Government control embraced individual regions and was, in the summer of 1920, entrusted to the Central Office of Imports and Exports. The Office classified commodities according to what could or could not be exported, which goods required export or import licences, etc. Customs offices played only a secondary role in foreign trade policy and tariffs of the partitioning powers remained in force. A uniform, although temporary, tariff was introduced in Poland in November 1919.

The first trade agreements signed with Austria, Czechoslovakia and Hungary were based on barter principles. Poland exported oil products, timber and semi-finished products in exchange for the necessary commodities. Polish trade with Germany was based on the Treaty of Versailles which obliged the Weimar Republic to allow Poland the 'most favoured nation' clause and to import goods produced in the former Prussian partition to the amount of the 1911-13 average for three years. This privilege was never enjoyed by Poland as in 1920-2 the German government boycotted trade with Poland on the grounds of German domestic trade control regulations. The boycott was aimed at gaining political concessions from Poland (mainly in relation to German property, which could be bought as provided by the Versailles Treaty) and at the problem of the citizenship option of Germans living in Poland. The German boycott was weakened by imports of German goods through other countries and by deliveries of international aid for countries affected by war. Poland, for example, obtained some raw materials necessary to start textile production, foodstuffs and medicines from relief credits. Considerable deliveries of armaments came mainly from France under credit agreements. Imports of armaments increased in 1919 and were continued in 1920.

Stabilisation of the economic situation in Poland and the ending of war in the east made it possible to liberalise foreign trade in June 1921. Free trade was introduced except where goods were specified as prohibited. The latter included above all those foodstuffs which could not be exported. But in the following years restrictions were gradually lifted. As government controls were removed, the major role in foreign trade policy was now played by tariffs. The tariff protection of the Polish market was relatively high. Customs allowances referred to imports of foodstuffs and capital goods. (24)

Soon afterwards negotiations were initiated with many countries which aimed at concluding trade agreements. Most frequently they covered one year and were then prolonged. Negotiations were also started with the Weimar Republic. In 1922, after the greater part of Upper Silesia was ceded to Poland, the German government recognised the futility of their economic boycott of Poland, and the more so since agreements concerning the division of Upper Silesia guaranteed Polish rights to export considerable quantities of duty-free Upper Silesian products to Germany until 1925. However a Polish-German trade agreement was not concluded and the bilateral exchange was based on agreements providing for the separation of Polish territory from the German Reich. This state of affairs lasted until June 1925 when regulations which concerned the division of Upper Silesia expired.

Creeping inflation stimulated exports and checked imports. Export prices of Polish goods abroad were more and more competitive, whereas imports of articles bought in stable currencies did not pay. Although exports seemed especially favourable, there was until 1922 a deficit in the trade balance. A foreign trade surplus occurred as late as 1923. Exports included mainly raw materials, foodstuffs and timber; imports were usually fully manufactured products. Poland's biggest trade partner at first was Germany and the Austro-Hungarian successor states. Despite the end of war with Russia and the subsequent conclusion of a peace treaty, Polish trade relations with the Soviet Union were very limited and this had a particular effect on industry as the former Kingdom of Poland had traditionally sold a major part of its production to the east.

Foreign trade was only a part of Poland's links with the world economy. A very important role was also played by foreign capital invested in enterprises in the Polish territories and by capital turnover.

It is not possible to estimate precisely the share of foreign capital in the economy of the Polish territories when independence was regained. In the Prussian partition there were large German investments. Mining, metallurgy, heavy industry and banks in Upper Silesia were entirely in German hands. In Greater Poland and Pomerania the share of German capital was also very high. In the former Kingdom of Poland German investments were accompanied by French, Austrian, and - to a lesser degree - Italian and Belgian capital. Foreign finance in the former Russian partition played a smaller role than in formerly Prussian Poland. In Galicia, Austrian investments prevailed but in the Galician oil industry capital from almost all the advanced capitalist countries could be found.

In view of war damage the Polish government adopted a positive attitude towards foreign capital investment. It was even suggested that without foreign capital it would have been impossible to reconstruct the Polish economy and heal the country's finances. Premier Ignacy Paderewski was of the opinion that Poland needed, above all, a 'large foreign loan'. (25) Thus the government sought foreign credits and encouraged foreign investment in Poland but the government's action was insufficiently coordinated and almost all ministries pursued foreign loans on their own account. This made any rational policy in this field wellnigh impossible. The demand for foreign credits increased in 1919-20 as a result of the Polish-Soviet war. During the Polish retreat on the eastern front in August 1920 the Economic Committee of Ministers authorised the government to contract foreign loans in exchange for various privileges and concessions. It was adopted that, for a one billion francs' loan,

> the minister of Treasury may conclude a contract of sale of mineral oil, petroleum products or sugar, allow foreign capital participation in exploitation of the tobacco monopoly and other state monopolies, give government coal mines on lease, sell areas of exclusive mining rights to foreign governments and private groups, allow the right of exploration and mining of minerals reserved to the Polish government, grant the right of construction and exploitation of new railway lines, allow exploitation of new shipping lines, airways, forests, water power, permit timber exports, concede other exploitation rights along with the right of founding and running joint-stock companies, insurance companies, factories, conclude agreements concerning the sale of government coal mines, iron and zinc works in Upper Silesia if this area is given to Poland, and finally - conclude trade agreements. (26)

When the Polish-Soviet war was over the policy

of attracting foreign capital was maintained both in the government and in private business circles. The problem was that the world's financial markets were unwilling to invest in Poland in view of her complicated political and economic situation. Foreign loans generally had a political content and most came from Western governments. For France and the United States credit supplies to Poland meant a possibility of getting rid of unnecessary or outdated wartime stocks. On the other hand private businessmen were very cautious about investing in Poland.

From 1918 to 1923 the Polish government received a total of $287 million in commodity credits and cash loans, the latter accounting for a mere 1 per cent of the total sum. The distribution of these credits over time was significant: in 1918 the government received $26 million; in 1919-20, that is during the war with Soviet Russia - $246 million; and from 1921 to 1923 - only $15 million. (27) This clearly points to the political nature of credits, of which 59 per cent were assigned for food supplies, 28 per cent for armaments, 8 per cent for government investments, and the remainder to health services, credit aid to private enterprises, public welfare, etc.

If the business circles of the Entente countries did show an interest in Poland, it was mainly to acquire shares in existing firms. This referred especially to some German enterprises. Frequently the transfer of shares was merely a purported operation aimed at preventing their redemption by the Polish authorities.

Poland's largest creditors were the United States and France. Public debts accumulated in 1918-23 and were mainly short term in nature. As 91 per cent of credits were assigned for consumption and only 9 per cent for investments, they hardly contributed to the creation of new sources of income. Foreign capital invested in private firms was usually aimed at producing quick profits which were rapidly sent abroad. German capital took the lead in this field, exporting to the Reich not only profits but also allowances for depreciation of industrial plant and floating assets. Capital withdrawn from the Polish part of Upper Silesia served as a source of considerable investment in the German part of the region.

LIVING CONDITIONS

Any review of changes in living conditions between 1918 and 1923 is a complex task in view of the severe and varied regional differences and the incomparability of subsequent annual data in money terms.

Immediately after regaining independence the main problem of the urban working population was a lack of work. Unemployment was highest in the former Kingdom of Poland: at the beginning of 1919, when the number of workers employed there in industry amounted to 90,000 people, unemployment reached a level of between 600,000 and 700,000. In other regions unemployment was lower. For the government this was not just an economic or social question: it was above all a political matter. The unemployed were generally more susceptible to agitation by the extreme left. The government consequently made great attempts to reduce unemployment by inaugurating public works, signing an emigration convention with France and encouraging the reconstruction of industry, etc. As these steps did little to improve the situation, a ystem of unemployment benefits was also developed.

Unemployment was only radically reduced when the Polish army was built up. From 195,000 soldiers and officers in November 1918, the army grew to more than 900,000 men by 1920. After the Polish-Soviet war a constantly improving market situation prevented a repeated increase in unemployment when the army was demobilised in November 1920. In December 1920 the number of unemployed in the former Russian and Austrian partitions was estimated at 51,000, a year later at 173,000, but in 1922 this number decreased to 62,000 people in the whole of Poland. In December 1923 there were 61,000 unemployed in Poland.(28) When compared with the figures for employed workers whose numbers had risen from 202,000 in 1920 (in contemporary frontiers) to 654,000 people in 1923 (including 201,000 workers employed in Upper Silesia), (29) unemployment seemed to maintain a moderate level.

Until mid-1921 increasing employment was accompanied by a growth in real wages (nominal wages grew constantly due to inflation). This occurred for a variety of reasons such as a very low level of real wages in 1918, the government's fear of revolution, strikes and so forth. From mid-1921 until the end of 1923 individual real wages gradually diminished. The total amount of real wages received by the working class grew until 1922, a result of a rapid increase in employment, but in 1923 even total real wages decreased. In the first half of 1921 individual real wages accounted for about 98 per cent of the 1914 level, but for only 57 per cent in late 1923. In the second half of 1923 individual wages were a mere 17 per cent higher than the starvation level of 1918. (30) This was one reason for the reappearance of a revolutionary climate in 1923. In November 1923 Cracow and some other towns in south Poland saw strikes, riots and scuffles between workers and the army. Several people were wounded and killed. These events forced the government to accelerate reforms.

On the other hand workers enjoyed essential changes in social legislation although benefits differed in various regions relative to the situation before 1918. The most advanced social legislation had existed in the Prussian partition, the least advanced in the Russian partition.

By November 1918 a decree had been issued introducing an 8-hour working day and a Saturday half-holiday which meant a 46-hour working week. In the former Kingdom of Poland the working day had been 10-11 hours long, whereas in the Prussian partition there had been no Saturday half-holidays. In January 1919 a government Inspection of Labour Office was established to monitor observance of this new legislation. At the same time another decree introduced obligatory health insurance. In February 1919 laws concerning the foundation and activity of trade unions were liberalised. Other regulations protected tenants and established a State Housing Fund aimed at financing construction of small flats for workers.

A lessening of revolutionary tension and more stable political conditions brought a slowing down of changes in social legislation. Regulations concerning leave for industrial workers introduced in May 1922 were the major exception. (31)

The introduction of labour legislation was resisted by entrepreneurs. Actual conditions of work were usually worse than those stipulated by existing legislation. Despite great efforts the Inspection of Labour Office was unable to prevent violations of the law, particularly in small factories.

Generally speaking, the Polish government considerably reduced the effects of unemployment in 1918-23 but did not succeed in checking the decrease in real wages which began in mid-1921 and led to a fall in demand and to a depression. Progress was however made in the field of social legislation.

As a rule the situation of the educated middle classes was better than that of industrial workers. There was a shortage of staff with higher or secondary education. The intelligentsia did not have to fear unemployment, had favourable labour legislation and was usually better paid. Living conditions were also better than those of industrial workers.

Farmers also had to contend with regional differences. Living conditions in the country were at first mostly determined by war damage. Peasants living in the areas affected by war between 1914-18 and 1919-20 tended to be worse off than those living in the western parts of Poland. The former had to expend both effort and capital on reconstruction, while the latter could utilise surplus production to develop their farms. Throughout most of this period prices for farm products were rather favourable for peasants. But as long as the obligatory quota system was in force, farmers had little chance of selling products at higher free market prices and most was sold to the government at low prices. Under these circumstances peasants received returns lower than they did before the First World War. The depreciation of the Polish mark was a positive stimulus as it diminished the real burden of state and local taxes and almost liquidated peasants' debts. A peasant politician mentioned in his memoirs that he had bought in 1920 about 2.5 hectares of land for 36,000 Polish marks borrowed from a credit institution. When he paid off the debt in 1924 the sum was worth only a box of matches. On the other hand any savings peasants might have had rapidly lost their value due to inflation.

It seems that between 1918 and 1923 the situation was far better (as compared with the pre-war period) for those farms which produced relatively small amounts of marketable goods than for the large privately-owned farms of the western provinces, which found themselves worse off.

Farm workers were an important social group and in the first post-war years their situation slightly improved due to radical movements which sprang up among agricultural workers. Numerous strikes were organised to disrupt large landed estates. One of their major achievements was the introduction of obligatory collective labour contracts throughout Poland. In many cases farm hands obtained rises of wages in kind, at a time when the role of cash wages was diminishing because of inflation.

Any evaluation of the financial standing of the city bourgeoisie and landowners seems impracticable. Industrial entrepreneurs benefited not only from market rallies but also from the privileges granted by the government in order to encourage reconstruction and stimulate employment. They also gained from the inflationary mechanisms that reduced indebtedness or diminished the tax burden, etc. The position of landowners was quite varied and often depended on the estate's location. Those who owned estates in the eastern territories affected by the 1919-20 war with Soviet Russia were in a rather tenuous position having lost all their moveables and buildings, while their capital was to be destroyed by inflation. On the other hand landowners from other regions were to benefit from a large demand for their agricultural products.

NOTES

1. E. Romer, I. Weinfeld (eds.), Rocznik Polski - tablice statystyczne (Gebethner i Spółka, Cracow, 1917), pp. 58-9.

2. Mały Rocznik Statystyczny 1931, (Główny Urząd Statystyczny, Warsaw, 1931), p.4.

3. Z. Landau, J. Tomaszewski, W dobie inflacji 1918-1923, (Książka i Wiedza, Warsaw, 1967), pp. 47-61.

4. Archive of New Records (quoted further as AAN), Protocols of the Council of Ministers, vol. 6, p. 629.

5. Report entitled 'W sprawie uruchomienia przemysłu', AAN, Protocols of the Council of Ministers, vol. 6, p. 632.

6. Z. Landau, J. Tomaszewski, W dobie, p. 81; AAN, Ignacy Paderewski Papers, vol. 518, p.2.

7. J. Dąbrowski, 'Rzut oka na rozwój przemysłu polskiego w latach 1918-1923', 'Przemysł i Handel', 1923, p. 687; Materiały do badań nad gospodarką Polski, part 1: 1918-1939 (Państwowe Wydawnictwo Naukowe, Warsaw, 1956), p. 1965.

8. Rocznik Statystyki Rzeczypospolitej Polskiej 1923 (Główny Urząd Statystyczny, Warsaw, 1923), pp. 47, 56, 59.

9. For details cf: J. Popkiewicz, F. Ryszka, Przemysł ciężki Górnego Śląska w gospodarce Polski międzywojennej (1921-1939) (Ossolineum, Opole, 1959).

10. Rocznik Statystyki Rzeczypospolitej Polskiej 1920/21 (Główny Urząd Statystyczny, Warsaw, 1920), part 2, p. 158; ibid., 1923, p. 64; ibid., 1924, p. 69.

11. Mały Rocznik Statystyczny 1937 (Główny Urząd Statystyczny, Warsaw, 1937), p. 107.

12. Położenie ekonomiczne rzemiosła wielkopolskiego w latach 1918-1939 (Państwowe Wydawnictwo Naukowe, Poznań, 1964), pp. 23-5.

13. E. Rose, Bilans gospodarczy trzech lat

niepodległości, (Gebethner i Wolff, Warsaw 1922), pp. 19-20, 23.

14.W. Grabski, J. Stojanowski, J. Warężak, 'Rolnictwo Polski 1914-1920', in Polska w czasie wielkiej wojny (1914-1918) (Towarzystwo Badania Zagadnień Międzynarodowych, Warsaw, 1936), vol. 3, pp. 52-3, 77, 110, 183-5.

15.Z. Ludkiewicz, Podręcznik polityki agrarnej (Komitet Wydawniczy Podręczników Akademickich, Warsaw, 1932), vol. 1, p. 38.

16.E. Szturm de Sztrem, Samowystarczalność Polski pod względem zbożowym (Ignis, Warsaw, 1922), pp. 31-2; Rocznik Statystyki Rzeczypospolitej Polskiej 1927 (Główny Urząd Statystyczny, Warsaw, 1927), pp. 31-2.

17.Z. Landau, J. Tomaszewski, W dobie, p. 273.

18.R. Rybarski, Ciężar podatków w Polsce (Ignis, Warsaw, n.d.), p. 89.

19.Parliamentary speech by MP J. Zdziechowski in Sprawozdanie stenograficzne z 81 posiedzenia Sejmu w dniu 23 XI 1923, szp. 23; T. Szturm de Sztrem, Żywiołowość w opodatkowaniu: podatek inflacyjny (Ignis, Warsaw, 1923), p. 49.

20.T. Szturm de Sztrem, Żywiołowość, p. 49; S. Starzyński, 'Myśl państwowa w życiu gospodarczym' in Na froncie gospodarczym 1918-1928 (Droga, Warsaw, 1928), p. 9.

21.E. Taylor, Inflacja polska (Poznańskie Towarzystwo Nauk, Poznań, 1926), pp. 1-37.

22.S. Karpiński, Pamiętnik dziesięciolecia (1915-1924) (F. Hoesick, Warsaw, 1931), p. 237.

23.H. Nowak, Bankowość w Polsce (Dom Książki Polskiej, Warsaw, 1932), vol. 1, p. 258.

24.S.F. Królikowski, Charakterystyka taryf celnych w Polsce (1919-1928) (Ministerstwo Przemysłu i Handlu, Warsaw, 1928), pp. 3-8.

25.Parliamentary speech by premier I. Paderewski in Sprawozdanie stenograficzne z 18 posiedzenia Sejmu w dniu 26 III 1919, szp. 1111.

26.Protocol of the meeting of the Economic Council of Ministers on 25 August 1920, AAN, Protocols of the Council of Ministers, vol. 11, p. 452, reprinted in Z. Landau, J. Tomaszewski, Kapitały obce w Polsce 1918-1939. Materiały i dokumenty (Książka i Wiedza, Warsaw, 1964), pp. 64-5.

27.Z. Landau, Polskie zagraniczne pożyczki państwowe 1918-1926 (Książka i Wiedza, Warsaw, 1961), p. 138; Z. Landau, 'The Foreign Loans of the Polish State in the Years 1918-1939', Studia Historiae Oeconomica, vol. 9, 1974, pp. 281-8.

28.J. Drecki, 'Bezrobocie w Polsce niepodległej' in Bilans gospodarczy dziesięciolecia Polski

Odrodzonej (Powszechna Wystawa Krajowa, Poznań, 1929), vol. 2, p. 379.

29.Z. Landau, J. Tomaszewski, Robotnicy przemysłowi w Polsce. Materialne warunki bytu, (Książka i Wiedza, Warsaw. 1971), pp. 145, 162.

30.S. Rychliński, Płace i zarobki robotników przemysłowych w dziesięcioleciu 1918-1929 (Instytut Gospodarstwa Społecznego, Warsaw, 1929), p. 10.

31.M. Święcicki, Instytucje polskiego prawa pracy w latach 1918-1939 (Państwowe Wydawnictwo Naukowe, Warsaw, 1960), pp. 11-77.

32.J. Madejczyk, Wspomnienia (Ludowa Spółdzielnia Wydawnicza, Warsaw, 1965), p. 126.

FROM DEPRESSION TO PROSPERITY, 1924-9

POPULATION

Although immediately after the end of the 1919-20 war with Soviet Russia the number of contracted marriages and the birth-rate increased considerably, between 1924 and 1929 population growth more or less stabilised. Natural increase remained relatively high, fluctuating between 16.6 per thousand in 1924 and 15.0 per thousand in 1929. By 1929 Poland was inhabited by 31.3 million people, the population having risen by almost 2.5 million over the previous seven years.

Emigration was still widespread in Poland although that which was due to the change of frontiers, repatriation of Poles and emigration of Germans to the Weimar Republic, had almost entirely ceased. Nevertheless there were substantial movements of population in search of work. More than 900,000 people emigrated for this reason in 1924-9 while about 395,000 people returned to Poland. These figures are not very precise but they generally show the order of magnitude of the problem. (1)

Most Polish emigrants leaving for Europe went to France and Germany. While emigration to France was as a rule permanent, Polish emigrants leaving for Germany usually undertook casual work in farming and returned after a certain time. Overseas emigrants headed for Canada and Argentina, but the United States by this time had begun to impose restrictions on immigration. Emigrants were mainly recruited from the peasant community, particularly from some southern and eastern provinces, including the Kielce and Łódź regions. Emigration meant a net outflow of half a million people and this to some extent eased agrarian over-population, as well as having a beneficial effect on the employment market in towns. Thus the government supported it.

There were also certain migrations inside the country, towns being a popular destination. Between the first census of 1921 and the 1931 census the share of the urban population in Poland had grown from 24 per cent to 27 per cent. Domestic migrations were mainly a flight from agrarian over-population and scarcity of work. Major cities like Warsaw or Łódź - a centre of the Polish textile industry - were the main attraction. Many people moved to the newly constructed Baltic port and city of Gdynia. The share of economically active and passive workers in the total population of Poland grew from 25.9 per cent in 1925 to 29.9 per cent in 1929, reflecting a gradual modernisation of the social structure.

Essential changes were made in education. At the end of the 1928/9 school year compulsory education embraced 93 per cent of children of school age, as against only 80 per cent four years earlier. Significant progress was made in the eastern provinces which were particularly backward in this respect. Secondary schools fared less well as they were rather hard to enter for most children coming from peasant or workers' families. Although secondary schools were free (with the exception of a few private schools), the cost of keeping children on at school was still beyond the financial abilities of most peasant and workers' families.

Higher education developed more rapidly and the number of students and graduates increased. Many graduates were employed in state and local administration, secondary and higher education, judicature, etc.

INDUSTRY

From the point of view of development trends during 1924-9, division may be made into two periods: a post-inflation depression from the autumn of 1923 to the beginning of 1926 and a period of prosperity which lasted until the autumn of 1929.

Hyperinflation impoverished society in general, producing cuts in consumption, investment and exports. Industrial production diminished and the currency stabilisation of 1924 only deepened the crisis. Polish commodities ceased to be competitive in foreign markets due to the high gold parity of the Polish złoty, whereas growing unemployment reduced home demand. These troubles were further aggravated by the expiration of agreements regulating duty-free exports of considerable quantities of Polish goods to Germany (for example, six million tons of coal per annum, some metallurgical products, etc.). The German government wished to gain the advantage and started an economic war with Poland in an attempt to impose what would be political concessions in Germany's favour. The reduction of Polish exports to Germany deepened economic depression in the Second Republic, an event not unwelcomed by the German government. A further collapse of the Polish currency in 1925 led to the reintroduction of the inflationary export premium. What is more, a long-lasting strike of British miners, which had started in May 1926, offered opportunities for Polish coal exports and contributed to a coal price rise. In February 1926 the index of industrial production in Poland began to show a rising trend. The Coup d'état in May 1926, organised by Józef Piłsudski, who overthrew a parliamentary government by military force and installed an authoritarian rule, did not influence the market situation as the new government continued the economic policy of former cabinets. (2) Piłsudski's associates included a group of adherents of a state-controlled economy headed by Stefan Starzyński and supported by some members of the civil service and the army. (3) This group was, however, not prevalent in the new government circles and had no support from Piłsudski who was not interested in economy, and except for finance, did not attach great importance to economic problems. The government economic policy after May 1926 was rather dominated by an organisation of business circles - the Central Association of Polish Industry, Mining, Commerce and Finance (called 'Lewiatan' in short) whose representatives took some seats in the ministries and the government's consultative bodies.

If the 1923 level of industrial output is taken as 100, the respective indices for the years 1924-9 would be: 85, 86, 84, 105, 118 and 121 per cent. This shows that in 1929 industrial production in Poland was higher by 21 per cent than in 1923, whereas in the years 1926-9 it had increased by almost 50 per cent. It seemed a success when compared with the post-inflation depression level, but still not much if compared with the 1913 level. World industrial production was also relatively much higher.

Although prosperity brought a considerable increase of output in all major branches of Polish industry, Poland's share of world industrial production had diminished and the 1913 level was not reached. According to an estimate Poland's industrial output in 1929 accounted for 91 per cent of the 1913 level, while world industrial output had reached 145 per cent of this level. Moreover, it must be remembered that even in 1913 the economy of the Polish territories was far behind more advanced countries. (4) Information on trends in industrial production can be found in Table 2.4.

The years between 1923 and 1929 brought certain changes in the structure of Polish industry. The loss of a large Russian market and trade difficulties with Germany forced entrepreneurs to cut production

Table 2.4: Production of Selected Industrial Goods in Poland, 1913, 1923, 1926 and 1929

Product	Unit	1913	1923	1926	1929
Hard coal	million tonnes	40	36	36	46
Oil	thousand tonnes	1,114	737	796	675
Natural gas	million cubic metres	687	390	481	467
Salt	thousand tonnes	189	363	339	407
Potassium salts	thousand tonnes	14	62	208	359
Iron ore	thousand tonnes	464	450	315	660
Zinc ore	thousand tonnes	510	260	305	377
Pig iron	thousand tonnes	1,055	520	327	706
Steel	thousand tonnes	1,619	1,132	788	1,377
Zinc	thousand tonnes	192	96	124	169
Lead	thousand tonnes	42	17	28	37
Coke	thousand tonnes	918	1,373	1,113	2,123
Fertilisers	thousand tonnes	400	282	613	579
Sugar	thousand tonnes	571	574	421	824
Cement	thousand tonnes	665	489	557	1,008
Electric power	million kilowatt-hours	660	1,511	1,441	3,048
Rolled goods	thousand tonnes	1,244	778	562	962
Paper	thousand tonnes	65	52	82	198
Sulphuric acid	thousand tonnes	225	-	168	233
Cotton thread	thousand tonnes	100	65a	-	67
Woollen yarn	thousand tonnes	48	37a	-	30

Note: a. Data for 1922.

Source: Z. Landau, J. Tomaszewski, Od Grabskiego do Piłsudskiego. Okres kryzysu poinflacyjnego i ożywienia koniunktury 1924-1929 (Książka i Wiedza, Warsaw, 1971), pp. 31, 52; Rocznik Statystyczny przemysłu 1945-1965 (Główny Urząd Statystyczny, Warsaw, 1967), pp. 798-801.

in traditional export industries and to concentrate on satisfying the improving Polish home market. Of particular importance was a breakdown of the traditional links between Polish enterprises and German industry after the tariff war began in 1925. The Polish market was badly affected by a lack of goods previously imported from the Reich. The gap began to be filled by home producers who started to invest in the production of formerly imported commodities.

Before the First World War most Polish workers were employed in the mining and textile industries, whereas employment in the metal-processing, engineering or chemical industries, which required a higher degree of processing, was rather low. Between January 1925 and December 1929 this situation changed. In January 1925 mining workers accounted for 28.5 per cent of the total employment in mining, metallurgy and processing industries (in factories of more than 19 workers), but in 1929 the comparable figure was 18.3 per cent, notwithstanding a growth in employment. At the same time the share of textile workers decreased from 21.0 per cent to 18.1 per cent. On the other hand employment in the mineral, food-processing and building industries rapidly increased. The share of metal-workers remained unchanged but they grew in absolute numbers. Employment in the metal-processing industry rose from 68,000 to 96,000 workers. It must also be remembered that during the entire period an increase in labour productivity was recorded.

In view of the cheapness of manpower, modernisation was not necessarily profitable at a time when inflation paradoxically brought a measure of prosperity and stimulated the export market. But the necessity to make Polish goods competitive after currency stabilisation made many entrepreneurs modernise their factories. Progress consisted mainly in replacing steam drive by electric power and combustion engines. This was common for all industries except metallurgy whose German owners withdrew their capital to the Reich.

Modernisation and investment soon raised the productive capacity of Polish industry. Nevertheless, even in the course of prosperity, certain lines of production could not fully utilise their potential. Of course capacity utilisation was much higher than it was during the post-inflation depression period when coal mining reached 56 per cent capacity, while that of sorting houses was 45 per cent, oil refineries 65 per cent, blast furnaces 40 per cent, open-hearth steelworks 57 per cent, and fertiliser factories 30-70 per cent. (5) According to a Polish economist the average capacity utilisation of industry in 1925-6 was between 30 per cent and 70 per cent. (6)

The major achievement during 1926-9 consisted in defining the basic lines of government economic policy. For a long time it was an open question as to whether Poland should develop along mainly agricultural lines or as an industrial-agricultural economy. The idea of agricultural Poland was supported not only by influential landowners but also by some foreign financial centres. After the introduction of the Dawes plan in 1925 those Western powers which allowed Germany substantial credits tried to provide German industry with new markets in order to prevent competition in the markets controlled by the creditor countries. (7) Therefore a theory was worked out that Poland should not develop her own processing industry but import the necessary industrial goods. This standpoint was most completely expressed by an American financial expert, Professor Edwin Walter Kemmerer who visited Poland in 1925 and 1926. In his report he wrote: 'The Polish industry is rather overgrown than underdeveloped in relation to agriculture and raw materials. It seems the best future for Poland would be production of agricultural articles and raw materials for the industrialised part of Europe.' (8)

Similar, though slightly disguised, was the attitude of the President of the Reichsbank, Hjalmar Schacht.

The contemporary Polish minister of industry and trade, Eugeniusz Kwiatkowski was advocating the idea of the industrialisation of Poland; he said agriculture might expand only on condition that Poland developed a well-developed industrial base. He believed that the only way to create a healthy market for farming products and absorb the manpower surplus from the over-populated rural areas was to speed up the industrialisation of Poland.

The period between 1923 and 1929 was characterised by a strong trend towards concentration of production and capital. The number of joint-stock companies increased along with their capital. But even more important was cartelisation. While on 1 January 1924 there were 31 domestic and six international cartels in Poland, on 31 December 1929 their number was, respectively, 133 and 48. (9) Cartelisation included all major industries and even some second-rank lines of production. Monopolisation caused an increase in prices of cartelised products in the home market. Domestic profits frequently covered losses resulting from exports. For instance, the price of coal in Poland in 1929 was 38 złotys per ton, while in exports it was 28 złotys; the price of sugar, respectively, 141 and 45 złotys per quintal and the price of petrol, 76 and 40 złotys per ton. Cartelisation in Poland was very advanced, a fact confirmed in the League of Nations' reports. (10)

An inflow of foreign capital into Polish enterprises was also typical for the years 1923-9. Usually it consisted in purchasing shares of already existing companies but from time to time new investments were also undertaken. Quite often foreign business circles took an interest in Polish industry by means of credits without direct participation in the joint-stock capital. This method seemed more convenient for those investors who wanted to be able to rapidly quit business in Poland. As there was little confidence in the stability of the Polish state due to German propaganda in the West, foreign capital did not expect long-term relations with Poland and counted on quick and ready profits. In 1927, a year for which there are the first relatively precise estimates, the share of foreign capital in the joint-stock capital of firms active in Poland amounted to 21.1 per cent and in 1929 to 33.3 per cent. The highest share of foreign capital occurred in oil mining (76.5 per cent in 1929), metallurgy (65.4 per cent), power plants, water-supply and gas works (75.6 per cent), chemical industries (40.6 per cent) and mining (38.8 per cent); the lowest share of foreign capital could be found in some light industries such as printing (1.5 per cent) or clothing manufacture (3.3 per cent), etc. Foreign capital was invested in the largest enterprises which influenced whole lines of production by means of cartel agreements. Thus the role of foreign capital was much higher than was apparent from the data concerning their share in the joint-stock companies.

The largest investments in Polish industry were undertaken by the French, the Germans, and, in the late 1920s, by the Americans. (11) The increased role of American business resulted from the entry of the Averell Harriman group to the Upper Silesian zinc and metallurgical industry where it represented the interests of German business circles.

Apart from manufacturing industry, an important role was played by handicraft production. The precise number of handicraft workshops is not known, as many craftsmen operated illegally or did not have to purchase official certificates and were therefore not included in the statistical evidence. It was estimated in 1928 that the number of handicraft workshops approached 450,000 and that they employed from 886,000 to one million people. In other words, handcrafts employed more workers than mining, metallurgy and all large and medium-size processing factories of more than 19 employees. In fact shoemaking engaged more workers than any line of manufacturing industry. Handicrafts were accompanied by domestic industry carried on mainly by peasants in the wintertime. It included about one million people working in 100,000 to 200,000 weaving shops, 2,500 pottery shops, etc. About 300,000 homeworkers working in the 'putting-out system' should also be mentioned. (12) It can be seen that small-scale market production was very extensive.

The role of handicrafts slightly diminished in 1926-9 as compared with the post-inflation depression period but the number of workshops and handicraftsmen was stable. It was estimated that in 1924 handicraft turnover amounted to 45 per cent of the turnover of large enterprises, whereas in 1928 it had fallen to 38 per cent; in relation to the whole industrial output the share of handicraft production declined from 14.7 per cent in 1924 to 10.5 per cent in 1928. (13) This was mainly due to a growing upturn in Polish industry.

AGRICULTURE

From the end of 1923 to mid-1926 farming was in a state of depression. Market trends for agricultural products in Poland were less favourable than in international markets due to industrial depression and to government policy. The Polish government wanted to prevent an increase in the cost of living in towns and reduced prices of farming products by imposing export restrictions. Improvements in the home and international markets began in the autumn of 1926 and as a result prices of farming products increased and improved the financial situation of the countryside. However, this favourable market situation broke down, after the harvest of 1928, and a period of recession began in the agricultural sector.

Farming production increased in the five years between 1924 and 1929. Profitability in agriculture was determined by the prices of articles sold (and bought) by farmers. Notwithstanding this relationship farmers were able to raise outputs, mainly due to an enlargement of the area under cultivation. During this time production of all basic grain crops, potatoes and sugar beet steadily expanded. The highest growth was recorded in the sugar beet plantations, the lowest in rye, although this crop was the most popular bread grain in Poland. The increase of crops was also due to a growing use of fertilisers. In 1923 about 334,000 tonnes of fertilisers were employed but in 1929 this had grown to 1,253,000 tonnes, that is four times more. However even in 1929 the pre-war level was not exceeded. The growth in fertiliser use was unequal in the various regions and types of farms. Fertilisers were mostly used in western provinces, much less in central Poland, while in the eastern regions their usage was very scarce. It was estimated that 70-80 per cent of fertilisers were applied by the large landed estates.

Modern land cultivation methods were gradually introduced at the behest of economic ministries, peasant organisations, etc. which by various means had begun to further agricultural knowledge throughout the countryside.

Yields per hectare grew in line with an improvement in economic results. A comparison of average yields in 1925-9 with those of 1909-13 shows an increase in barley, oats, potato yields and a decrease in sugar beet yields. Total crops changed in a different way. The rye, potato and sugar beet crops grew (mainly due to an increase of the area under crop), but the wheat, barley and oat crops were still below the pre-war level. Increasing farm production meant that Poland was able to reach self-sufficiency in foodstuffs. Crop fluctuations led to a surplus in the good harvest years, while a certain shortage appeared in less fertile years.

Considerable differentiation in yields in various provinces was another characteristic feature of Polish farming. For instance in 1925-9 wheat yields per hectare amounted to 19.7 quintals in the western provinces and in Polesie to only 7.9 quintals, whereas yields of potatoes were, respectively, 128 quintals and 77 quintals. In the early 1920s these differences diminished slightly due to a growth of yields in the most backward eastern provinces and a decrease in the leading provinces.

Animal husbandry was also developing. With the exception of sheep, numbers of all other animals increased but growth in this area was slower than crop production. Hog breeding was limited by a lack of foreign markets but milk-cow husbandry developed quite well due to domestic and export demands. (14)

The controversy over land reform principles continued in 1924-5. The interests of landowners and other social groups were incompatible. The Land Reform Act was finally passed by the Seym on 28 December 1925. It was mainly aimed at setting in order the parcelling out of large estates. As a rule it was adopted that all surplus land above 180 hectares of cropland on each estate would be redistributed. In the eastern provinces this limit was raised to 300 hectares and - for industrialised estates - to 350-700 hectares. Voluntary parcelling was to include 200,000 hectares per annum for the following ten years. Unless the yearly quota was reached the government was to apply compulsory measures. Compensation was to cover the market price of land and buyers could be granted credits for the purpose of purchasing land. (15) These principles remained in force until the Second World War.

The 1925 Land Reform Act only sanctioned the principles of land redistribution which had in fact been going on since 1919. In 1919-25 more than 740,000 hectares were divided up. After the Land Reform Act was passed the area of parcelled land increased, mainly due to an improving market situation in farming and to the growing financial capability of the peasantry. In 1926 about 210,000 hectares of land were parcelled; in 1927, 245,000; in 1928, 228,000; but in 1929, when the economic situation began to deteriorate, only 165,000 hectares were apportioned. (16)

Land redistribution was one of the concepts promoted at that time which aimed at the transformation of the agricultural system. The Polish minister for land reforms, Witold Staniewicz, postulated a change from peasant farms running an almost subsistence economy over a large part of Poland to commercial farming. In his opinion both the large estates and peasant farms should intensify production. He thought the major task of the government was to consolidate peasant lots, to liquidate easement rights and to accelerate drainage and watering. At the same time he expected the surplus peasant population to emigrate. This amounted to a capitalist transformation of Polish agriculture based on the assumption that most of the agrarian over-population would have to leave the country so that self-sufficient commercial farms could then be created. This programme hung in midair as there was little or no employment in towns. The realisation of the programme was therefore limited to consolidation, amelioration and the ending of easement rights. These latter measures did stimulate the development of agriculture but did nothing to alter radically the agrarian structure.

FINANCE

Hyperinflation led to a reduction in the standard of living and, consequently, to strikes and riots. The November 1923 events shook the country. It was thought that any further delay in implementing financial reforms would inevitably lead to an increase in political tension or even to revolution. All the Polish Seym parties which supported the maintenance of the capitalist system proclaimed a Treuga Dei and accepted a non-parliamentary government to carry out budgetary and monetary reforms.

On 19 December 1923 Władysław Grabski became premier and minister of the Treasury. (17) He had already twice held the Treasury post and had worked out a clear-cut and realistic programme. In his opinion reform should aim at the replacement of the depreciated Polish mark with another monetary unit and, at the same time, deal with the basic cause of inflation - the budget deficit. Financial means for this purpose had to be sought within Poland as the inflow of foreign capital played only a minor role.

Grabski then asked the Seym to authorise the President to issue decrees having the force of parliamentary law. This power, aimed at accelerating legislative prodedure, was accepted for a period of six months.

Hoping to achieve budget equilibrium Grabski made use of two laws, passed by the Seym at the end of 1923, referring to valorisation of taxes and to an extraordinary property tax in the sum of 1,000 million francs in gold. Property tax was to be paid in instalments for three years in order to cover budget deficits. The prime minister expected business activity to provide the budget after that time with sufficient, regular revenues. At the beginning of January 1924 the government decided to accelerate payment of the first instalment of the property tax and at the end of the same month sped up payment of other taxes and imposed severe penalties for delay. Reducing expenses was another way to help reach budget equilibrium. This time government expenditure cuts were to affect both the army and the state-controlled railway company. Some central government institutions were also dispensed with.

Grabski tried to charge various social groups

with the cost of monetary reform according to their financial means. The propertied classes were to bear the highest burden paying a large property tax. In addition, entrepreneurs paid an increased turnover tax, while landowners were obliged to pay a higher rate of tax on their landholdings. Working people had to pay increased taxes on their earnings. Peasants and landowners were also affected by a raised land-value tax. At the same time indirect taxes also grew. According to (one of the authors of this book) Jerzy Tomaszewski: 'Although the Władysław Grabski cabinet increased indirect taxes raising the tax burden of the working masses, the increment of budget revenues mainly affected the propertied classes.' (17)

Simultaneously Grabski was preparing for monetary reform. The government announced that they would cease using bank note issues to cover budget deficits. After temporary stabilisation of the Polish mark, Grabski wanted to replace it with the Polish złoty. The new monetary unit was to be issued by the Bank Polski - a joint-stock private bank independent of the government. On 20 January 1924 a special decree was issued setting out the principles of the future monetary system. The new currency - the złoty - was to be based on the gold parity of the Swiss franc and be secured by gold and currency reserves amounting to 30 per cent of its circulation. The Bank Polski began trading the złoty on 28 April 1924. (18)

Polish marks were exchanged at the rate of 1.8 million to one Polish złoty. The exchange lasted until 1 July 1924 and in the meantime both monetary units were temporarily allowed to circulate.

Within the first few months the reform seemed a success. The government managed both to check inflation and to introduce a new currency. This success changed the attitude of various social groups towards reform in general. The proletariat was appeased but the propertied classes were no longer interested in paying further taxes. Budget revenues began to decrease again. While at the beginning of 1924 payments of property tax accounted for 80 per cent of the estimated sums, at the end of 1924 this had plunged to only 30 per cent (19) and the budget deficit returned. Grabski tried to cover it by means of various extraordinary revenues but in 1925 the government was unable to prevent further widening of the deficit.

Fearing collapse of the reform Grabski modified his plans. He attached more and more importance to foreign loans and managed to receive some credits from abroad. The loans obtained were insubstantial as well as expensive; creditors demanded not only high interest rates but special privileges also. For example, Italian businessmen who granted Poland a loan of 400 million lire were given precedence in supplying the Polish Tobacco Monopoly with raw tobacco; Swedes were given the match monopoly on lease in exchange for a $6 million loan, etc. On the whole, however, Poland's difficult economic situation in 1925 dissuaded foreign business circles from offering the Polish government really worthwhile aid.

The growing deficit obliged the government to cover expenses by means of new coin issues (coins were Treasury monies independent of the Bank Polski). In the first half of 1925 the circulation of coins was growing rapidly and the Bank Polski refused to accept them for major payments or for exchange into foreign currencies. Thus the Polish złoty had two rates of exchange - that of the Bank Polski notes and that of the Treasury coins. As a result foreign money exchanges showed an increasing distrust towards the stability of the Polish currency. While at the beginning of the Grabski reform the Polish złoty was accepted without question, in 1925 its position became more and more complicated. Flight from the złoty diminished the Bank Polski's note coverage, especially after the outbreak of the Polish-German economic war which deepened the trade balance deficit. Because of an excessive supply of the Polish złoty abroad its rate of exchange collapsed on 20 July 1925. Monetary intervention started by the Bank Polski at the request of the prime minister proved ineffective. The złoty rate of exchange had fallen from 5.14 to 6 złotys to one US dollar. In September 1925 it crumbled again. To peg the złoty the Polish government managed to obtain small intervention credits from foreign banks. But when the Bank Polski refused to continue intervention purchasing of Polish złotys in domestic and foreign monetary exchanges, Grabski resigned. (20) On that day - 12 November 1925 - the złoty rate of exchange was already 6.9 złotys to one US dollar.

Having decided to issue more coins the Polish government initiated a second period of inflation, sometimes called the 'coin inflation'. The rate of inflation was not really so damaging, as in February 1926 Poland's financial situation began to improve due to a general market recovery and to rapidly increasing exports (a result of the British coal-miners' strike, and other reasons). (21)

Władysław Grabski's successor in the Treasury ministry, Jerzy Zdziechowski, aimed at a gradual balancing of the budget. But while Grabski tried to attain this end by increasing the tax burden of the better-off groups, Zdziechowski, who represented business finance, made attempts to shift this burden upon consumers. Therefore he stressed the need to raise taxes on consumption and to introduce new indirect taxes. Along with a further cut in government expenditure these steps gradually diminished the monthly budget deficits. Improving the budget also strengthened the position of the złoty.

One reaction to the *coup d'état* of May 1926 was an immediate fall in the złoty rate of exchange. Before the coup one US dollar cost 10.05 złotys but by 20 and 21 May the rate of exchange had reached 11.1 złotys. Piłsudski's intentions were unknown and business circles feared that he would tend towards a state-controlled economy and social reforms. But soon after the *coup d'état* members of a new cabinet headed by Kazimierz Bartel made several pronouncements which allayed misgivings in the business world. But even more encouraging was the continuation of the previous financial policy by a new Treasury minister and rapid recovery in the market. By September 1926 the new Treasury minister was able to state in his parliamentary speech:

> The anxiety for our currency is gone. The situation of the Bank Polski is sound... The złoty rate of exchange, which reached 11 zł to one US dollar in May, was brought down to 9 zł to one US dollar in July and has been maintained since that time. (22)

In 1927 budget targets had been achieved and there were considerable surplus margins. The monetary situation was in order. Nevertheless the Piłsudski government wanted to attract foreign capital to Poland. Therefore, despite full monetary stabilisation, the government decided to contract a foreign 'stabilisation loan'. It was arranged not to improve the already sound position of the złoty but to demonstrate to foreign business circles that stabilisation of the Polish economy had at last gained international acceptance.

The terms of the loan were initially prepared by the Kemmerer mission whose report became the foundation for negotiations between the Polish government and foreign bankers. On 13 October 1927 a decree was issued in Poland concerning the stabilisation of the złoty and the raising of the loan, which amounted to $US 62 million and £2 million. The stabilisation plan included ways to strengthen the złoty and certain changes to the Bank Polski's statute. The Polish złoty was devalued. Whereas previously one kg of gold would cover 3,100 zł, this sum was now raised to 5,924.44 zł. Thus the złoty gold parity decreased by 42 per cent and its rate of exchange was fixed at 8.91 zł to one US dollar. (23) The złoty was to remain convertible in gold and foreign currencies, but with gold this was only possible for amounts of 20,000 zł or more. The Bank Polski was obliged to raise gold and currency coverage to 40 per cent (previously 30 per cent) of note circulation. The stabilisation plan also imposed obligations on the budget economy. The government's compliance with the stipulations of the stabilisation plan was to be monitored by a special adviser to the Polish government, Charles Dewey, who was the former US Treasury under-secretary. He published quarterly reports, (24) supplying material for foreign businessmen which would enable them both to evaluate Poland's economic performance and to be briefed on government policy. It is noteworthy that this was the only exception when the Polish government had agreed to such a far-reaching concession.

The new reform finally set the Polish monetary system in order. A proportion of coin money was exchanged for Bank Polski notes and the gold and currency reserves of the bank were increased. From this point of view the stabilisation loan came up to expectations. However, it did not succeed in its original intention of stimulating an inflow of long-term capital investment to Poland. A favourable monetary climate then prevailed until the end of the 1920s.

Currency stabilisation also had its effect on banks. Some were in adverse financial positions and bankruptcy was frequent among those banks which had indulged in speculation. At the same time the role of the state-controlled banks grew as they began to enjoy more confidence in Polish society. Soon after the Grabski reform banking deposits began to increase but the collapse of the złoty in the autumn of 1925 resulted in a banking crisis. Depositors began to withdraw their money and many banks faced insolvency. Under these circumstances the government decided to grant considerable credits to several major joint-stock banks.

An improvement in economic conditions stimulated a banking recovery but led to a drop in the number of banks. Whereas in 1923 there were 111 private banks and 655 branch banks, in 1929 their number had fallen to 51 banks and 164 branch banks. Banking operations were growing rapidly and the rate of interest was stabilised. In 1929 the Bank Polski discount rate was 9 per cent and decreasing rates were an incentive to further economic progress.

DOMESTIC TRADE

In the course of post-inflation depression the number of trading shops slightly diminished but increased from 1926 onwards - although problems in the agricultural sector after the 1928 harvest caused a further decline. The number of wholesale enterprises had in any case radically decreased in 1924 due to centralisation of trade, normalisation of supply, and to the fact that speculative transactions were out of favour. Between 1924 and 1925 one half of wholesale enterprises in Poland were forced out of business. In 1926 this process continued, but at a slower rate. Concentration of turnover in the hands of the largest wholesale dealers made it possible to control purchasing and retail shops as was the case with slaughterhouses and fruit imports. The emerging export syndicates were supported by the government. Concentration was correlated with the spread of cartels and many of them established their own retail outlets. The sugar cartel was one of the strongest monopolies. The oil syndicate organised in 1927 under government pressure was aimed at eliminating intermediary agents and this policy forced several thousand small dealers into bankruptcy. Even without their own outlets, cartels could drastically reduce the profits of individual dealers and regulate the parameters of trade profit margins. Those merchants who broke cartel rules were punished by having their supply of goods withdrawn.

The centralisation of trade destroyed many small dealers but it could be said to have improved the quality of services, and the organisation of trade, etc.

In 1924-9 the trade network also changed. In the western provinces the number of shops increased by 42 per cent; in Central Poland by 17 per cent; in the south by 14 per cent, while in the eastern provinces an increase of only 5 per cent was recorded. Thus the imbalance between various regions was as noticeable as ever.

At the end of 1926 a certain rise in business

was recorded which lasted until mid-1928. The recovery in the market was connected with an improvement in the financial circumstances of both workers and peasants. To increase sales traders developed the hire-purchase system and introduced credit sales. A narrowing of the market in the second half of 1928 led to growing competition and controversies connected with regional differences, the latter becoming more and more the focus of continuing political struggle.

Co-operative trade was playing a minor, though gradually increasing role, especially in the country. Urban consumer co-operatives were more important immediately after the war when they improved the supply of goods in towns but later on they were less prominent. A general improvement in market supply lessened public interest in developing co-operatives. (25) Farming co-operatives expanded, however, particularly in south-east Poland where Ukrainian organisations regarded them as an instrument of policy.

FOREIGN ECONOMIC RELATIONS

Polish foreign trade policy during 1924-9 concentrated on maximum protection of the domestic market and on the promotion of exports. Though methods serving these ends were modified, their essence remained unchanged.

Tariffs were of basic significance in the protection of the domestic market. On 9 February 1924 several tariff rates were introduced but fearing a growth of social discontent, the government prevented price increases for articles of everyday use and maintained import tariffs for these at a relatively low level. In June 1924 customs tariffs were radically altered but the general policy of domestic market protection did not change. In May and November 1925 many tariff rates were raised and this strengthened the anti-import effects of the złoty collapse. At the same time controls on various commodities, whose export or import had been prohibited, were relaxed.

The economic quarrel with Poland started by the Weimar Republic on 15 June 1925 left the Polish government no alternative but to change its foreign trade policy. The conflict began when the German coal commissioner announced that after the expiry date of the convention concerning the division of Upper Silesia (which had obliged Germany to purchase certain quantities of duty-free coal from Poland), he would no longer grant permits for Polish coal imports. In return the Polish government imposed a partial embargo on exports from countries which prohibited the import of Polish goods, and regulations to this effect were enacted on 27 June 1925. The German government's response on the 1st and 2nd of July was to prohibit the import of many Polish goods, and impose high tariff rates on other Polish articles. On 11 July 1925 Poland extended its list of articles whose import from Germany was prohibited. Their value amounted to about 57 per cent of the previous Polish exports to Germany and to 27 per cent of total Polish exports. For Germany it meant a mere 3 per cent of the value of imports. Polish restrictions affected 47 per cent of German exports to Poland but only 3 per cent of the total exports of the Reich. Undoubtedly the consequences were much more severe for Poland than they were for Germany. (26)

The conflict immediately brought a slump in Polish exports at a time when the Polish economy was already under pressure. The German government thought the war would lead to a deepening of the depression and the collapse of the złoty. Redirecting Polish export goods to other markets was possible but required time.

The outbreak of economic war with the Reich coupled with an outflow of foreign currencies from the Bank Polski compelled the Polish government to introduce import restrictions. In July 1925 control of the import of goods prohibited in relation to Germany was extended to include all other countries. This affected about 30 per cent of the total value of Polish imports.

The depreciation of the Polish złoty diminished the real value of tariff rates. Valorisation was required and this was carried out in February 1928. Individual rates were calculated according to various coefficients. Thus the duty charge structure was changed. At the beginning of 1928 maximum tariff rates were introduced for goods imported from the countries which had no trade agreements with Poland. The Polish government had thus introduced another measure of trade policy. (27)

Polish exports were also promoted by means of the so-called duty refunds. The government had the right of specifying goods whose exporters were repaid the duty charged while importing raw materials or tools necessary to manufacture the exported goods. The duty refunds were often not limited to the real value of the import duties but served as a kind of bounty or premium for exporters. One of the main state-controlled banks - Bank Gospodarstwa Krajowego - set aside a special fund for export promotion. At the same time exporting cartels benefited from privileges in the domestic market.

It was essential for Polish foreign trade to have access to a Baltic port. Although international treaties provided Poland with the right of usage of the 'Free City' - the port of Gdańsk - in practice there were certain difficulties. At the beginning of the 1920s the Polish government decided, therefore, to build a port and sea town in the fishing village of Gdynia. Construction of the Gdynia port was accelerated in 1926 when new markets opened for Polish coal exports in Scandinavia, the state of public finances improved and when the construction of this new port began to receive special support from the Minister of industry and trade, Eugeniusz Kwiatkowski. In 1924 the new port handled 10,000 tonnes of goods but by 1929 this had reached 2,823,000 tonnes. As the capacity of Gdynia port had then not reached the level of tonnage handled by Gdańsk, the Polish government oversaw the development of both ports. The rapid construction of Gdynia and expansion of Gdańsk, as well as a policy of directing Polish maritime trade through these ports, led to stiff competition with ports of the German customs area.

Trade agreements were another method of export promotion. As a rule they were based on the 'most favoured nation' clause. Only in the Polish-French agreement of 9 December 1924 Poland granted France an unlimited most favoured nation clause, without appropriate retaliation the result of a certain degree of political and military dependence on France. Although negotiations were under way, Poland did not at that time have a trade agreement with the USSR. Thus the Second Republic had not signed agreements with her two largest neighbours.

The commodity structure of Polish foreign trade changed very little. Poland still exported mainly coal, timber and other raw materials and semi-finished products and imported machinery, raw materials lacking at home, fertilisers, etc. Imports showed an acceleration in investments but it was frequently observed in Poland that the structure of foreign trade turnover was unfavourable to the country and unprofitable in view of the existing terms of trade. But any major change would require long-term effort and application.

On the other hand, Polish foreign trade was beginning to expand in new directions. The significance of the German market diminished but there was an increase in trade with the Austria-Hungary successor states (Austria, Czechoslovakia, Hungary) and some other countries. The United States, for example, played an important role in Polish imports.

From 1924 to 1929 Poland's foreign trade balance was not favourable. Only in 1926 was a certain surplus recorded, (the 1924-5 deficit was a major reason for the collapse of the złoty). In the years of prosperity foreign trade deficits were covered by inflowing, mainly short-term credits. These deficits badly affected Poland's balance of payments. From 1923 to 1929 credits totalling almost 4 billion zł (according to the 1927 parity) were spent on covering foreign trade deficits: they amounted to about $US 445 million. (28)

LIVING CONDITIONS

The standard of living of industrial workers was of course related to the general trend of economic activity. During the post-inflation depression the number of employed workers diminished and unemployment grew. Wages decreased as mass unemployment usually led to a reduction in wage rates.

Employment in Polish industry was dramatically cut in 1924-5. It was estimated that the total number of workers employed in large and medium-sized industrial plants fell by one-third. A more precise estimate seems impossible as statistical methods of measuring employment used by the Główny Urząd Statystyczny (Central Statistical Office) have since changed. From 1926 to 1929 employment constantly increased but in December 1929 it had fallen again to a level lower than the year before. If the data for June of each year are compared, total employment in mining, metallurgy and processing industries (factories of more than 19 workers) shows a 37 per cent increase from 632,000 to 865,000 people.

Increasing employment did not fully solve the problem of all those without work. Their number is hard to estimate as there were no accurate unemployment statistics in Poland. The evidence that is available refers to workers seeking jobs through government employment agencies. Not all jobless workers were recorded and some of those entitled to register either did not or did not re-register each month. The actual number of unemployed was as a rule higher than that of the registered unemployed. In December 1924 the registered unemployed numbered 102,000 while actual unemployment was estimated at

151,000. One year later the figures were to 204,000 and 252,000 respectively. The years of prosperity brought a gradual reduction in unemployment. In 1926 there were 168,000 people seeking work (data for December), in 1927 138,000, in 1928 94,000 but in 1929 the number had risen to 125,000 people. Unemployment remained a permanent feature of Polish society.

Apart from unemployment there was the problem of part-time working. It was constantly diminishing. While in February 1924 the average number of working days in a week was 4.88 per worker, between mid-1926 and the end of 1928 this had increased to 5.97. In practice, part-time work was virtually non-existent and in 1929 the situation deteriorated again.

Unemployment insurance was introduced in Poland in 1924. It included all workers employed in factories of more than five workers. The insured had the right to obtain a small benefit for 13 weeks and later for 17 weeks from the moment of losing work. The government also made attempts to support the unemployed by organising public works but as a rule it was impossible to employ all those who sought work.

The ending of hyperinflation checked the decrease in real wages. Notwithstanding a deterioration of the market situation employers still tended to reduce nominal wage rates. As a result growing costs of living caused a fall in real wages from 1924 to 1925. The general purchasing power of workers was also negatively affected by declining employment. In 1925 the real value of wages fell by 19 points. Moreover, employers delayed wage payments.

Rising economic prosperity brought an end to this situation. Individual nominal wages grew by 30 per cent between December 1926 and December 1929. Real wages grew less rapidly. Individual real wage rates increased by 19 per cent but in view of rising employment the total amount of all real wages actually grew by more than 40 per cent. (29) Some improvement had been made. By 1929, the 1913 level of real wages had been exceeded.

In the course of post-inflation depression employers demanded that the government reduce workers' rights that had been introduced as a result of social legislation. Under this pressure the working day in Upper Silesian metallurgy was extended to ten hours in 1924. At the same time the number of holidays was limited and the working-day hours in mining were increased. At the same time new legislation was enacted in the interests of workers. This included an extension of accident insurance to the former Russian partition and the protection of female and juvenile labour. The latter law was considered then to be progressive but its realisation was strongly opposed by employers who were unwilling to bear the costs involved.

Economic prosperity was one of the principal factors in the development of social legislation. The functioning of the Inspection of Labour was improved, new regulations referring to the prevention and treatment of occupational diseases were introduced as well as others concerning work safety and employment contracts. Special labour courts were called into being to settle matters in dispute between workers and employers. Between 1927 and 1928 the 8-hour working day was reinstated in metallurgy. This positive trend was halted in the spring of 1929 by the increasing signs of economic depression and the government's policy of limiting workers' self-management. The regulations which were introduced were aimed at restraining the influence of left-wing parties on organisations and institutions acting among workers. Self-management in health insurance, for example, was abolished.

Generally speaking the years between 1926 and 1929 were quite favourable for the working class. The situation of the intelligentsia was even better. The demand for qualified staff was still very high. Thus there were hardly any problems with finding a job, and salaries were increasing. Legislation referring to white-collar workers was more favourable than that for manual workers. Social insurance, for instance, was much more developed.

The financial situation of farmers changed according to market trends. In 1924-5 economic conditions in agriculture were rather poor. But at the end of 1925 a gradual improvement began which lasted until the autumn of 1928. Then the first signs of depression brought a deterioration in the market which altered the balance between the prices of goods sold by farmers and that of goods purchased. Only between 1927 and 1928 was the balance restored to anything like a favourable one in the agricultural sector.

The tax burden of farming considerably increased in 1924 and remained unchanged afterwards. In view of increasing returns in agriculture, taxes were actually decreasing in relative terms, and it was estimated that taxation accounted for only 3 per cent of total earnings.

Although the financial position of the peasantry had improved with the general upturn in the economy, their standard of living was much lower than that of other social groups. According to an estimate of two outstanding Polish economists, Michał Kalecki and Ludwik Landau, small farmers received in 1929 only 8.7 milliard zł out of 23.9 milliard zł of the consumed part of the national income. This meant that the average monthly income (the figures are approximate) of a peasant family of four persons amounted to 175 zł (about $US20), while a similar family of non-agricultural workers might earn 265 zł and a professional family 640 zł. (30)

The small improvement in the financial situation of the peasantry did not however lead to any long-term benefits. The basic problem of unemployment still remained and peasant holdings were not extended to any great extent. From 1925 to 1929 the peasant population was gradually buying land but in view of relatively high market prices most purchases were on credit terms which more often than not carried exorbitant rates of interest. Thus the increasing area of land in peasant hands did not radically raise the standard of living of this social group: a large proportion of earnings was spent on loan repayments (interest rates often reached 50 per cent per annum). The situation of agricultural workers was gradually improving. Their wages in złotys grew. Whereas in 1924/5 the average annual wage in agriculture was 932 zł, in 1928/9 it had increased to 1853 zł. Work was regulated by collective agreements and a system of health insurance was developed. Certain regional differences still remained, with the western provinces usually dominant economically. In the most backward regions landowners preferred to employ seasonal workers recruited from rural areas rather than seek more expensive permanent labour. Sometimes poor peasants were employed under near-feudal conditions - working in return for a leased plot of land, for a hired horse or for small loans received in pre-harvest time. Such cases were relatively frequent in the east and south but were exceptional in the western provinces.

After a decline in business activity during the second period of inflation, a gradual recovery began in 1926. Dividends paid by joint-stock companies to their shareholders were growing, while increasing profits made it possible to invest in new projects. Large landowners found themselves better off as a result of enhanced crop yields and higher prices for farming products.

For the urban population and for industry in general the years between 1926 and 1929, and for agriculture the period between 1926 and 1928, were relatively prosperous. Increasing production stimulated employment growth as well as wage rises, but the fall in prices of cereals in the autumn of 1928 and, later, a fall in demand for some light industrial products (mostly textiles) were early signs of the depression to come.

NOTES

1. For more details cf. H. Janowska, Emigracja zarobkowa z Polski 1918-1939 (Państwowe Wydawnictwo Naukowe, Warsaw, 1981), p. 338 ff.; E. Kołodziej, Wychodźstwo zarobkowe z Polski 1918-1939 (Książka i Wiedza, Warsaw, 1982), p. 88.
2. Z. Landau, 'Impact of the May 1926 Coup on the State of Polish Economy', Acta Poloniae Historica, vol. 35 (1977), pp. 169-87.
3. This group has presented its concepts in several publications, e.g: Na froncie gospodarczym 1918-1928 (Droga, Warsaw, 1928), p. 442; Pięć lat na froncie gospodarczym 1926-1931 (Droga, Warsaw, 1931) vol. 1, p. 719; vol. 2, p. 665.
4. J. Stachniuk, Państwo a gospodarstwo. Geneza etatyzmu w Polsce (F. Hoesick, Warsaw, 1939), p. 34.
5. Z. Landau, 'Industrial Recession in Poland 1924-1925', Acta Poloniae Historica, vol. 43 (1981), pp. 189-90.
6. R. Battaglia, O programie gospodarczym Polski oraz o warunkach rozwoju poszczególnych gałęzi wytwórczości (Bank Gospodarstwa Krajowego, Warsaw, 1927), pp. 135-49.
7. W. Fabierkiewicz, O konsekwencjach gospodarczych planu Dawesa (Instytut Gospodarstwa Społecznego, Warsaw, 1925).
8. E.W. Kemmerer, Sprawozdanie oraz zalecenia komisji doradców finansowych pod przewodnictwem..., vol. 3. Waluta i kredyt (Ministerstwo Skarbu, Cracow, 1926), pp. 63-4.
9. Mały Rocznik Statystyczny 1937 (Główny Urząd Statystyczny, Warsaw, 1937), p. 107.
10. Étude sur le régime des ententes industrielles préparée pour le Comitée Economique de la Société des Nations (Société des Nations, Geneve, 1930), p. 87.
11. J. Kożuchowski, Kapitał zagraniczny w przemyśle polskim (Przemysł i Handel, Warsaw, 1928), p. 16; M. Smerek, Bilans płatniczny Polski za rok 1929 (Główny Urząd Statystyczny, Warsaw, 1931), p. 89.

12. C. Ptasiński, Rzemiosło w Polsce współczesnej (C. Ptasiński, Lublin, 1934), pp. 40-4; W. Hauszyld, 'Rzemiosło i przemysł ludowy w Polsce w ostatnim lat dziesięciu' in Bilans gospodarczy Polski Odrodzonej (Powszechna Wystawa Krajowa, Poznań, 1929), vol. 1, pp. 528-30.

13. Rocznik Ministerstwa Skarbu 1927-1930, (Ministerstwo Skarbu, Warsaw, 1931), pp. 110-11.

14. For more details concerning farming production cf. Zarys historii gospodarstwa wiejskiego w Polsce, vol. 3 (Państwowe Wydawnictwo Rolnicze i Leśne, Warsaw, 1970); Z. Landau, J. Tomaszewski, Od Grabskiego do Piłsudskiego. Okres kryzysu poinflacyjnego i ożywienia koniunktury 1924-1929 (Książka i Wiedza, Warsaw, 1971), pp. 148-60.

15. Dziennik Ustaw RP 1926, no. 1, item 1. The land reform is described in Cz. Madajczyk, Burżuazyjno-obszarnicza reforma rolna w Polsce (1918-1939) (Książka i Wiedza, Warsaw, 1956), p. 460.

16. These data differ in various sources. Cf. Rocznik Statystyki Rzeczypospolitej Polskiej 1930 (Główny Urząd Statystyczny, Warsaw, 1930), pp. 38-9; Mały Rocznik Statystyczny 1937 (Główny Urząd Statystyczny, Warsaw, 1937), p. 65.

17. J. Tomaszewski, Stabilizacja waluty w Polsce. Z badań nad polityką gospodarczą rządu polskiego przed przewrotem majowym (Książka i Wiedza, Warsaw, 1961), p. 53.

18. Z. Karpiński, Bank Polski 1924-1939, Przyczynek do historii gospodarczej okresu międzywojennego (Państwowe Wydawnictwa Gospodarcze, Warsaw, 1958), pp. 21-32.

19. AAN, S. Kauzik Papers, vol. 30: Sprawozdanie z działalności Departamentu Podatków i Opłat Ministerstwa Skarbu za rok 1924.

20. W. Grabski, Dwa lata pracy u postaw państwowości naszej (1924-1925) (F. Hoesick, Warsaw, 1927), pp. 241-3.

21. E. Taylor, Druga inflacja polska. Przyczyny, przebieg, środki zaradcze (Gebethner i Wolff, Poznań, 1926), p. 135.

22. Cz. Klarner, Dorobek czterech miesięcy (dwie mowy programowe) (Przemysł i Handel, Warsaw, 1926), p. 12.

23. Z. Landau, Plan stabilizacyjny 1927-1930. Geneza, założenie, wyniki (Książka i Wiedza, Warsaw, 1963), pp. 169-88; J.F. Dulles, Poland. Plan of Financial Stabilization 1927. Documents relating to the realization of the Plan of Stabilization (publishing house not given)(New York, 1928), pp. 24-8.

24. Combined reprint of the Quarterly Reports

of the Financial Adviser to the Polish Government (Bank Polski, Warsaw, 1930), p. 339.

25. W. Rusiński, Zarys historii polskiego ruchu spółdzielczego. Part one - 1919-1939 (Zakład Wydawnictw CZRS, Warsaw, 1980), pp. 49-126.

26. For details cf. B. Puchert, Der Wirtschaftskrieg des deutschen Imperialismus gegen Polen 1925-1934 (Akademie-Verlag, Berlin, 1963), pp. 48-79; K. Błahut, Polskoniemieckie stosunki gospodarcze w latach 1919-1939 (Ossolineum, Wrocław, 1975), pp. 85-136.

27. S. Królikowski, Zarys polskiej polityki handlowej ze szczególnym uwzględnieniem polityki celnej, (Instytut Społeczny, Warsaw, 1938), pp. 123-59.

28. Calculated according to: J. Piekałkiewicz, 'Bilans płatniczy Polski' in Bilans gospodarczy, vol. 2, p. 432; M. Smerek, 'Bilans płatniczy Polski za rok 1928', Kwartalnik Statystyczny, no. 1 (1931).

29. J. Ettinger, 'Wskaźnik stawek płac zarobkowych w Polsce w latach 1923-1930', Statystyka Pracy, no. 2 (1931), p. 5; W. Skrzywan, 'Próba szacunku dynamiki konsumpcji robotniczej w Polsce', Koniunktura Gospodarcza, no. 12 (1930).

30. M. Kalecki, L. Landau, Szacunek dochodu społecznego w r. 1929 (Instytut Badania Koniunktur Gospodarczych i Cen, Warsaw, 1934), p. 34.

THE GREAT DEPRESSION, 1930-5

POPULATION

The Great Depression brought a sudden fall in marriage- and birth-rates, the result of a common pauperisation and anxiety about setting up a family or having more children. The natural annual increase in population had declined from 15 per thousand in 1929 to 12.1 per thousand in 1935. The total population of Poland, however, was constantly growing. At the end of 1935 it amounted to 33.8 million people, an increase of 2.2 million people since 1929.

A characteristic feature of economic depression was that migratory movements diminished, especially those of people seeking work abroad, a situation mainly due to the severe immigration restrictions introduced in most countries. Between 1930 and 1935 emigration from Poland totalled 448,000 people, whereas in the previous six years more than 900,000 Poles had emigrated. At the same time about 334,000 emigrants returned to Poland during the Great Depression - a net outflow of 114,000 people, but in some years the number of emigrants returning to Poland was higher than those leaving for abroad.(1)

Emigration and re-emigration patterns slightly changed. From 1933 onwards the proportion of people leaving for overseas began to grow. Re-emigration came mostly from France where the authorities had placed restrictions on employment for foreigners.The situation of re-emigrants in Poland was also very difficult as high unemployment hampered their chances of finding work which in turn increased tension in the labour market. The Polish government realised the importance of this problem and examined the possibility of overseas colonisation, an idea promoted by an organisation called the Maritime and Colonial League. Nevertheless, the colonial programme was quite unrealistic, given the economic and social conditions of the time.

A lack of jobs in towns halted the flow of population from rural areas to industrial centres. Indeed, many people who had lost work returned to the country, though their number is not known.

The second population census carried out in December 1931 made it possible to assess the changes that had taken place in the social and occupational structure of Polish society in 1921-31. To make the 1921 census data comparable (not all the constituent parts of Poland had been included) one must calculate accordingly. The share of the population depending on agriculture and horticulture diminished from 63.9 per cent to 60.8 per cent; those depending on industry and mining increased from 17.2 per cent to 19.2 per cent, while the share of people employed in trade and insurance decreased from 6.2 per cent to 5.7 per cent. The share of employment in transport grew by 0.2 per cent, in public service by 0.5 per cent, in health services by 0.2 per cent and in household service by 0.3 per cent. The Great Depression slightly changed these proportions. For instance the number of workers at first fell but afterwards exceeded the pre-depression level. (2)

In 1930-5 there was a noticeable decline in the standards of the educational system. The actual number of children in schools fell throughout the country, especially in the eastern provinces where some 25 per cent remained outside the school system altogether in the 1935/6 school-year. The number of secondary schoolchildren also dropped - the only exception being in higher education, where more places were taken up, particularly in the jurisprudence and philosophy faculties. Technical colleges developed more slowly, a reflection no doubt of the troubled economic conditions in Poland at that time.

INDUSTRY

The industrial recession started in the autumn of 1929. In 1932 the crisis reached its low-point, with business activity remaining relatively static in 1933-5, although there was a very slight increase in production, but not enough to exceed the pre-depression level. Poland was one of the worst-affected countries, the depression biting deeper and industrial production falling faster than the world average. For example, industrial production in the United States fell to 51 per cent of its pre-depression level, in Germany to 53 per cent, in Canada to 55 per cent, and in Poland to 58 per cent. (3) This may be partly due to a certain polarisation of economic sectors in Poland: small-scale production farming ceased to be a selling market for industry as it tended more and more towards a subsistence economy and Polish industry began to depend on the urban market, as in the highly advanced countries. (4)

Recovery was also slower than that in countries of a similar agricultural/industrial structure. Thus while in 1935 Poland had reached 76 per cent of its 1928 production level, similar figures for Hungary were 113 per cent, Spain 97 per cent, Romania 131 per cent, Finland 122 per cent, Estonia 107 per cent,

Greece 143 per cent and Italy 102 per cent. The Great Depression in Poland may therefore be considered to have had certain specific features.

The industrial crisis mainly concerned the dramatic decrease in production levels. Compared with the 1928 level, industrial output in 1930 amounted to 86 per cent, in 1931 to 74 per cent, in 1932 to 58 per cent, in 1933 to 63 per cent, in 1934 to 71 per cent and in 1935 to 76 per cent. According to other estimates production at the height of the crisis amounted to 54-64 per cent, and in 1935 to 66-85 per cent of the 1928 level. Investments both generally and in industry were quite seriously affected by the depression, certainly more so than the production of consumer goods. The recovery which began in 1933 was due to a slight increase in investments and renewed activity in export markets. Table 2.5 gives more detailed information relating to changes in industrial production in 1929-35.

Table 2.5 shows that the production of all industrial goods, with the exception of radio sets, decreased during the Great Depression. The largest decline was recorded in farm machinery, with production of fertilisers also badly affected. In 1935 only five commodities exceeded the 1929 level of production. But by that time the total industrial output of Poland accounted for only 67 per cent of the 1913 level, while that calculated per capita for 61 per cent. (5)

The years of the Great Depression brought further structural changes in Polish industry. The number of mining workers and metallurgists in employment was decreasing although there was no change in the metal-processing industries. However, the number of workers employed in newly-developed industries was on the increase. In electro-engineering, for example, figures record a rise in employment from 0.82 per cent in 1929 to 1.56 per cent in 1935. Similar increases can be found in the chemical industries (4.76 per cent to 5.73 per cent), and in the paper industry (1.57 per cent to 2.03 per cent). Although rather small, the figures indicate that a process of modernisation and unification of the Polish economy was under way. The number of textile workers in employment also grew. The textile industry - which employed 21.87 per cent of the Polish workforce - still had the largest share of manpower, followed by the metal-processing industries (17.10 per cent) and mining (13.61 per cent). These three areas employed 53 per cent of workers in factories of more than 19 employees.

Table 2.5: Comparison of Production of Selected Industrial Goods in Poland, 1929, 1932 and 1935

Product	Unit	1929	1932	1935	1932/1929	1935/1929
Hard coal	million tonnes	46	29	29	63	63
Oil	thousand tonnes	675	557	515	83	76
Natural gas	million cu. metres	467	437	486	94	104
Salt	thousand tonnes	407	387	368	95	90
Potassium salts	thousand tonnes	359	299	384	83	107
Iron ore	thousand tonnes	660	125	340	19	52
Zinc ore	thousand tonnes	413	73	138	18	33
Pig iron	thousand tonnes	706	199	394	28	56
Steel	thousand tonnes	1,377	564	946	41	69
Zinc	thousand tonnes	169	85	85	50	50
Lead	thousand tonnes	37	12	10	32	27
Coke	thousand tonnes	2,123	1,288	1,562	61	74
Fertilisers	thousand tonnes	579	212	263	37	45
Sugar	thousand tonnes	824	376	400	46	49
Cement	thousand tonnes	1,008	354	843	35	84
Electric power	million kWh	3,048	2,257	2,817	74	92
Rolled goods	thousand tonnes	962	404	674	42	70
Paper	thousand tonnes	128	109	137	85	107
Sulphuric acid	thousand tonnes	233	120	139	52	60
Cotton thread	thousand tonnes	67	54	72	81	108
Woollen yarn	thousand tonnes	30	21	30	70	100

continued/...

Table 2.5 continued

Product	Unit	1929	1932	1935	1932/1929	1935/1929
Metal-working machines	pieces	3,232	903	-	28	-
Farm machinery	thousand tonnes	40	2a	5	5	13
Radio sets	thousand pieces	7b	11	91	157	1,300

Note: a. Data for 1933; b. Data for 1930.

Source: Z.Landau, J. Tomaszewski, Wielki kryzys 1930-1935 (Książka i Wiedza, Warsaw, 1982), p.42.

During the depression, employers, businessmen and entrepreneurs cut back on investments and modernisation plans. It has been estimated that a sizeable proportion of factories simply allowed their capital assets to depreciate, without bothering to replace them, a practice that was more widespread in private enterprises than state-controlled firms. Decapitalisation was greatest in the tanning, oil and textile industries. On the other hand electric power supply developed rapidly; this was connected with the general transition from steam to electric power. The decline in industrial investments is illustrated by the fact that imports of investment goods decreased from 63,724 tonnes in 1929 to 6,834 tonnes in 1933, that is, by 89 per cent.

The main reason for the lack of interest in investment was the fact that large reserves already existed - industrial capacity utilisation was estimated at only 40-45 per cent. If and when an upturn in the economy occurred therefore, increased demand could be met without much difficulty. According to Leon Grosfeld, the utilisation rate in mining was 40 per cent; in pig-iron production 15 per cent; in zinc 58 per cent; in steel 25 per cent; in metallurgy 44 per cent; in sugar-refining 42 per cent; in engineering 10 per cent and in cement mills 12 per cent. (6) The figure for engineering, however, is probably an underestimation.

As with the rest of society, the Great Depression took the Polish government completely by surprise. Only a year before economists had predicted an uninterrupted economic expansion and the gradual deterioration that took place in economic conditions was treated as only a temporary phenomenon. Even when the fact of depression could no longer be questioned, the government hesitated in providing assistance to industry. Much more attention was paid to maintaining the stability of the złoty and trying to obtain some sort of budget equilibrium. Consequently the government's economic policies were subordinated to these two objectives, and this resulted in a period of financial restraint and cut-backs in investment. In 1932, when the depression had reached its most serious level, vice-premier Władysław Zawadzki told the Seym:

> Whereas the government have managed to control the budget, they can only indirectly assist the progress of economic life. The government can neither animate nor stimulate business activity. It is up to business circles. Only some facilities which are at the government's disposal will be utilised. (7)

Until the autumn of 1932 the Polish government pursued something that was afterwards called the 'policy of survival'. This programme was aimed at reducing the prices of cartelised articles and, consequently, at increasing domestic sales and improving the competitiveness of Polish goods abroad. In order to weaken the resistance of cartels the government tried to reduce certain costs of production (for example, clearing of debts, credit aid, reduction of railway tariffs, facilities in discharge of back taxes, decrease of tax rates, limitation of social legislation, increase of government orders, etc.). The government, however, still refused to stimulate business activity in more radical ways, and the effects of the policies undertaken were rather modest, especially with regard to the reduction of cartelised prices.

Difficulties faced by private enterprise often involved the threat of closure and this was important in the case of those businesses producing goods for Poland's defence industry, or those employing large numbers of workers. Although the government did not openly adhere to any policy of state control, in practice they were forced not only to finance private firms but also to take over companies whose owners were unable to repay debts incurred through formerly contracted credits. Thus the government took over many industrial plants which were then controlled by the Bank Gospodarstwa Krajowego. At the end of the depression revenue from government enterprises accounted for 17-18 per cent of the total industrial turnover. In many lines of production the state controlled most of the output - this was particularly the case with potassium salts, the motorcar industry, aircraft industry, spirit and tobacco processing, dyestuff semi-manufactures, salt, metallurgy and the telecommunications industry. (8)

Generally speaking, the government's policy had only a limited influence on what was already a low level of business activity and the steps that were taken arose more from necessity than from any planned intention.

The problems that beset industrial plants accelerated the process of cartelisation: the number of domestic cartel agreements increased from 133 to 274 between 1930 and 1935 and international agreements increased from 48 to 106. Most of the cartel agreements were aimed at regulating prices (80 per cent), terms of payment (70 per cent) and at introducing the supply quota system (54 per cent). In 1934 about 30 per cent of domestic and 49 per cent of foreign joint-stock companies operating in Poland participated in cartels. They were some of the largest enterprises, as they controlled, respectively, 67 per cent and 80 per cent of the total industrial joint-stock capital. Estimates of the share of cartelised production differ considerably; it seems, however, that at the end of the depression cartels handled about 60 per cent of the total industrial output in Poland. (9)

In the early years of the depression the Polish government supported cartels in order to stimulate exports. But soon this policy changed. Cartels were strongly criticised by peasants and non-monopolised industries alike. Public opinion was against them. In 1933 a cartel law was passed stipulating the government's rights to intervene in cartel affairs. Those cartels whose activities were recognised as contrary to the public interest could be dissolved by a special Cartel Court. (10) In the same year the Cartel Court dissolved the cement cartel and, later, many others. Although the prohibition of these cartels did actually reduce domestic prices, most of the cartels that were dissolved were small and did not deal in exports.

To oppose the monopoly of the cartels was (in theory) to bring about a reduction in prices but Table 2.6 illustrates that despite government action prices of raw materials and cartelised semi-manufactures were higher than those of other articles throughout the depression. A journalist of an independent periodical, Gospodarka Narodowa, explained that the government price policy towards cartels meant:

> Wagging of the finger. Afterwards even this kind of threat was given up so that the children [i.e. cartels] were not frightened. But cartels, like children, do not stop scaring the government. They use simple but meaningful arguments: if you reduce prices, cartels will break down; but if so, we shall close some factories and the unemployed will cause trouble for the police. (11)

Table 2.6: Price Indices in Poland, 1929-35
(1928 = 100)

Prices	1929	1930	1931	1932	1933	1934	1935
Wholesale total	96	86	75	66	59	56	53
Industrial goods total	99	90	77	67	61	59	57
Industrial raw materials and semi-manufactures	97	86	73	64	59	57	55
Within: cartelised prices	108	109	107	103	92	88	82
Goods bought by farmers	101	99	90	81	73	70	66
Goods sold by farmers	76	49	54	48	40	34	33

Source: Mały Rocznik Statystyczny 1935 (Główny Urząd Statystyczny, Warsaw, 1935), p. 145; 1937 (Główny Urząd Statystyczny, Warsaw, 1937), p.227.

The high prices imposed by the cartels only reduced domestic demand and so helped to prolong the depression in Poland.

The Great Depression also brought about a further increase in the share of foreign capital in joint-stock companies in Poland. But this was not because of new investments but because previously invested money could not be rapidly withdrawn. Polish enterprises indebted abroad, not being able to pay off sums that fell due, were forced to give up some of their shares to creditors. Thus, despite a tendency to withdraw investments from Poland, the dependence of Polish industry on foreign business circles was actually increasing. In 1929 the share of foreign capital in the joint-stock capital of companies domiciled in Poland amounted to 33.3 per cent; in 1934 to 47.1 per cent, and in 1935 to 44.2 per cent. The 1935 decrease was due to the government's take-over of a few large enterprises, dominated by German capital, which faced bankruptcy. From 1929 to 1935 foreign shares grew in oil mining from 76.5 per cent to 86.7 per cent, in coal mining from 38.8 per cent to 67.4 per cent, in metallurgy from 65.4 per cent to 82.5 per cent, in chemical industries from 40.6 per cent to 60.0 per cent, in metal processing from 11.3 per cent to 31.5 per cent, in timber industry from 16.7 per cent to 44.5 per cent, etc. A slight decrease in foreign shares was only recorded in the paper and mineral industries.

These data do not fully reflect the degree of dependence of Polish industry on foreign capital. Credits and cartel connections were also involved. Enterprises dominated by foreign capital as a rule played a leading role in cartels. Foreign business interests controlled the largest firms in each line of production (with perhaps textiles as an exception).

The ownership structure of foreign capital did not change: the largest share was still in the hands of the French (24.4 per cent in 1935), Americans (21.8 per cent) and Germans (19.3 per cent). They were followed by the Belgians, the Swiss, the British, the Austrians, etc. The position of German capital was slightly weakened when the government took control of some large metallurgical plants which had been brought to the edge of bankruptcy by previous German owners.

The Great Depression badly affected handicrafts also, but despite diminishing turnover and a narrowing of the market the number of workshops increased. This resulted from attempts by unemployed workers to find any kind of work at any cost. Some of the newly established workshops acted legally, others illegally, so it is rather difficult to quote precise numerical data. But according to an expert in this field in 1933 every 100 workshops included 77 legal and 23 illegal ones. (12) Official statistics showed an increase in the number of handicraft workshops from 182,000 in 1929 to 222,000 in 1935. The actual number was estimated, however, at 450,000 workshops.

The increasing number of handicraft workshops was not accompanied by any growth in employment. On the contrary, it diminished. Workshop owners employed fewer journeymen and apprentices and sometimes even limited employment to close relatives.

The decreasing demand for handicraft services went hand in hand with falling prices for handicraft products and services, bringing about a dramatic decline in the value of production from 3.7 billion zł in 1929 to 2.0 billion zł in 1932. It may be assumed that in 1933 the total volume of handicraft production in Poland was already one half of that before the depression.

A similar crisis affected domestic industry. Essential operations were handled by a growing number of employees but the demand for their products was diminishing.

AGRICULTURE

Whereas industrial depression was expressed mainly by falling production, in agriculture the major symptom of crisis consisted in ever-decreasing prices. The reaction of small farmers to market difficulties was quite different from that of industrial capitalists. If for the latter it was essential to gain profits, farmers were more concerned with trying to earn a living. In view of falling profits capitalist entrepreneurs checked expansion, whereas small-scale producers in agriculture tried to make up for diminishing prices and increased production or market supply. Given a falling demand, the growth of supply of farm products inevitably led to a further reduction in prices. It was a kind of vicious circle, unlikely to be broken under the conditions then existing in Poland.

The fall in prices of farm products began in the autumn of 1928 and gradually deepened until the 1935 harvest. More detailed data can be found in Table 2.6. The price decline affected all lines of farming production. In 1935 average prices amounted to 33-34 per cent of the 1928 level. This resulted in an unprecedented impoverishment of the peasantry. Farmers found that as prices of industrial goods bought in the country fell by 34 per cent, taxes, insurance costs or debt obligations remained unchanged, and the so-called 'hunger supply' system appeared in Polish agriculture: being forced to gather the necessary financial means for taxes, insurance and discharge of debts, peasants had to sell not only any commodity surplus they possessed but also that part of production which before the depression had been kept for their own consumption.

The depression in agriculture in Poland was one of the most serious in the developed world at that time. Most of the countries that were included in international farming statistics recorded their lowest price levels in 1933-4; only in Ireland, Lithuania, Poland and Switzerland did the depression last until 1935, and only Bulgaria, Lithuania and the United States recorded greater falls in farm prices.

The decline in agricultural prices forced the government to take some action to counteract the growing problems experienced in rural areas. At first the government encouraged the export of farm products in the hope that this would diminish domestic supply and thereby halt the decline in prices. However, Polish foodstuffs that were exported had to contend with opposition in the form of restrictions imposed by the importing countries to protect their own agricultural markets. Intervention purchases of grain were started but these were limited by small budget resources. In view of the failure of previous farming policies - particularly in the autumn of 1932 and at the beginning of 1933 - the government introduced a plan which had as its objective the financial reform of Polish agriculture. Conversion of debts was undertaken and interest rates were lowered in order to contain the problem of 'hunger supply'. The debt clearing action slightly improved the position of farms indebted to financial institutions, but small farms which had received credits at punitive rates of interest from private sources were unable to benefit as their creditors simply did not respect the new debt regulations. Although there was therefore an improvement for some farms, the main purpose of the government's plan - to increase the price of farm products - had not been achieved. (13)

But agricultural production, as already mentioned, was in fact growing, if very gradually, throughout the depression. The area under crop had grown by 4 per cent. The only crop which actually recorded a decrease in production was sugar beet and this was only a reflection of the falling demand for sugar. Against this must be set the fact that methods of cultivation had grown more backward - in 1933 the demand for farm machinery amounted to only 10 per cent of the 1928 level and instead of purchasing new machinery farmers made do with equipment that was often virtually obsolete. The use of fertilisers rapidly decreased: in 1928/9 farmers spent 236 million zł on fertilisers but in 1934/5 purchases amounted to only 42 million zł. Commercial farms in the western provinces were most affected by these developments.

The decreasing use of machinery and fertilisers

did not reduce production which grew as a result of the increasing area under crop. In 1935/6 total crops exceeded the 1928/9 level by about 9 per cent. Only yields per hectare diminished. If we compare the 1931-5 average crops with those of the years 1926-30, a fall in wheat, barley, oats and sugar beet yields may be noticed with a rise in rye and potato yields. This meant that yields of the more exacting crops decreased whereas yields of those requiring less care grew slightly. It was characteristic that yields of almost all basic crops diminished in the western provinces, while in the more backward southern and eastern regions they increased. The differences between average yields in peasant holdings and large landed estates also diminished. Peasant farms and the landed estates of west Poland were badly affected by the decrease in the use of fertilisers and by the return to less efficient cultivation methods. Low prices for farm products also brought about a non-profit situation for all investments requiring capital expenditure. (14)

The number of livestock increased, with the exception of horses. This intensification in animal husbandry was the result of small farms, which were dominant in animal production, doing everything possible to gain extra earnings. With surplus labour and over-population in the agrarian sector, husbandry was often the only way to supplement what were already meagre incomes. The government also helped by giving their support to meat and dairy exports, and this was coupled with the introduction of more productive strains of cattle and pigs.

The Great Depression did not help the realisation, however, of the 1925 land reforms. Despite growing demand for land (caused by population increases in the rural areas and a reduction in overseas emigration), the general shortage of capital in the country made the purchase of land extremely difficult. In 1929 the minimum figure of 200,000 ha, which was to have been redistributed annually, was not reached and only 165,000 ha were parcelled out. In the following years there was a further decrease - to 56,000 ha in 1934, although this rose to 80,000 ha in 1935. The Seym gave their approval to a lower level of land redistribution as it was feared that any major increase might have led to a disastrous fall in land prices. Other development policies continued; for example, the consolidation of the very small plots into larger farms, improved drainage, etc., but the trend towards reform was clearly curtailed by the financial difficulties experienced by both farmers and government.

FINANCE

The Polish government decided to maintain the 1927 gold parity of the złoty, opposed the idea of suspending its convertibility in gold, and did not introduce currency restrictions. In the early stages of the depression, this policy seemed justified and even recommended by the prevailing economic doctrine. The Treasury minister, Ignacy Matuszewski, made the protection of the złoty the cornerstone of the government's economic policy, a policy that was to be maintained until the end of the Great Depression. (15) In 1931, when many countries abandoned traditional monetarist policies and devalued their currencies, the competitiveness of Polish exports slumped. A deflationary programme was continued, the government not wanting to introduce foreign exchange restrictions although at the time an outflow of foreign capital from Poland led to near exhaustion of the Bank Polski's gold and currency reserves. It was thought that any major change in policy would make foreign loans, which were eagerly sought after, less likely.

A deflationary policy meant a limitation in note circulation. By 1932 this had dropped by 16 per cent, but grew again by 5 per cent in 1934/5. The share of coins and small denomination notes in total circulation was increasing, the result of both the Treasury's wish to find a way of covering the budget deficit and the shrinking gold and currency reserves. In 1929 złoty coverage was 62 per cent but fell in 1933 to the minimum level of 41 per cent, although there were fewer notes in circulation. Official data here are clearly overestimated, the actual decrease being much greater, as the statistics that were published failed to take into account foreign debt obligations of the Bank Polski. If these are added, then the gold and foreign exchange reserves of the Bank Polski fell by some 1,000 million złotys (81 per cent), proof, it would seem, of the negative effect of a general lack of currency restrictions. (16)

Alarmed at the prospect of wholesale depletion of the gold and foreign exchange resources, the government embarked on a costly programme of 'dumping' exports abroad; without this action the złoty, faced with large and sustained foreign capital outflow, might well have collapsed.

With the slowing down of the economy came a

deterioration in the budget situation. A budget surplus was in fact recorded in 1929/30 but large deficits followed, despite a reduction in expenses, and these accounted for between 2 to 17 per cent of the budget in various years. In practice, however, the figures were even higher as the authorities were sometimes reluctant to reveal actual figures.

The government plan was to limit the budget deficit by reducing expenditure and raising revenue, mainly through taxes. Expenditure cuts were by no means even-handed: the Ministry of Military Affairs spent less in absolute terms but its share of budget expenses increased; the share of the Ministry of Internal Affairs was maintained at the same level. Spending cuts therefore mostly affected agriculture, education and civil servants, whose salaries were reduced.

These reductions alone, however, were not enough to solve the problem. Taxes began to be raised in a selective manner, the government's taxation policy being the increase of budget revenues without penalising business enterprises through excessive taxation. Indirect taxes were introduced, and some direct ones reduced, the aim being to ensure that private firms would not simply close which would only have aggravated their economic problems. When tax revenues proved insufficient, the government, in 1933 and 1935, decided to introduce two internal loans. In theory they were voluntary, but in practice compulsory. The loans brought the Treasury considerable receipts, mainly from employees, with wage-earners and salaried workers purchasing 44 per cent of the value in 1933 and 57 per cent of the value in 1935. (17)

The government continued to seek foreign credits but those which it managed to obtain were relatively small. The loans were insufficient to restore budget equilibrium, and served only to bolster up the dwindling foreign exchange resources of the Bank Polski.

Budget equilibrium was not restored despite these measures. In August 1935 the government, led by Walery Sławek, decided to abandon previous economic policies; a balanced budget was to be achieved by increased taxation and more drastic spending cuts.

Although during the years of the Great Depression national income decreased, it was subject to more and more taxation, the result of the policy followed by subsequent Treasury ministers: Ignacy Matuszewski until 26 May 1931, Jan Piłsudski until 5 September 1932 and Władysław M. Zawadzki until 12

October 1935. The ministers put budget performance before the rest of the economy;this had a negative impact on Polish economic life, with the Treasury draining the market as much as it could.

Banking was also affected by the depression. Private banks suffered from a withdrawal of deposits. At first it was rather slow but from the beginning of 1931 the rate of withdrawal increased, causing the bankruptcy of several banking institutions. Real panic set in in May 1931 after the collapse of the Rothschild banks in Austria. Within a few months almost half of all deposits in private banks in Poland had been withdrawn. (18) Deposits were withdrawn not only by domestic investors but by foreign depositors also. Altogether during the Great Depression deposits in private banks in Poland fell from 1,092 million zł to 507 million zł. At the same time deposits in public banks increased as they began to enjoy the confidence of depositors. Financial difficulties reduced the number of private banks by 35 per cent, of their branch banks by 49 per cent and of the foreign branch banks acting in Poland by 37 per cent.

Private banks which survived the pressure of depositors continued to function only because of financial aid from the government. In his justification of the top secret motion for the Economic Committee of Ministers, the Treasury minister wrote in February 1935:

> It must be pointed out that government aid to private credit institutions in Poland is necessary not only to support private banks but also due to more general reasons. Any more serious weakening of private banks may bring about unpredictable consequences for the whole credit system. (19)

The aid was granted only to major banks in which the government had taken an increased share. For instance, having improved the lot of the Bank Związku Spółek Zarobkowych SA in Poznań the government took over a block of its shares which made practical control of the bank possible. Thus the growing power of state banks was accompanied by increasing government influence over private banks.

The situation in the credit market can be precisely illustrated by the data relating to credits granted by various banks. In 1929-35 private banks decreased the total sum of credits granted by 57 per cent, state banks by 10 per cent, whereas the Bank

Polski increased them by 11 per cent. This meant a certain 'nationalisation' of short-term credits.

The official rate of interest was gradually reduced in the course of the depression. The maximum legal interest rate on credits was reduced from 13 to 9.5 per cent. In the unorganised market, however, rates were higher. For example, most farmers paid between 18-24 per cent interest on cash loans. The situation in handicrafts and small trade was similar but the rate of interest reached 28 per cent. (20) This explains why philanthropic societies providing small, interest-free loans were organised, offering financial aid to the poorest strata of the petty bourgeoisie.

A high rate of interest (that of the Bank Polski was among the highest in Europe) raised production costs and caused difficulties for private entrepreneurs. Nevertheless, its further reduction was impossible in view of the scantiness of financial means caused by the government's deflationary policy.

Though not always consistent, deflation proved rather useless in Polish conditions. Reduction in wages and agricultural earnings limited the already narrow market, a stable currency checked exports, while decreasing note circulation raised the cost of credits. Deflation as a remedy was not only unpopular; it had dangerous side-effects.

DOMESTIC TRADE

Pauperisation of society and a decline in productivity had a direct effect on home trade. Until 1934 the number of shops slowly diminished, with a slight increase seen in 1935. In 1929 there were 466,000 trading shops, but in 1934 only 404,000. This decrease referred mainly to the larger enterprises and wholesale trade which fell by one half. At the same time small shops grew in number. Though many small traders were forced out of business, their place was soon taken by others, the result of the collapse of bigger firms and the desire of the unemployed to find any means of subsistence. The latter turned to peddling, much of it often illegal.

The Great Depression also changed the pattern of trade. Whereas in 1929 the smallest shops accounted for 41 per cent of the total number of trading enterprises, in 1935 their number grew to 71 per cent of all shops in Poland. The situation in the most backward provinces deteriorated and the trading network shrank as compared with 1924.

Trade turnover diminished until 1933. In 1931

(for later years there are no figures) the average turnover of small enterprises decreased to 7,000 zł per annum, that is, to less than 600 zł monthly ($US100). Under these circumstances small traders were frequently living in poverty, all the more so when trading costs were high, due to tax and insurance charges and high rates of interest on cash and commodity credits. Traders tried to help themselves by creating credit co-operatives but this failed to solve the problem. Small dealers faced the growing domination of cartels which supplied goods at high prices leaving the retail traders only a small margin of profit. The number of shops going bankrupt increased as well as the number of protested bills.

With turnover decreasing, capital in short supply and a growing tax burden, the competitive struggle between individual traders was becoming even more acute. Of course, competition had existed even in the years of prosperity but then the problem had been to gain maximum profits, whereas during the depression the question was how to survive. Shopkeepers tried to fight competition from pedlars. In the course of the competitive struggle Poles were encouraged to buy in Polish shops, Ukrainians in Ukrainian co-operatives, etc. Anti-Semitic slogans became commonplace, as a weapon against Jewish shopkeepers and pedlars.

FOREIGN ECONOMIC RELATIONS

During the Great Depression all countries made efforts to maintain a foreign trade surplus and promote exports. At the same time stricter control was imposed on imports. As with other debtor countries, Poland had to earn a considerable surplus in the balance of trade to cover the deficit of the balance of capital movements. In 1929 this problem turned out to be particularly grave in view of the withdrawal of foreign capital from Poland. Credits withdrawn from private banks had amounted to 192 million zł in 1931, to a further 77 million in 1932 and to 37 million zł in 1933. Large sums were also withdrawn from industrial enterprises. Apart from withdrawing capital, foreign businessmen exported from Poland immense sums in the form of interest, dividends, patent charges, etc. Only a fraction of their value was included in government statistics. In many cases capital transfers were concealed in trading operations or in discharge of imaginary debts. The total sum of interest and dividends withdrawn from Poland in 1930-5 amounted, according to official statistics, to 1,781.1 million zł. This sum did not include short-term loans. Altogether the outflow of foreign capital reached 2,570 million zł, (21) - more than an average yearly budget of the Polish state. For a country affected by depression this was an immense burden.

The outflow of foreign capital was partially covered by the gold and foreign exchange reserves of the Bank Polski. When these reserves were exhausted the only solution for the government (which did not want to introduce currency restrictions) was to try to increase foreign trade surplus. And this was what the Polish government did.

A foreign trade surplus could be achieved either by reducing imports or by export promotion; the Polish government tried both methods. In the summer of 1930 certain import duties were raised with a further increase in 1931. The Treasury minister was empowered to apply reduced rates whenever imports were connected with simultaneous exports. Tariffs thus became an instrument of export promotion. In March 1932 a maximum tariff was introduced for imports from Germany. It was a reply to a similar tariff introduced in the Reich which had affected Polish exports. In the summer of 1932 a draft of a new Polish tariff was published, to come into force in October 1933. In many cases it raised the tariff protection rate. The protectionist nature of the new tariff was reinforced by the two-column system. Higher rates were applied to countries which had not signed trade agreements with Poland, whereas lower ones were offered to countries possessing such agreements.

In the years of the Great Depression, however, the role of tariff protection in the domestic market was gradually falling. Even high tariff barriers could be overcome by means of 'dumping'. Import prohibitions and currency restrictions proved more efficient and were more and more widely used. In Poland a system of import prohibitions, which had had their foundation in the Polish-German economic war, was maintained. Within this system individual countries received appropriate import quotas. Import prohibitions were gradually extended and the import quota system was written into trade agreements.

The protection of the domestic market was accompanied by various methods of export promotion. A system of export bounties on farm products was developed. Gradually the bounty system was extended to metallurgical products, machinery, chemicals, textiles, clothes, etc. Sums paid in this connection were constantly growing. While in the financial year 1929/30 the government spent 29 million zł for this purpose, in 1935 expenses had increased to 73 million zł. This policy made it possible for exporters to reduce export prices - sometimes even below the cost of production. Several cartels also had as their aim the financing of export dumping by means of maintaining high domestic prices. For instance, the price of sugar in Poland in the early 1930s was 1.41 zł per kg, whereas the export price amounted to 0.17 zł per kg.

It is difficult to estimate the total costs of dumping to the Polish economy. The dumping charge on domestic consumers was estimated at 300-500 million zł per annum. (22)

The government's export promotion policy also included the construction of a railway line joining the Upper Silesian coal mining region with the port of Gdynia. The first sections of this line were ready in 1930 and the whole of it was brought into operation in 1933. The port of Gdynia was constantly developed as it handled most of Poland's foreign trade. Imports going through Gdynia or Gdańsk benefited from reduced duties.

Foreign exchange controls introduced in other countries made the Polish government stick to the principle of strict compensation of the bilateral turnover as foreign importers were unable to settle their obligations in monetary terms.

Trade agreements concluded before the depression had to be renegotiated. Additional protocols were signed with many countries regulating barter trade and the payments involved. The ending of the Polish-German economic war in 1934 and the conclusion of a bilateral trade agreement in 1935 were significant events for Poland.

The government's policy of supporting foreign trade surplus was a success, though it had been costly. More details relating to Poland's foreign trade during the Great Depression can be found in Table 2.7.

The data in Table 2.7 show that Polish foreign trade turnover dramatically decreased during the Great Depression. While the physical volume of exports fell by 36 per cent, its value diminished by 65 per cent. This was the result of the structure of prices in the world market and the costs of 'dumping'.

Table 2.7: Polish Balance of Foreign Trade, 1929-35

Year	Polish turnover in million złotys			Value of turnover %	
	Import	Export	Balance	Poland	World
1929	3,111	2,813	-298	100.0	100.0
1930	2,246	2,433	+187	79.0	87.1
1931	1,468	1,878	+410	56.5	57.9
1932	862	1,084	+222	32.8	39.2
1933	827	960	+133	30.2	35.2
1934	799	975	+176	29.9	33.9
1935	861	925	+ 64	30.1	34.7

Source: Mały Rocznik Statystyczny 1936 (Główny Urząd Statystyczny, Warsaw, 1936), p.106; 1937, p.152.

The geographical structure of Polish foreign trade also changed. Trade relations with Germany diminished as did turnover with the former Dual Monarchy successor states. While in 1929, regardless of the economic war, about 31 per cent of Polish exports went to Germany, in 1935 this share fell to 15 per cent. At the same time Polish imports from the Reich decreased from 27 per cent to 14 per cent of total Polish imports. On the other hand trade relations with overseas countries developed. The commodity composition of Polish foreign trade also changed. The import of fully manufactured products decreased due to the tariff protection of the domestic market, while the share of these products in exports was on the increase.

LIVING CONDITIONS

The decline in industrial production and fall in the price of agricultural products led to a sharp fall in national income. There are various estimates available but all of them show a similar trend. The decline was not so steep (15-33 per cent between 1929 and 1932) when we take into account the fact the fixed prices formed the basis. The decrease, estimated at current prices, was about 50 per cent.(23)

A diminishing national income meant fewer investments and a fall in the standard of living. However, it should be pointed out that the national income available was lower than that produced, due to foreign trade surplus.

The depression affected all social groups;those who suffered most included the peasantry whose share in the national income diminished from 46.8 per cent in 1929 to 39.7 per cent in 1935, and the gap between the living standards of urban and rural populations widened. If the real value of consumption in 1929 is treated as 100, its 1933 level will be as follows: clerks - no change; the rentiers class and the professions - 92 per cent; landowners - 82 per cent; the petty bourgeoisie - 78 per cent; workers - 75 per cent and peasants - 44 per cent. (24)

These data illustrate trends of the real value of consumption but not the level of the standard of living of various groups. Taking consumption of an average worker's family of four persons as 100, consumption of a similar petty bourgeoisie family would be 137, a clerk's family 329, while a family living on profits or profession would be 529. The situation of workers in general was mainly determined by growing unemployment, diminishing wages, increasing labour intensity and by changes in labour law.

The decrease of employment in large and medium-size industrial plants was 36 per cent over the years 1929-32. Even in countries which faced a decline in industrial production similar to Poland's, the reduction in employment was lower; for instance, in the United States it reached 35 per cent, in Germany 28 per cent, in Canada 25 per cent, in Czechoslovakia 24 per cent, etc. In 1933 employment in Poland began to grow but in 1935 it was still lower by 25 per cent than before the depression. To illustrate the degree of unemployment one must rely on estimates as there were at that time no unemployment statistics in Poland. These estimates are shown in Table 2.8. From the various estimates available it may be assumed that the Moraczewski estimate approximated to the upper limit and the Lewy estimate to the lower limit of urban unemployment in Poland. The Moraczewski estimate was confirmed by a secret report of the Ministry of Internal Affairs which said that urban unemployment in 1935 numbered about a million people and unemployment in major industrial centres amounted to about 750,000 people. (25) There seems no reason to doubt these data.

In relation to total employment the number of unemployed amounted to 3 per cent in 1929, while in the years 1930-5, respectively, figures available are: 10.5 per cent, 25.4 per cent, 40.7 per cent, 43.5 per cent, 40.4 per cent and 39.9 per cent. Apart from total unemployment there was an increase in part-time working. Both can be estimated on the grounds of the number of worked labour-hours in industry. In 1929-32 this number diminished by 45 per cent.

Table 2.8: Estimates of Unemployment in Poland, 1929-35

Year	Estimate by S. Lewy		Estimate by J. Moraczewski
	Manual and professional workers	Manual workers	Manual and professional workers
1929	139	71	-
1930	327	239	-
1931	655	524	-
1932	914	755	713
1933	940	781	937
1934	908	743	1,072
1935	830	683	1,156

Source: S. Lewy, 'Szacunek bezrobocia pracowników najemnych poza rolnictwem w latach 1929-1935', Studia i Materiały Instytutu Spraw Społecznych, no.1 (1938), p.14; J Moraczewski, Rozważania nad położeniem politycznym i gospodarczym Polski (J. Moraczewski, Warsaw, 1938), p.63.

Increasing unemployment led to a reduction in nominal wages. Pay per hour fell on average by 29 per cent. As a result the total sum of wages paid to workers in large and medium-size industrial plants fell rapidly. Taking the 1928 level of the total wage fund as 100, in 1933 this level had decreased to 44 per cent. On the other hand real wages did not fall so quickly as living costs dropped. Thus the real value of sums paid to workers decreased more slowly than nominal wages. In 1932 the real wage fund in Polish industry fell to 62 per cent of the 1928 level. In practice it meant that during the depression Polish workers could buy only two-thirds of the goods and services they had bought before the crisis.

Wages were strongly differentiated according to the line of production, size of a factory, its location and the employee's age and sex. The best paid printing workers earned 1.19 zł per hour; the lowest pay per hour in the timber industry amounted to

0.49 zł. The average pay per hour in Warsaw was 1.04 zł, whereas in the Nowogródek province it was only 0.36 zł. In large factories wages were, on average, 20 per cent higher than those in smaller ones. Women were usually paid 20-40 per cent less than men for the same kind of work. All this resulted in considerable differentiation in wages. In 1933 as many as 47 per cent of workers earned less than the level of bare subsistence. The highest proportion of people earning less than the level of subsistence occurred among the unemployed (77 per cent), home-workers (75 per cent) and in handicrafts (61 per cent).

Labour legislation did not change until 1932. The government did not wish to antagonise workers but since 1933 government policy had been more and more concentrated on protecting the interests of producers. The working week was extended from 46 to 48 hours and the Saturday half-holiday was ended. Paid leave was limited and the pay involved was also reduced. A radical reform of the social insurance system was introduced in 1933. It consisted of a limitation of benefits available from health insurance, and a rise in social insurance contributions paid by workers, etc. On the other hand insurance for the old and retired was introduced for the first time and accident insurance benefits were increased. The 1933 reform has been a matter of controversy ever since - some authors said it favoured workers, others argued that it discriminated against them.

The situation of those workers who had kept their jobs was much better than that of the unemployed; despite diminishing wages, increasing labour intensity and a deterioration in some of the labour legislation regulations, they were still better off. There was small likelihood of finding a job. The unemployed received benefits for 13-17 weeks on condition that they had worked continuously for 20-26 weeks before being laid off. Moreover, unemployment benefit was only paid to workers formerly employed in factories obliged to insure their employees against unemployment, that is in practice employing more than five workers. Under these circumstances the share of the unemployed entitled to benefits decreased from 43 per cent in 1931 to 13-14 per cent in 1933-4.

Receiving only small casual earnings, estimated at about 19 zł per month per person in the unemployed family (a little less than $US4), the standard of living of the unemployed was rapidly deteriorating. Food was scarce, barely adequate, their clothes and housing conditions very poor. (26) Assistance rendered by the government, various charities, and social organisations provided some relief but it was not enough radically to change living conditions for the unemployed. Public works, whose development was somewhat limited due to the shortage of budgetary means, did nothing to alleviate the situation either. (27)

The effects of the Great Depression were also relatively serious for the petty bourgeoisie engaged in handicrafts and trade. According to an estimate, in some lines of handicraft unemployment reached 60-80 per cent. In 1929 the unemployed accounted for 29 per cent of all Polish handicraftsmen. As with industrial workers, handicraftsmen suffered from part-time working. As employees in handicraft were rarely insured against unemployment, their situation was often worse than that of the unemployed.

Those who depended on handicrafts and small trade had their standard of living reduced by lower earnings. Therefore it was in handicrafts and domestic industry where the share of people earning less than the level of subsistence was the highest.

Unemployment due to the depression also affected white-collar workers. According to the 1931 census unemployed professional workers accounted for 12 per cent of all the economically active members of this social group, and later this share grew to almost 24 per cent. With the deepening of the crisis unemployment here was on the increase but it still remained relatively lower than among manual workers. (28)

Between 1930 and 1935 salaries showed a slightly downward trend. As the cost of living rapidly diminished, individual real salaries actually increased. This explains why the taxation of salaries was raised considerably.

Apart from the unemployed in towns the depression seriously affected those peasants who depended for their livelihood on small farms. Their situation arose from the fall in prices for farm products, an increase in the real tax burden and the necessity to discharge debts. Moreover, there were fewer possibilities of finding an extra job and falling incomes had to be distributed among a growing number of the peasant population. Unemployment in the towns and immigration restrictions abroad made it impossible for the surplus population to leave the already over-populated countryside. It was estimated that the agrarian over-population amounted to 3-4.5 million people who could have left their villages without harming agricultural production in

Poland. (29)

The depression made its influence felt upon each group of the agrarian population in different ways. Landowners and rich peasants faced a fall in income and profits. They were sometimes forced to sell some of their land or livestock but never felt the real poverty which became the fate of the very poor in the country and most of the owners of medium-size farms. Differences in the standard of living of landowners and the rural poor may be illustrated by the fact that in 1933-5 the annual per capita consumption of the former was 10,204 zł, whereas that of the latter was a mere 158 zł.

Decreasing agricultural incomes forced farmers to reduce their expenses, both for consumption and for productive purposes. Shrinking cash incomes served in the first place to pay taxes and debts. Productive expenses came second, with personal consumption last. The most backward eastern and southern provinces were the most seriously hit by the depression. The example of sugar consumption figures is very representative here. In 1933 a peasant household in the eastern provinces consumed 0.33 kg of sugar (per month), in the southern provinces 0.56 kg, in Central Poland 0.83 kg, and in the western provinces 1.12 kg. Consumption of other processed goods was similar. For instance, farmers of East and South Poland almost ceased to buy coal. (30)

Almost all money-bought foodstuffs disappeared from the daily menu of the peasant and the consumption of much food produced at home (eggs, meat, corn, milk, etc.) was radically reduced. In the poorest regions of Poland bread was available in most smallholdings of 0.5 to 1 ha until the New Year. To save flour it was then baked with various admixtures. Later on peasants consumed more potatoes but in the pre-harvest period even these were sometimes lacking. And this meant hunger. In 1933 the government had to develop a food relief programme especially for the north-eastern provinces.

The impoverishment in the country also affected clothing; in many regions the demand for clothes was entirely met by homespun textiles of wool and flax. Shoes became a real problem as only in some regions bast moccasins had been traditionally produced. In the country everybody saved what he or she could. Electricity was only supplied to a minority of households and there was usually not enough money for fuel nor kerosene for lighting. Evenings were usually spent in the dark. Oil lamps and torches given up at the end of the nineteenth century were brought back into use. Cigarettes and matches were no longer bought as, for peasants, they were too expensive. Matches were frequently bought by the piece and divided. Wherever there was still too little money, tinder-boxes were used. (31) Even salt appeared too expensive.

The situation of farm workers was also deteriorating. Smallholders were becoming more and more competitive, offering labour to landed estates for extremely low pay. Many landed estates reduced the number of permanent farm hands and the remaining workers were paid less. Farm labourers were also affected by unfavourable changes in social insurance regulations which restricted their right to medical care.

The government was aware of the problems but its capacity to improve living conditions was limited. The Great Depression spread throughout the world and Poland was not able to distance itself from the general economic trends of the time. The government was simply too poor to improve standards of living in more radical ways. To provide worthwhile assistance to agriculture would have required large-scale intervention purchasing of farm products, a reduction in taxation and the clearance of debts. Such action involved large expenditure which the government could not afford. The same applied to the workers. Reducing urban unemployment would mean having to develop a new system of benefits and initiating large public works which would entail immense expenditure from a budget which was already overspent.

Of course, this does not mean that the government made no errors in its economic policy or that it did not discriminate against the workers in favour of the propertied classes. Even the most efficient government policy was unlikely to reverse the effects of the depression; it could only ameliorate some of its more negative effects.

The Great Depression did help to bring about changes in the development of the Polish economy. Private business circles proved too weak to offer much resistance. During the depression the role of the state grew, not only as controller and organiser of the labour market but also as manager of industrial, banking, foreign trade enterprises, etc. In Poland the Great Depression became the turning point between the monopolistic stage of capitalism and the state controlled capitalism. (32)

NOTES

1. Z. Landau, 'The Employment-seeking Emigration from the Second Republic 1918-1939 (Selected Topics)', Zeszyty Naukowe Uniwersytetu Jagiellońskiego. Prace Polonijne, no. 1 (1975), pp. 111-13.

2. Statystyka Polski, series C, no. 62, p. 54.

3. Two different indices of industrial production were used in the Polish Second Republic. Here we use the so-called 'compromising' index according to J. Tomaszewski, 'Ogólny wskaźnik produkcji przemysłowej' in Z. Landau and J. Tomaszewski, Druga Rzeczpospolita. Gospodarka, społeczeństwo, miejsce w świecie (Książka i Wiedza, Warsaw, 1977), pp. 9-42.

4. Z. Landau, 'Polish Village as a Selling Market for Industry in the Period of the Great Depression 1930-1935', Studia Historiae Oeconomica, vol. 7 (1972), pp. 171-88.

5. Materiały do badań nad gospodarką Polski. Cz. 1 - 1918-1939 (Państwowe Wydawnictwo Naukowe, Warsaw, 1956), p. 165.

6. L. Grosfeld, Polska w latach kryzysu gospodarczego 1929-1933, (Wydawnictwo Ministerstwa Obrony Narodowej, Warsaw, 1952), p. 27.

7. Przemówienie pana wicepremiera W. Zawadzkiego o sytuacji gospodarczej, Polska Gospodarcza, 1932, p. 657.

8. Sprawozdanie Komisji do Zbadania Gospodarki Przedsiębiorstw Państwowych (Ministerstwo Przemysłu i Handlu, Warsaw, 1939), pp. 241-2.

9. Z. Landau,'The Extent of Cartelization of Industries in Poland 1918-1939', Acta Poloniae Historica, vol. 38 (1978), pp. 163-7; Statystyka karteli w Polsce, Statystyka Polski, 1935, series C, no 28.

10. Z. Landau, 'Le developpement de la legislation sur les cartels pendant la IIe Republique et la politique du gouvernement vis-à-vis de ces associations', Studia Historiae Oeconomica, vol. 11 (1976), pp. 119-40.

11. K. Karłowicz, Kartele, Gospodarka Narodowa, no. 23 (1935), p. 340.

12. C. Ptasiński, Rzemiosło w Polsce współczesnej (C. Ptasiński, Lublin, 1934), p. 41.

13. J. Ciepielewski, Polityka agrarna rządu polskiego w latach 1929-1935 (Książka i Wiedza, Warsaw, 1968), pp. 137-264.

14. J. Orczyk, Produkcja rolna Polski w latach wielkiego kryzysu gospodarczego (1929-1935), (Poznańskie Towarzystwo Przyjaciół Nauk, Poznań,

1971), pp. 50-64.

15. For more details relating to the deflationary policy see: Z. Knakiewicz, Deflacja polska 1930-1935 (Państwowe Wydawnictwo Ekonomiczne, Warsaw, 1967), pp. 15-132.

16. Z. Landau, J. Tomaszewski, Wielki kryzys 1930-1935 (Książka i Wiedza, Warsaw, 1982), pp. 250-3.

17. K. Ostrowski, Polityka finansowa Polski przedwrześniowej (Państwowe Wydawnictwo Naukowe, Warsaw, 1958), p. 227.

18. Sprawozdanie Związku Banków w Polsce za r. 1932 (Związek Banków w Polsce, Warsaw, 1933), p. 9.

19. 'Uzasadnienie do ściśle tajnego wniosku ministra skarbu na Komitet Ekonomiczny Ministrów w sprawie rozrachunku między Skarbem Państwa a Banca Commerciale Italiana w Mediolanie oraz Bankiem Handlowym w Warszawie z 12 lutego 1935', AAN, Komitet Ekonomiczny Ministrów, vol. 1258.

20. T. Sołowij, Rynek pieniężny i stopa procentowa w Polsce, ('Bank', Warsaw, 1939), pp. 86-9; Z. Landau, J. Tomaszewski, Wielki kryzys, p. 299.

21. Z. Landau, J. Tomaszewski, Zarys historii gospodarczej Polski 1918-1939 (Książka i Wiedza, Warsaw, 1981), pp. 229-30; Z. Landau, J. Tomaszewski, 'The International Movement of Capital in Central and South-eastern Europe before the Second World War' in Studies in Economic Theory and Practice. Essays in Honour of Edward Lipiński (North-Holland Publishing Company, Amsterdam, 1981), p. 32.

22. K. Sokołowski, Dumping (Polska Gospodarcza, Warsaw, 1932), p. 133; R. Battaglia, Zagadnienie kartelizacji w Polsce. Ceny a kartele (Izba Przemysłowo-Handlowa, Warsaw, 1933), p. 145.

23. Z. Landau, 'National Income in Historical Research (On Material from the Period of Interwar Poland)', Acta Poloniae Historica, no. 33 (1976), pp. 116-18.

24. M. Kalecki, L. Landau, Dochód społeczny w roku 1933 i podstawy badań periodycznych nad zmianami dochodu (Instytut Badania Koniunktur Gospodarczych i Cen, Warsaw, 1935), p. 29.

25. 'Tajne sprawozdanie Referatu Zawodowego Wydziału Bezpieczeństwa Ministerstwa Spraw Wewnętrznych z dn. 24 III 1936', Archive of the Party History Department, Military Institutions, no. 296/III, vol. 1. This document was published by M. Drozdowski in Najnowsze Dzieje Polski. Materiały i Studia z okresu 1914-1939, vol. 4.

26. H. Krahelska, S. Pruss, Życie bezrobotnych, Badania ankietowe (Instytut Spraw Społecznych,

Warsaw, 1935); A. Minkowska, Rodzina bezrobotna (Instytut Gospodarstwa Społecznego, Warsaw, 1935).

27. M. Ciechocińska, Próby walki z bezrobociem w Polsce międzywojennej (Państwowe Wydawnictwo Ekonomiczne, Warsaw, 1965).

28. T. Czajkowski, J. Derengowski, Bezrobocie wśród pracowników umysłowych w Polsce w latach 1927-1932, (Instytut Spraw Społecznych, Warsaw, 1933), p. 33; J. Żarnowski, Struktura społeczna inteligencji w Polsce w latach 1918-1939 (Państwowe Wydawnictwo Naukowe, Warsaw, 1964), p. 193.

29. M. Stańczyk, 'Przeludnienie agrarne w Polsce kapitalistycznej', Ekonomista, no. 1 (1955), p. 106; L. Landau, J. Pański, E. Strzelecki, Bezrobocie wśród chłopów (Instytut Gospodarstwa Społecznego, Warsaw, 1939), p. 146.

30. Z. Sobańska-Kieniewiczowa, Zużycie wyrobów przemysłowych na wsi w r. 1932-1933 w zależności od położenia geograficznego i stopnia zamożności gospodarstw wiejskich (Państwowy Instytut Naukowy Gospodarstwa Wiejskiego, Warsaw, 1939), pp. 33-6.

31. Pamiętniki chłopów. Seria I (Instytut Gospodarstwa Społecznego, Warsaw, 1935); Pamiętniki chłopów. Seria II (Instytut Gospodarstwa Społecznego, Warsaw, 1936); J. Michałowski, Wieś nie ma pracy (Instytut Spraw Społecznych, Warsaw, 1935); J. Ciepielewski, Wieś polska w latach wielkiego kryzysu 1929-1935. Materiały i dokumenty (Książka i Wiedza, Warsaw, 1965).

32. Z. Landau, 'The Great Depression in Poland (1929-1935) and its Consequences', Studia Historiae Oeconomica, vol. 8 (1973), pp. 337-54.

THE DIRECTED ECONOMY, 1936-9

POPULATION AND TERRITORY

Although the depression was over, the Polish countryside was still in deep economic trouble, reflected in basic demographic statistics. The number of newly contracted marriages diminished along with the birth-rate. In 1935 there were 8.4 new marriages and 26.2 births; in 1938 there were 8.1 marriages and 24.6 births (per 1,000 inhabitants). The population of Poland reached 35.1 million people in 1939 including 241,000 inhabitants of the so-called Zaolzie, incorporated in 1938. As compared with 1935 this meant an increase of 1.3 million inhabitants, relatively less than in previous years.

In the 20 years of the Second Republic the population of Poland had increased by almost 8 million people and the density of population had risen from 70 to 90 persons per sq km. Basic demographic indices changed. The birth-rate declined from 30.5 per thousand in 1919 (in 1923 it was even higher at 35.6 per thousand) to 24.6 per thousand, the number of newly contracted marriages diminished from 12.7 per thousand in 1919 to 8.1 per thousand in 1938, whereas the death rate fell from 26.9 per thousand to 13.9 per thousand between the same dates.

In 1936-9 emigration was slightly higher than during the Great Depression but still lower than in the 1920s. Altogether 286,000 people emigrated and 178,000 returned in the last three years of the Second Republic. Most of the emigrants left for European countries.

An improvement in the industrial situation encouraged migration from village to town as people sought work in the industrial regions. But most regions had high unemployment, and the unemployed had a better chance of obtaining work than the newcomers from the villages. The latter were usually employed as household servants, caretakers, unskilled labourers, etc.

In the inter-war period both the occupational and social structure of Polish society changed. (1) The most characteristic feature of changes in the former was the increase in the number of people depending on industry and mining - from 17.2 per cent in 1921 to 23.2 per cent in 1938; on public service from 3.7 per cent to 4.2 per cent; and on household services from 1.1 per cent in 1921 to 1.4 per cent in 1938. On the other hand the agricultural population decreased from 63.8 per cent to 59.1 per cent.

There was little change in the number of people depending on trade, insurance, transport and communications. The changing social structure of Poland is illustrated in Table 2.9.

Table 2.9: Changing Social Structure of Poland, 1921-38

Category	1921	1931	1938
	%	%	%
Total population	100.0	100.0	100.0
Independent persons			
hiring workers	8.6	5.9	5.7
self-employed	56.2	57.5	56.9
Professionally employed	4.2	4.3	4.8
Manual workers	26.6	28.4	30.1
Indefinite social standing	4.4	3.9	2.5

Source: J. Zarnowski, Społeczeństwo Drugiej Rzeczypospolitej 1918-1939 (Państwowe Wydawnictwo Naukowe, Warsaw, 1973), p.22.

It is difficult to draw conclusions from Table 2.9. Some of the changes were due to a decrease in the number of people of 'indefinite social standing'. But undoubtedly it was an important feature of inter-war Poland that the number of workers (along with the unemployed) and clerks was growing while the number of independent persons employing hired workers was falling. This could mean either a concentration in production or, more likely, a gradual splitting up of peasant farms employing hired workers into smallholdings cultivated only by family hands.

The increase in the number of workers and clerks was accompanied by urbanisation. While in 1921 about 24 per cent of the population lived in towns, in 1938 the share of the urban population was estimated at about 30 per cent. A relatively rapid urbanisation was accompanied by migrations from the country to towns in search of work.

An improvement in the economic situation led to an increase in the number of primary and secondary schoolchildren. Compared to the 1934/5 school year, in 1938/9 the former increased by 6 per cent, the latter by 41 per cent.

There were still considerable regional differences with regard to compulsory schooling. In the

Silesian province 99.3 per cent of children of school age went to schools in 1937/8; in Wołyń province only 71.6 per cent; in Polesie 79.9 per cent and in Nowogródek province only 81.4 per cent. Despite efforts made to balance inter-regional differences, the eastern provinces were still behind the western regions.

At the beginning of October 1938 Poland annexed from Czechoslovakia a part of the Teschen Silesia called Zaolzie. Poland's participation in the dismemberment of Czechoslovakia by the Third Reich was one of the greatest errors of Polish interwar diplomacy. The area incorporated into Poland had 906 sq. km. It included 16 coal mines, 5 coking plants, 2 briquette factories, 4 blast furnaces, 13 open-hearth furnaces, 8 roll lines, etc. (2) More than a half of its population depended on industry and mining. Most of this population was Polish, particularly in the districts of Teschen and Frysztat. After the incorporation of Zaolzie, the Polish authorities started resettlement of the Czechs to Czechoslovakia and tried to absorb local enterprises in the Polish economy and to find markets for their products. (3)

INDUSTRY

The gradual improvement of economic conditions in industry, which had begun in 1933, turned into a market rally in 1936. It was due to an ending of world depression, to a certain recovery in Polish agriculture and to the government's incentives to business activity. This latter policy was initiated by the Felicjan Sławoj Składkowski cabinet in which economic problems were the responsibility of Eugeniusz Kwiatkowski who was vice-premier and Treasury minister. He remained true to his idea of industrialisation and saw in it a means of strengthening Poland's defences and economic independence, as well as being the only chance for improvement in the country, lowering urban unemployment, and progress in general.

In mid-1936 the government formulated a programme known as the four-year investment plan. It included the period between 1 July 1936 and 30 June 1940 and foresaw total investments of 1,650-1,800 million zł. (4) It was not an extravagant sum but Poland simply could not afford more. Apart from the four-year investment plan the Ministry of Military Affairs and the General Staff envisaged a six-year plan of development and modernisation of the Polish armed forces which were rather out of date in relation to neighbouring countries. Both plans were not sufficiently co-ordinated and this led to certain difficulties in their fulfilment.

A revival of the market accelerated the realisation of the four-year plan. It was fulfilled not only ahead of time (by March 1939) but its targets were outstripped. Altogether 2,400 million zł were spent on investments. The investments - dissipated over too wide an area - were barely noticeable. The public did not see any important progress. So the government decided to concentrate investments in a few major fields. These included a rapid increase in Poland's defensive capacity, the creation of conditions for systematic industrialisation, the development of economically backward regions, neutralising differences between the advanced western provinces (so-called Poland A) and the backward eastern regions (Poland B). (5)

The programme was very ambitious. It had, however, to be compared with the government's financial ability. In February 1937 the idea of developing the Central Industrial Region was put forward, to include some parts of the Kielce, Lublin, Cracow and Lvov provinces. Its area accounted for almost 15.4 per cent of the total area of Poland and was inhabited by 18 per cent of Poland's population. The Central Industrial Region (COP in Polish), relatively far away from the western and eastern frontiers, was to safeguard the security of the region in case of war. The area was also selected because of the considerable agrarian over-population. The surplus manpower in the region was estimated at 400,000 - 700,000 people. Economic reasons were also taken into account. They included the possibility of creating a market for farm products from East Poland and for raw materials and semi-manufactures from West Poland, as well as to utilise the gas and water power resources of southern regions.

The Central Industrial Region was not a uniform area. It was divided into three sub-regions: the so-called A Kielce zone supplying raw materials, the B Lublin zone supplying foodstuffs and the C Sandomierz zone of processing industries. The construction of large industrial plants started to include power plants, iron and steel mills, armament plants, aluminium mills, engines, machine tools, aircraft, truck and chemical factories, etc. The investments were put into effect efficiently, making use of the latest engineering equipment, etc. Nevertheless most of the plants had not been completed by September 1939. (6)

New industrial plants and their accompanying enterprises started in handicrafts, and trade provided 107,000 new jobs. This was the first economic success since 1930, although in relation to the country's needs the number of new jobs was by no means sufficient.

The construction of the COP required considerable finance, but Polish and foreign business circles held back from major investment, fearing the growing possibility of war. Investment had to be financed by the government and public enterprises. Despite the importance of the scheme, the construction of the COP absorbed only 60 per cent of total government investment expenditure. The remaining 40 per cent was spent on developing the port of Gdynia and other industrial centres.

Nevertheless the Central Industrial Region could not solve the most urgent problems of the Polish economy. A Polish journalist had put it correctly when he said: 'The Central Industrial Region cannot exist as an oasis of happiness in an underinvested country of backward agriculture and insufficient road systems. It may become not a blessing but a burden for such a country.' (7)

The government took heed and announced the formulation of a wider, long-term programme of economic development. On 2 December 1938 Vice-Premier Kwiatkowski made a parliamentary speech presenting a draft programme of government economic policy for the next 15 years (from April 1939 to March 1954). The programme was divided into five three-year parts, each of which was to deal with different socio-economic problems. The major task of the first stage was to develop the defence sector so that armament production could meet the army's requirements. Further stages were to improve the transport and communication systems, to develop education, agricultural production and trade, to extend industry and towns, and - by the fifth stage - to eliminate differences between so-called Poland A and B. (8)

The 15-year plan was hardly likely to be realised. Poland faced the approach of war. The government plan did not include any analysis of the sources of investment finance. The first three-year stage was, however, more concrete: the government planned to spend 2 milliard zł on investments, 60 per cent of which was to be for military expenditure.The investment plan was to be based on budgetary means, as well as on domestic and foreign loans (in 1936 a loan for rearmament was raised in France). In addition the Polish government raised deposits in the Pocztowa Kasa Oszczędności (a savings bank) and in government insurance institutions.

Insufficient government funds forced the cabinet to encourage private business circles to invest in the COP. Special tax and credit privileges served this purpose. Nevertheless the range of private investments was limited and the larger part of the cost was borne by the government. This was conducive to interventionist policies and led to a state-controlled economy.

The years 1936 to 1939 brought a rapid increase in industrial output, which exceeded the 1928 level, and some lines of production reached capacity limits. In relation to 1935 the general index of industrial production grew by 7 per cent in 1936. The 1937 yearly increment was 15 per cent and that of 1938 8 per cent. Coal output increased by 24 per cent, while steel production rose by 25 per cent and that of pig iron by 50 per cent. This necessitated the reopening of those businesses which had closed down during the Great Depression. The production of investment goods grew more rapidly than that of consumer goods, particularly in industries connected with armament production. Civilian industries, especially in agricultural regions, showed signs of recession in 1939. This was due to a repeated collapse of the price of farm products. More details concerning industrial production in 1936-8 (for 1939 there is no statistical evidence) are given in Table 2.10.

A rapid increase in industrial production in 1936-9 cannot hide the fact that it was related to a rather low starting level. By that time Polish industry had considerably exceeded production levels achieved during the first few years after the war.In 1938 industrial output in Poland was more than 50 per cent higher than in 1922. On the other hand the 1938 level of industrial production oscillated around the 1913 level. This meant that the Polish economy had managed to reconstruct the damage of war but had not succeeded in making up for the backwardness brought into the independent statehood. It was a disquieting phenomenon as in view of the growing population the per capita industrial output had diminished by 13-15 per cent in relation to 1913. As most other countries developed their industry, inter-war Poland lagged behind all those countries whose industrial production in 1938 was higher than in 1913. This applied particularly to the agro-industrial and agricultural countries. (9) Increasing

Table 2.10: Comparison of Production of Selected Industrial Goods 1913, 1935 and 1938

Product	Unit	1913	1935	1938
Hard coal	million tonnes	40	29	38
Oil	thousand tonnes	1,114	515	507
Natural gas	million cubic metres	687	340	872
Salt	thousand tonnes	189	368	417
Potassium salts	thousand tonnes	14	434	567
Iron ore	thousand tonnes	464	340	872
Zinc ore	thousand tonnes	510	130	498
Pig iron	thousand tonnes	1,055	394	879
Steel	thousand tonnes	1,619	946	1,441
Zinc	thousand tonnes	192	85	108
Lead	thousand tonnes	42	19	20
Coke	thousand tonnes	918	1,562	2,292
Fertilisers	thousand tonnes	400	263	498b
Sugar	thousand tonnes	571	400	491
Cement	thousand tonnes	665	843	1,719
Electric power	million kWh	660	2,817	3,977
Rolled goods	thousand tonnes	1,244	674	1,074
Paper	thousand tonnes	65	136	205
Sulphuric acid	thousand tonnes	225	112	189
Cotton thread	thousand tonnes	100	72	85
Woollen yarn	thousand tonnes	48	30	34b
Metal-working machines	pieces	-	1,327a	4,285b
Farm machinery	thousand tonnes	-	5	22
Radio sets	thousand pieces	-	91	142

Note: a.Data for 1933; b.Data for 1937.,
Source: Mały Rocznik Statystyczny 1938 (Główny Urząd Statystyczny, Warsaw, 1938), pp. 117-18; 1939, pp. 128-9; Rocznik statystyczny przemysłu 1945-1965 (Główny Urząd Statystyczny, Warsaw, 1967), pp. 798-801.

world production and stagnation in Poland (comparing the years 1913 and 1938) changed Poland's position in the world economy. The share of output in Poland related to world production decreased in most cases for which there is adequate evidence. Only in a few lines was any progress recorded although sometimes there was a considerable advance. Table 2.11 includes such a comparison for basic industrial products.

Table 2.11: The Share of Polish Industrial Production in World Output, 1913 and 1938

Product	Share of Poland in world production		Ratio of the share of production
	1913	1938	1938:1913
Hard coal	3.37	3.11	92.3
Oil	2.05	0.18	8.8
Salt	1.03	1.76	170.8
Lead ore	4.63	2.45	52.9
Zinc ore	44.17	26.67	60.4
Coke	0.83	1.38	166.2
Pig iron	1.39	1.08	77.7
Steel	2.21	1.28	57.9
Zinc	19.65	6.96	35.4
Lead	3.76	1.20	31.9
Paper	0.57	0.68	119.3
Superphosphate	1.60	1.12	70.0
Cement	1.67	2.02	120.9
White beet sugar	6.70	5.13	76.5

Source: Z. Landau, 'An Appraisal of Poland's Economic Development in 1918-1939', Oeconomica Polona, no.3 (1979), p.302.

At the same time the structure of Polish industry changed, adjusting to the needs of the domestic market and to new directions in foreign trade. For instance, a fall in production of woollen and cotton yarn as compared with 1913 was, as with metallurgical output, due to the difficulties faced in exporting these commodities to the Soviet Union. These changes were characterised by a rapid increase in the number of workers employed in electrical industries (the 1928-38 increase of 190 per cent, earlier data being unavailable), in power plants and waterworks (an increase of 36 per cent), in the chemical industry (24 per cent), paper industry (20 per cent) and metal processing (an increase of 9 per cent). At the same time employment diminished in building (a fall of 28 per cent), mining (27 per cent), metallurgy (18 per cent), textile industry (12 per cent), etc. This meant that traditional industries developed in the Polish territories in the course of the partitions (such as metallurgy, mining, or textiles) were gradually losing their importance to new lines of production. It was a positive process although the newly developed industries employed fewer workers than traditional ones. In 1938, for example, the electrical industry employed 18,000 workers, power plants and waterworks 9,000, whereas metallurgy employed 162,000, the textile industry 154,000, mining 105,000, etc. The total employment in large and medium-size industrial enterprises amounted to 808,000 people in 1938 - 42,000 workers less than in 1928. (10)

Increasing production and diminishing employment meant a growth in labour productivity, this last being recorded throughout the duration of the Second Republic, due not only to technical progress but also to the workers' fears of losing work and being pushed down among the unemployed. The continued existence of unemployment, which had seemed transitory until the Great Depression - but inevitable since 1930 - made it possible for businessmen to lay off less productive workers.

The increase in industrial output was also due to investments. Between 1935 and 1938 gross investments grew by 78 per cent, while net investments rose by 126 per cent. The general level of investments exceeded the amount of inputs in 1928. Most investments were financed from public resources. Private investments accounted only for 39 per cent. (11) The role of the government and the public sector was constantly growing.

The government was not only a major investor. The purchase of some private enterprises by the government still continued. After the depression the Polish government owned one of the largest metallurgical concerns and a major textile company. Assuming that all enterprises in which the government shared 75 per cent of the capital were state controlled, in many lines of production the Polish government controlled 100 per cent of the output, particularly in potassium salts, the motor-car and aircraft industries, production of spirit and tobacco, etc. In many other lines the government controlled more than 50 per cent of the output - in salt mining, metallurgy, dye semi-manufactures, and communication engineering. Coal mines and oil refineries were also controlled (19 per cent), natural gas production (23 per cent), cement mills (40 per cent), quarries (32 per cent), machine tools (29 per cent), dyestuffs (20 per cent) and the electrical industry (13 per cent). Most of the armaments production was in the hands of the government. The tendency towards a state-controlled economy was more and more noticeable. Though it was still treated as a mal nécessaire, its necessity was mainly due to the weakness of Polish private capital and to the disinclination of foreign business circles to invest in Poland. At the same time authoritarian tendencies which took the upper hand in government after the death of Józef Piłsudski in May 1935 seemed conducive to the ideology of a state-controlled economy.

This, for instance, was expressed in the government's policy towards cartels. In November 1935 the government empowered the minister of trade and industry to dissolve cartels without a hearing before the Cartel Court. By December 1935 the minister had dissolved 93 cartel agreements (out of 274 existing cartels) and several dozen others were wound up in 1936-7. In most cases they were local agreements but some large cartels were also dissolved. The government coupled this action with pressure on the remaining cartels to reduce prices. Cartels which refused price reductions could be dissolved or reorganised by the government. This action brought certain results: the domestic price for sugar decreased by 20 per cent, kerosene by 12 per cent, salt by 11 per cent, iron and coke by 10 per cent, coal by 13 per cent, etc. Cartel prices, however, were still higher than those of non-cartelised products (see Table 2.12). Another amendment to the cartel law issued in July 1939 additionally increased their dependence on the state.

Despite the dissolution of many cartels, the role of the remaining agreements did not diminish. It was estimated in 1938 that 'the share of cartelised production accounted for two-thirds of the total industrial output and for about 75 per cent of the production of large and medium-size industrial enterprises'. (12)

This was mainly the result of the cartels' role in exports. The outstanding Polish economist, Ferdynand Zweig, said:

> The whole export policy was based on the cartels. Many export branches, especially sugar, coal, steel, oil, zinc, were based on the price discrimination between internal and export

prices, the deficit in export prices being covered by the excess of internal prices. (13)

Increasing government intervention also diminished the role of foreign capital in industry. This tendency, which began in 1935, gained momentum in 1936 when the share of foreign capital in the joint-stock capital of Polish companies fell from 44.8 per cent to 39 per cent. In 1937 this share grew again to 40.1 per cent. For later years there are no data. But foreign capitalists still controlled 87.5 per cent of shares in the oil industry, 81.3 per cent in power plants and waterworks, 66.1 per cent in the electrical industry, 59.9 per cent in the chemical industry and 52.1 per cent in mining and metallurgy. In other lines of production this share was lower.

Foreign influence in Polish industry not only limited Poland's freedom of movements but also caused an immense capital outflow. In view of her geographical position Poland did not seem suitable for long-term investments. If it was decided to face the risk, foreign investors usually tried to withdraw their money as quickly as possible. Finally, capital outflow (connected with the foreign capital service) was higher than capital inflow in the inter-war period. It was estimated that in 1924-37 the inflow of long-term capital investments amounted to 3,194.9 million zł, and their outflow to 1,865.9 million zł. At the same time 3,702.6 million zł were transferred out of Poland in the form of interest, dividends and other obligations. Thus the total outflow of capital was 2,373.6 million zł higher than the inflow. It must be pointed out that this does not include sums omitted in the statistics. (14) Poland was therefore rather deprived of the capital necessary for long-term economic development.

When the Great Depression was over the situation of handicrafts improved. The incomplete data that are available show that the number of handicraft cards issued by the Chamber of Handicrafts increased from 347,000 in 1935 to 374,000 in 1937. It may be assumed that this trend was maintained in further years. However, it is difficult to find out whether the actual number of cards issued represented the real increase in the number of persons running handicraft enterprises. It is possible that it only showed the registration of formerly illegal workshops.

The most widespread handicrafts included tailoring, shoemaking, butchering, smithery, carpentry and baking - which employed the majority of handicraftsmen. The territorial distribution of workshops was still uneven. The eastern provinces were handicapped in view of the lack of industry and backwardness in agriculture and this situation did not change at all through the inter-war period. For instance in 1938 about 29,000 workshops bought industrial licences in the Poznań province, but in the eastern provinces only 5,000-6,000 workshops did so.

Differences between various regions were still rather high. In 1935 as little as 20.4 per thousand inhabitants of Poland worked in large and medium-size industrial enterprises. In the most backward provinces of Tarnopol, Polesie, Nowogródek, Wilno, Lublin, Wołyń, Stanisławów, Białystok and Lvov this coefficient varied between 3.3 to 9.8 whereas in the more industrialised provinces of Łódź, Upper Silesia and Warsaw, it varied between 48.3 to 82.4.

AGRICULTURE

Falling prices, the basic reason for depression in Polish agriculture, were halted in the autumn of 1935. Bad harvests in the United States and an increase in the consumption of farm products in industrial countries which entered the market rally period in 1933 improved the outlook for Polish farming. This is illustrated in Table 2.12.

Table 2.12: Price Indices in Poland, 1935-9 (1928=100)

Prices	1935	1936	1937	1938	March 1939
Wholesale total	53	54	59	56	55
Industrial goods total	57	57	61	58	57
Industrial raw materials and semi-manufactures	55	56	61	57	56
of which: cartelised prices	82	75	77	78	78
Goods bought by farmers	66	65	66	65	65
Goods sold by farmers	33	35	52	44	37

Source: Mały Rocznik Statystyczny 1939 (Główny Urząd Statystyczny, Warsaw, 1939), pp. 245-6.

In 1937 prices of farm products increased but in the following year another drop came as a result of a drop in world prices. Even in the best year (1937) prices of agricultural goods were not only much lower than in 1928 but also less satisfactory than those of all other goods and of industrial articles bought by farmers in particular. The 'price scissors' (see pp. 93,95) were unfavourable for agriculture from 1929 to 1939. This made progress impossible and the Polish village was not restored to the standard of living it enjoyed in 1926-8 until 1939. Nevertheless a certain increase in earnings in 1936-8 enabled farmers to buy industrial products again.

The government's policy mainly concentrated on the development of industry, while agricultural problems were treated as not so urgent. But some attention was still given to preventing the 'hunger supply' (see pp. 95), intervention purchasing was continued, farmers were granted credits and so on. None of these measures could really raise the prices of farm products as their range was rather limited.

The government considered programmes to improve the structure of the basic agricultural system. It was thought, however, that in many parts of the eastern provinces landowners were the main support of the Polish administration and the realisation of the 1925 land reform still faced difficulties. Instead of the planned 200,000 hectares per annum, the area of parcelled land amounted in 1936-8, respectively, to 97,000, 113,000 and 119,000 hectares. This was due to the shortage of financial means in the rural areas. Colonisation of the parcelled large landed estates in the eastern regions by Polish settlers was planned as a substitute for land reform. (15)

Altogether 2,655,000 hectares were parcelled out between 1919 and 1938, accounting for about 7 per cent of arable land. This meant a reduction in the area of large landed estates and a transfer of some land into peasant hands. But 26 per cent of cultivable land still belonged to farms of more than 50 ha, while the number of these farms was only 0.5 per cent of the total number of farms in Poland. Parcelling created 154,000 self-sufficient farms and made it possible to increase the area of a further 503,000 farms.

Compared with the increase in the agricultural population (3.5 million people, emigrations and migrations to town deducted) this was very little. The splitting-up of peasant holdings continued. Between

1921 and 1938 the number of farms of 0 to 2 ha grew by 36.4 per cent; of farms of 2 to 5 ha by 34 per cent, and of farms from 5 to 10 ha by 25.4 per cent. However, the expanding number of farms was not accompanied by an adequate increase in their area. The actual increase in the area of farms below 2 ha amounted to 25 per cent, of farms from 2 to 5 ha to 22.4 per cent and of farms from 5 to 10 ha to 15.7 per cent. (16) The average area of holdings in each category therefore fell. The division of holdings was thought to be an answer to the difficulties that peasants faced when migrating to towns in search of work in underdeveloped industries. However, emigration ceased to play a noticeable role after 1930.

The splitting up of peasant holdings and continued use of old-fashioned methods of land cultivation led to a decrease in average earnings, all this compounded by the fact that the number of 'redundant' people in the country was constantly growing. Because peasants in the total population of Poland were the majority, the domestic market was determined by their purchasing power. Industrialisation was possible only if the farmers' demands for industrial goods could be voiced and met. But this also depended on the peasants' incomes. Unfortunately the renunciation of radical land reform, which would have considerably increased the amount of land in peasant hands without throwing them into debt, checked economic advance in Poland. Similar radical land reforms had been carried out in some European countries (for example, the Baltic states) in the interwar period. In Poland, however, it could not be accomplished in view of the close relationship between the ruling elite and landowners. Thus the vicious circle of backwardness could not be broken. The countryside was too poor to buy industrial goods and industry was therefore unable to develop. The relative underdevelopment of industry made it impossible for the 'redundant' agricultural population to leave for the towns, which consequently exacerbated the poverty felt in the countryside.

It was estimated that reducing the upper limit of large estates to 50 ha, even in 1938, could have satisfied about 60 per cent of the demand for land among smallholders and landless peasants. (17) The consolidation of peasant holdings played some part in the improvement of the agrarian structure. In 1919-38 it included 859,000 farms of an area of almost 5.5 million ha. Nevertheless some of the consolidated holdings were afterwards split up again as a result of reapportioning among and within families.

Between 1936 and 1938 farming production did not change, only the area under crop increased slightly. Yields per hectare were also relatively stable. An increase was recorded in the number of horses, cattle and pigs. In 1935-8 the number of horses grew by 4 per cent, of cattle by 8 per cent and of pigs by 12 per cent.

A comparison of agricultural statistics during the Second Republic with the level before the First World War (to allow for weather conditions, five-year average data are quoted) shows that total crops increased. Harvests of the four basic grain crops (rye, wheat, barley and oats) were growing in proportion to the increasing area under crop. Between 1909 to 1913 the four grain crop harvests amounted to 117 million quintals (q), and in the years 1934-8 to 125 million q. However, the per capita crop diminished from 3.8 q to 3.6 q. The total potato crop rose from 248 to 346 million q, the per capita potato crop from 8.2 q to 10.1 q. The increasing potato crop was due to the fact that the potato formed a major part of the staple diet as well as to the development of pig husbandry. On the other hand the sugar beet crop diminished from 41 to 32 million q. Animal breeding developed considerably. According to adequate estimates (data for the years preceding the First World War are only approximate) the number of horses grew by about 10 per cent, of cattle by 20 per cent and of pigs by as much as 40 per cent. Only the number of sheep diminished.

While total industrial production did not change much compared with the 1913 level (only its structure having been different), there was some progress in agriculture, although cultivation methods remained much the same. This can be seen from a comparison of yields of basic crops before both world wars (Table 2.13). Yields of oats and rye grew, while those of the wheat and sugar beet decreased.

The variation between the economic results of the eastern and western provinces slightly diminished. This can be shown by yields per hectare; in the west these were decreasing, while a certain increase was recorded in the east. However, the level of development in both parts of Poland still differed. For example, the highest yields per hectare (the 1934-8 five-year annual average) as regards wheat were recorded in the Silesian province (15.8 q), the lowest in the Wilno province (7.5 q); the highest rye yields in the Silesian province (14.8 q) and the lowest in the Wilno province (7.9 q); the highest potato yields in the Lublin province (136 q) and the lowest in the Wilno province (95 q); the highest barley yields in the Pomeranian province (16.7 q) and the lowest in the Polesie province (7.4 q).

Table 2.13: Average Yields of Basic Crops in Poland before the First and the Second World War (Five-year Averages in q per Ha).

Period	Wheat	Rye	Barley	Oats	Potatoes	Sugar beet
1909-13	12.4	11.2	11.8	10.2	103	245
1934-8	11.9	11.2	11.8	11.4	121	216
Difference	-0.5	0.0	0.0	+1.2	+18	-29

Source: Mały Rocznik Statystyczny 1939 (Główny Urząd Statystyczny, Warsaw, 1939), p. 77.

It is also interesting to compare Poland's share in world agriculture between 1909 and 1913 and between 1934 and 1938 (Table 2.14). Here also Poland seemed to lag behind.

Table 2.14: The Share of Polish Crop Production in World Output in 1909-13 and 1934-8.

Crop	Share of Poland in world production		Ratio of Poland's share in
	1909-13	1934-8	1934-8:1909-13
Four grain crops	4.65	4.31	92.69
of which:			
wheat	1.63	1.48	90.79
rye	12.67	13.97	110.26
barley	3.92	3.42	87.24
oats	4.28	4.02	93.92
Potatoes	16.65	15.43	92.67
Sugar beet	7.56	3.80	50.26

Source: Z. Landau, 'Poland's Economy Against the Background of World Economy 1913-1938', Acta Poloniae Historica, no. 20 (1969), p. 93.

FINANCE

The posts of Treasury minister and vice-premier for economic affairs were held until the Second World War by Eugeniusz Kwiatkowski who belonged to a group of politicians connected with the president of Poland, Ignacy Mościcki. This group, called 'the Castle', shared power with politicians connected with the General Inspector of the Armed Forces, General Edward Rydz-Smigły. The two competing groups divided power within the government and economic problems fell within the competence of 'the Castle'. The Rydz-Smigły followers often criticised the government's economic policy. Monetary policy was particularly in dispute. Kwiatkowski rejected the idea of monetary experiments and instead followed a rather traditional policy. But his opponents thought it necessary to dispense with traditional methods and use limited inflationary issues as an incentive to the economic development and modernisation of the army. At that time the economic policy was a kind of compromise between different tendencies.

Foreign exchange restrictions, introduced on 26 April 1936, were notably significant. They were aimed at checking the gold and foreign exchange outflow from Poland, but the restrictions were introduced in Poland much later than in other countries, so gold and foreign currency reserves of the Bank Polski decreased to a level hardly securing the złoty. The delay made it difficult for the government to follow a more radical policy. Currency restrictions were unable to prevent the outflow of all foreign capital but this process was finally stopped in September 1936 when the Polish government suspended payments on foreign loans contracted up to that date. Foreign exchange settlements were then regulated by the Foreign Exchange Commission.

The decreasing gold and foreign currency reserves of the Bank Polski were limiting the growth of note circulation. In this connection the Rydz-Smigły group managed to force a so-called fiduciary issue of 800-1,200 million zł in 1939. The Bank Polski was entitled to raise note circulation regardless of coverage. Thus złoty circulation increased from 1,412 to 1,866 million zł over the years 1935-8, while note coverage decreased from 39.8 per cent to 28.6 per cent. (19) The increased circulation was utilised for financing government investments. Inflation was unlikely because the growing number of notes in circulation helped to stimulate production and the construction of new factories. The złoty maintained its 1927 gold parity until the outbreak of war in 1939.

The principle of balancing the budget, formulated in 1935, was carried into effect by means of further budgetary cuts and simultaneous tax increases. The latter charged mainly consumers and not producers. In December 1935 a special tax charged earnings connected with public expenditures, income tax was raised while pensions were cut. Thus in March 1936 budgetary revenues appeared higher than expenses for the first time since December 1931. The budget surplus was maintained in later years. Revenues were growing, mainly due to the market recovery, and this made it possible for the government to spend more without necessarily fearing inflation.

Special funds established for certain purposes were playing a growing role in the government's financial policy, though they were not included in the budget. The most important of them all, the National Defence Fund, was created in April 1936. It accumulated state subsidies, private donations and grants from public institutions and was aimed at gathering additional finance for the army. Moreover, it made military expenditures more independent of the Treasury ministry. The National Defence Fund obtained more than two milliard francs from a loan granted by the French government. Other credits were of minor importance.

The last years of the Second Republic brought a further decline in private banking. The number of private banks decreased from 32 to 26 over the years 1935-8. The balance-sheet totals grew when compared with the depression level but they still remained lower than in state banks. The years 1938-9 were rather difficult for Polish banking. The growing danger of war caused periodic withdrawals of banking facilities and savings deposits. A run on the banks, connected with the incorporation of Zaolzie by Poland in 1938, deprived the Pocztowa Kasa Oszczędności of deposits of about 400 million zł, which accounted for 20 per cent of all its deposits. On the eve of German aggression in August 1938 more than 800 million zł were withdrawn from banks. (20) Thus private banks had to seek help from the Bank Polski which had already been practically dependent on the government and on state banks.

DOMESTIC TRADE

The increasing number of commercial enterprises was the first sign of recovery in domestic trade. Their number grew from 421,000 in 1935 to 469,000 in 1938 (that is by 11 per cent). More importantly the number of large enterprises had also grown. The number of wholesale warehouses, for example, increased by 37 per cent and that of large retail shops by 34 per cent. Turnover was also growing, particularly in towns. Rural trade was expanding much more slowly and this was connected with the financial difficulties of farmers who, despite a certain improvement in the market situation, could purchase less goods than before the depression. A plough, for example, cost 100 kg of rye in 1927/8 and 221 kg of rye in 1939, 100 kg of superphosphate (in the same years) cost 31 and 69 kg of rye, a pair of shoes cost 99 and 191 kg, 10 kg of salt 8 and 24 kg, 1 kg of tobacco 141 and 575 kg, while 10 litres of kerosene cost 13 and 29 kg of rye, etc.

Polish domestic trade remained split up into any number of small units, which was expensive and hardly cost-effective. The trade turnover supported a whole hierarchy of agents. Commercial credits were expensive, taxation still relatively high and profits of trading enterprises remained at a rather low level. Consequently there was keen competition in the home market.

Shortly before the Second World War broke out, in July 1939, the Polish domestic market had a much increased turnover in connection with the buying up of foodstuffs. This caused a speculative increase in prices which in turn was quite effectively counteracted by the government.

FOREIGN ECONOMIC RELATIONS

The introduction of foreign exchange controls in 1936 played a very important role in Polish foreign trade. The development of foreign trade control systems in many countries gradually diminished the significance of duties and tariff policies. In fact no major changes were made in the latter field in Poland in 1936-9. Import tariff reductions, however, were of some importance. These referred to imports of machinery and raw materials for investment purposes. As the government lent its support to any form of investment, these reductions could be as high as 80 per cent of the tariff rates. At the same time duty refunds (bounties) were limited - in 1937 duty refunds for grain and milling products (with the exception of barley) were ended. Until that time most of the duty refund sums were paid for grain export promotion (in 1936/7 the latter absorbed 67.2 million zł but figures for industrial exports amounted to only 11.4 million zł). (21)

The imposition of foreign exchange controls in April 1936 was followed by closely connected foreign turnover control regulations which were effective from May 1936. Export licences were granted subject to the submission of a certificate guaranteeing that the exporter would return all foreign currency to Poland. Such certificates were not required for exports within the clearing agreements. The Polish foreign trade system was different in relation to the free-exchange countries with which Poland had an active trade balance (Great Britain, Belgium, Netherlands, the Scandinavian countries and Baltic states), and in relation to the free-exchange countries with which Poland had a passive trade balance (France and Czechoslovakia) - and to the clearing countries. Settlement of clearing accounts was carried out by the Polish Clearing Institute established in November 1936.

The necessity to adjust trade agreements and conventions signed by Poland to these new methods of payment obliged the Polish government to renegotiate many agreements or conclude new commercial treaties or additional protocols.

Growing difficulties in foreign trade had not limited turnover. Polish exports increased by 28 per cent and imports by 51 per cent between 1935 and 1938. (22) This rapid increase in turnover resulted mainly from the government's ambitious investment programme whose realisation depended to a great extent on imports of machinery and equipment. In 1935 Poland's share of world exports amounted to 0.89 per cent, but by 1938 had grown to 1.14 per cent. The share of Polish imports increased in the same period from 0.79 per cent to 1.18 per cent. (23)

As imports grew more rapidly than exports a deficit appeared in the Polish trade balance in 1937, which widened in the two following years (in 1938 the deficit amounted to about 10 per cent of exports).

Under these circumstances the government made attempts to reduce the burden of repayments resulting from previous foreign loans. At first the government suspended the transfer of obligations to owners of treasury bonds until new terms of payment had been negotiated. Amounts due to foreign creditors were gathered in złotys in a special account in the Bank Polski. Then obligations resulting from Polish loans issued abroad to Polish citizens were converted into special bonds issued in Poland in złotys. It appeared that a greater part of the Polish treasury bonds were bought by Polish citizens.

This kind of measure largely decreased Polish foreign exchange commitments due to loans contracted by the Polish government abroad. In this way, for example, $US8 million (out of $US16.6 million) due to a loan contracted in the US bank of Dillon, Read and Co in 1925 were converted into internal government bonds in the late 1930s.

After the conversion of these loans the government returned to servicing loans in foreign currencies. The time of discharge of the Dillon loan was extended by 13 years and the interest decreased from 8 per cent to 3 per cent. (24) Allowances gained as regards other loans were similar. Thus the total indebtedness of the Polish state rapidly diminished along with sums paid from the budget for servicing foreign loans. Devaluation of some foreign currencies had a similar effect. The Polish government's foreign indebtedness fell from 3,345 million zł to 2,558 million zł over the years 1935-8 while bonded debts diminished from 928 million zł to 470 million zł. At the same time the debt service burden of the budget decreased from 119 million zł to 89 million zł.

Nevertheless Poland's financial problems grew again with the accelerated outflow of foreign capital. In 1936 the deficit due to foreign capital outflow from Poland amounted to 162 million zł and in 1937 to 52 million zł.

LIVING CONDITIONS

There are relatively precise estimates of Polish national income for 1935-9. They show that the national income of Poland had grown from 19.7 to 23.7 milliard zł between 1935 and 1938, that is, by 20 per cent. Other estimates differ a little in numerical terms but confirm a rapid increase in Polish national income at fixed prices. In view of the fact that the 1938 level of prices for farm products and many industrial goods was much lower than in 1928, Polish national income at current prices indicated a decrease of about 30 per cent. (25) The first estimate, however, is more important as it puts economic development in a more realistic light. It must be added that the 1936 active trade balance meant that the national income to be distributed was lower than that generated whereas in the two following years the proportions were opposite in view of the passive trade balance. It is also noteworthy that in 1938 the national income exceeded the 1928 level.

Improvements in the standard of living of various social groups can only be approximately evaluated as there are no detailed studies or reliable estimates of these changes. It seems that the increasing national income was hardly noticed by farmers. The narrow market for farm products led to low prices for these articles and the country remained heavily over-populated.

The working classes felt the improving economic situation both through rapidly growing employment and real wages. Between January 1936 and January 1939 employment in mining, metallurgy and processing industrial plants of more than 19 workers (excluding the Zaolzie incorporated in 1938) increased from 587,000 to 766,000 people, that is, by 31 per cent.

At the same time, however, unemployment remained an important social problem. Despite the improving situation in industry, the number of people registered as seeking work remained at a very high level. In December 1935 the number of unemployed seeking work amounted, according to official statistics, to 403,000, in 1936 to 466,000, in 1937 to 470,000 and in 1938 to 456,000 people. The number of all unemployed workers in towns (including those formerly working in small enterprises) was estimated at 713,000 in 1935, in 1936 at 1,114,000, in 1937 at 933,000, and in 1938 at 798,000 people. (26) The situation seemed a little better than during the Great Depression but improvement was very slow and the number of unemployed was still higher than that of workers employed in large and medium-size industrial plants.

Part-time work was diminishing. In 1933 the number of part-time workers accounted for 27 per cent of all workers employed, but by 1936 this had decreased to less than 23 per cent. Nevertheless it was still more than in 1928. Unemployment mainly affected unskilled workers. Qualified workers could more easily find a job at one of the investment sites designated for development.

The government tried to counteract unemployment through its investment policy. The activities of the so-called Fund of Labour were also significant as it organised public works. Moreover, the settlement of south-eastern provinces by landless Polish families was encouraged. In many districts Ukrainian emigration was openly supported, the land left by emigrants being seen as available for Polish settlers. All these policies aimed at ensuring work for the unemployed but there was still a disastrous lack of jobs. Living conditions for the unemployed were partially mitigated by a benefits system but this applied to only a part of the jobless population. In 1935 unemployment benefits were paid to 18 per cent of those registered as unemployed and in 1938 to 24 per cent of this number. In these circumstances various forms of emergency aid were developed.

An improvement in the labour market influenced the rate of growth in nominal wages. Nevertheless, they did not reach the pre-depression level. In 1936 nominal wages in Poland amounted to 70 per cent of the 1929 level and in 1938 to 77 per cent (comparison of mean annual industrial rates per hour). It is noteworthy that the more and more frequent strikes contributed to the increase in nominal wages. The Great Depression had checked or rather limited the number of strikes. However, in 1936 there were 2,056 strikes involving 675,000 workers and 3,950,000 working days were lost. In 1937 the number of strikes amounted to 2,078 in which 565,000 workers participated and 3,315,000 working days were lost. (27)

The increase in nominal wages was higher than that of the cost of living. Therefore personal real wages increased in 1935-8, exceeding the 1929 level. Whereas 1938 nominal hourly wages accounted for 77 per cent of the 1929 level, the 1938 cost of living index totalled 59 per cent of this level. (28) This resulted mainly from the cheapness of food on which most of the workers' earnings were spent (apart from rents). Total real wages paid to workers employed in large and medium-size industrial factories amounted to 88 per cent of the 1929 level in 1936, to 98 per cent of this level in 1937 and to 113 per cent in 1938. In smaller factories improvement was less pronounced.

After the Great Depression labour legislation began to be changed in favour of the working class. The government wished to gain support in this social group and the introduction of regulations concerning collective labour contracts, payment for overtime, working hours in mining and the settlement of collective conflicts were of particular importance. However some regulations were a step back in relation to the previous stipulations. The president's decree concerning the protection of certain public interests issued in 1938 may be considered such a step as it limited the right to strike. The situation of professional workers was also improving. Their nominal and real salaries grew and there were better employment prospects. In 1931-8 employment of professional workers increased by about 20 per cent. (29) Nevertheless, even in this social group unemployment did not cease. Official data relating to 1938 recorded that there were still 27,000 professional workers seeking jobs. In practice this number must have been higher.

The financial position of the peasantry in 1936-9 is very difficult to assess in view of the lack of statistical evidence. Thus many problems can only be described with partial knowledge of the actual situation.

Increasing earnings from sales of farm products and from casual work undertaken outside the farm were of essential significance for farmers. In farms of 2-50 ha the cash revenue per hectare of arable land increased from 143 zł in the economic year 1934/5 to 204 zł in 1937/8, that is, by 43 per cent. In the following year income fell once again due to further decreases in prices obtained for farm products. Though the increment of cash earnings in the country seemed quite considerable, this was still lower than in 1928/9 when income per hectare amounted to 506 zł. Income in 1937/8 accounted therefore for only 40 per cent of the pre-depression level. (30)

Most of the cash received by peasants was spent on taxes, compulsory insurances and the discharge of debts. Remaining sums were used for investment and personal consumption. In 1937/8 the annual cash expenditure for food, household equipment, light and fuel per person in farms of 2-50 ha amounted to 52 zł, that is less than 5 zł monthly. On the other hand expenditure for clothing, shoes, furniture, medical care and medicines, education, newspapers, books, travels, tobacco and cigarettes, spirits, etc., amounted to 129 zł per person, that is less than 11 zł monthly. Total consumption expenditure remained at the level of 15 zł monthly or a little less than $US3. It must be pointed out that these data refer to the leading peasant farms including both medium-size, and small, poor peasant lots.

The quoted data show that living conditions in the Polish countryside were still very difficult. The government was only able to improve this situation slightly through the conversion of loans and debt clearing. In 1936-8 almost 2.5 million agreements were signed, changing the terms of debt payments. This was a serious and welcome relief for the countryside. On the other hand taxation was not reduced.

In 1936-9 farm workers were affected by two contrary trends. On the one hand their wages increased, but on the other the area of land owned by large landowners diminished which limited the demand for manpower. Farm workers still faced competition from landless peasants and smallholders who were willing to accept wages lower than those of permanent farm-hands.

Little is known of the standards of living of the landowner and industrial entrepreneur on the eve of the Second World War. It may be presumed that increasing profits gave industrial entrepreneurs and shareholders higher incomes. The same may be said of landowners with large estates, but it is not possible to state precisely whether their situation improved as compared with the years preceding the Great Depression.

NOTES

1. J. Żarnowski, Społeczeństwo Drugiej Rzeczypospolitej 1918-1939 (Państwowe Wydawnictwo Naukowe, Warsaw, 1973), p. 22.
2. J. Ignaszewski, Śląsk Zaolziański w życiu gospodarczym Polski (publishing house not given, Katowice, 1938), pp. 10-26.
3. J. Tomaszewski, 'Zaolzie' in: Encyklopedia historii gospodarczej Polski do 1945 roku (Wiedza Powszechna, Warsaw, 1981), vol. 2, pp. 542-3; Z. Landau, J. Tomaszewski, 'Československo-polské obchodní vztahy 1930-1939', Slovanský přehled, no. 5 (1980), pp. 379-83.
4. Ku przebudowie gospodarczej. Wytyczne inwestycji państwowych (Polska Gospodarcza, Warsaw, 1937), p. 10.
5. M. Drozdowski, Polityka gospodarcza rządu polskiego 1936-1939 (Państwowe Wydawnictwo Naukowe, Warsaw, 1963), pp. 127-34.
6. H. Radocki, COP w Polsce (Myśl Polska, Warsaw, 1939), p. 25; S. Zawadzki, 'Centralny Okręg Przemysłowy', Przegląd Geograficzny, no. 1 (1963), p. 59 ff.
7. K. Bobiński, Centralny Okręg Przemysłowy. Przyczyny powstania i warunki rozwoju, (Kozierkiewicz, Warsaw, 1939), p. 65.
8. E. Kwiatkowski, O wielkość Rzeczypospolitej. Przemówienie wygłoszone w Sejmie w dniu 2 grudnia 1938 r. (Polska Gospodarcza, Warsaw, 1938), pp. 58-9.
9. I. Svennilson, Growth and Stagnation in the European Economy (United Nations, Geneva, 1954),

p. 207.

10. Mały Rocznik Statystyczny 1939 (Główny Urząd Statystyczny, Warsaw, 1939), pp. 261-2.

11. Materiały do badań nad gospodarką Polski. Część I - 1918-1939 (Państwowe Wydawnictwo Naukowe, Warsaw, 1956), pp. 178-9.

12. Materiały, p. 191.

13. F. Zweig, Poland between Two Wars. A Critical Study of Social and Economic Changes (Secker and Warburg, London, 1944), p. 104.

14. R. Gradowski, Polska 1918-1939. Niektóre zagadnienia kapitalizmu monopolistycznego (Książka i Wiedza, Warsaw, 1959), pp. 193-4.

15. Odpis tajnego pisma Ministerstwa Rolnictwa i Reform Rolnych do Urzędu Wojewódzkiego w Stanisławowie z dn. 27 kwietnia 1939 r., AAN, Prezydium Rady Ministrów, vol. 148-50, p. 2.

16. M. Mieszczankowski, Struktura agrarna Polski międzywojennej (Państwowe Wydawnictwo Naukowe, Warsaw, 1960), pp. 310, 331 and 333.

17. Młodzież sięga po pracę (Instytut Spraw Społecznych, Warsaw, 1938), p. 75.

18. In English: cf. A. Polonsky, Politics in Independent Poland 1921-1939. The Crisis of Constitutional Government (Clarendon Press, Oxford, 1972), pp. 391-447; E. Wynot Jr, The Polish Politics in Transition. The Camp of National Unity and the Struggle for Power 1935-1939 (University of Georgia Press, Athens, 1974), pp. 21-258.

19. I. Weinfeld, Skarbowość polska, (Biblioteka Prawnicza, Warsaw, 1939), vol. 1, pp. 86-9.

20. H.Gruber, Wspomnienia i uwagi (Gryf Publications Ltd, London, 1968), pp. 383 and 390.

21. S. Królikowski, Zarys polskiej polityki handlowej ze szczególnym uwzględnieniem polityki celnej (Instytut Społeczny, Warsaw, 1938), p. 143.

22. M. Drozdowski, Polityka, p. 161.

23. J. Krynicki, Problemy handlu zagranicznego Polski 1918-1939 i 1945-1955 (Państwowe Wydawnictwo Naukowe, Warsaw, 1958), p. 170.

24. Z. Landau, Pożyczki zagraniczne państwa polskiego 1918-1926 (Książka i Wiedza, Warsaw, 1961), p. 249.

25. Z. Landau, 'National Income in Historical Research (On Material from the Period of Interwar Poland)', Acta Poloniae Historica, vol. 33 (1976), pp. 116-17; C. Clark, The Conditions of Economic Progress, 3rd edn, (MacMillan and Co, London, 1957), p. 177.

26. J. Moraczewski, Rozważania nad położeniem gospodarczym kraju (J. Moraczewski, Warsaw, 1938), p. 63; J. Tomaszewski, 'Liczba robotników w Polsce

w latach 1925-1938', Roczniki Dziejów Społecznych i Gospodarczych, vol. 26 (1964), p. 71.

27. Mały Rocznik Statystyczny 1939 (Główny Urząd Statystyczny, Warsaw, 1939), p. 284.

28. H. Jędruszczakowa, Płace robotników przemysłowych w Polsce w latach 1924-1929 (Państwowe Wydawnictwo Naukowe, Warsaw, 1963), p. 250.

29. J. Żarnowski, Struktura społeczna inteligencji polskiej w latach 1918-1939 (Państwowe Wydawnictwo Naukowe, Warsaw, 1964), p. 123.

30. J. Curzytek, Położenie gospodarstw włościańskich w 1937/38 r. (Państwowy Instytut Naukowy Gospodarstwa Wiejskiego w Puławach, Warsaw, 1939), p. 17.

CHAPTER THREE

NAZI OCCUPATION

TERRITORY

On 1 September 1939 Germany invaded Poland without any declaration of war. Poland could not resist the German aggressors in view of the military and economic supremacy of the Reich, Poland's unfavourable strategic situation and encirclement by Germany in the north, west and south, as well as the lack of any immediate assistance from the Western allies (France and Great Britain). The Polish army fought a forlorn war for five weeks. It continued even after Soviet troops entered the eastern territories of the Second Republic on 17 September 1939. Besieged Warsaw was defended until 28 September, the fortress of Modlin until 29 September and the marine garrison of the Hel peninsula until 2 October. The last organised Polish resistance ended on 5 October. The war against Poland proved longer and more exhaustive than had been thought in Berlin and Hitler had to postpone the already planned attack westwards.

The Polish-German war resulted in serious population and material losses, affecting not only battlefields but areas situated beyond the reach of direct military operations. Most were due to air raids by the Luftwaffe against which the Polish defence system was powerless. Poland's main industrial centres, however, did not suffer too much except for the oil mining region and Warsaw industry in general. Total industrial losses were estimated at about $US100 million. (1) The countryside was also seriously hit. Agricultural losses comprised mainly farm buildings, standing crops, and horses which had been mobilised for the war effort. The war had cost thousands of lives, both of soldiers and civilians, with many wounded.

As a result of war the Polish territories

situated westward of the Bug river fell under Nazi occupation, while territories lying eastward of this river were taken by the Soviet army, the result of an agreement between Hitler and Stalin for a new division of Poland. 48.4 per cent of the area of the Polish state (389,000 sq km in 1939) was occupied by the Third Reich, 50 per cent was incorporated into the Soviet Union and 1.6 per cent went to Lithuania. Proportions relating to the number of population differed as the territories eastward of the Bug river were less populated. Thus the Nazi occupation embraced 62.9 per cent of the population of the Second Republic, whereas areas incorporated into the Soviet Union were inhabited by 35.8 per cent and those taken by Lithuania by 1.3 per cent of the population of inter-war Poland. (2)

The territory occupied by the German Reich was divided. A large area was incorporated into the Reich as an integral part of Germany on 8 October 1939. These were the most economically advanced parts of inter-war Poland and included the Pomeranian and Poznań provinces with highly efficient agriculture, Upper Silesia with its industrial potential, the Łódź province with well-developed textile industries and part of the Kielce province with its metal-processing factories. The territory incorporated into the Reich produced 100 per cent of Polish coal, 97.5 per cent of its pig iron, 90 per cent of its steel, as well as 70 per cent of the textile and sugar production. (3) Non-economic considerations such as historic or ethnic backgrounds were disregarded, as Germany incorporated not only the areas of formerly Prussian Poland but also a considerable part of the Polish territories which had belonged to the Russian partition. The share of the German population in the incorporated areas was a mere 6.4 per cent.

The remaining part of the Polish territories occupied by the Germans was organised into the so-called General Gouvernement in October 1939. This territorial body was to be the provisional seat of the Polish population. The capital of the General Gouvernement was established in Cracow while Warsaw was reduced to one of the four district towns.

Further territorial changes were the result of the outbreak of the German-Soviet war and there followed a German takeover of the whole of Polish territory as it was before 1 September 1939. Part of the conquered area was actually (though not formally) incorporated into the Reich (the Białystok region) while East Galicia was incorporated into the

General Gouvernement as its fifth district. Other areas which had been included in the Soviet Union were re-organised within two newly established Reichskomissariats - Ukraine and Ostland.

The areas incorporated into the Reich and the General Gouvernement were subject to different policies. The former were to be united with the Reich as quickly as possible. This was connected with their legal and economic unification and with a specific Nazi germanisation policy. The German language was introduced as the only official tongue, all geographical names were germanised, all Polish institutions were banned and their property confiscated, Polish schools were suppressed but, above all, Poles were murdered and resettled. The incorporated areas were cut from the General Gouvernement by a state frontier. There were also customs tariffs and separate currencies which made it possible for the Nazi authorities to pursue different economic and monetary policies and to maintain various prices and wages in the two divided parts of the Polish state. Both of them were subject to the occupation administration but Nazi organisation and policy towards them differed.

This discrimination in the Nazi attitude towards both parts of occupied Poland was the outcome of various plans formulated by the occupation authorities. The incorporated areas were to be Germanised in the course of war and this process was to be completed by 1949. According to Adolf Hitler Germanisation was not to be achieved by denationalisation of the local population but by means of their resettlement, mass deportation or execution. The Polish population was to be replaced by German colonists. Hitler had emphasised this in Mein Kampf: 'Only the land can be Germanised.' (4)

The General Gouvernement was at first thought to be the provisional seat of the Polish population but Poles were deprived of all independence. The Gouvernement was ruled by a so-called 'government' composed of Nazi functionaries directly subordinate to Hitler and headed by Hans Frank. Poles did not participate in this 'government'. The German occupation authorities had suppressed all Polish political, self-governing, cultural and educational organisations maintaining only primary schools and secondary trade schools. All other secondary and higher schools were abolished. Cultural life and social activities were pushed underground. Thus conspiracy developed on a large scale including not only the underground state apparatus and secret army but also a rich and differentiated political life together with an under-ground system of secondary and higher education. An extensive secret press was also published. Clandestine activities included representatives of all political parties from the extreme left to the extreme right.

POPULATION

German population policy in the Polish territories was directed at three objectives: (i) getting rid of their inhabitants; (ii) crushing all opposition and (iii) maximum exploitation of the manpower resources in the course of war. These objectives could not all be realised at the same time. The first task, for example, was sometimes contrary to the third one. A too rapid resettlement of Poles, given a slow inflow of German colonists, would lead to a shortage of manpower which might reduce industrial or agricultural output. Thus the Nazi occupation authorities postponed the final deportation of the Polish population until the expected victorious end of war.

These plans were formulated in the Generalplan Ost worked out in the course of war and foreseeing resettlement of all Poles eastwards, mainly to Western Siberia. The Polish population was to be dispersed over vast tracts of Siberian land so that it would be unable to create compact concentrations. In this manner the Germans intended to denationalise those Poles who would survive the war. Only a small part of the Polish population was to remain in the former territory of the Second Republic to do the hard manual work from which the Germans, as representatives of the Herrenvolk, were to be relieved. The Generalplan Ost was to be carried into effect within 20-30 years. The slow rate of its realisation was mainly due to the German colonisation capacity which limited the progress of the plan. Thus the Generalplan Ost took into account the Germanisation of 3 to 4 million Polish peasants who were to remain in the Polish territories, dispersed among the German colonists. (5)

The Generalplan Ost was of course subject to the defeat of the USSR. However, the occupation authorities made preparations for its realisation and even tried to resettle the Polish population from the Zamość region and to colonise this area with German settlers in 1942-3.

The basic Nazi population policy, which continued from 1 September 1939 to the liberation of the Polish territories, resolved itself to the use of overwhelming terror. It took various forms, in intensity and practice, but always remained the basic occupation policy. Terror was aimed at weakening the Polish liberation struggle and at destroying the resistance movement. Nevertheless, Nazi policy, directed against the whole of society regardless of political attitudes, social position, views or activities, helped to consolidate Polish society in an act of resistance against the invaders.

Mass murders began to take place almost immediately after German troops invaded the Polish territories. In order to terrorise the population scores of prominent Polish citizens were shot in most of the occupied towns. In Bydgoszcz several thousand people were murdered. Mass murders continued throughout the years of occupation. They included both the Polish and Jewish population. The death penalty was introduced not only for acts directed against the German occupation system but also for the baking of white bread, illegal trade or slaughtering, failure to deliver foodstuff quotas, keeping Jews in hiding, etc. Sending people to concentration and death camps was a similar kind of extermination policy. Death camps killed everybody who got there while concentration camps took the lives of most of the prisoners. Deportation to a concentration camp was not the result of a judicial sentence. Anybody who fell into Nazi hands, no matter if he acted against the occupation system or not, could be sent to the camp for an unlimited time.

Apart from a physical extermination the German occupation authorities applied other means of oppression; resettlement of inhabitants without the right to take possessions, forced Germanisation of selected groups of people, deportations for forced labour in Germany and so on. All these inhuman activities cannot be described here in detail but they have an extensive bibliography. (6)

The Nazi terror affected both Polish and Jewish populations. The German authorities did not wait until the expected victorious end of war for the 'final solution' of the Jewish problem, when they planned to do the same to most of the Polish population, but started the deliberate, physical extermination of Jews during the war. At the same time the Nazis tried to deepen nationality conflicts between various groups of people living in the Polish territories, attempting to fan anti-semitic feelings or oppose the more privileged Ukrainians against Poles. They also endeavoured to provoke spurious hostility between regional groups within the Polish population such as the Tatra highlanders, the Kashubes or the Mazovians, nominated separate nations, and the remaining Poles. The occupation authorities believed that nationality conflicts would facilitate the isolation of various social groups and, consequently, that this would help Nazi population policies.

The persecution of Poles and Jews started the moment the German army entered Poland. At first, oppression of the Jewish population was limited to enforcing various kinds of labour services, plunder and beating. But soon a system of regulations was introduced forbidding Jews to possess more than 2,000 zł in cash per family, to practise some professions, compelling them to wear armbands with the Star of David, depriving them of pensions or the liberty of choice of the place of residence, etc. In January 1940 mass confiscations of Jewish property were started and soon the Jewish ghettos began to be created in many towns. All Jews were compelled to move to separate quarters. At first they could enter and leave the ghettos but afterwards the Jewish quarters were closed, surrounded by walls and controlled by guards. The inhabitants were deprived of the right to leave the ghettos and the non-Jewish population, called the 'Aryans', forbidden to enter the ghettos. This meant that the overwhelming majority of Jews were no longer able to work and earn their living. Food supplies were cut because the Germans intended to starve out the Jewish population. In the second half of 1941 food rationing coupons satisfied only about 10 per cent of the minimum daily requirement and in view of very high prices and scarcity of wage-earning most of the Jewish population could not afford to buy food on the black market. Thus within a year and a half about 15-20 per cent of the inhabitants of the Warsaw ghetto died as a result of hunger and disease. The Warsaw ghetto was the largest in Poland; according to studies carried out inside it, about 50 per cent of its population were dying of hunger, 30 per cent were gradually starving, 15 per cent ate too little and only 5 per cent fed normally. (7) A similar situation was recorded in other ghettos. Enormous over-population of relatively small areas aggravated this situation because the German authorities usually located the ghettos in the most neglected quarters. One room was frequently inhabited by up to a dozen people. (8)

Under these circumstances the extermination of people recognised as Jews (the German authorities treated as a Jew anyone who had Jewish grandparents, regardless of his knowledge of the language, religion or connections with the Jewish community) seemed inevitable within a few years. But even this rate of extermination seemed too slow for the Nazis. In the autumn of 1941 there began the infamous deportations of ghetto inhabitants to the death camps where Jews were murdered in gas chambers and cremated. All the belongings of victims were confiscated for the Reich. Even gold teeth were removed from corpses. The last ghetto of the General Gouvernement was destroyed in mid-1943. As a result of this genocidal action the overwhelming majority of the Jewish community living in the Polish territories, numbering 3.2 million people, were killed. Only a small number of Polish Jews survived - in concentration camps, compulsory works or in the shelter of Poles who were subject to the death penalty for hiding Jews. There also survived those Jews who had lived in the areas incorporated into the USSR and found themselves deep in Russia before June 1941.

The Jewish holocaust also had an economic background; the Nazis had simply grabbed all the property of their victims. The extermination of the Jewish population had a significant impact on the post-war Polish state - since Jews had dominated certain trades before the Second World War, their extermination substantially aggravated post-war reconstruction problems.

The extermination of the Jewish population was considered by the Nazi invaders as an introduction to a similar extermination of most of the Polish population. In view of a shortage of manpower during the war the German authorities were unable to realise all their plans. This is why they tried above all to crush any form of national resistance - and this meant the execution of all Poles active in the political, economic, cultural, professional or even sporting life of the country. This action started immediately after the occupation of the Polish territories. At first Nazi policy was mostly confined to the areas incorporated into the Reich but soon persecution was also intensified in the General Gouvernement. The cruelty and ruthlessness of Nazi activities may be illustrated by the statement of the General Governor, Hans Frank, who told a representative of the Nazi newspaper Völkischer Beobachter that the difference between the situation in the Protectorate of Bohemia and Moravia and that of the General Gouvernement could be realised:

> by means of the following example. In Prague big, red posters announced the shooting of seven Czechs. Then I told myself if I wanted to print one poster for every seven Poles shot, all the Polish forests would not suffice to produce enough paper. (9)

The Nazi terror took various forms. People were shot in the streets, in prisons, others died in concentration camps or during Gestapo interrogations.

Concentration camps played a particularly big role in Hitler's system of extermination. They were populated not only by people acting against the invaders but also by several hundred thousand people who were politically passive; their only 'crime' to be born Polish. The precise number of concentration camps situated in the Polish territories has not yet been stated. In many cases none of the victims survived and the German authorities thoroughly destroyed any trace of the camps as well as their archives. It is estimated that there were several hundred camps. The largest of them included Auschwitz-Birkenau and Majdanek where several million people from many countries were killed. It has been estimated that about 2-3 million Poles (not counting Jews of Polish citizenship) went through the concentration camps and only some 863,000 survived. On the other hand only about 25 per cent of prisoners survived the Auschwitz-Birkenau camp. The average duration of a prisoner's life was about six months. (10)

The camp system was only a part of the extermination policy. There were also others, like the principle introduced in the autumn of 1943 that at least ten Poles would be shot in a public execution for each German or collaborating Pole. Executions of hostages captured by chance took place in the streets. In Warsaw more than 1,500 people were shot in this way within less than five months (between October 1943 and 15 February 1944); even more victims were shot in secret executions.

The Warsaw Rising which began on 1 August 1944 and lasted for 63 days was drowned in blood. As a result of fighting and mass murders between 150,000 and 200,000 civilians were killed along with 16,000 insurgents. (11)

It must be stressed again that the killing of Poles was limited only by the demands of the Third Reich for manpower. No doubt, after a victorious ending of the war the extermination policy would have been accelerated. The already-quoted Hans

Frank said at an NSDAP meeting:

> One day when we have finally won this war I will not mind hacking all these Poles, Ukrainians and everybody else who is gadding about here ... But today the point is to keep working in peace and discipline about 15 million people of the hostile tribe which is organising against us. (12)

The extent of population losses was really tragic. As a result of war about 6 million Poles and Polish Jews were killed. Most of these victims died because of Nazi terror. Various forms of mass extermination brought about the deaths of almost 5.4 million people living in the Polish territories. The range of Nazi terror becomes clear when it is known that direct military operations cost only 10.7 per cent of the population losses while 89.3 per cent were a result of Nazi genocide. More details about population losses in Poland in the course of the Second World War can be found in Table 3.1.

If the data quoted in Table 3.1 are compared with the number of Poles and Jews living in Poland on 31 August 1939 it will be seen that the victims of war and occupation accounted for 22.2 per cent of this number. This was the highest proportion in the world. The population losses of the Soviet Union amounted to 124 people per thousand inhabitants, in Yugoslavia to 108, in Greece 35, Albania 24, Netherlands 22, Czechoslovakia 21, France 13, Belgium 12 and in Great Britain to 8 people per thousand inhabitants. (13)

The bibliography of the subject includes some other estimates of population losses in Poland, the differences between them being mainly due to the consideration of various areas of the Polish territories (within the 1939 or 1945 frontiers) or to the inclusion or exclusion of victims of Jewish origin. A strict separation of losses among the Polish and Jewish populations is unfeasible as there is no precise criterion of definition as to who was a Jew and who was not.

Most of the population losses occurred in towns. This was mainly due to the almost entire extermination of the Jewish community which mostly inhabited urban settlements as well as to deliberate extermination of the intelligentsia. This may be illustrated by the fact that 67 per cent of dentists, 58 per cent of lawyers, 38 per cent of doctors and 26 per cent of professors and other scholars were killed in

Table 3.1: Population Losses in Poland in the Course of the Second World War

Cause of death	Number of casualties (thousands)	%
1. Direct military operations	644	10.7
a. the military	123	2.0
b. civilians	521	8.7
2. Nazi terror	5,384	89.3
a. concentration and death camps, pacifications, executions, liquidation of ghettos, etc.	3,577	59.3
b. prisons, POW camps and other places of isolation, epidemics, rough treatment, etc.	1,286	21.3
c. casualties outside prisons and camps due to wounds, excessive labour, etc.	521	8.7
Total	6,028	100.0

Source: Sprawozdanie w przedmiocie strat i szkód wojennych Polski w latach 1939-1945 (Biuro Odszkodowań Wojennych przy Prezydium Rady Ministrów, Warsaw, 1947), p.25.

Poland during the years of war and occupation. (14) At the same time the German authorities suppressed all secondary and higher education, therefore limiting the progress of new generations. Underground education, such as it was, could not fill this gap.

Apart from the direct losses discussed above, there were also considerable indirect population losses in the form of a declining birth-rate (by about 1.2 million children as compared with the inter-war average), an increase in the death-rate due to the rapid spread of disease (for instance more than a million people fell ill with tuberculosis), etc. The number of cripples with various kinds of handicap grew by 590,000 people. (15)

The German authorities consciously attempted to limit natural growth of the Polish population not only by means of mass terror and deterioration of living conditions but also through legislation. In the areas incorporated into the Reich the lower age limit of people entitled to marry was fixed at 25 years for women and 28 years for men. Persons deported to Germany for compulsory work had no right to marry.

The calculated extermination of more than 6 million Poles and Polish Jews was not the only population policy pursued by the Third Reich in Poland. It also included the above-mentioned resettlement of Poles and Jews, colonisation of the Polish territories by German settlers, attempts to Germanise part of the Polish population (this deviation from Nazi racial doctrines resulted from huge losses suffered by the Reich on all fronts and from the desire to fill the gap by germanised Poles) and so on.

Czesław Łuczak estimated the number of those resettled at 1.7 million people, without taking into account Jews transported to the ghettos. (16) Resettlement of the Polish population referred mainly to the areas incorporated by the Reich from where the intelligentsia and all the better-off people were deported along with entrepreneurs and landowners. Property belonging to displaced persons was taken over by the Nazi authorities without compensation. As a rule those deported were allowed to take several kilograms of necessary items but not jewellery, money, securities and the like. There were also cases of resettlement of Poles from the General Gouvernement, this being connected with the construction of military ranges and camps. Between November 1942 and August 1943 the occupation authorities tried to put into effect the principles of the

Generalplan Ost by resettling Polish peasants from the Zamość region in the General Gouvernement. (17) The action was aimed at the German colonisation of this area. About 100,000 people were displaced, most of the ousted population being sent to Germany for forced labour, others to concentration camps, while a small number consisting mainly of children separated from their parents were to be indoctrinated for their eventual Germanisation. The extreme brutality of this action made many people join the Polish resistance. Since the action coincided with the Stalingrad defeat of the German army, no further attempts were made to complete the Generalplan Ost. Displacement also affected the population of Warsaw after the collapse of the 1944 uprising. Apart from the Praga quarter situated on the right bank of the Vistula, all other inhabitants of the Polish capital who survived the insurrection were resettled. This action embraced about half a million people. All the displacement actions led to pauperisation of the Polish population. The same applied, of course, to the resettlement of Jews in the ghettos.

These were only a part of the mass migrations caused by war and occupation. Movements of the front line in 1939 and in 1944-5 also resulted in mass migrations. Other migratory movements were due to the spontaneous evacuation of civilian populations from the areas occupied by Germany to those incorporated into the USSR and vice versa. Large deportations of Poles also took place in the territories incorporated by the Soviet Union.

The displaced population was supplanted by German colonists. The number of German settlers in the Polish territories incorporated into the Reich is estimated at 631,000 people. (18) The colonists were given the property taken from Poles and Jews as well as substantial financial and organisational aid. Notwithstanding this colonisation the occupation authorities could by no means guarantee a rapid Germanisation of the Polish territories. Each 100,000 settlers could only raise the share of the German population by 1 per cent. The speeding up of this action was thought by the occupation authorities to be possible by means of a compulsory 'option' of Poles inhabiting some areas incorporated into the Reich (mainly Upper Silesia and Pomerania) to take up German nationality. (19) Various forms of pressure were exercised to make people enrol on the so-called Volksliste. Some voluntarily joined the Volksliste; there is information to suggest that the occupation authorities were eager to extend the

Volksliste merely to recruit more manpower and planned to have the list verified after the war.

The Polish territories were treated by the Nazi invaders as a large reservoir of gratuitous manpower which ought to be utilised for the economic purposes of the Reich. These requirements were related to the calling up of young German recruits. Their place in production had to be taken by forced labour. In the first years of occupation the German authorities had already begun to employ Polish prisoners of war - estimated at about 300,000 soldiers. However, this was a mere drop in the ocean when compared to German needs. Forced labour was therefore brought to Germany from the occupied areas. These actions faced the opposition of local occupation authorities who feared shortages of manpower in the areas under their control. Finally, the reservoir of forced labour was found in the General Gouvernement. By October 1939 work had become a legal obligation for all inhabitants between 18 and 60 years of age. In December 1939 this was extended to those of 14 years upwards.

At first the GG occupation authorities sought to encourage voluntary emigration to work in Germany with references to the pre-war tradition of seasonal or permanent work-seeking emigration from Poland to the Reich. But propaganda of that kind held no attractions, all the more so now that people who went to Germany discovered very poor living and working conditions. Voluntary recruitment was gradually replaced by administrative action and since this too proved in vain the occupation authorities resorted to force. The Labour Offices (Arbeitsamt) were helped by the Nazi police to organise łapanki (round-ups). Those captured were sent to Germany regardless of their family situation, the nature of the work, state of health or fitness to work. Only from time to time were a few people set free if they could prove employment in factories working for the Reich. The Nazi round-ups in Polish streets even included children of 14 or 15 years old. Apart from the round-ups forced labour was organised by means of personal summons to leave for the Reich. If the summons was ignored and the person failed to appear his family could be taken instead, not to mention a host of other penal sanctions. Personal summons were the most frequent form of forced manpower recruitment in the areas incorporated into the Reich. The total number of people forced to go to work in Germany from all the Polish territories amounted to more than 2.8 million persons. (20) In 1941 Poles accounted for 55 per cent of all foreign workers in Germany. In the middle of 1944 their share fell to 28 per cent but in absolute terms the number of Poles forced to work in Germany constantly grew. The high share of Polish workers demonstrated the growing intensity of exploitation of the manpower resources in Poland by the German authorities.

The legal duty to work was also extended to Polish Jews who were forced to perform all kinds of compulsory work services imposed by the Nazi administration. Some were transported to labour camps whose conditions hardly differed from those of the concentration camps. The employment obligation referred to workers who seemed normally employed as well. In many factories they had no right to give notice and, if they tried to do so, they were liable to deportation to a concentration camp or for forced labour in the Reich.

Summing up the Nazi population policies in relation to Poles and Jews it must be repeated that 22.2 per cent of them were killed, a further 3.2 per cent went through the concentration camps and prisons (to count only those who survived), 10.5 per cent were deported as forced labour and about 6 per cent suffered from resettlement or displacement. These data show that about 40 per cent of the population was directly affected by Nazi terror. This meant not only untold physical and moral suffering; the ghastly workings of terror led to a substantial deterioration in the quality of life and in the living conditions of people who had lost their property, their normal employment and ability to earn a living.

The Nazi population policies also caused certain changes in the social structure of the Polish territories. These are hard to measure but undoubtedly the number of Polish landowners and entrepreneurs diminished along with the number of professional workers.

INDUSTRY

The Nazi policy towards industry in the incorporated areas and of the General Gouvernement was not uniform. These differences were highly significant in the first years of occupation.

From the very beginning the German authorities tended towards the inclusion of the industry of the areas incorporated into the Reich within the all-German division of labour. This meant a change in the structure of industry, the liquidation of some factories and changes in the pattern of production of many others. However the need to develop industry in these areas was not questioned. As regards the General Gouvernement industry, the German plans foresaw its almost entire liquidation. (21)

Hans Frank wrote in his diary:

> It was said it would be useful for this area not to have its own economy. Therefore we shall take from this land all the valuable machinery, dismantle all the valuable factories, destroy, if possible, all its valuable communication lines. There were even plans to send abroad all the telephone and telegraph cables, to maintain only the most necessary one-track railway lines and to take other railway facilities to the Reich. (22)

The German authorities removed from the GG facilities for armament and munitions production with particular regard to the most modern machinery. Several large plants constructed and equipped in 1936-9 were dismantled and sent to Germany along with other facilities. Apart from that several thousand train-loads of raw materials and semi-manufactures were taken away to the Reich.

The changing concepts referring to the future fate of the General Gouvernement, which was to become a part of the German Reich as a result of the Generalplan Ost, made the Nazi authorities change their industrial policy. Destruction of the GG industrial potential was no longer useful. Moreover, the GG cheap manpower resources, the German attack on the USSR and the more and more intensive air raids of the Allied air forces in the Third Reich - all this made it expedient to leave some industry in the General Gouvernement. Nevertheless, it was still considered necessary for the Gouvernement to concentrate on farm and raw material production within the four-year economic plan, while industrial output was designated a minor role.

Industry in both parts of the Polish territories under occupation was subordinated to the German four-year economic plan aimed at the inclusion of the whole economy to provide for the realisation of German military objectives. Thus the plan provided for the maintenance and development of production for military purposes or satisfying the requirements of German citizens. Light industry was reduced. Since 1941, when the Reich faced growing economic problems, the productive capacity of the Polish territories had been more and more intensively utilised for the needs of the German army. Production was concentrated in factories requiring less manpower while small enterprises were either liquidated or consolidated. Factories that had been closed down were scrapped regardless of their technical condition due to a scrap-metal shortage in German metallurgy.

According to estimates available about 75 per cent of handicraft and trade shops were destroyed in the areas incorporated into the Reich by the end of 1942. In Łódź production was stopped in 40 per cent of textile factories and in 66 per cent of factories in Warsaw. (23) This applied to other lines of production as well. It was estimated that the total number of industrial and handicraft enterprises in the Gouvernement diminished by the end of 1942 by a half as compared with the pre-war period, while by 1944 this had fallen to about 33 per cent of the pre-war level. It is notable that this process developed despite the evacuation of some factories from the German industrial regions exposed to Allied air raids on the Polish territories.

The last stage of German industrial policy in the occupied Polish territories began along with the withdrawal of German armies under pressure from the Soviet Army. The Nazi authorities tried to evacuate all major industrial plants engaged in production for military purposes. The rapid advance of Soviet troops often made this impossible. The Polish underground also worked to counteract these moves. In many cases the Germans managed to evacuate only essential machinery, measurement apparatus, power generation facilities, etc. If there was too little time to dismantle and take away machinery, abandoned factories were in most cases destroyed. Warsaw is a case in point since almost all her industrial plants were either destroyed or largely damaged. Wherever the Soviet offensive surprised the Germans, most of the industrial potential was saved as in Łódź or Upper Silesia.

Substantial changes also took place in the system of ownership. Industry in the areas incorporated into the Reich was expropriated without compensation and taken over for the use of the German state. This also applied to Polish government and municipal property. Major handicraft workshops were also confiscated. This action was directed by the Haupttreuhandstelle Ost (Central Trusteeship Administration for the East). The range of confiscations in the General Gouvernement was less. Some enterprises in light industry and food processing remained formally in Polish hands but all were given special German trustee managers (Treuhänder) who took all major decisions. By the middle of 1942 about 2,000 large private factories had been taken over by the Germans. At the same time enterprises belonging to foreign businessmen were bought out.

Heavy industry, raw material production and large and medium-size enterprises in other lines were taken over by the occupation authorities. In the incorporated areas only a small number of handicraft workships survived in Polish hands, while in the General Gouvernement most handicraft and some small and medium-size industrial enterprises remained under Polish control.

The consequences of the German take-over were not confined to a simple change of ownership but affected the whole system of production, capital and co-operative interrelations. The Haupttreuhandstelle Ost kept most of the requisitioned enterprises under its own control (after the war they were to be sold to prominent members of the NSDAP), whereas some parts of the largest enterprises were subordinated to major companies of the Third Reich.

The changing system of ownership resulted in a modification of the division of labour between individual firms, both in the Polish territories and within the Grossdeutsches Reich. The occupation authorities disregarded the compactness of the Polish economic system which had existed before 1 September 1939 and its self-sufficiency in the field of industrial output. Those lines which the Germans thought unnecessary were liquidated and their facilities dismantled. These changes proved of substantial importance for the economic redevelopment of People's Poland after 1944 since the lack of several lines of goods and factories made it impossible to start production again.

It is not easy to give data regarding trends in industrial production. Only piecemeal information is available and accuracy here is questionable. Undoubtedly raw material output was developing. Hard coal production, for example, grew from 38 million tonnes in 1938 to 52 million tonnes in 1943. (24) This 36 per cent increase was due to the wasteful exploitation of mines; extraction of the most accessible seams, little preparatory work, reduction of casing and silting up, all of which led to growing mining damage. Certain investments were continued until 1943 but afterwards entirely ceased. Coal mines and their facilities gradually depreciated in economic value. At the same time oil output jumped by about 20 per cent as compared with the 1939 level while that of natural gas grew by 13 per cent. Production of iron ore increased until 1941 but later it was neglected in view of the seizure of more efficient Soviet resources. Upper Silesian steel and pig iron production was growing but this was also achieved at the cost of a depreciation in facilities. Light industry and food-processing production fell both in the incorporated areas and in the GG; Łódź textile production, for example, fell to 25-30 per cent of the pre-war level. At the same time production of paper decreased by 65 per cent, leather by 35-40 per cent and foodstuffs by 50 per cent. Mineral and chemical industries failed to reach the inter-war level of output. (25)

The General Gouvernement industrial production decreased by 63 per cent in 1938-40/1. In 1941-3 a certain increase was recorded and in December 1942 it was estimated at 60 per cent of the 1938 level. Only those industries working for the German army exceeded the pre-war level of output. The year 1943 was the culminating point of GG industrial production and the following years brought a relatively rapid decline.

A similar trend was recorded in the incorporated areas. After a sudden collapse in production at the beginning of the occupation, industrial output gradually grew. But from 1943 a decline set in, the Upper Silesian region with its relatively stable production being an exception.

The basic reason for the 1943 decline in production concerned supplies - progressively more difficult to obtain. Raw materials, fuel, spare parts, etc., were always in short supply and the troubles were aggravated by a disorganised transport system, the growing deficit of skilled manpower and decreasing labour productivity. Even the growing use of terror failed to prevent falling manpower efficiency. Working 10-12 hours a day, frequently on Sundays and holidays, badly fed and deprived of leave, Polish workers could not maintain pre-war levels of labour productivity.

The utilisation of Polish industry for the military purposes of the Reich was made more and more difficult by the developing Polish resistance movement. There were frequent acts of sabotage and the popular motto was 'work slowly'. The sign of a tortoise drawn on walls was an everyday reminder of it. From time to time workers used machinery and raw materials to produce goods designed for the black market. The Polish underground movement organised guerrilla or diversionary groups which blew up railway lines and bridges, interrupting supplies not only for the front but also for industrial plants. (26)

German investment activity in the Polish territories was quite limited. But the Nazi authorities completed the construction of some industrial plants in the Central Industrial Region and built a few new factories like those producing synthetic petrol, rubber or carbide. In 1942-3 certain factories were transferred from areas in western Germany to the Polish territories. Nevertheless the range of these transfers was limited in view of the shortage of power generating capacity.

Investments and the transfer of German factories were unable to counterbalance the damage done to Polish industry as a result of the 1939 and 1944-5 military operations, the disassembly of many factories, and the removal and scrapping of machinery and equipment. Serious losses were also caused by a lack of general maintenance and machinery was usually subject to extremely intensive exploitation, the German authorities preferring production growth to the upkeep of productive potential. Apart from the destruction of productive potential the Polish economy suffered from the changing pattern of production and the breakdown of traditional co-operation links between individual factories. The elimination of Polish design offices and research institutions which all played their part in the development of industry was also a serious shock. All these institutions ceased to exist and their equipment and personnel were dispersed or physically destroyed.

AGRICULTURE

The German Reich was not self-sufficient in foodstuffs. Thus the development of Polish farming and the creation of a system in which local consumption was reduced in favour of the seizure of the largest possible part of production for the Reich became prime targets for the occupation authorities. Maximum supplies of foodstuffs to Germany was always the top priority of the Nazi administration both in the incorporated areas and in the General Gouvernement. The German authorities intended to change the farming system by increasing the area of farms, improving the breeding of cattle as well as by extending the use of machinery and artificial fertilisers.

This programme began in the early years of occupation but with growing war difficulties the Nazis abandoned it later on. Afterwards emphasis was put on the exploitation of existing agricultural resources and the wasteful treatment of farming became more and more drastic. (27)

As with industry, the Germans aimed at a takeover of Polish and Jewish landed property. In the areas incorporated into the Reich the Nazi authorities expropriated all large Polish estates without compensation and the landowners were displaced. The expropriation of land belonging to peasants advanced much more slowly. It was easier to take over 3,600 large landed estates than several hundred thousand peasant farms. However, in 1939 the ousting of peasants had already begun in the incorporated areas, its rate being subject to the number of incoming German settlers. As a rule German colonists were given more prosperous farms situated on fertile soils. Where there was a lack of adequate buildings several Polish farms would be joined together, unnecessary premises demolished and Polish owners resettled. In this way the Germans tried to bring about the idea of extended peasant farms producing a large commodity surplus. By 1942 the Nazi authorities had take over about 59 per cent of arable land formerly belonging to Polish peasants in the incorporated areas. More than 9 million ha had been confiscated by 1 July 1942. 'Afterwards only undersized holdings remained in Polish hands or some unprofitable farms for which no German applicant could be found.' (28)

However, even peasants who remained on their farms were deprived of their property rights. They were compelled to pay all income into special banking accounts from which money could only be withdrawn with the approval of a German district farm adviser. These advisers determined detailed production targets, areas under individual crops, numbers of livestock, system of crop rotation, etc. All surplus production had to be delivered to the occupation authorities at officially fixed prices. Farmers were allowed to keep only limited amounts for sowing, maintenance of livestock or as very poor subsistence for their families. The whole output was scrupulously recorded so that peasants could not practically conceal even the smallest amount from the German administration. Thus, Polish farmers working on their own holdings became, in effect, poorly-paid hired employees.

The situation in the General Gouvernement was

a little more favourable. Some large estates remained in Polish hands though each was allotted a German manager. However, in many cases these managers were merely stooges who undertook little, if any, active participation. Expropriation included at least one-third of all large estates, most of them being the richest and the best-managed ones. On the other hand the mass ousting of peasants was not a regular practice except for the instances mentioned above. The expropriation of peasants' land was mainly due to the construction of military installations, claims of local German settlers or carried out as a punishment for giving shelter to resistance fighters or failing to deliver the compulsory quotas of farm products. German plans prepared for the post-war future were aimed at repeating the pattern introduced in the incorporated areas and in the Zamość region.

The German administration pushed hard for increases in farm yields and encouraged this by means of extra machinery, artificial fertilisers, pedigree cattle, etc. These supplies were mostly delivered to Germans and Polish peasants hardly benefited from them. German administration aid declined with the growing military difficulties of the Third Reich. In order to encourage peasants in the use of artificial fertilisers prices were reduced. The occupation administration's aim was to adjust agricultural production in the Polish territories to the requirements of the Third Reich and to accomplish this the area under grain crops was limited while that of root, pulse and oil plant crops was increased.

It is difficult to ascertain whether Polish farm production improved as a result of these policies. It seems there were regions where agricultural output rose, others where it diminished, particularly with reference to crop production since the number of cattle and pigs dramatically declined due to an extremely thorough collection of the meat quotas. In fact the idea of increasing agricultural production was subject to the current supply requirements of Germany. The prevailing tendency was to gather all the commodity surplus output from the Polish countryside so that farms were not guaranteed a simple reproduction of capital. This trend became more pronounced as war dragged on and took the form of a wasteful exploitation of Polish agriculture. In the last year of war, when it became clear to the Germans that their occupation was coming to an end, the exploitation of Polish farming reached a dismal climax. Just before withdrawing from the Polish territories, the German army tried to plunder all existing food reserves, cattle, pigs, horses and sheep and send them to Germany or made use of them on the spot.

Whereas in the incorporated areas the system of control was based on a take-over of the entire farming production (above defined internal consumption standards), in the General Gouvernement a system of quotas was introduced in 1940. It consisted in the duty to supply definite quantities of various products at fixed prices which were much lower than black market prices. The quota standards were raised from year to year and the range of products included was gradually extended. Thus farmers were obliged to supply grain, potatoes, cattle, pigs, wool, milk, straw, etc. The growing scale of these compulsory deliveries can be illustrated by reference to the increasing grain supplies. In 1940 the grain quota amounted to 383,000 tonnes, in 1941 to 685,000 tonnes, in 1942 to 1.2 million tonnes and in 1943 to 1.5 million tonnes. (29) This represented a fourfold increase in four years.

Payments for compulsory supplies were only symbolic. In order to encourage peasants to fulfil their quotas the German authorities supplied them with small quantities of industrial goods at official prices. For instance in 1942/3 suppliers of 100 kg of grain had the right to purchase half a litre of vodka, 0.25 l of kerosene and some textiles for 10 per cent of the official price of the grain supplied. The vodka supply is especially worth attention as it served to spread bouts of drunkenness among Polish peasants. Large estates were allowed to buy farm machinery and fertilisers in exchange for quotas fulfilled. This kind of compensation, however, was much lower than the returns which farmers could earn on the black market. Thus it was hardly an incentive to quota supplies which were frequently collected by force. Landowners failing to supply quotas could have their manors confiscated while peasants were deprived of livestock, beaten and, later on, sent to concentration camps or executed. The terror connected with the quota collection was constantly spreading. In 1942 the death penalty was introduced for a 'spiteful' failure to supply quotas, the term 'spiteful' being interpreted as widely as possible. These harsh regulations remained in force in the years following.

Peasants nevertheless sabotaged the quota supplies, resorting to various methods, one of the most frequently used being the bribery of German officials who lowered the quota rates or issued false certificates of quota fulfilment. As a result some surplus commodities remained in peasant hands and were sold on the black market or secretly supplied to towns with chronic food shortages.

The German quota system was supplemented by various regulations which had as their aim the limitation of the farmers' consumption or use of agricultural products. These regulations included, for example, a prohibition on domestic slaughter, standards of grain milling per peasant or a prohibition of milling of higher quality flour. The milling standards were so low that they did not suffice to meet even basic needs. Peasants therefore returned to querns to avoid the strictly controlled mills. The possession of querns, in consequence, was severly punished.

Most of the quota supplies were taken to the Reich. Only limited amounts were intended for food rationing supplies to towns. In 1940/1, for example, about 40,000 tonnes of grain were exported from the General Gouvernement to Germany - and in 1942/3 as much as 572,000 tonnes. Potato supplies (in the same periods) amounted to 121,000 and 434,000 tonnes, sugar supplies to 4.5 and 28.7 thousand tonnes, and fat supplies to 0.8 and 7.2 thousand tonnes. (30) Large quantities of foodstuffs were also taken from the incorporated areas.

Polish farming suffered great losses not only from the take-over of Polish property, collection of quotas or robbery but also from military operations and the Nazi terror. A considerable part of these losses could hardly be reversed once the war was over. (31)

FINANCE

The monetary, banking and budgetary policies of the occupation authorities were quite different in the areas incorporated into the Reich and in the General Gouvernement. The annexed territories were included in the legal system of the Third Reich. Some tax law regulations differed slightly to allow for an increased tax burden on the Polish population for the benefit of the German state.

The Polish territories incorporated into the Reich were embraced by the all-German budget. The taxation system of these areas gave privileged benefits to the German population: they paid much lower taxes than Poles which were also lower than those paid by Germans living within Germany. This policy was clearly aimed at encouraging German settlers to move to annexed Polish territories. On the other hand Poles had to pay special taxes: the so called 'Polish tribute' (Polenangabe) and a 'social compensatory tax' (Sozialausgleichabgabe). The 'tribute' consisted in paying Polish employees working in the annexed areas wages 10 to 30 per cent lower than those paid to German workers. The 'social compensatory tax' collected in some regions amounted to 15 per cent of wages. Moreover Poles did not benefit from normal tax reductions such as child maintenance, etc.

The General Gouvernement had a separate budget whose expenses were covered by local revenues. Most of these expenditures were designed for the maintenance of the German army, police force and administration. Expenses serving the GG population played only a secondary role. The pre-war taxation system remained in force to supply the GG budget with necessary revenues. This system was gradually changed by raising tax rates and the introduction of new taxes. As a rule the tax burden of the German inhabitants of the Gouvernement was much lower than that of the Polish or Jewish population. Enterprises belonging to Germans enjoyed numerous tax privileges. (32) Monopoly profits from the sale of vodka and lottery tickets increased substantially.

The Polish population was also subject to 'contributions'. These were treated as a kind of punishment for disobedience to the occupation authorities. Warsaw, for examples, was laid under contribution three times: in October 1942 (1 million zł), in February 1943 (10 million zł) and in February 1944 (100 million zł). (33) The last contribution was an act of revenge for the assassination of the SS and police commander of the Warsaw district, SS-Brigadeführer Franz Kutschera who was responsible for many mass murders and atrocities.

The monetary policy in the annexed territories was based on the exchange rate of Polish złotys for German marks in the autumn of 1939. This rate of exchange meant a 75 per cent loss for all owners of Polish currency. Moreover, Poles were allowed to exchange only 500 zł for 250 marks (in some regions Poles were refused any right of exchange whatsoever). Remaining złoty resources had to be deposited in banks and these were confiscated. When this had been done, the monetary system of the annexed areas did not differ from that of other parts of the Grossdeutsches Reich. The German financial policy within the Reich was mainly aimed at counteracting inflation by means of a freeze on wages and prices.

The General Gouvernement, on the other hand, was subject to a different monetary policy. This consisted of a freeze on wages linked to an inflationary growth in prices. Some surplus products which the Poles could not afford were utilised for German needs while the standard of living of the Polish population decreased.

Immediately after the termination of military operations the pre-war złotys issued by the Bank Polski were maintained in the GG. In view of the withdrawal of Polish złotys from circulation in the territories annexed by the Reich and those situated eastward of the Bug river (exchanged into marks and roubles) the Polish pre-war currency flowed into the General Gouvernement in great quantities. This precipitated an inflationary spiral and the buying up of goods. In order to prevent insolvency in the GG market caused by Polish purchasers and to preserve goods necessary to the Nazi administration the occupation authorities ordered the placing of all banknotes of 100 and 500 zł on deposit - promising to pay the equivalent in future. This manipulation deprived the Polish and Jewish populations of a great part of their financial assets which in this case were usually gathered in banknotes of a higher nominal value. Exchanging 100 and 500 zł banknotes for those of a lower nominal value was rather difficult and involved hefty additional costs. As late as the end of January 1940 exchanges of 200 zł per adult person were started, the Jewish population being excluded.

Since the Bank Polski had managed to ship abroad all its equipment for printing banknotes, further issuing of the złoty in Poland was impossible. Therefore, in December 1939, the German occupation authorities announced the formation of a new bank of issue under the name of the Bank Emisyjny w Polsce. This was the only case where the name 'Polska' (Poland) was used in the occupation territories. Moreover, the Bank Emisyjny was directed by a Pole - Feliks Młynarski. It seems that in this case the occupation authorities wanted to ensure that the new currency gained the confidence of Polish society. The Bank Emisyjny began its activities in April 1940. The pre-war złotys of the Bank Polski were exchanged for new złoty banknotes without limitation on a one-for-one basis. The equivalent rate for the 100 and 500 zł banknotes already deposited was also paid in the new złotys of the Bank Emisyjny which was in practice strictly controlled by the German authorities. The monetary policy of the Bank Emisyjny was subject to the German administration's intention to provoke inflation with all its negative effects. (34) Whereas the GG note circulation increased 20 times over the occupation years, wages were practically frozen and this meant pauperisation for the majority of the population.

The German policy towards Polish banks was also different in both parts of the occupied territories. In the incorporated areas the Nazi administration was resolved to suppress all Polish credit institutions and to create German branch banks in their place. The method of suppression was based on special German regulations. The general objective was to enforce payment of all credits and to pay out deposits and shares only to German citizens. Polish and Jewish deposits were confiscated along with valuables and foreign exchange stored in safe-deposit boxes. Polish branch banks whose central offices were situated in the General Gouvernement were also closed down, their managing boards not being notified. (35)

The liquidation of Polish banking and the looting of deposits and safes was, as with the confiscation of agricultural and industrial property, illegal in international law. The Hague convention concerning conditions of occupation in wartime stipulates that private property cannot be seized by occupation authorities, who are only entitled to demand certain services for the army, to sequester means of transportation and communication, armament stocks and military equipment.

In the General Gouvernment the Bank Emisyjny w Polsce worked in association with German credit institutions and some Polish banks which received German managers and which were subject to the new banking regulations. Transactions with German institutions were reserved for banks controlled by the German administration, while Polish banks were confined to dealing with small enterprises usually belonging to Poles. The occupation authorities introduced a principle that the financing of current operations was the only way to utilise assets gathered in the years of occupation. Paying out pre-war deposits was in this way impeded. Similarly, as in the areas incorporated into the Reich, all gold and foreign exchange reserves stored in credit institutions or kept by their customers in safe-deposit boxes were liable to confiscation.

The Bank Polski (whose administration left Poland in September 1939) functioned in London throughout the war years. The evacuation of the Bank Polski included its gold reserves which had provided cover for the złoty banknotes issued by the bank. The Bank Polski's administration tried to prevent its gold reserves from falling into German hands and in this were totally successful. (36) The Bank Polski's activities abroad were also aimed at preparing for its regular functioning in post-war Poland. In this connection a new series of złoty banknotes was printed in the United States and Great Britain. Managing boards of other Polish banks who found themselves abroad as a rule succeeded in preventing the Germans from taking over their debts in the banks situated in third countries.

INTERNAL AND EXTERNAL TRADE

The years of Nazi occupation brought a rapid development in illegal trade about which little is known. This makes research into the problem quite difficult.

The trading network was constantly diminishing, both in the annexed territories and in the General Gouvernement. This was due to a number of reasons including a planned policy of the German administration to reduce employment in trade, a decreasing market supply, extermination of Jews who played a leading role in Polish trade (except for the western provinces) and so on. According to Polish underground estimates the number of wholesale firms in the General Gouvernement fell from 8,000 to 700 or 800, while the number of retail shops dropped from 195,000 to about 50,000. (37) The trading network in the annexed territories seems to have declined in a similar way. As in other fields of economic life, the elimination of Poles and Jews was also typical for trade in occupied Poland. In the incorporated areas only very small shops remained in Polish hands, all other enterprises being taken over by the Germans. In the General Gouvernement the German takeover was not so extensive though most of the wholesale firms and larger shops were Germanised or made subject to German control. Co-operative stores played an important role in the General Gouvernement as they dealt with rural trade and provided the quota collection with technical service. Apart from shops serving the local population, special Nur für Deutsche shops were introduced in the General Gouvernement. These served Germans only.

Official trade was entirely regulated. Trade control included food rationing based on a coupon system. The coupon rations were differentiated according to the nationality of workers. Rations designed for the Germans satisfied actual needs, those given to Poles covered about 20-30 per cent of the basic minimum (rations were changed from time to time and were different in various parts of occupied Poland; in the annexed areas they were usually higher), but rations designed for Jews covered on 5-8 per cent of the basic minimum requirement (see Table 3.2).

Table 3.2: Daily Food Rations in Warsaw, 1940-3

	Grams			Calories
	Protein	Fat	Carbohydrates	
Physiological standard (basic requirement)	70.0	50.0	400	2,400
Unemployed worker in Poland (1932)	48.0	33.0	384	2,087
Food ration for Poles (1940)	12.1	1.1	163	740
Food ration for Poles (1941)	12.9	3.3	142	669
Food ration for Poles (1942)	11.1	1.6	125	576
Food ration for Poles (1943)a	7.0	0.9	93	415
Food ration for Germans (1941)	82.4	95.6	338	2,613
Food ration for Jews (1941)	3.2	0.2	41	184

Note: a. Before 1 October 1943 when the ration was raised to 939 calories.

Source: W. Jastrzębowski, Gospodarka niemiecka w Polsce (Czytelnik, Warsaw, 1946), p. 344.

Industrial goods were distributed on the grounds of special tickets. The Jewish population was entirely excluded from this system while Poles were only occasionally given these tickets. Prices of rationed goods were fixed or only slightly increased. For all that the point was that the Polish population received rations which did not cover even the minimum needs and these had to be supplemented by purchases on the black market.

The illegal market existed both in the incorporated areas and in the General Gouvernement. But in the latter case it was much more widespread. The black market was supplied mostly with food from Polish farms. In the GG farms were more numerous than in the annexed territories and could more easily conceal and sell part of their products. Thus the illegal market for foodstuffs was more developed in the Gouvernement. Some black market supplies originated from the illegal production of Polish handicraftsmen or - through bribed German officials - from German institutions. The occupation administration in the General Gouvernement was highly corrupt which encouraged the development of a black market. Illegal trade included not only food and industrial products but also foreign exchange. There was even an illlegal stock exchange which recorded share and currency-rate quotations.

Delivery of black market supplies was a high risk. The supply of foodstuffs to towns was prohibited except for small retail quantities. Notwithstanding, large deliveries were frequently tolerated by bribed Germans. These operations were dealt with by a growing number of people called szmuglerzy (smugglers). They bought food in the country, conveyed it to towns and sold at high profits. Most of the supplies were sold well away from official shops which led to a long chain of black market agents. A smuggler sold his products to one receiver who resold them to several other pedlars and so on. Final consumers usually bought small quantities of foodstuffs (such as 10-20 decagrams of pork fat) in view of their relatively high prices. Smugglers and sellers were liable not only to confiscation of their goods but to beating or deportation to a concentration camp. There were cases when people caught while smuggling food were shot on the spot. Smugglers supplying food to the ghettos were particularly liable to death.

It seems the range of illegal trade in the General Gouvernement was higher than that of the legal trade turnover. A well-known interpreter of these problems, Wacław Jastrzębowski, estimated that in 1941 black market supplies covered 73 per cent of the demand of the Polish urban population for protein, 90 per cent of the demand for fat and 63 per cent for carbohydrates, or 75 per cent of the nutritional value. In his opinion the average in 1942 of food supplies to the illegal market grew to 80 per cent of the total demand. (38)

The black market also played an important role in meeting the requirements of the countryside. Wacław Jastrzębowski estimated that the demand of the GG countryside for industrial goods was covered in 20 per cent of cases by legal supplies, in 50 per cent through selling by the urban population and in 30 per cent by other illegal sources.

Black market prices differed from region to region. This was mainly due to the supply available, to the degree of satisfaction of local demand, to the risk connected with illegal deliveries and so forth. The highest prices were recorded in the ghettos where demand was extremely high and where illegal supplies were liable to the greatest risk. Black market prices in the General Gouvernement were also very high though levels were lower than in the ghettos. The dynamism of prices as compared with the pre-war level is presented in Table 3.3. Black market prices in the annexed areas were also many times higher than the official ones. In view of the wage-freeze purchases on the black market had to be limited and were mostly subject to extraordinary non-wage sources of earnings.

It is of course difficult to discuss foreign trade in the annexed areas since they were treated as a part of Germany. On the other hand the General Gouvernement was a separate administrative body within the Grossdeutsches Reich marked off by a customs frontier from other parts of Germany. Thus it may be thought that the General Gouvernement had its exports and imports although the term 'foreign trade' does not seem adequate as most of the GG exports included plundered government, municipal and private property. Goods imported from the Reich were charged duty. The costs of production in the General Gouvernement were therefore higher than in the Reich. There are no reliable data concerning the turnover between Germany and the GG. The obligatory clearing accounts were managed so that the Reich was always in debt to the Gouvernement. The value of property confiscated by the German authorities was not included in official records. (39)

LIVING CONDITIONS

The following remarks will be limited to a presentation of some basic elements of living conditions since the consequences of the Nazi extermination policy have already been described.

One of the major problems here was lack of work. War damage and the closing of many factories as well

Table 3.3: Free Market Prices of Some Articles in Warsaw, 1940-4 (1938=100)

Article	1940	1941	1942	1943	1944
Rye bread	933	2,496	3,380	3,430	1,490
Potatoes	320	2,350	2,890	3,310	3,310
Pork	548	1,410	3,523	8,828	8,800
Pork fat	1,002	2,575	6,170	14,030	11,100
Eggs	675	1,762	3,800	6,612	8,525
Milk	552	1,348	2,474	5,029	6,367
Sugar	628	1,870	5,395	9,083	8,135
Coal	335	2,417	2,807	3,212	3,663
Kerosene	1,008	2,121	5,081	11,205	12,894
Soap	2,700	3,143	3,911	8,959	9,702

Source: Cz. Łuczak, Polityka ludnościowa i ekonomiczna hitlerowskich Niemiec w okupowanej Polsce (Wydawnictwo Poznańskie, Poznań, 1979), p. 430.

as their disassembly and removal to Germany - all these factors seriously hit the working classes. The elimination of the state apparatus, limitation of education, dissolution of political organisations and the suppression of social or cultural institutions led to considerable unemployment among the intelligentsia. Only in the Radom district was the number of people seeking work higher in the autumn of 1939 than in the whole of Poland in 1938. The situation in the three other districts was similar in that a part of the adult male population found itself in captivity while others emigrated along with the Polish government. Unemployment was gradually decreasing due to a slight rise in production and to deportations for forced labour in Germany. But the fall in unemployment did not apply to Jews and the intelligentsia. The creation of the ghettos dramatically raised the number of the unemployed while members of the professional classes could only find jobs if they were prepared to undertake manual work.

Official employment as such was gradually losing its economic importance - this being due to the freezing of pre-war wages or even reduction of the highest wages. Since free market prices were rapidly growing the significance of wages diminished accordingly. In 1943, for example, the monthly wage of a Polish worker was equal to the black market price for one kg of butter which was withdrawn from legal trade. Thus wages could not cover even the minimum cost of living. Nevertheless finding a job was necessary for other reasons. In many cases employment gave protection against deportation for forced labour to the Reich or against forced services in the General Gouvernement.

In order to gain the means of subsistence almost the entire urban population had to search for extraordinary sources of earnings. This was not easy. At the beginning of the Nazi occupation most of these earnings came from selling personal belongings but exhaustion of this source forced people to seek various odd jobs such as trafficking in the black market, smuggling, brokerage, services or domestic industry.

Additional earnings were usually of a temporary nature. Thus most of the urban population suffered from poverty and hunger. Even as early as the beginning of 1940 the death rate in Warsaw almost doubled compared with the pre-war level (not to mention the Jewish population dying at a much higher rate). Besides hunger the majority of townspeople suffered from lack of clothing and fuel.

Housing conditions were also very difficult. In many towns the occupation administration created separate German quarters. As a rule they were situated in the most modern parts of towns from where the previous dwellers were ousted. The remaining quarters were overcrowded, all the more so since the September 1939 military operations had caused serious damage to dwelling houses. Population density in the ghettos was even higher. Most flats were underheated or not heated at all because of high coal prices. Lighting was also a problem as the occupation authorities allowed the Polish population to use electricity for only about a dozen hours a week.

Working conditions rapidly deteriorated. Most of the pre-war Polish labour and social insurance legislation was suspended. Workers were deprived of the right to organise trade unions and were forbidden to strike. In practice all employees were subordinate to decisions of the occupation administration or local managers. Working time was extended and leave was shortened. In some factories work was continued on Sundays and public holidays. Work safety suffered markedly. In many factories German managers punished employees by sending them to labour or concentration camps. All this led to a sharp decrease in labour productivity. In the autumn of 1943 the German authorities, concerned about low productivity, decided to raise food rations by a small amount. The improvement was only partial and had hardly any significance in terms of productivity which had decreased still further as a result of the physical exhaustion of the workers.

The situation in the GG countryside was somewhat different. At first, farmers experienced a slight improvement in their standard of living. This fact might seem paradoxical in view of the previously mentioned exploitation of Polish agriculture through the quota system. But at the same time the price structure had changed in favour of the farmers. Consequently, those farmers who managed to retain even a small commodity surplus could sell, thus earning relatively high incomes. The reversal of the 'price scissors' mechanism in favour of farmers was mainly due to the shortage of foodstuffs in towns and to the selling of industrial goods by urban dwellers - thereby limiting the growth of prices for manufactured goods bought in the country. The decrease in the real value of debts due to currency depreciation was also of significance in this respect.

Variations between the economic situation of rural dwellers and that of the urban population led to a changing distribution of national income. The share of peasants became higher than in the Second Republic though the absolute value of the national income decreased. The decline of the latter can hardly be estimated as there have been no reliable studies in this respect and the various estimates differ. Nevertheless, the improvement of the situation in the GG countryside was only temporary. A rise of quotas in 1942 and violent methods of collection dramatically reduced surplus commodities. The volume of marketable foodstuffs also diminished; many people resettled from the areas incorporated into the Reich were placed by a Polish mutual aid organisation, Rada Główna Opiekuńcza (Central Protective Council) in large estates and peasant farms which maintained them. The same applied to the inhabitants of Warsaw, who were displaced in the autumn of 1944. Meeting the food requirements of so many people was by no means an easy burden for farmers. Although there was a certain improvement of the economic situation in 1939-41, this does still not take into account farms affected by war damage, occupation terror, deportations to Germany, the requisition of living accommodation to German troops, etc. Only those farms with a considerable surplus of marketable goods - the larger estates and peasant farms - could really benefit from price increases.

Peasants in the annexed areas, however, fared much worse. Administrative and police supervision made it practically impossible to keep surplus products. This is why Polish farmers in the incorporated areas were rapidly impoverished. They lost not only the right of disposal over their farms but were also deprived of the control of their own crops. They could not even eat what they wanted - consumption was limited by special standards and monetary returns could only be spent with the approval of the district farm adviser.

Polish urban dwellers in the incorporated areas found themselves in a slightly different situation. While the price-freeze in the General Gouvernement referred only to coupon rations and prices for compulsory deliveries, in the annexed territories all prices were frozen in February 1941. As a result the black market was not so extensive as in the GG but real wages were higher. What is more, coupon rations were also higher: the occupation authorities had realised the demand for manpower, and knowing how scarce illegal food supplies were, had deduced there was no alternative but to supply the Polish population with enough food to make them work. Notwithstanding, the rations for Poles were much lower than those for the German population.

Generally speaking, however, conditions for urban workers in the annexed areas were extremely harsh. They were faced with deportation, forced labour, confiscation of flats and equipment, lower wages as compared with the inter-war level, limitation of social benefits, etc. All health benefits and pensions were abolished. A Polish worker who fell ill was not paid for the time he remained at home. Workers were also deprived of extra pay for children, all bonuses and premiums, while their leave was restricted and working hours extended. Moreover, the Polish population in the annexed areas had to contend with various kinds of petty annoyances. At the end of 1940, for example, Poles living in Poznań were forbidden to travel by tram between 7.00 and 8.00 a.m., so as not to meet German children. In Łódź and some other towns Poles were not allowed to enter many shops, restaurants and parks or to buy wheat flour and bread. In other shops Poles were only served after German customers. Poles could not become clerks and practising other professions was subject to obtaining special permits. There were, for example, some Polish doctors and chemists but no Pole was allowed to practise as a lawyer, notary, veterinary surgeon, etc.

The decline in the financial standing of Poles was also due to wage policy. Polish workers were paid less than Germans - even if they held higher positions or were better qualified. The wages of Polish workers were charged with special taxes as discussed above. The occupation authorities aimed at equalising the wages of Polish workers to the prices of coupon rations, rents and communal services, etc. Poles had to make their living at a very low standard determined by wages and rations. In this connection the situation of workers in the General Gouvernement was, despite lower real wages, better than in the annexed territories. They, at least, had the possibility to gain 'extraordinary earnings' and to buy the products they needed on the black market which existed in the General Gouvernement.

Representatives of the pre-war propertied classes of Jewish nationality were entirely pauperised and mostly murdered. Polish entrepreneurs were also frequently deprived of the whole of their real and moveable assets, particularly those persons inhabiting the areas incorporated into the Reich, whereas Polish landowners and the bourgeoisie of the General Gouvernement suffered less. The propertied classes were replaced by a group of nouveaux riches who made fortunes from speculation, the take-over of Jewish property, illegal handicrafts, etc. In the latter case the highest profits were made in illegal distilleries or tanning.

Nazi policies in the Polish territories led to a scale of destruction which set back the Polish economy by several decades. War damage in the First World War accounted for 10 per cent of the national property of the Polish territories; the 1939-45 losses amounted to 38 per cent.

Despite the machinations of terror and difficult living conditions Polish society never lost hope of eventually gaining independence. Polish soldiers fought for it on the western and eastern fronts, and organised a mass underground army to resist the occupation authorities. At the same time various programmes of socio-economic reform were formulated both in the occupied country and abroad. Various concepts of post-war reconstruction and frontier changes were also prepared from different political points of view. Some of these programmes were planned by the Polish government in exile in France and, after 1940, in Great Britain, as well as by its home representation (Delegatura Rządu) headed by a vice-premier. Quite different, however, were the programmes worked out by radical leftists who found themselves in the USSR and who were represented by the underground Polish Workers' Party created in 1942.

NOTES

1. *Prowizoryczne zestawienie strat wojennych państwa polskiego sporządzone na koniec lutego 1940 r. (pierwsze przybliżenie)*. Opracowanie dokonane przez Ministerstwo Przemysłu, Handlu i Żeglugi Rządu Polskiego w Londynie. *AAN*, Ministerstwo Przemysłu, Handlu i Żeglugi, vol. *159*, p. 54.

2. L. Landau, *Kronika lat wojny i okupacji* (3 vols., Państwowe Wydawnictwo Naukowe, Warsaw, 1962-63), vol. 1, pp. 52-3.

3. W. Jastrzębowski, *Gospodarka niemiecka w Polsce* (Czytelnik, Warsaw, 1946), p. 103.

4. For more details concerning Nazi plans cf: Cz. Madajczyk, *Polityka III Rzeszy w okupowanej Polsce* (2 vols., Państwowe Wydawnictwo Naukowe, Warsaw, 1970). This book contains an extensive bibliography of this subject.

5. Cz. Madajczyk, 'Generalplan Ost', *Przegląd Zachodni*, no. 2 (1961), pp. 66-103; Cz. Madajczyk, 'Dalsze dokumenty dotyczące Generalnego Planu Wschodniego', *Dzieje Najnowsze*, no. 3 (1975), pp. 195-203.

6. For instance cf: Cz. Łuczak, *Polityka ludnościowa i ekonomiczna hitlerowskich Niemiec w okupowanej Polsce* (Wydawnictwo Poznańskie, Poznań, 1979) (including an extensive literature of the subject); Cz. Madajczyk, *Polityka* (see Bibliography).

7. B. Mark, *Powstanie w ghetcie warszawskim na tle ruchu oporu w Polsce* (Żydowski Instytut Historyczny, Warsaw, 1953), p. 26.

8. Literature concerning the extermination of Polish Jews is very wide. For instance one should mention: *Eksterminacja Żydów na ziemiach polskich w okresie okupacji hitlerowskiej. Zbiór dokumentów*, T. Berenstein, A. Eisenbach, A. Rutkowski (eds.), (Żydowski Instytut Historyczny, Warsaw, 1957); A. Eisenbach, *Hitlerowska polityka zagłady Żydów* (Książka i Wiedza, Warsaw, 1961); R. Sakowska, *Ludzie z dzielnicy zamkniętej* (Państwowe Wydawnictwo Naukowe, Warsaw, 1975).

9. *Okupacja i ruch oporu w Dzienniku Hansa Franka 1939-1945* (2 vols., Państwowe Wydawnictwo Naukowe, Warsaw, 1972), vol. 1, pp. 147-8.

10. J. Gumkowski, K. Leszczyński, *Okupacja*

hitlerowska w Polsce (Wydawnictwo 'Polonia', Warsaw, 1961), pp. 91-2.

11. B. Ratyńska, Ludność i gospodarka Warszawy i okręgu pod okupacją hitlerowską (Książka i Wiedza, Warsaw, 1982), p. 65.

12. Speech made by Hans Frank on 14 January 1944 quoted according to: S. Piotrowski, Dziennik Hansa Franka (Państwowe Wydawnictwo Naukowe, Warsaw, 1957), p. 510.

13. Cz. Łuczak, Polityka, p. 640.

14. Sprawozdanie w przedmiocie strat i szkód wojennych Polski w latach 1939-1945 (Biuro Odszkodowań Wojennych przy Prezydium Rady Ministrów, Warsaw, 1947) p. 36.

15. Straty wojenne Polski w latach 1939-1945 (Wydawnictwo Zachodnie, Poznań, 1960), p. 24.

16. Cz. Łuczak, Polityka, p. 136. For details cf: W. Jastrzębski, Hitlerowskie wysiedlania z ziem polskich wcielonych do Rzeszy w latach 1939-1945 (Instytut Zachodni, Poznań, 1968).

17. Zamojszczyzna - Sonderlaboratorium SS. Zbiór dokumentów polskich i niemieckich z okresu okupacji hitlerowskiej, Cz. Madajczyk (ed.) (2 vols., Ludowa Spółdzielnia Wydawnicza, Warsaw, 1977).

18. Cz. Łuczak, Polityka, p. 194.

19. Cz. Madajczyk, 'Polityka narodowościowa władz hitlerowskich na Pomorzu', Najnowsze Dzieje Polski 1939-1945, no. 9 (1965), pp. 5-33; E. Serwański, 'Hitlerowska polityka narodowościowa na Górnym Śląsku', ('Pax', Warsaw, 1963).

20. Cz. Łuczak, Polityka, p. 161.

21. T. Kłosiński, Polityka przemysłowa okupanta w Generalnym Gubernatorstwie (Instytut Zachodni, Poznań, 1947).

22. Speech made by Hans Frank on 19 January 1940 quoted according to: S. Piotrowski, Dziennik, p. 402.

23. W. Jastrzębowski, Gospodarka, p. 308.

24. J. Jaros, 'Górnictwo w czasie II wojny światowej' in Zarys dziejów górnictwa na ziemiach polskich (2 vols., Stowarzyszenie Inżynierów, Katowice, 1960-61), vol. 2, p. 259.

25. T. Kłosiński, Polityka, pp. 95-100; 'Polska. Położenie gospodarcze przemysłu, rzemiosła i handlu w III kwartale 1942 r.', Ekonomista Polski , no. 7 (1943).

26. M. Walczak, Walka ekonomiczna narodu polskiego 1939-1945 (Wydawnictwo Ministerstwa Obrony Narodowej, Warsaw, 1983).

27. Z. Mańkowski, 'Wieś polska i chłopi w latach 1939-1945' in Historia chłopów polskich

(3 vols., Ludowa Spółdzielnia Wydawnicza, Warsaw, 1980), vol. 3, pp. 498-603.

28. Cz. Łuczak, Polityka, p. 236.

29. S. Piotrowski, Dziennik, pp. 107, 112 and 487.

30. Cz. Madajczyk, Polityka, vol. 1, p. 533.

31. For instance cf: Wieś polska 1939-1948. Materiały konkursowe, K. Kersten, T. Szarota (eds.) (4 vols., Państwowe Wydawnictwo Naukowe, Warsaw, 1967-71).

32. K. Ostrowski, Hitlerowska polityka podatkowa w Generalnym Gubernatorstwie (Uniwersytet Jagielloński, Cracow, 1977).

33. Cz. Łuczak, Polityka, p. 387.

34. F. Skalniak, Bank Emisyjny w Polsce 1939-1945 (Państwowe Wydawnictwo Ekonomiczne, Warsaw, 1966).

35. Z. Landau, J. Tomaszewski, 'Bank Handlowy w Warszawie S.A. w latach drugiej wojny światowej', Przegląd Historyczny, no. 2 (1969), pp. 445-53.

36. Z. Karpiński, 'Losy złota polskiego podczas drugiej wojny światowej', Najnowsze Dzieje Polski 1939-1945, no. 1 (1957), pp. 97-154.

37. B. Ratyńska, Ludność, p. 352.

38. W. Jastrzębowski, Gospodarka, p. 356.

39. F. Skalniak, Bank, pp. 183-95.

CHAPTER FOUR

PEOPLE'S POLAND

RECONSTRUCTION AND REFORMS

PROGRAMME OF THE NEW AUTHORITIES

On 21 July 1944 Soviet troops liberated Chełm - the first town taken from under German occupation on the changed territory of the Polish state. At the same time the Home National Council, presided over by Bolesław Bierut and representing left-wing Polish underground groups declaring co-operation with the USSR, created the Polish Committee of National Liberation - the first *de facto* government of People's Poland headed by Edward Osóbka-Morawski. In the following months the Committee tried to get in touch with the Polish Government in exile whose Prime Minister was Stanisław Mikołajczyk, but these attempts proved in vain. On 31 December 1944 the Home National Council replaced the Committee by a Provisional Government. Only as late as 28 June 1945, after several days of negotiations held in Moscow by representatives of Polish political circles from the country and from abroad, under pressure from the big powers, was a compromise concluded and a Provisional Government of National Unity established. Its main purpose was to carry out elections and to stabilise the political situation in Poland.

On 22 July 1944 the Polish Committee of National Liberation proclaimed its manifesto to the Polish nation presenting a programme formulated by the new authorities. It was the result of long discussions within the left-wing conspiracy at home and among Polish emigrants in the USSR. The manifesto considered it essential for the new authorities to regain independence through a continuing struggle with the Germans, to create a democratic state in which conditions would be different from those prevailing before 1939 and to carry out various social reforms. The predicted reforms included above all land reform for all estates of more than 50 hectares. At the same time the manifesto said: 'The property robbed by the Germans from individual citizens - peasants, merchants, craftsmen, small and middle-class entrepreneurs, from the Church and other institutions, will be returned to its legal owners. All German property will be confiscated.' (1) Enterprises under German management were to be taken over by the Provisional Government Administration.

Such an economic programme did not predestine the future socio-political system of Poland. The declared land reform only meant the ending of the process of splitting up the large landed estates which had survived the agrarian reforms of the nineteenth century. For a long time suggestions of this kind formed the principal component of the Polish peasant movement programme. They were also approved of by other democratic parties, which differed as to the methods of realisation but were in agreement as to the necessity of land reform. The political significance of land reform seemed beyond doubt as without it no party could ensure the support of the peasants. Simultaneously, land reform made it possible to reconstruct Polish farming and to extend the market for industrial goods.

The confiscation of all German property - including that of collaborators - was a consequence of occupation and provided the Polish economy with the means to end its considerable dependence on German capital. Before the Second World War a large part of mining and industry, mainly in Upper Silesia, was in German hands. During the Second World War German ownership still expanded. The formation of the Provisional Government Administration was a temporary solution to be applied until property rights could finally be settled. Property was also administrated where the fate of the owners remained unknown. In this way the state organs began to manage all major industrial plants and this facilitated reconstruction. The return of property to the legal owners, provided for in the manifesto, could therefore refer only to non-German owners. Apart from capital in the hands of the Allied and neutral countries, the private sector referred in practice mainly to small enterprises. In spite of the preservation of private ownership, if the objectives of the manifesto were to be realised there had to be some far-reaching transformations in the property structure of the Polish economy.

The manifesto did not proclaim construction of a socialist system in Poland. Though Polish Workers' Party activists tended to agree (along with Polish Socialist Party members) with such a system, they treated it as a future consequence. Reforms proclaimed in the manifesto were to pave the way for socialism in Poland but the latter was not yet a matter of immediate concern.

In international relations the Committee and, later, the Provisional Government adopted the Teheran conference provisions of November 1943 as the foundation for the frontiers of the Polish state. The main principle of both bodies was co-operation with the Soviet Union, the closest neighbour among the Big Three. This meant reconsideration of the past, when lack of agreement with the USSR facilitated the aggressive policies of the Third Reich and the assistance of Western Allies proved inefficient.

FRONTIERS AND TERRITORY

During the Second World War the Soviet government had already told the Polish government in exile in London that it could not accept a mutual frontier which would leave a considerable number of Belorussians and Ukrainians in Poland. At the same time Moscow suggested a shift of Poland's western frontier to the Oder line.

The rejection of these requirements by the Polish government in exile raised tension between both governments and afterwards became one of the reasons for the break in diplomatic relations. At the Teheran conference Joseph Stalin, Winston Churchill and Franklin Delano Roosevelt agreed to the formula put forward by the British Prime Minister:

> It is thought in principle that the home of the Polish State and nation should be between the so-called Curzon Line and the line of the Oder, including for Poland East Prussia [as defined] and Oppeln; but the actual tracing of the frontier line requires careful study, and possibly, disentanglement of the population at some points. (2)

The new frontiers of Poland were confirmed at Yalta in February 1945. The Polish Committee of National Liberation took over power on the territories situated westward of the new Polish-Soviet frontier line, formally settled in an agreement signed in Moscow on 16 August 1945. On the grounds of an agreement of 25 May 1951 the frontier line between Poland and the Soviet Union was altered and about 480 sq km were exchanged from both sides.

The western and northern frontier of Poland was determined at Potsdam in August 1945. Although the Potsdam conference settlements reserved that 'the final delimitation of the western frontier of Poland should await the peace conference' (3) the signatories defined principles of displacement of the German population from Poland. This meant therefore that in settling the Polish western frontier, representatives of the Big Three postponed only its formal confirmation.

Under these circumstances the basic Polish frontier problems were settled in 1945. The Potsdam decisions substantially changed the territorial shape of the Polish state which now resembled its form at the end of the tenth century. This must have brought far-reaching demographic and economic consequences. The Soviet Union incorporated mostly agricultural areas with hardly any industry. Poland gained territories which had been peripheries of the German state and - except for Upper Silesia - belonged to the less economically advanced parts of the Reich. However as compared with the eastern parts of the Second Polish Republic their level of development - industrial plants, urban and rural settlements or infrastructure - was higher. In other words, from the economic point of view the change of frontiers brought Poland benefits which may be regarded as partial compensation for war damage caused by the Germans.

The territories regained in Poland, however, had been devastated in the last stages of war. Heavy fighting had gone on in many places, and German troops made futile attempts to defend several towns which were badly damaged as a result. Wrocław, for example, was one of the worst-hit towns in Europe. Population problems were also very complicated. In some regions of the regained territories there were native Polish populations but elsewhere these were almost exclusively German.

The new Polish state had to face enormous problems; it had to find a way of revitalising economic life, of reconstructing the regained territories - areas which now had to be integrated with other Polish lands. It must be remembered that for centuries the regained territories had developed within the German economic system. In practice the Polish authorities had to reconstruct not only war damage but also had to establish a new system of co-operation in production, transportation, etc. After the Second World War no other European country faced problems on such a scale. Poland, it should be remembered, gave the USSR about 46 per cent of her 1937 territory while the regained territories accounted for about 33 per cent of the area of Poland after the Second World War. (4)

After 1945 there also remained an open dispute with Czechoslovakia over the frontier in the Teschen and Kłodzko regions. As a result of negotiations in 1946 it was agreed that the 1937 frontier would be maintained in Teschen Silesia while the Kłodzko Region would become a part of Poland.

These settlements altered the area of the Polish state to 311,730 sq km and the total length of frontiers to 3,538 km. The Polish frontier with Czechoslovakia was now 1,310 km long, with the USSR 1,244 km, with Germany 460 km, while the sea coast was 524 km long. (5) The western frontier of Poland was recognised by the German Democratic Republic in a treaty signed in Görlitz/Zgorzelec on 6 July 1950, whereas the German Federal Republic recognised it in a treaty signed in Warsaw on 7 December 1970.

POPULATION

As a result of war losses and the alteration of frontiers the population of Poland considerably diminished. The February 1946 census showed 23.9 million inhabitants, that is about 11 million people less than in 1938. These data must be treated approximately in view of the fact that at the same time mass migrations were still going on. They included movements in various directions. Poles were returning from forced labour and concentration camps or prisons of the Third Reich, wartime emigrants were coming back home from Western Europe (including soldiers of the Polish Armed Forces in the West and the Allied armies), Polish citizens were returning or resettling from Soviet up-country or from the eastern territories of pre-war Poland on the grounds of appropriate Polish-Soviet agreements, Germans were being displaced to Germany and Belorussians and Ukrainians to the USSR. Data concerning the magnitude of these migrations are also approximate as they tended to start spontaneously, before the end of military operations, and were frequently not recorded.

The resettlement of Germans began at the end of 1944 on the orders of Hitler's authorities in view of the approaching Soviet Army. At first, the evacuation was well organised but it soon turned into a stampede frequently forced by the army, police and SS. This migration is estimated at about 7 million people. In the autumn of 1945 a planned displacement of Germans by the Polish authorities began; according to the February 1946 census there were still 2.3 million Germans within the new Polish state. Mass resettlements ended in autumn 1947. Small scale migrations lasted until 1950. Altogether about 3.2 million Germans left Poland in organised resettlements. Lack of evidence makes it impossible to estimate precisely how many Germans remained.

From the autumn of 1944 to the end of 1946 mass migrations took place between Poland and the USSR. About 489,000 Ukrainians left Poland along with 36,000 Belorussians and a small number of Lithuanians. On the other hand about 160,000 Ukrainians remained in Poland (most of them were resettled to the northern and western parts of Poland in 1947) along with more than 150,000 Belorussians and almost 10,000 Lithuanians. At the same time about 1.5 million people came to Poland from the Soviet Union as well as 2.3 million people from Germany and other West European countries.

Among those coming back to Poland there were also Jews; some of them decided later on to emigrate to Palestine or to other countries. Rough estimates show that around 1950 Poland was inhabited by not less than 100,000 people of Jewish nationality. Other minorities (Slovaks, Gypsies, Czechs) were much less numerous. After 1947 political refugees came from Greece. Altogether it may be estimated that around 1950 Poland had about 600,000 inhabitants representing national minorities. As compared with inter-war Poland their share was now quite small. (6)

A considerable number of the immigrants from the Soviet Union went to the regained territories. People from other regions moved there, too, especially from the most over-populated southern provinces. In December 1950 the regained territories were inhabited by 5.9 million people, almost exclusively Poles, both those living there for generations and the post-war newcomers. Mass migrations in 1945-6 also concerned the return of people to their homes from which they had been removed during the occupation.

All these migrations took place at the end of war or directly afterwards when the whole economy faced heavy war damage and transport was disorganised. All this aggravated the problems which had somehow to be solved but, on the other hand, a rapid conclusion of the post-war migrations was a precondition for political stabilisation and economic reconstruction.

AGRICULTURE

Immediately after the liberation of Polish territories situated eastwards of the Vistula (beyond which fighting still continued) the new authorities faced three basic problems in the field of agriculture: to secure foodstuffs for the army, for the population of towns and the devastated countryside and to carry out land reform. The Soviet Army lent aid to the most hard-hit regions but this was treated as emergency aid only. Food supplies were to be organised by the new authorities, and became one of their main tasks from the beginning.

In August 1944 the Polish Committee of National Liberation issued a decree concerning obligatory deliveries of corn, potatoes, meat and hay, appropriate quotas being lower than those imposed during the Nazi occupation. Quotas were set according to the size of farms; the smallest of them or those that had suffered most damage could be released from delivery obligations.

Implementing the new decrees encountered difficulties, of an economic as well as of a political nature. Opposition was effectively organised against obligatory quota deliveries and other regulations.

By mid-December 1944 the planned deliveries of corn were 60 per cent fulfilled, of meat 90 per cent, potatoes 80 per cent, while those of hay reached 120 per cent. Thus army requirements could be almost entirely satisfied, but food supply for the population covered only 60 per cent of the volume demanded by the rationing system. (7) Deliveries from the USSR, mainly corn supplies, partially filled the gap. All in all the food supply system was unsatisfactory and there was the threat of severe hunger. The situation would only improve when new crops were planted and when the UN Relief and Rehabilitation Administration deliveries started.

The development of agriculture depended on the speed of land reform. On 6 September 1944 a decree was issued defining principles of the reform. It was aimed at enlarging existing farms so that they could support their owners and families, the creation of new farms for agricultural workers hitherto employed on parcelled estates and the preservation of some land for other purposes (centres of agricultural engineering, seed farms, etc.). Parcelling referred to estates belonging to Germans and their wartime collaborators, to the state and to all private owners. The latter provision included estates whose 'total size exceeded either 100 hectares of overall area or 50 hectares of arable area; whereas in the Poznań, Pomorze and Silesian province - 100 hectares of overall area, irrespective of the arable land area within'. (8)

Separate settlement of the problem in the three provinces resulted from their different development in the nineteenth century when they belonged to the Prussian partition. Expropriation for land reform purposes also applied to farms whose owners had left for the USSR.

The expropriation of large estates was without compensation. Previous owners received only a small independent farm elsewhere or a monthly pension equal to an average salary. The land taken over was distributed among agricultural workers and smallholders. Beneficiaries were to pay a sum equal to their mean annual crop value paid in 10-20 yearly instalments.

At first land reform was effected by the state administration apparatus. It acted slowly while political and economic conditions demanded a rapid end to parcelling, so that peasants could start cultivation. Moreover, some civil servants, opposing the reforms, delayed and were content to wait for the new system to collapse. In some regions fulfilment of the reform faced armed resistance. The upshot was that peasants frequently adopted a passive and suspicious attitude towards reform. Rumours said it was only an introduction to collectivisation based on Soviet patterns.

At the beginning of October 1944 the Polish Committee of National Liberation appointed its plenipotentiary for land reform who was charged with its realisation by various methods. The Polish Workers' Party, headed then by secretary-general Władysław Gomułka, who played a leading role in the Committee, sent worker activists to help peasant commissions expropriating estates and parcelling land. With few qualified surveyors, these activities were as simple as possible so that work in agriculture could begin as soon as possible. After the liberation of territories westwards of the Vistula in the winter and early spring of 1945, parcelling was extended to all estates in those regions.

By this time the peasants' distrust was not so marked; some even began to demand allotments. In the former Russian and Austrian partitions land reserves were smaller than the social and economic needs.Thus the commissions had frequently to distribute land in small plots which could not become independent farms. Lack of livestock and tools because of war damage was another grave problem. Particularly difficult was the situation of former agricultural workers without farm buildings. They had to be helped by the government though its financial ability was limited.

Further westwards, in the former Prussian partition, land reserves exceeded requirements. Thus, farmers demanded bigger allotments in accordance with traditional conditions of farming in these areas. On the other hand, some agricultural workers refused to take land, realising the problems they would have to face in order to create independent, self-sufficient farms. In addition, the social standing of agricultural workers there was, contrary to other regions of Poland, usually thought higher than that of poor peasants. Thus workers desired to change some large estates expropriated in the course of land reform into socialised property. However, the Central Committee of the Polish Workers' Party declared itself against these economic communities in order to avoid accusations of preparing for collectivisation. After this many farm workers returned their allotments but an increase in the average size of land allotments and government assistance for the newly established farms put an end to this process. Nevertheless many estates in western parts of Poland remained non-parcelled; they became state farms.

As a result of land reform former large landowners ceased to exist as a social group; some chose other professions or lived on private savings, others could barely make a living.

The division of large estates in Poland could not satisfy the hunger for land - reserves were limited and, what is more, peasant families coming from the USSR also had to be given land. The acquisition of land left by the resettled Germans, Belorussians and Ukrainians extended available land reserves but reconstruction of the basic property structure of Polish agriculture could not really get under way without mass settlement of peasants in the regained territories given to Poland in the Potsdam agreement.

The mass migration of Poles to the regained territories began in the spring of 1945, almost immediately after the liberation of these areas. In autumn 1945 and in the following year colonisation began in earnest. Newcomers mainly took over farms formerly belonging to German peasants but the management of large estates, particularly in north-western regions, proved much more complicated. A general lack of buildings suitable for peasant needs led to settlers establishing co-operatives which were to be dissolved after a few years. Some large estates were taken over by the state. The state farms were assumed to supplement peasant farms. At the First Congress of the Polish Workers' Party in December 1945 Edward Ochab, Secretary of the Central Committee said: 'The national interest requires as many peasants as possible to settle on the Oder and Neisse, to make medium-sized (about a dozen acres) peasant farms prevail, exist and develop without hired labour.' (9)

Altogether, land reform and colonisation in 1945-9 included 6,070,000 hectares, 3,686,000 hectares of which were situated in the regained territories. The average area of newly-created farms amounted to 6.9 hectares. A total of 347,000 new farms were created and 254,000 farms increased in area in the regions belonging to Poland before 1939, while 467,000 farms were created in the regained territories. In 1949 there were 3,342,000 peasant farms in Poland. On 1 January 1949 there were 4,823 state farms of 1,506,000 hectares, while 696,000 hectares belonged to other types of state or collective management. The property composition of land ownership was therefore considerably changed. In 1931 only 35.8 per cent of farms in Poland had more than 5 hectares but in 1950 their share had grown to 42.8 per cent, the number of smaller farms having particularly fallen. (10) Henryk Słabek seems right when he summed up the change in Polish agriculture: 'land reform made the farm structure in 1950 sounder than before 1939 despite the atomisation of plots'. (11)

But land reform and colonisation of the regained territories could not solve all the inherent social problems of Polish farming. In southern parts of Poland especially, there were still over-populated areas, though this congestion was less than in the inter-war period. It would seem that Nicolas Spulber was exaggerating when he remarked: 'Thus the expulsion of the German population made possible the creation of an important stratum of medium-sized peasant holdings in the West without relieving *in toto* the pressure of rural over-population in the former Polish provinces.' (12)

After 1944 the problem of peasant indebtedness was finally solved. Peasants received land free of mortgage charges. The pre-war obligations of many farms depreciated due to war inflation. Polish post-war monetary reforms and changes in the price structure practically cleared the country of its former indebtedness.

Land reform was accompanied by the reconstruction of war damage in the agricultural sector. Rough estimates show that in 1946 about 87 per cent of arable land was sown in the former Polish provinces; in the regained territories 38 per cent of arable land was under cultivation. (13) The efforts connected with this revival were considerable. Peasants could only begin to cultivate their land after unexploded mines and shells had been removed. Sometimes, however, they ploughed without waiting for sappers. There was a general lack of tools, seeds, farm buildings and horses - with which to plough the land. Some of the country folk had to live in dug-outs and bunkers. It may be presumed that without land reform agrarian reconstruction would have been much slower in such conditions.

The state assisted to some extent with the recovery programme. In 1945 the government had already assigned financial means for the rebuilding of farm buildings. Though the sums spent by the government constantly grew, these could only partially supplement the farmers' own efforts and inputs in view of the large scale of needs. Government aid was mainly granted to medium-sized farms situated on good land as these farms brought the highest yields. Supplies of fertilisers started in 1945, both from home factories and from abroad. By 1945/6 the supply of nitrogen and calcium fertilisers per hectare of cropland had exceeded the 1937/8 level, whereas in 1948/9 it amounted to 282 per cent of pre-war nitrogen fertiliser consumption, to 177 per cent of phosphate and to 322 per cent of calcium fertiliser consumption. (14) This was mainly due, however, to the very low levels of consumption before 1939. In 1946 production of farm machinery reached the pre-war level, though it was still low and the demand very high. Electrification of the country was commenced. Seeds were distributed, industrial goods supplied but their sale was usually tied to the purchase of farm products.

Important aid was also granted by the UN Relief and Rehabilitation Administration (UNRRA) which supplied fertilisers, cattle, horses, incubative eggs, etc. In 1946 Poland received from the UNRRA 122,000 horses (7 per cent of the total number of horses in Poland) and 17,000 cattle (0.5 per cent of the total number in Poland). (15)

Rapid development of land cultivation did not mean restoration of the pre-war level of production. According to rough estimates the total farming production of 1946 amounted to about 47 per cent of the 1934-8 average value, while in 1949 it reached 91 per cent, the per capita indices being 66 per cent and 127 per cent respectively. (16) This was connected with the large decrease in the population in Poland. Within a few years the per capita farming output had exceeded the pre-war level but it did not necessarily mean a similar improvement of supply in towns. The large supply of farm products before 1939 mainly resulted from the poverty of country folk who were forced to limit their consumption.Land reform destroyed large estates which had previously produced market surplus products. Land distribution and debt clearing allowed peasants to increase their consumption. As a result total market surplus production considerably decreased, causing serious difficulties with food supplies in towns.

Under these circumstances the government decided to maintain obligatory quota deliveries.Prices paid for these were much lower than free market prices, so that deliveries amounted to a tax in kind paid along with normal taxes in terms of money. For instance, in December 1945 the price for wheat within the system of obligatory deliveries was about 2 per cent of the free-market price, while that of the price of potatoes was about 5 per cent. At the same time however the tax impost assessed in money was quite inconsiderable. (17)

The increase in agricultural production, peasants' dislike of obligatory deliveries and the sheer unworkability of this system dictated the government's abolition of it in the summer of 1946. At the same time a tax reform increased the real value of the tax impost. Food supplies to towns were then secured by means of 'tie-in' sales. Farmers could buy industrial goods at relatively low prices in exchange for farm products sold at prices controlled by the government. Simultaneously a system of supply contracts was developed consisting in agreements signed by farmers with state-owned enterprises for the delivery of agricultural products. These contracts mostly concerned sugar beet crops.

In 1947-9 the growth of farming production proved slightly higher than was expected in the three-year plan of economic reconstruction passed in September 1946. Rough estimates show that the total agricultural output in 1949 was 95 per cent higher than in 1946; corn yields exceeded the planned level by 12.8 per cent and livestock number by 36 per cent. (18)

Polish agriculture was dominated by peasant farms. State farms played a minor role and their area, though gradually growing, accounted for no more than 10 per cent of arable land. Development of stock, improvements in machinery and other investments made it possible for the state farms to obtain higher than average yields. In 1949, for example, average yields of wheat in Poland amounted to 12.3 per hectare but in the state farms the figure was 15.4 q. (19) At the same time yields of potatoes and sugar beet were lower than average.

In the second half of 1948 the government's agricultural policy was changed and the socialist reconstruction of agriculture was advanced. This resulted from discussions in the international workers' movement and from the Soviet-Yugoslav dispute in particular. In July 1948 Trade and Industry minister, Hilary Minc, said at the Central Committee meeting:

> Within the socio-economic system of a people's democracy farm co-operatives are the simplest and easiest way, within the grasp of a common peasant, to develop a new system of large-scale economy, capable of utilising all the benefits of modern technology and agricultural knowledge. (20)

At the same time he warned that reconstruction of agriculture in this way would neither be easy nor rapid, that it would require development of those industries producing the means of production, large credits and other aid, and would therefore take a long time to accomplish. Minc also pointed out the need for peasants to be convinced that collective methods would work or, in other words, that is, ensure that changes would be accepted voluntarily.

In autumn 1948 the government began a programme of agricultural reconstruction. The programme was also announced at the First Congress of the Polish United Workers' Party in December 1948. By the end of 1949 there were already 243 co-operatives, most of them composed of farms created in the course of land reform or belonging to settlers in the regained territories. State Centres of Agricultural Machines came into being aimed at rendering technological services to agriculture. Differentiation in tax rates was also increased. In 1946 these rates varied (according to the lowest and the highest income groups) from 4 per cent to 8 per cent, but from 2 per cent to 18 per cent in 1949. Farm co-operatives were granted allowances and paid no more than 8 per cent of the tax base, a move to encourage peasants to create co-operatives. A compulsory saving system was also introduced hitting medium-sized and better-off farms. (21) Although collectivisation was in principle voluntary, in 1949 the first attempts appeared here and there to exert administrative pressure on peasants.

INDUSTRY

Reconstruction of war damage in industry began very quickly after the end of the war. When Polish troops arrived in Lublin a workers' meeting decided to create factory committees to take over management and to start reconstruction. As the power plant and the water supply system were not destroyed, work could begin at once. In all the liberated towns the less damaged factories were soon repaired. The attitude of workers played a major role. At the end of the Nazi occupation workers frequently hid the most important pieces of machinery to protect them against destruction or removal. The moment the Germans evacuated, men frequently stood on guard defending factories against plunder. If they could not prevent the removal of machinery, the workers often tried to specify the property taken away and the probable direction of shipment. Sometimes this proved very useful when the recovery of Polish property from Germany began.

Getting industry on its feet was no easy task. Managers and qualified workers, machinery, tools, raw materials and foodstuffs for employees were all in short supply. The authorities appointed 'plenipotentiaries' whose task was to organise industrial plants. Their experience was then utilised by the so-called 'operation groups' created in November 1944 and headed by Alfred Wiślicki. These groups included engineers, qualified workers, economists and active party members who were responsible for organisation, the protection of factories, representation of Polish interests before Soviet military authorities, etc. They started work when the January 1945 offensive began. Though the operation groups lasted for only a few months, they played an important role in protection and reconstruction of industrial activity and stimulated the initiative of workers. They also created the first organisational forms of state-controlled industry.

In spring 1945 the take-over of administration from the hands of Soviet military commanders began in the regained territories. Industrial plants were secured, gradually reconstructed and set to work. The Potsdam conference decisions finally determined the destiny of these territories which accelerated their reconstruction. With the exception of Silesia, the regained territories belonged to the less developed parts of the Reich, their productivity and income being lower than the all-German average.Their economic role in Poland was different. The regained territories had industries hardly developed in pre-war Poland, raw materials and important lines of communication. The most advanced mining and manufacturing centres were situated in their southern part - in western Upper Silesia and in Lower Silesia. These industries, however, were seriously damaged during the Second World War, about half of their productive potential having been lost. Reconstruction was checked by the displacement of the German population and the necessity to organise new colonisation. War booty was another problem. As long as the ownership of German property had not been legally settled by international agreement, it was treated by the Soviet authorities as war booty or as a part of war reparations from Germany. In the summer of 1945 this question was settled by a Polish-Soviet agreement defining the term 'war booty' throughout Poland. The Soviet troops were not 'to treat as war booty or subject of requisition all property belonging to private owners, co-operatives, industrial enterprises and municipalities in the territory of Poland'. (22)

Another, even further reaching agreement was signed in Potsdam on 16 August 1945. It said that the Soviet government would cede to Poland 15 per cent of the due reparation deliveries from Germany while Poland would:

> supply to the Soviet Union coal at special prices from 1946 on, as long as Germany is occupied; within the first year of delivery - 8 million tons, within the following four years - 13 million and afterwards until the end of occupation of Germany - 12 million tons of coal per annum. (23)

The same agreement stipulated that:

> The Soviet government cedes to Poland all claims

> to German property and other assets, as well as to the shares of German industrial and transport enterprises all over the Polish territory including this part of German territory which is passing to Poland.

Protecting and starting the remaining enterprises was only the beginning of reconstruction. The provisional state management faced more and more complicated problems. The most dramatic raw material difficulties were solved by Soviet supplies. From autumn 1945 UNRRA deliveries were growing. The most important home material was coal. In February 1945 the first mines commenced output and in 1946 the pre-war level of coal production was exceeded.

The state-controlled industry included all major enterprises in Poland, as in most cases their legal status had not been settled or they were treated as abandoned property. Only a few minor firms remained in private hands. Sometimes their owners returned but could not afford the capital cost of reconstruction. In some lines of production co-operatives played an important role and were supported by the government. The large - and medium-size - industries of liberated Poland had been practically nationalised.

Under these circumstances it was necessary to create a uniform management system in industry. In December 1944 the Polish Committee of National Liberation called into being its Department of Industry (on 1 January 1945 it became the Ministry of Industry) headed by Hilary Minc. The objective of the Department was to guide the government's industrial policy and to manage enterprises provisionally controlled by the government by means of their Central Administrations.

The organisation of the industrial management system was based on Soviet models and on some conclusions resulting from the Polish economic policy of the late 1930s. Many experts employed before the Second World War in the administration of private syndicates and other economic organisations turned their knowledge over to the requirements of People's Poland. The new state apparatus also absorbed many officials and clerks who had gained experience in state economic institutions before 1939. The post-war Polish naval economy, for instance, was started by Eugeniusz Kwiatkowski who was Minister of Treasury in 1935-9. Economic management, however, faced a serious shortage of personnel, as the professional classes had been a particular target of Nazi occupants. Some experts were in the army, others - having served in the Polish Armed Forces in the West - remained abroad. It was therefore thought necessary to draw the most experienced and politically conscious workers into administration of the national economy. Special courses were organised and great importance was attached to worker participation in industrial management. In early 1945 a decree concerning trade-union councils in factories was passed entitling them to control working conditions, to participate in fixing output rates and working regulations, to control food supply and to have a decisive voice in engagement and dismissal of employees.

Workers' participation in factory management accelerated reconstruction. In the first few months people worked without waiting for wage payments, their solidarity sometimes expressing itself to the extent that moderate food rations were accepted in lieu of wages. Production rapidly increased. In April 1945 the index of production of selected industrial goods amounted to 19 per cent of the 1937 level, but in late 1946 it had reached the pre-war level. (24) Such a rapid increase was in part due to the westward shift of Polish frontiers.

The reconstruction of industry based on workers' self-sacrifices could not last indefinitely. The negative effects were soon noticed and in spring 1945 problems with food supply caused short strikes in several factories, mainly in Łódź. This made it necessary to put the wage system in order. A new system introduced in summer 1945 determined that wage levels would depend on productivity.

A gradual stabilisation of the internal situation in Poland, expressed by the recognition of the Provisional Government of National Unity by all the big powers, made it essential to regulate property rights in industry. In spring 1945 some owners claimed their enterprises back according to the July 1944 manifesto and in many cases property rights were restored. Some decisions concerning the takeover of factories by private owners were opposed by workers, some of whom went on strike.

The political situation changed however. In summer 1945 ex-premier of the London government in exile Stanisław Mikołajczyk returned to Poland and founded the Polish Peasant Party adducing to the tradition of popular movement but in practice uniting various political forces standing in opposition to the government. The Mikołajczyk programme did not intend to restore pre-war social relations but rejected socialism as represented by the workers' movement. The Mikołajczyk group criticised land reform. Likewise before the Second World War they wanted large peasant farms based on hired labour.The Polish Peasant Party also opposed - just as in prewar years - monopoly domination but at the same time defended so-called 'private initiative', that is, small and medium-size businesses and criticised the extension of government interference in private economic activity. In other words, it was a programme of stabilisation of socio-economic relations and the formation of a reformed capitalist economy in Poland.

Under these circumstances the struggle for further reforms sharpened in the second half of 1945. The workers' parties formulated principles of nationalisation for large- and medium-size industrial enterprises and approved the private ownership of minor firms. An appropriate draft bill entered the agenda of the Home National Council (playing the role of a provisional Parliament) in December 1945 and was passed after a few amendments on 3 January 1946. (25)

The nationalisation bill stipulated that all enterprises formerly belonging to Germans, to joint-stock companies controlled by them or to people who escaped to the enemy would be nationalised without compensation. This referred not only to industry but also to other branches of the national economy. All enterprises in 17 specified industries (for example, mining, heavy industry, power production, large and medium-size light industry, etc.) were to be nationalised and their owners paid indemnities. The same rules were applied to all other industrial enterprises employing more than 50 workers per shift, except for co-operatives and communal enterprises. Firms controlled by the provisional state management and not coming under the nationalisation bill were to be returned to their owners.

Simultaneously another bill was passed concerning the government's support for private firms. The bill defined conditions and kinds of private business activity but its practical importance proved rather limited in the years to come.

The nationalisation of industry was to secure favourable conditions for a rapid reconstruction and development of the national economy. It was also aimed at freeing the Polish economy from the influence of foreign capital. The nationalisation bill was the forerunner of a socialist system.

In the following months many factories returned

to their former owners; it should of course be remembered that some of them did not survive the Second World War. The discharge of indemnities was spread over many years. As regards arrangements for foreign citizens, these were based on appropriate international agreements. An agreement on economic and financial co-operation signed by Poland and the United States on 24 April 1946 stipulated mutual obligation to pay compensation in the case of nationalisation. In the following years detailed agreements concerning indemnities were signed. (26) The discharge of all indemnities is due to be completed by 1990. (27)

Nationalisation diminished the role of private industry in the Polish economy. According to Nicolas Spulber in 1947 employment in the state-controlled sector accounted for 86.8 per cent of the total employment in Poland, in co-operatives for 4.1 per cent, and in private enterprises for 9.1 per cent. In 1949 these proportions were respectively: 89.3 per cent, 6.1 per cent and 4.6 per cent. (28) Nationalisation of the key branches of the national economy made it possible to begin preparing for the introduction of economic planning. By 1945 segmental plans had been elaborated, including the most important of them - a coal output plan worked out in April 1945. On 1 January 1946 the Economic Committee of the Cabinet (including premier and economic ministers) passed a plan for 1946 embracing all major industries. In autumn 1945 the Central Planning Office was established under the direction of Czesław Bobrowski. The Office prepared an investment plan for the period between 1 April and 31 December 1946. The experience gathered by the Office served as a foundation for the preparation of the first long-term plan.

It is now difficult to estimate industrial production in Poland in 1946 as compared to pre-war levels. According to Hilary Minc, in autumn 1946 it reached about 70 per cent of the 1938 level, (29) while later statistical publications showed slightly higher figures. Lack of exact data makes all estimates very approximate.

On 21 September 1946 the Home National Council passed a resolution including the guidelines of an economic plan for 1947-9. In January 1947 a general election brought a defeat of the Polish Peasant Party and in autumn 1947 Mikołajczyk illegally left the country. The office of the president was taken over by Bolesław Bierut and Józef Cyrankiewicz became premier. On 2 July 1947 the Seym passed a bill concerning the objectives of the three-year plan. It read: 'the basic task of the national economy in the years 1947-9 is to raise the standard of living of the working population above the pre-war level'. (30) This was to be obtained by means of:

(a) stabilisation of the political system and reconstruction of the socio-economic structure;
(b) reconstruction of war damage;
(c) consolidation of the regained territories with the rest of Poland and a comprehensive utilisation of the sea coast;
(d) extension of the country's participation in the world economy;
(e) repatriation of Poles who found themselves abroad in connection with the 1939-45 war and those who emigrated in search of work;
(f) reduction of costs of production and services along with an increase of efficiency of basic factors of production.

Specifying these general guidelines the bill stipulated an increase in the share of industry and services in the total output, development of foreign trade and increases in production of basic consumer goods. It also read: 'a shift from the priority of consumer goods toward investment goods will take place in the course of realisation of the plan, particularly at its end'.

The bill also determined the planned volume of industrial and agricultural production; in 1949 Polish industry was to exceed the 1946 level of production by 40 per cent. In other words the reconstruction of the Polish economy was to be generally completed. The plan did not foresee the construction of new plants. Most of the planned investments were designed for rebuilding the least-destroyed factories which would bring a rapid increase in production. At first the plan accorded priority to the production of consumer goods in order to improve living conditions. It was planned that in the last year of the three-year plan the priority would be shifted to new plants and capital goods.

The plan's first year brought serious problems. Some of them resulted from the increasing tension in international relations which had affected Polish foreign trade. Hard frosts in the winter of 1947 hampered transportation and raw material supplies. Poor harvests in the same year caused an increase in free market prices for foodstuffs. All these obstacles, however, did not restrain the growing productivity. In 1947 the output of large-and medium-size industrial enterprises almost reached the pre-war level; (31) however the production of small enterprises and handicrafts remained far below it.

The fulfilment of targets for 1947 made it possible to start the shift of investments from consumer goods to heavy industry. This led to a conflict between the two major bodies running the national economy. The Central Planning Office was criticised for aiming to increase investment in consumer industries and restraining inputs in producing the means of production. Its planning methodology was also questioned. These charges were exaggerated and the real reasons for the dispute were growing differences of one kind or another between the two workers' parties. The Ministry of Industry and Commerce (this name was adopted in March 1947 by the Ministry of Industry which was responsible for economic decisions) aimed at far-reaching centralisation of management, a gradual end to private business and the subordination of co-operatives to the government. In spring 1948 the Polish Workers' Party won and changed the direction of the Central Planning Office. Another reorganisation took place in the following year. The State Commission for Economic Planning was called into being under the direction of Hilary Minc while the Ministry of Industry and Commerce was divided into a number of branch ministries of lesser authority.

There were also other changes. In the summer of 1948 the Secretary-General of the Central Committee of the Polish Workers' Party and Vice-Premier, Władysław Gomułka was accused on serious political charges and dismissed. From September 1948 the Central Committee was headed by Bolesław Bierut. Controversy developed in the Polish Socialist Party. In December 1948 both parties fused into the Polish United Workers' Party whose Central Committee was headed by Bolesław Bierut. The PUWP was dominated by a policy of acceleration in production of investment goods and limitation of private business. These guidelines determined the government's economic policy in succeeding years.

Rapid progress in reconstruction made it possible to exceed the three-year plan industrial targets. In 1947-9 the rate of growth in production was extremely high and amounted to 33 per cent, 37 per cent and 22 per cent in the following three years. (32) This increase, however, was uneven in individual industries. There was a fall in private industry and stagnation in handicrafts; in 1947-8 employment in the former sector diminished by 54 per cent and in the latter it grew by 34 per cent to decrease in 1949. (33)

There was also considerable inequality of development and fulfilment of planned targets in the nationalised industries. Though only few lines failed to reach the target, these noticeably included the production of consumer goods which adversely affected market supplies.

The most significant achievement was undoubtedly the reconstruction of major plants in the regained territories. Thanks to precisely determined investments the three-year plan led to the economic integration of Poland in these new frontiers.

FINANCE

At the end of July 1944 the monetary and credit system of the liberated Polish territories was in utter disarray. The Polish Committee of National Liberation had at first neither a concept of policy nor a way to act in this field. Not until the end of August 1944 did new złoty banknotes arrive from a Moscow printing-house. In the first weeks, therefore, the occupation złotys remained in circulation along with German marks and Soviet roubles. Gradually new banknotes were introduced. They were actually issued by the new Treasury though formally they bore the name of a still non-existent Narodowy Bank Polski (it was created on 15 January 1945 as a central issuing bank).

From the end of October 1944 a gradual changeover to the new złoty banknotes began. The principle was quite simple. According to the final decree of 6 January 1945 the exchange in the former General Gouvernement was limited to 500 złotys per person. This meant a far-reaching reduction in circulation which might also curb increasing inflation. At the same time the government was able to raise circulation without any negative results for a certain time.

The budgetary situation was difficult. Revenues of the emerging state were very low, while expenditure had at first to be extremely high. According to the estimate for the last quarter of 1944 it was expected that the budget deficit would amount to 97 per cent of expenditure; in practice it proved possible to reduce it to 67 per cent between 22 July and 31 December 1944. (34) Despite the government's efforts the following year also brought a deficit covered by the growing indebtedness of the Treasury to the Narodowy Bank Polski. The situation slightly improved in 1946 but Treasury debts still grew. However, in 1947 and 1948 the budget had surplus sums which helped discharge these debts. The Premium Reconstruction Loan of 1946 also contributed to the solution of the debt problem.

All credit institutions in Poland were dramatically weakened by the Second World War. Some of them were practically ruined as the war had destroyed all their assets. Monetary reform was also a serious blow as it deprived all resources in occupation złotys of their value. All this made general reform of the banking system inevitable.

Apart from the Narodowy Bank Polski, in January 1945 other government banks were made functional again: the Bank Gospodarstwa Krajowego, the Państwowy Bank Rolny and the Pocztowa Kasa Oszczędności, along with communal and co-operative banks (some credit co-operatives were destroyed during the war) and three joint-stock banks: the Bank Polska Kasa Opieki SA (its shares belonging to the Pocztowa Kasa Oszczędności), the Bank Związku Spółek Zarobkowych SA in Poznań (directly before the war a great part of its shares were taken over by the government) and the Bank Handlowy SA in Warsaw (most of its shares had belonged to private sugar mills and other enterprises nationalised, therefore it also belonged to the state). Other private banks were refused concessions and went out of business. Therefore there was no nationalisation as such of banks in Poland. In view of huge losses during the Second World War most private banks were unable to function without some assistance. Private banking was not necessary as far as the government was concerned as it had its own banks established before 1939 and these comprised a sufficiently developed banking system.

At first credit institutions retained their traditional working methods. Future planning, however, made it necessary to adjust the banking system to new requirements. In 1946 gradual changes were introduced and these were completed by a comprehensive reform of the banking system which took place during the course of the three-year plan according to Soviet patterns.

The centrally planned economy required above all the concentration of business accounts in one bank so as to keep them under full financial control. This was connected with the centralisation of free capital and specialisation of banks.

In 1946 the Narodowy Bank Polski was given the

right to grant credits to enterprises in key branches of the national economy; the Economic Committee of the Cabinet recommended a limitation to bill discounting. In 1947 all acceptance credits for state-controlled enterprises were banned. At the same time enterprises were forbidden to give credits to one another and obliged to settle their accounts through banks. Former methods of lending were maintained only in the private sector. Last but not least, investment funds were closely scrutinised. All these changes increased the role of the Narodowy Bank Polski which became the country's main centre for financial and credit planning.

In the summer of 1948 a banking reform decree was passed. The Narodowy Bank Polski was designated as the central institution concentrating accounts of enterprises and financing their current activity. The financing of investments was entrusted to the newly established Bank Inwestycyjny. Moreover, the decree called into being the Bank Rolny (financing agriculture),the Bank Komunalny (financing self-government and in existence until 1952), the Bank Rzemiosła i Handlu (financing private enterprises and in existence until 1950) and the Powszechna Kasa Oszczędności. Two other joint-stock banks were maintained - the Bank Polska Kasa Opieki SA and the Bank Handlowy SA in Warsaw - whose purpose was to engage in foreign dealing. The accomplishment of banking reform took several years.

DOMESTIC TRADE

Within a few months after liberation trade turnover was entirely disorganised. An overall shortage of goods and public distrust of the Polish currency made normal trade suffer. The direct exchange of goods appeared instead. In the course of 1945 the situation slightly improved. The regulation of supply brought about two separate markets with different prices. Goods supplied by state-controlled trading organisations for rationing and for farmers within the tie-in sale system had relatively low prices. Apart from that there was a free-trade market where prices were much higher. The shortage of goods and market dualism invited speculation which had adverse effects for consumers. Certain articles in common use (for example, matches) were sometimes in short supply and traders would often sell them at inflated prices.

Post-war home trade began to follow a different pattern as most firms had either suffered war damage or gone out of business altogether during the Second World War. The vacuum was filled by new tradesmen who were often accustomed both to illegal operations and speculation under the Nazi occupation. Established merchants faced previously unknown obstacles and the distrust of the authorities.

Besides private trade there were co-operatives but these, too, had been so badly hit that they were unable to start regular activity immediately after liberation, and had to set up in business gradually. Co-operative shops, however, played an important role in the distribution of rationed articles. State-controlled commerce was at first limited to wholesale institutions.

The Polish Committee of National Liberation declared in favour of free trade, though according to a long tradition of popular and workers' movements, it pointed out the development of co-operatives. In November 1944 an Economic Association of Polish Co-operatives (Społem) was created including consumer co-operatives. At the end of December 1944 a Peasant Mutual Aid Union was called into being to take up the initiative of creating local supply and marketing co-operatives in the country.

In spring 1945 Hilary Minc put forward a plan for the nationalisation of home trade. State-controlled central wholesale offices developed along with a newly established State Central Trade Organisation whose purpose was to purchase foodstuffs for the rationing system. The new enterprise was mainly concerned with wholesale trade but later on it began to open retail shops as well. In 1946 a few shops attached to industrial plants were also organised for promotional purposes. Nevertheless in 1946 private trade still took precedence over socialised trade. Out of 157,830 retail shops in Poland there were 141,530 private ones, 15,530 co-operatives and only 800 state-controlled shops. (35)

Speculation, lack of market supplies and differences between political parties concerning the property structure of the national economy and trade in particular - all led to the formulation of the PWP programme of the so-called 'battle for trade' in spring 1947. It was proclaimed that it aimed at precluding a take-over of a growing part of the national income by private merchants and at improving the turnover between country and towns. It may be presumed, though, that the government's intention was to gain control of an important sphere of economic activity on which the standard of living depended. The hampering of co-operatives dominated by the

Polish Socialist Party was another matter of concern for the PWP.

In the second half of 1947 restrictions on private trade began through new regulations concerning price fixing, profit control, taxation and the granting of concessions. In 1947-9 the number of private wholesale firms fell from 3,307 to 1,128, while the number of private retail shops dropped from 131,218 to 76,728. At the same time the number of socialised trade enterprises grew. In 1949 the state-controlled wholesale trade included 1,834 enterprises and 1,163 co-operatives, whereas the number of government shops grew to 4,131, the number of co-operative retail shops to 41,451. (36) Still more significant were changes in turnover. In 1948 the share of private wholesale was a mere 7 per cent of the total turnover and private shops accounted for 44 per cent of the total retail turnover in 1949. (37)

The reorganisation of commerce undermined private incomes and gradually led to the subordination of all trade under state control. It proved, however, that the restrictions mainly affected tradesmen who observed the law and who could therefore be more easily controlled while profiteers adapted to the new conditions and continued trading - despite penal sanctions.

In late 1947 the reorganisation of co-operatives began according to the PWP pattern. A Consumer Co-operative Centre Społem was set up to act in towns and an Agricultural Co-operative Centre Samopomoc Chłopska was established to carry on trade in the country. Within a short time urban consumer co-operatives transferred their food-processing factories and wholesale trade to the state-controlled organisations. Co-operatives were subordinated to the central economic plan and their independence limited. Joseph V. Yakowicz is therefore right when he says: 'Thus, by the end of 1948, the economic activities of the co-operatives, like those of the central administration boards for state industry, were under the direct guidance of the state planning apparatus.' (38)

FOREIGN ECONOMIC RELATIONS

In the second half of 1944 and at the beginning of 1945 Poland's foreign economic relations were practically limited to the Soviet Union due to the fact that there were no transport connections with other countries. The revival of Polish industry was made possible by deliveries of Soviet raw materials, while exports hardly existed at all. Relations with other countries did not begin to develop until the second half of 1945 when sea ports and railway connections were brought into operation again.

Foreign trade was from the beginning in the hands of state-controlled enterprises which usually took the form of limited liability companies.

Throughout this period trading with the Soviet Union played a major role in total turnover but when relations with other countries were gradually resumed, its share diminished. Trade exchange with the capitalist world rapidly grew.

Table 4.1: Foreign Trade of Poland, 1945-9 (million $US)

Countries	1945		1946		1947		1948		1949	
	Ex.	Imp.	Ex.	Imp.	Ex.	Imp	Ex.	Imp	Ex.	Imp
Socialist	36	31	76	114	109	111	235	245	281	269
of which: USSR	35	31	59	101	71	81	111	120	120	119
Capitalist	3	3	51	32	137	209	296	271	338	363
Total	38	34	127	146	246	320	531	516	619	632

Source: Rocznik Statystyczny Handlu Zagranicznego 1971, p. 2; Gospodarka Polski Ludowej 1944-1955, vol. 2 (Warsaw 1976), pp. 284, 317.

Apart from normal trade exchange in 1945-6 significant deliveries came to Poland from UNRRA. They were not included in the foreign trade statistics.

In the first post-war years the major Polish export article was coal which in 1949 already accounted for 48 per cent of total Polish exports. Foodstuffs took second place from 1948. The export of machinery was quite inconsiderable and imports were dominated by foodstuffs and raw materials. However, in 1947 the share of machinery imports increased - this being related to the reconstruction of industry and credits received from the USSR and the United States.

The development of Polish foreign trade largely depended on establishing an efficient transport network. As late as 1946 the export of coal, or even its delivery to distant parts of the country, was still checked by transport difficulties. In December 1945 Hilary Minc said:

> We can export any amount of coal obtaining in exchange the goods we badly need but provided that the country which needs our coal receives it with its own means of transportation. So far only two countries have accepted such terms: the Soviet Union and Sweden. (39)

Rapid development of Poland's foreign economic relations faced problems after 1947 when the international political situation deteriorated. On 12 March 1947 the President of the USA, Harry S. Truman, made his famous Congress speech in which he said:

> I believe that it must be the policy of the United States to support free peoples who are resisting attempted subjugation by armed minorities or by outside pressure... The world is not static, and the status quo is not sacred. But we cannot allow changes in the status quo in violation of the Charter of the United Nations by such methods as coercion, or by such subterfuges as political infiltration. (4)

A practical interpretation of the so-called 'Truman doctrine' was considered by some to mean giving economic aid to countries threatened with the overthrow of their capitalist systems. In the summer of 1947 the US Secretary of State George Marshall put forward a programme of economic aid for the reconstruction of post-Second World War Europe (1948-52). Despite general wording making no mention of current political conflicts, the hidden purpose of the plan was to restrain the growing influence of Communism in Europe. Poland considered the Marshall Plan along with other allied countries. There were opinions in favour of the offer but finally the arguments of economists and politicians prevailed; they feared Poland's economic and political dependence on an overseas partner. The final decision was made for general political reasons, as Poland's closest ally - the Soviet Union - negatively evaluated the Marshall Plan.

Such a decision considerably checked Polish economic relations with the West European countries. The purchase of investment goods in the United

States and from their allies was limited, and UNRRA deliveries suffered; in 1947 this organisation ceased to grant aid to Poland anyway.

Under these circumstances at the beginning of 1949 representatives of Bulgaria, Czechoslovakia, Poland, Romania, Hungary and the Soviet Union met in Moscow to create the Council for Mutual Economic Aid. According to the announced communiqué the Council's purpose was to exchange economic experience, technological aid, raw material supplies, foodstuffs, machinery, etc. The creation of the Marshall Plan and foundation of the Council for Mutual Economic Aid meant the formation of two separate economic and political blocks in Europe. Poland was becoming closely connected with the Soviet Union.

LIVING CONDITIONS

As a result of war and the Nazi occupation, living conditions for the Polish population after liberation were poor and sometimes even tragic. The devastation of cities and villages had made living conditions more than inhospitable. In most towns people lived in provisional quarters, ruins or even dug-outs. Those flats which remained were often overcrowded; the countryside lacked food and faced hunger. Food supply in towns was very poor. Large numbers of people who were not engaged in agriculture could not find work and regular pay.

Survival in the hardest months of late 1944 and 1945 was made easier by food supplies from the USSR and UNRRA. At the same time reconstruction was bringing direct results and production began again in the factories which had escaped serious damage. In the second half of 1945 the first peacetime crops radically improved the country's food supplies.

In the first weeks and months after liberation wages were mainly paid in kind. Thus factory workers who were producing articles in heavy demand (for example, yeast, alcohol, textiles etc.) were better off as they could exchange their allotments for food and even get extra profits. The situation gradually stabilised but the wage system remained quite complicated for a long time. One such complication concerned cash wages for the purchase of rationed goods at fixed prices which were lower than the free-market prices. Rationing included basic foodstuffs such as bread, sugar, flour, etc. In practice, however, shop supplies were irregular and long queues were seen at most shops. Employees also obtained various allotments in kind (foodstuffs, shoes, clothes, etc.) including articles which came to Poland as foreign aid. In the first half of 1946 it was estimated that pay in kind accounted for 40-50 per cent of the average wage and it is thus very difficult to compare changes in real wages. According to a rough estimate in 1945, the real wage outside agriculture amounted on average to about 40 per cent of the 1938 level, whereas in 1946 it reached 50 per cent of the 1938 level. (41)

Even such rough estimates cannot be made for changes in the incomes of the agricultural population. No doubt, land reform, the discharge of debts and increasing free-market prices for farming products considerably improved the financial standing of those living in rural areas. This particularly applied to farmers whose property had not been damaged and who were fortunate enough to own larger farms. Living conditions, however, of peasants deprived of houses or farm buildings and possessing tiny plots were very difficult.

A further, relatively rapid improvement in the living conditions of the Polish population took place in 1947-8. Increases in farming production and reconstruction of the countryside improved the standard of living of farmers, although the rate of this improvement slightly diminished. Even more significant was the development of the educational system; soon after the war was over literacy classes were introduced which were of particular benefit in some rural regions. The school system was developed while the government was particularly eager to facilitate access to education for the less socially mobile in the population. Country people in general and peasant youth in particular faced new prospects of social advancement, previously unknown in Poland.

Life in the country was also influenced by the reconstruction and development of industry. New chances of finding work outside agriculture appeared and this offered the means to end the traditional burden of agricultural over-population.

The wage system outside agriculture was gradually set in order. The policy of payment in kind was limited thanks to stabilisation of the market situation. In December 1948 it was estimated that various allotments accounted for about 10 per cent of the whole wage and that of the rationed supply for 8 per cent. At the beginning of 1949 allotments in kind were continued in only a few lines of the national economy - mining, power and transportation, for example. (42)

The wage system was repeatedly changed but

generally speaking wages rapidly grew. Rationing was abolished at the beginning of 1949. Since free-market prices were higher than those of rationed articles, employees received additional increments. These changes, however, make it extremely difficult to estimate trends for average real wages. Rough calculations show that in the first half of 1947 real wages slightly fell but afterwards they increased, though the rate of increase is estimated in various ways. It seems likely that in 1949 the average real wage amounted to 158 per cent of the 1946 level but was still lower than in 1938. (43) These figures, however, cover diverse changes for various groups of employees and workers. Salaries, for instance, were much lower than before 1939, whereas the wages of lowest paid labourers grew considerably.

At the same time noticeable changes in standards of living occurred in 1945-9 and these cannot be calculated into figures comparable to real wage fluctuations. Modification of the labour laws and social insurance brought several changes favourable to employees. Social insurance contributions were to be paid by employers in full. All charges for doctors' consultations, medication and medicines were lifted. Agricultural workers were included in the social insurance system. Laws were amended to settle the question of working hours, young workers were entitled to additional benefits (especially those facilitating their education) and women were given maternity benefits.

These changes were accompanied by developments in the health service and the creation of a holiday system enabling workers to spend their holidays in health resorts. In 1949 about 360,000 people enjoyed workers' holidays. (44) It is notable that the share of workers going on such holidays systematically increased, whereas before the Second World War such holidays had been the exception rather than the rule.

Housing conditions were also slowly improving. Since most of the population were very poor, it was decided to fix rents at a low level. There were places where housing conditions even exceeded pre-war standards, particularly in the regained territories which had been less extensively damaged. Elsewhere, however, the outlook was still bleak, especially in Warsaw. The most overcrowded cities included Łódź and Cracow, as their population had considerably increased, mainly due to an influx of refugees from Warsaw.

Although average standards in Poland seemed to

show an improvement as compared to the inter-war period, in practice the housing problem was very serious. It must be pointed out that most of the remaining housing resources were either of very low quality, overcrowded or partially damaged; most repairs being at first only provisional.

In 1946-9 resources were mainly allocated to repairs and rebuilding war-damaged property. New development projects began in 1947. According to the 1946 data there were 5.05 million flats including 11.5 million dwelling units (in towns there were 1.95 million flats and 4.5 million dwelling units). Reconstruction undertaken in 1945-9 provided about 635,000 flats (including 320,000 flats in towns) and 1.5 million dwelling units. (45) The rate of increase in housing resources was higher than that of the population which meant a steady improvement in housing conditions. Nevertheless, conditions were still very adverse, especially in some towns, as the urban population was constantly growing.

NOTES

1. Konstytucja i podstawowe akty ustawodawcze PRL. Zbiór tekstów (Wydawnictwo Prawnicze, Warsaw, 1952), p. 9.

2. Cf. E. Wiskemann, Germany's Eastern Neighbours. Problems Relating to the Oder-Neisse Line and the Czech Frontier Regions (Oxford University Press, London, 1956), p. 75.

3. A Decade of American Foreign Policy. Basic Documents, 1941-49 (US Government Printing Office, Washington, 1950), p. 43.

4. Calculated according to: Mały Rocznik Statystyczny 1937, p. 12; Rocznik Statystyczny 1947, p. 14.

5. Rocznik Statystyczny 1981, p. 1. These data refer to the latest survey; they slightly differ from the data quoted previously.

6. Data concerning migrations, based on various sources, have been gathered by J. Tomaszewski, 'Mniejszosci narodowe w Polsce po drugiej wojnie światowej', Mówią Wieki, 1983, no. 2.

7. Z. Landau, B. Skrzeszewska (eds.), 'Sprawozdania resortów Polskiego Komitetu Wyzwolenia Narodowego', Polska Ludowa, 1965, vol. 4, p. 144.

8. Konstytucja, p. 15.

9. E. Ochab, Wieś polska na nowych drogach (Książka i Wiedza, Łódź, 1946), p. 14.

10. Rolniczy Rocznik Statystyczny 1945-65, (Główny Urząd Statystyczny, Warsaw, 1966), pp. 115-17;

Rocznik Statystyczny 1949, p. 43. Data relating to effects of the land reform differ in various sources which probably results from the inaccuracy of post-war statistics.

11. H. Słabek, Polityka agrarna PPR. Geneza, realizacja, wyniki (Książka i Wiedza, Warsaw, 1978), p. 478.

12. N. Spulber, The Economics of Communist Eastern Europe, (The Technology Press of Massachusetts Institute of Technology, John Wiley & Sons, Inc., Chapman & Hall Ltd, New York/London, 1957), p. 234.

13. Rocznik Statystyczny 1948, pp. 44-6.

14. Rocznik Statystyczny 1949, p. 65.

15. W. Miś, Od wojny do pokoju. Gospodarka Polski w latach 1944-1946 (Wydawnictwo Ministerstwa Obrony Narodowej, Warsaw, 1978), pp. 184 and 186.

16. Rolniczy Rocznik Statystyczny 1945-65, p. 28.

17. R. Winiewska, Obciążenie podatkowe gospodarstw chłopskich w Polsce w latach 1944-1955 (Polskie Wydawnictwa Gospodarcze, Warsaw, 1961), p.9.

18. J. Kaliński, Plan odbudowy gospodarczej 1947-1949 (Książka i Wiedza, Warsaw, 1977), pp. 158-60.

19. Ibid., p. 163.

20. H. Minc, 'Wytyczne w sprawie naszego ustroju gospodarczego i społecznego. Referat wygłoszony na plenum KC PPR dnia 6 lipca 1948 r.', Nowe Drogi, 1948, no. 10.

21. R. Winiewska, Obciążenia, pp. 42-5, 57-60; J. Kaliński, Plan, p. 166.

22. According to: J.W. Gołębiowski, Walka PPR o nacjonalizację przemysłu, (Książka i Wiedza, Warsaw, 1961), p. 116.

23. E. Basiński, T. Walichnowski (eds.), Stosunki polsko-radzieckie w latach 1945-1972. Dokumenty i materiały (Książka i Wiedza, Warsaw, 1974), p. 40. In March 1947 this amount was reduced to 6.5 million tonnes per annum.

24. Rocznik Statystyczny 1947, pp. 2-3.

25. Konstytucja, p. 21-6.

26. Their specification according to the early 1974 status: cf.: W. Dudek, Międzynarodowe aspekty nacjonalizacji w Polsce (Państwowe Wydawnictwo Naukowe, Warsaw, 1976), pp. 75-9, 138.

27. According to information by deputy Minister of Finance Julian Kole in Polityka, 1964, no. 13.

28. N. Spulber, Economics, p. 63.

29. Plan Odbudowy Gospodarczej (Centralny Urząd Planowania, Warsaw, 1946), p. 49.

30. Dziennik Ustaw i Rozporządzeń RP, 1947, no.

53, item 285.

31. Rocznik Statystyczny 1970, p. 38.
32. Rocznik Statystyczny Przemysłu 1945-1965, p. 130.
33. Rocznik Statystyczny 1950, p. 30.
34. Z. Landau, 'Pożyczki wewnętrzne w Polsce w świetle sytuacji skarbowej państwa' in J. Kaliński and Z. Landau (eds.), Gospodarka Polski Ludowej 1944-1955 (Książka i Wiedza, Warsaw, 1976), vol. 2, p. 230.
35. J. Kaliński, Bitwa o handel 1947-1948 (Książka i Wiedza, Warsaw, 1970), p. 53.
36. Rocznik Statystyczny 1950, p. 69.
37. J. Kaliński, Plan, p. 214.
38. J.V. Yakowicz, Poland's Post-war Recovery. Economic Reconstruction, Nationalization and Agrarian Reform in Poland after World War II (Exposition Press, New York, 1979), p. 30.
39. H. Minc, Aktualne zagadnienia i perspektywy gospodarcze demokratycznej Polski (Książka i Wiedza, Łódź, 1945), p. 23.
40. Decade, p. 1256.
41. S. Jankowski, 'Warunki bytu ludności' in J. Kaliński and Z. Landau, Gospodarka, vol. 2, pp. 64-5.
42. J. Kaliński, Plan, pp. 261-2.
43. Ibid., p. 276.
44. Ibid., p. 284.
45. A. Andrzejewski, Sytuacja mieszkaniowa w Polsce w latach 1918-1974 (Państwowe Wydawnictwo Ekonomiczne, Warsaw, 1977), pp. 140.

ACCELERATED INDUSTRIALISATION, 1950-6

POPULATION

At the end of 1950 the population of Poland amounted to 25,035,000 people and by the end of 1956 it had reached 28,080,000 people. (1) The natural increase in population amounted to 3,040,000 people and remained relatively high which seems typical for the post-war period. External migrations were quite insignificant. Their total balance for 1951-5 brought an increment of 5,000 persons. It was not until 1956 that the number of immigrants grew to 33,200 while the number of those who left Poland reached 33,000 people. But in the total balance it was of minor importance. (2)

On the other hand internal migrations remained very high. In 1946-50 about 1,186,000 persons moved from the country to towns while in 1951-5 this kind of migration included 630,000 people. It must be pointed out that these data seem only approximate in view of the inaccuracy of current evidence.

Large migrations from the country to towns in the post-war period were mainly due to effects of war. Wartime losses in the urban population had to be supplemented and the regained territories could only be populated in this way. In the following years the main reasons for mass migrations were rooted in the industrialisation process which absorbed the growing number of urban workers. On the grounds of a detailed study Michał Pohoski found that: 'Migrations to towns in the years 1946-50 were mainly connected with the extraordinary post-war situation but later on industrialisation became the major factor determining the range of migration movements.'(3)

Questionnaire surveys show that in most cases migration to towns included young people from smallholders' families. The traditional over-population of the Polish countryside diminished and the phenomenon of the so-called 'superfluous' people whose manpower remained idle was almost entirely eliminated. Notwithstanding, in some regions there remained agricultural manpower reserves which were not fully utilised in autumn and wintertime.

Socio-economic changes were closely related to the changing educational system. The country's economic development required more and more qualified workers in all lines of production, particularly since the number of professionally qualified and skilled workers had decreased as a result of the war.

A rapid development of trade and higher schools was typical for this period. The number of students increased from 86,500 in 1946/7 to 157,500 in 1955/6, whereas the number of trade school pupils jumped from 263,700 to 440,100 students. At the same time the number of pupils in secondary grammar schools fell from 228,400 to 201,400 over the same period. (4) Moreover, the system of adult education was extended. On the other hand, the primary education system was relatively stable.

For the national economy the development of education meant an increase in the number of qualified employees. In the first post-war years and in the early 1950s increasing employment was available for thousands of unskilled workers mostly coming from the countryside. But in the course of time more and more young people who completed their education in trade or higher schools were entering the labour market. At first economic development was hampered by the lack of qualified staff but in the mid-1950s this problem slowly disappeared. In the course of the three-year plan the government had to take into account the shortage of qualified staff capable of making economic decisions. This is why most qualified managers were concentrated at mid-management level. Thus the centralisation of planning and management, begun in 1948-9 was to a certain extent a temporary necessity. In the mid-1950s the situation in this respect improved and although some regions still felt the shortage of qualified staff some attempts were made to modify the excessively centralised economic apparatus.

INDUSTRY

A new economic plan for 1950-5 was considered at the unification congress of the Polish workers' movement in December 1948. The congress resolution said the plan would lead to the construction of economic foundations for socialism in Poland. The economic results of 1949 proved better than expected. As a result the authorities adopted an optimistic attitude and raised the primary targets of the Six-Year Plan. This modification was also due to the changing international atmosphere. As a result of growing tension between the capitalist world and the Council for Mutual Economic Aid (CMEA) countries investment imports from the United States and West Europe faced increasing difficulties. Economic plans had to take this into account but there was no doubt that the development of national industries was becoming an urgent priority. Although Poland imported some machinery and equipment from the socialist countries, these imports could not satisfy growing demand, especially since other socialist countries were in the process of developing their own industries. All this obliged the Polish government to develop heavy industry in order to extend the foundations of the whole economy. At the same time rapid progress in agriculture seemed of major importance as food supplies remained unsatisfactory. Presenting the modified draft of the Six-Year Plan Hilary Minc told the plenum of the Central Committee of the Polish United Workers' Party on 15 July 1950:

> The present draft of the Six-Year Plan foresees a much higher rate of development and a higher progress in production than was stipulated in the congress instructions. The congress resolution forecast an increase in production of our socialist industry by 85-95 per cent as compared with the 1949 level. The present draft stipulates an increase in socialist industrial production by 158.3 per cent. The congress resolution expected the six years' increment of agricultural production to amount to 35-45 per cent... in relation to the 1949 crops. The present draft forecasts agricultural production to grow by 50 per cent as compared with the actual 1949 production though it proved much higher than had been expected. (5)

On 21 July 1950 the Seym passed the Six-Year Plan Act which put forward the construction of socialist foundations in Poland by 1955 as the major general target. According to the act this meant:

> 1. A considerable development of productive resources with special regard to production of means of production.
> 2. Restraint and restrictions of capitalist elements in those branches of the national economy where they still appear as well as their gradual removal and subsequent liquidation as a social class.
> 3. Voluntary transformation of a significant part of small- and medium-size farms into collective farms - socialist co-operatives - in order to cut off sources of capitalism.
> 4. Deepening and closening of mutual economic relations and aid based on the principle of socialist solidarity and aimed at the widest

possible development of the productive resources within the economic plans of Poland, the USSR and the countries of people's democracy.

5. A considerable increase in the material prosperity, improvement in living conditions, culture and activity of the working people. (6)

In order to accomplish these targets the act required nationalised industries to increase production by 158 per cent. Particularly rapid growth was to be achieved in the metallurgy, metal-processing and chemical industries. The increase in production of means of production was planned at 154 per cent (large and medium-size industrial plants), while production of 'means of consumption' was to grow by 111 per cent. At the same time the output of small nationalised enterprises was to increase by 384 per cent. This required an acceleration of investment. Most investment inputs were designed for industry (along with building it was to receive 46 per cent of the total value of investments, while farming and forestry were to receive a mere 12 per cent); 76 per cent of industrial investments were designed for industries producing means of production.

The expected growth in industrial production was to be reached by increasing employment by 60 per cent and through a 66 per cent rise in labour productivity.

Therefore the initial project was extended, this being brought about by the raising of investment targets. Relatively low inputs in agriculture and consumer industries made prospects for an improvement in living standards quite doubtful. It may be assumed that the final stipulations were the result of an overestimation of Poland's economic reserves and of the international situation. The plan assignments were modified in the early stages of the cold war when NATO was established. The Polish government was also anxious about the creation of the Federal Republic of Germany whose leading politicians questioned the Potsdam stipulations concerning the Polish western frontier. Thus investment programmes had to include the development of military industry as stated by Hilary Minc at the July 1950 plenum of the Central Committee of the PUWP.

The Six-Year Plan involved the formation of a centralised management system based on directives from the ruling centre of decision. The Six-Year Plan Act served as the foundation for subsequent annual plans - which usually raised the average plan targets - while current problems were solved by means of ministerial orders and instructions from the central economic organisations. Within this system there was hardly any room for independent enterprises. Its task consisted solely of seeking ways to exceed centrally fixed targets. In the early 1950s the advantages of this system outweighed its shortcomings. Given limited material resources, a relative abundance of manpower and a shortage of qualified economists, the system of central planning and management made accelerated economic growth a distinct possibility. The international situation also seemed to justify this kind of system.

Within the first year of the plan investments grew by as much as 38 per cent as compared with 1949. The investment programme began with basic lines of production - metallurgy, semi-manufactures, etc. Industrial production grew by 28 per cent, that is more than was expected. The production of consumer goods increased at the same rate due to previous reconstruction and development trends.

However the Six-Year Plan assignments were soon changed again. International tension reached a new height when the Korean war broke out in 1950. The growing danger of war led to a reconsideration of investment policy and to further acceleration in the development of military industries. The resolution of the CC PUWP plenum held in July 1956 described these changes as follows:

> Already in 1951, in view of a dramatic worsening of the international situation, the necessity had arisen to build a large defensive industry as quickly as possible and to raise the current expenditure for the national defence. In this connection the primary Six-Year Plan assignments were actually changed. (7)

In 1952 the cost of military production was still growing but other targets were not revised. Consequently more and more serious imbalances began to be seen in the national economy.

The initial version of the plan was too optimistic based as it was on high expectations and prospects for the Polish economy. This mainly referred to the coal output which was the basis of power production and the major Polish export commodity. Investments in lines which neither supplied consumer goods nor extended heavy industry would, inevitably brought about the limitation of total consumption. The demand for various investment goods constantly increased but their production was growing relatively slowly. This led to difficulties which could only be resolved by extraordinary methods. In mining, for instance, work continued throughout the week - including Sundays. Overtime work was extended. In 1955 an average worker worked 138 overtime hours per annum. (8)

Changing economic policy led to a rapid increase in investment expenditure which exceeded budget limits. In 1953 investments at fixed prices were more than twice higher than in 1949 and heavy industry was still given preferential treatment and received huge inputs. Total industrial investments were ten times higher than before the Second World War and accounted for a much higher share of the national income than in most capitalist countries. As a result production grew but the rate of growth was different in various lines of industry. New lines of production were started: shipbuilding, motor cars, aircraft - and plastics industries which hardly existed in inter-war Poland. One of the largest plants built in this time was the steel mill Huta Im. Lenina near Cracow. An entirely new town, Nowa Huta, was constructed around this large plant. A number of other large factories were to be started at the end of the Six-Year Plan. These included among others a high quality steel mill in Warsaw, cotton industry in Fasty near Białystock and so forth. Data concerning industrial investment and production between 1949 and 1956 are presented in Table 4.2.

The great aims of the Six-Year Plan aroused the enthusiasm of younger generations. Participation in the plan was treated as something of an honour and a contribution to the future of the nation. Extensive investment undertakings, for which there was neither adequate equipment nor qualified staff, required the mobilisation of a large number of unskilled workers. Many of these were provided by a special organisation, <u>Służba Polsce,</u> in which young people could also learn a profession. One of the SP members remembered:

> As a member of the SP brigades I was going to Silesia to set my hand to reconstruction of my country. Cattle-trucks on which we were embarked... reminded me of some heroic fragments of wartime movies. But I must point out that I really wanted to take part in this action. Służba Polsce... was a road to a new world for me and

Table 4.2: Major Data Concerning Polish Industry, 1949-56

	1949	1950	1951	1952	1953	1954	1955	1956
National income	100.0	115.1	123.7	131.4	145.1	160.4	173.5	188.2
Percentage of accumulation	15.6	20.7	20.3	22.8	27.9	23.2	22.2	20.2
Industrial investments	100.0	164.5	214.3	282.0	325.3	333.9	312.8	330.5
Industrial output	100.0	127.7	156.0	185.4	217.8	242.6	270.3	294.6
Means of production	100.0	128.5	160.5	197.0	234.5	266.3	295.9	327.3
Means of consumption	100.0	127.0	151.3	173.4	200.0	217.9	243.6	261.1
Employment	100.0	116.8	126.6	132.8	141.2	147.4	154.0	160.4

Source: Rocznik Statystyczny 1957 (Główny Urząd Statystyczny, Warsaw, 1957), p. XXIX; Rocznik Statystyczny Przemysłu 1945-1965 (Główny Urząd Statystyczny, Warsaw, 1965), pp. 130-2, 134, 284-5, 633.

for many country girls and boys. (9)

Many industrial plants which employed large numbers of unskilled youths also organised trade schools to train qualified workers for the future.

'Work competition' also played a certain role in stimulating production and overcoming difficulties inherent in the investment process. The CC PUWP resolutions recommended that work competition should be adopted by all factories. Before very long competition results became an important means of evaluating the standard of administration, trade unions and party activities,etc. This led to a distortion of the movement which started as a workers' initiative. Factories presented overestimated lists of competitors to become worthy of praise. In fact the work competition movement was frequently decreed by administrative measures. There were even cases when competitors did not know anything at all about obligations adopted in their names.

The changing assignments of the Six-Year Plan and the concentration of effort in selected lines of production resulted in unequal development in various fields. Processing industry grew much more rapidly than mining. Between 1950 and 1956 coal production increased by 34.0 per cent, whereas power generation (mainly based on coal) rose by 97.3 per cent. At the same time engineering output jumped by 390.8 per cent and a similar increase was recorded in other heavy industries. However, it must be remembered that their starting levels were rather low. Food-processing production increased by 55.9 per cent and textiles by 90.6 per cent. (10)

The growth of production was mainly due to investment and better employment prospects, and only slightly to the modernisation of existing factories. In some lines (for example, power plants, cement mills or sawmills) productivity rapidly grew but in coal mining it fell; this was probably connected with the low qualifications of newly employed workers (prisoners included) and with the exploitation of less favourable seams. There were cases when labour productivity in new factories was lower than that of the old ones. This was often due to faulty organisation and lack of plant maintenance. Having thoroughly considered the results of the Six-Year Plan Andrzej Karpiński found that:

> The major reason for that (inadequate success - ZL and JT) was an undoubtedly defective system of central management and an inefficient system

> of wages which created no incentives for the introduction of technological experiments and progress. Isolation of technical thought from world achievements and faulty treatment of engineers and technicians were also conducive to such a situation. (11)

At first it was planned that the newly-built industrial plants would be equally distributed. In other words, new factories were to be built mainly in regions with surplus manpower and no industry. This kind of policy, however, was more expensive than constructing new factories in traditional industrial centres since it required large inputs in infrastructure. As a result plans for many factories intended for non-industrialised regions were abandoned. This led to an increased concentration of pollution while the shortage of means meant that plans for the construction of waste treatment plants were also given up. The cost of rapid economic development was growing pollution of the natural environment. The actual location policy also caused an increased migration of workers to the traditional industrial regions which placed extra demands on housing requirements.

All these factors led to new economic and social problems. At the end of 1953 these had grown so serious that they blocked further economic development. It became inevitable that further changes in economic policy would be introduced. The international political atmosphere was becoming more favourable. In July 1953 an armistice was signed in Korea which considerably eased global tensions. Growing discontent within society had also to be taken into account. There were riots in Plzeň in Czechoslovakia in May 1953, the result of monetary reform and lifting of the rationed supply system. Similar demonstrations but on a larger scale broke out in the German Democratic Republic soon after. It seemed that a modification of economic policy was now more likely as a result of political changes in the USSR following the death of Joseph Stalin in March 1953.

In October 1953 Bolesław Bierut told the plenum of the CC PUWP:

> In order to accelerate the improvement of the living standard of the working people it is necessary to adequately shift investments to agriculture, to raise the farming output, to stimulate production of consumer goods, housing

and culture as well as development of the social infrastructure. (12)

Decisions made there led to cut-backs in the level of industrial investment. From the point of view of national income distribution and the direct objectives of economic policy this manoeuvre was very important. Janusz Beksiak thought it was a new programme 'aimed at increasing production and mainly at raising consumer goods' output'. (13) The changes were, however, not accompanied by any reform of the planning and management system and mainly concerned the restitution of targets foreseen in the Six-Year Plan. Thus it can hardly be treated as an essential change to the programme adopted in 1950.

Reducing investments meant much postponement and delay in starting the production in new factories. As some of them were connected with other enterprises supplying them with raw materials or semi-manufactures this produced a reduction in the possible results of the whole investment effort in previous years. The manoeuvre was also connected with personal changes. Though he remained vice-premier, Hilary Minc was replaced by Eugeniusz Szyr in the State Commission for Economic Planning in March 1954.

The draft Five-Year Plan for the years 1956-60 prepared in 1955 was a continuation of the policy adopted in 1954 and 1955. At the same time, however, the changes in the international communist movement influenced the state of affairs in Poland. The growing criticism, often underestimating previous developments, among workers and intellectuals induced the necessity of further, far-reaching reforms. Excessive centralisation of economic decisions made it impossible to adjust production to current requirements. Social unrest grew due to some phenomena contrary to the socialist principles. Strikes and demonstrations of Poznań workers in June 1956 led to scuffles, and the deaths of many people were a warning to the government that such a policy could not continue. The turning point came in October 1956 when a plenum of the CC PUWP criticised its former policies and realistically appraised the situation.

Further change was inevitable. In March 1956 Bolesław Bierut died. In July the former head of the Polish economy, Hilary Minc, resigned and the State Commission for Economic Planning was taken over by Stefan Jędrychowski. A far-reaching reorganisation of the planning and management system was expected. In October 1956 the office of the party's first secretary was given to Władysław Gomułka on whom Polish society laid high hopes.

AGRICULTURE

Relatively good harvests in 1949 encouraged the authors of the 1950 version of the Six-Year Plan to set very high targets for agriculture. It was expected that Polish farming, having real development possibilities, would produce increasingly high returns despite reduced investment. It was also thought that a gradual collectivisation and application of machinery would suffice to raise production. The development of large collective farms was also expected to make it possible for the manpower to migrate to industry.

The contemporary agitation for co-operatives stressed the fact that large farms would invest more economically as in relation to smallholdings they required fewer building materials. It was also expected that large co-operative farms would provide for a more rational utilisation of machinery and land, as well as for the introduction of modern cultivation and zootechnical methods. These arguments were acceptable but they neglected the fact that Polish agriculture already had an adequate network of farm buildings for the existing structure of ownership and that the creation of co-operatives would require a lot of new machinery. In other words, collectivisation required large investments in farming. But supplies of goods required in agriculture were quite insufficient. The production of tractors was started as late as 1947; in 1948 farmers were supplied with only 1,201 tractors. More complicated machines were even scarcer. In fact the transformation of agriculture could not be achieved without a similar development in industry.

The above-mentioned changes in economic policy made in 1951-2 badly affected agriculture. As the main effort was concentrated in industry, investments in other branches were limited. There were not enough building materials for rural areas and other goods were also in short supply. It was believed that farmers would be able to solve their own problems and, despite all, raise production. These hopes were based on the fact that before 1939 the peasant economy over a large part of Polish territory had an almost subsistence nature - peasants saved cash and tried to manufacture as many necessary items as possible at home, even tools.

In 1951-3 total investment in farming diminished by about 24 per cent as compared with the 1947-50 level; investments in private peasant farms fell more than three times. The 1951 cement supplies to farming were almost three times lower than in 1949. (14) Tractor and fertiliser supplies grew but they were unable to meet the demand.

To make things worse in 1951-2 unfavourable weather conditions affected harvests and as a result farming production temporarily levelled off. General trends in Polish agriculture in 1950-6 are shown in Table 4.3.

The unfavourable situation in agriculture in the first stage of the Six-Year Plan negatively influenced the market and food supplies to towns in particular. This was reflected in an increase in free-market prices for farm products. Since there were not enough investment goods for the countryside, the increasing prices and incomes of the rural population were accompanied by growing consumption of food by farmers, additionally limiting the supplies to towns. All this made the reality of economic plans quite doubtful and the government decided to change the purchase system for agricultural products. In 1950 the so-called planned purchase of grain was introduced; this required peasants to supply definite quantities of grain according to the government plan. Farmers who did not fulfil this duty had their land taxes raised and had to pay for them in kind. Nevertheless this step proved rather ineffective and in 1951 obligatory deliveries of grain were reintroduced. In 1952 they accounted for more than 90 per cent of grain sold by farmers. Afterwards this proportion diminished. (15) In the following years the obligatory delivery system included other commodities such as animals for slaughter, milk or potatoes. The purchasing organisations bought these articles at fixed prices which more and more departed from free-market prices. On the other hand this system made it possible to maintain retail prices of foodstuffs at an unchanged level. At the same time the decrease in market production was lower than that of the total agricultural output.

All estimates of the real value of the burden placed on peasant farms by obligatory deliveries and taxes raise doubts connected with the question as to

Table 4.3: Major Data Concerning Development of Polish Agriculture, 1950-6

	1950	1951	1952	1953	1954	1955	1956
Rural population (millions)	15.7	15.3	15.4	15.6	15.7	15.4	15.4
Gross agricultural production (1950-2 = 100)	104.6	96.8	98.6	101.3	107.2	109.9	118.0
Market agricultural production (1950-2 = 100)	101.5	100.1	98.5	104.4	107.7	117.7	122.3
Area under crops (million ha)	15.0	15.1	15.1	15.1	15.2	15.4	15.4
of which: socialised farming (%)	10.3	14.8	16.1	19.8	21.5	23.1	23.9
Wheat yields in q per ha	12.8	12.2	13.5	12.5	12.8	14.9	14.5
Potato yields in q per ha	138	102	106	124	135	100	140
Cattle (millions)	7.2	7.2	7.3	7.4	7.7	7.9	8.4
Pigs (millions)	9.4	8.5	8.6	9.7	9.8	10.9	11.6
Tractors (thousands)	28.4	31.9	38.0	41.0	43.9	48.3	51.8
Fertiliser use in kg per ha of arable land	17.7	18.2	21.0	21.0	23.3	26.7	28.8

Source: Rocznik Statystyczny 1977 (Główny Urząd Statystyczny, Warsaw 1977), pp XXX, XXXVIII.

what prices should be adopted in order to calculate total peasant production value. Bearing this in mind an estimate can be quoted showing that in 1949 the total tax burden of peasant farms in favour of the government accounted for 9 per cent of their net income, in 1950 for about 11 per cent and in 1952 for about 23 per cent. The rate of increase is worth attention. In 1952/3 smallholdings paid about 10 per cent - larger farms about 38 per cent - of their net income. (16) The growing fiscal burden of the countryside seemed inevitable in view of such ambitious plans to accelerate the development of the whole economy, the different rates being aimed at a gradual elimination of capitalist elements. Nevertheless the effects could be felt even by peasants who did not employ hired workers. Theoretically, the employment of hired manpower was treated as a criterion distinguishing capitalist and non-capitalist farms but in practice all better-off peasants were suspiciously watched by local authorities which saw symptoms of 'capitalism' even in the mere existence of solid farm buildings standing out from the poor countryside of the central and eastern provinces.

The planned development of co-operative farms was soon accelerated. In May 1949 the Organisation Bureau of the CC PUWP warned against 'a harmful pressure, superficiality and hurry resulting from a desire to obtain quantitative effects in the organisation of co-operatives'. (17) Notwithstanding this statement quantitative plans were soon elaborated for co-operatives. In order to keep to their appointed dates local administration and party committees exercised economic and administrative pressure on farmers and put forward various bogus promises. Local organisations of the United Peasant Party were ignored. Though its leadership declared in favour of collectivisation, masses of ordinary UPP members usually remained doubtful.

Strict instructions issued by district party secretaries to organise productive co-operatives in the country were executed by devoted young activists who tried to persuade farmers of the superiority of socialist farming. Sometimes this led to scenes like this one described by an activist remembering the autumn of 1950:

> To the surprise and horror of our hosts we made them almost prisoners in their own home. When the night came the worst thing in my life started. My companion proved to be a master in keeping the hosts awake. Unmilked cows mooing

> for mercy, hungry pigs squeaking and horses neighing were accompanied by his monotonous voice repeating over and over again until madness 'You won't go to bed... You'll sign the declaration and we shall leave you alone.' (18)

Abuses of power were not stopped by the CC PUWP declarations of 1949 and 1950. As long as party organisations were judged by increases in the number of co-operatives the situation lent itself to the use of formally condemned methods. The Gryfice events made themselves especially well known - there were illegal searches and the peasant property was destroyed by brigades purchasing farm products. Those responsible for these actions were severely punished. But it was soon disclosed that the authorities in another district had violated the law while establishing co-operatives. In September 1951 the CC PUWP passed a resolution saying:

> The leadership and the apparatus of the District Committee... have frequently broken the voluntary character of the organisation of co-operative farms, widely using illegal surtaxes, groundless administrative penalties or even unlawful detention by the Security [Urząd Bezpieczeństwa] and Civic Militia [Milicja Obywatelska] organs. (19)

People responsible for the abuse of power in this case were also punished but the need for rapid development of co-operatives was still stressed. Pressure on farmers still continued though it hardly ever took such drastic form as in the Gryfice affair.

Such policies led to a lack of investment by peasant farmers. Unwilling to join co-operatives, farmers usually avoided any extra expenses. Overloaded with taxes and obligatory deliveries some farms collapsed and their owners left for the towns.

Polish agricultural policy was based on the Soviet patterns of the 1930s. Collectivisation of Soviet farming was accelerated in view of growing international tension and the need to ensure fulfilment of the first five-year plan. The same pattern was applied to Poland without regard to her different historical and economic heritage. Cold war tension and acceleration of industrial development seemed similar in both cases. But in the USSR it was possible to raise production by extending the area under crops, while in Poland such a possibility was out of the question. The only solution for

Polish farming was to intensify production through investments, but there were too little means for that within the framework of the Six-Year Plan.

In order to stimulate the development of co-operatives and to raise farming output 'State Centres of Agricultural Machines' were created according to the Soviet pattern. They were aimed at lending tractors and other farm machinery to farmers. Co-operatives were granted credits, tax reductions and other kinds of aid. Some land owned by the government was given to co-operatives. If they lacked manpower the work was done by workers' and youth brigades.

Farming co-operatives developed quite rapidly. The number of co-operatives grew from 2,199 at the end of 1950 to 10,510 at the end of September 1956. In mid-1956 co-operatives covered an area of 1,963,000 ha while the area of individual farms amounted to 15,630,000 ha. In the Koszalin, Szczecin and Wrocław provinces most land was in the hands of co-operatives, while the role of co-operatives in the Warsaw, Kielce, Lublin, Cracow, Katowice and Białystok provinces was only marginal.

The difference in production levels in farming was a grave problem. In 1950-5 co-operatives usually achieved relatively high grain yields (average wheat, rye, barley and oat yields of 13.6 q per ha as compared with 12.4 q in state-owned farms and with 12.6 q per ha in private farms). On the other hand individual holdings were much more efficient in potato and sugar beet crops and husbandry. (20) Apart from a few well managed, properly equipped and efficient co-operative farms, many co-operatives lagged far behind the average level of Polish farming. As they did not possess adequate machinery, most of the work was done manually as it was on individual farms. Too few farm-hands could not secure good results, especially when farmers forced to join co-operatives were unwilling to work efficiently.

The economic manoeuvre begun in 1954 included, though inconsistently, the problems of agriculture. In his report for the party's Second Congress Bolesław Bierut said in March 1954:

> More than 3,000 co-operatives were created in 1953. Previous experience leads to an assumption that the same rate of development of co-operatives will be continued in the two forthcoming years... Particular attention ought to be paid to a more even development of co-operatives and to their wider spread in the cen-

tral and eastern provinces.

This meant a continuation of the former policy. But then Bierut went on to say:

> Industrial achievements have made it possible to extend the aid for farming including individual holdings which produce the major part of farm products necessary for the country... Now we can give small and medium-size farm holders growing aid in equipment, machinery, fertilisers, seeds, pedigree animals, building materials and more professional advice from agronomists, zootechnicians and the veterinary service, as well as spreading agricultural knowledge. (21)

This seemed an announcement of a change of policy towards individual farmers though collectivisation still remained the basic long-term objective of the government.

In 1954 investments in farming began to grow. The compulsory delivery quotas were stabilised which encouraged individual farmers to produce more. Thanks to changing government policy and to more favourable climatic conditions the total farming production of 1955 exceeded the 1950 level. Nevertheless this was much less than the plan targets. The forced collectivisation of agriculture proved a failure. The methods applied not only failed to transform social relations in the Polish countryside but also discouraged farmers to work for the collective economy; hence production temporarily declined.

Under these circumstances discussions concerning the state and prospects of the Polish economy which started in 1956 were to a large extent concentrated on policy towards farming. Undoubtedly previous principles had to be given up. In the autumn of 1956 the CC PUWP stated:

> While continuing efforts to strengthen co-operatives it is necessary to agree with the possible dissolution of co-operatives which do not have prospects of development and bring shame upon the idea of agricultural co-operation. All attempts to support them by means of government subsidies must be considered harmful. (22)

This was a break with previous policy and a return to concepts realised before 1948. At the same time the CC PUWP resolved to decrease obligatory deliveries and improve supplies to the rural markets. An eminent farmer from Greater Poland remembered:

> The world of farmers was especially sensitive to the new lines of agricultural policy related to the countryside and the ownership system... The official announcements seemed to show clearly that the attitude towards bigger farms would be changed... and that a green light was switched on for farming. (23)

The changing agricultural policy did not mean a freedom to restore capitalist farms. The economic changes which had taken place in the whole country made hired manpower become less and less profitable for well-off peasants. Good prospects of getting a job outside agriculture limited the hidden overpopulation of the countryside which had been a cheap manpower reservoir since before the Second World War.

FINANCE

The accelerated industrialisation of Poland created difficult tasks for the financial system. Above all the issue of banknotes had to be set in order. As already mentioned, the preceding years brought an increase in money supply, which was connected with budget deficits. Restoration of the budget balance in the course of the Three-Year Plan only partially decreased the excess of money. The investment effort had to bring about another increase in wages without a similar increase in market supply. Inflation was becoming a real threat and the government decided to carry out monetary reform which had been planned as a top secret operation.

On 28 October 1950 a closed sitting of the Seym (closed in a literal sense - the MPs were not allowed to leave the conference room to declare the news) passed the monetary reform regulations. The ratio of the new złoty to the old one was fixed at 3:100 but cash was to be exchanged at the rate of 1:100. Saving deposits were exchanged at the rate of 3:100 to the amount of 100,000 złotys. (24) This method of exchange was explained by the desired objective - to deprive speculators of two-thirds of their currency resources. In practice this kind of effect was limited as illegal dealers kept most of their capital in gold or foreign exchange. This is why about 40 per cent of banknotes were submitted for exchange by representatives of small producers or capitalist enterprises, whereas the rest belonged to hired workers. From the government's point of view the reform diminished circulation and savings by almost 3 milliard new złotys, that is by about $US750 million in gold. The exchange reform, therefore, had important economic consequences.

The temporary effects of the reform were serious as note circulation diminished from 6.0 milliard zł at the end of September 1950 to 4.6 milliard zł at the end of December 1950. Soon, however, circulation grew again, reaching 6.2 milliard zł at the end of 1952, 11.6 milliard zł in 1955 and 17.4 milliard zł in 1956. Apart from this, saving deposits constantly grew, reaching 3.6 milliard zł at the end of 1956. (25)

Increasing production and investment by state-owned enterprises were accompanied by a growth of budget revenues and expenses. Total revenues increased from 47.4 milliard zł to 135.7 milliard zł between 1950 and 1956. Expenditure was lower and the budget was balanced. (26) Budgetary receipts were based on payments from the state-owned enterprises (64.0 per cent of revenues in 1950 and 75.0 per cent in 1956), the role of receipts from the private sector diminishing. Most government expenses were investments for economic development. Expenditure for health protection, physical culture and social benefits grew in absolute terms though their share in the budget expenses decreased (7.5 per cent in 1951; 7.0 per cent in 1956). The same applied to military expenditure (7.4 per cent in 1951; 10.2 per cent in 1955; 9.5 per cent in 1956). In view of the fact that the major industrial means of production were state-owned and that the planning and management system was largely centralised, the budget became the main link in the country's financial chain and showed the basic trends of economic development.

The credit system established earlier was only slightly modified. The scope of the Narodowy Bank Polski was extended when it took over the granting of credits for agricultural enterprises from the Bank Rolny in 1953. The Bank Rolny was left to finance farming investments. Thus, the Narodowy Bank Polski had become a financial centre for the countryside Communal Co-operative Banks as well.

The government's credit action was mainly directed towards the socialised sector. In 1950 it received 91 per cent of the total value of credits (of which 7 per cent went to farming and forestry). In 1952 this proportion grew to 94 per cent but the credits included for farming and forestry fell to 5 per cent. Afterwards these shares only slightly changed reaching 88 per cent and 11 per cent respectively in 1955. On the other hand private farming received only 1.9 per cent of credits in 1950 while in 1952-5 its share oscillated between 0.9 per cent and 1.0 per cent. (27)

DOMESTIC TRADE

Within a short time revolutionary changes in the ownership and organisation system called the 'battle for trade' resulted in the almost entire disappearance of traditional and well-organised private trade. Small stands, booths or petty shops were the only exception.

The number of state-controlled retail trading posts increased from 57,881 in 1950 (including 56,654 shops while the rest were small stands, booths and the like) to 123,081 in 1956 (including 92,352 shops). The number of private trading posts fell from 43,388 in 1950 to 14,059 in 1955 to grow again to 15,150 (including 7,576 shops) in 1956.(28)

By the end of the Six-Year Plan only a small part of the retail turnover (about 3 per cent) was in private hands. Large co-operative and state-owned trade enterprises monopolised trade in industrial goods. State-owned shops became bigger and better equipped, especially in towns. The first department stores were opened.

Private trade was usually limited to foodstuffs. Under the growing tax burden aimed at the elimination of private dealers, small and primitively equipped stands and booths proved the most resistant as their owners avoided the expense of investment to prevent losses in the event of liquidation. At the same time various forms of illegal trade were continued, thus exploiting the short supply of the market. The range of illegal dealing can hardly be estimated since it largely depended on various random and variable circumstances.

The deteriorating market supply compelled the government to introduce meat rationing in the middle of 1951. Prices of articles included in the coupon system were lower than their free-market prices which were constantly growing.

On 3 January 1953 the coupon system was abolished and a general price reform introduced. Socialised trade prices were fixed at a new level which was lower than that of the previous free market prices but much higher than the previous controlled prices. At the same time wages were raised but much less than prices. At the end of 1953 some prices were reduced and until the end of 1956 socialised trade prices as a rule remained stable. On the other hand private trade prices were gradually growing. For example 1 kg of pork cost 27 zł in state shops without any changes but the free market price of pork grew. In 1953 it differed according to various towns from 24 to 29 zł, while in 1956 it varied from 27 to 31 zł (the average price having grown from more than 26 zł to more than 28 zł). (29) It must be pointed out, however, that records of free-market prices were none too accurate.

Modification of the economic policy after 1953 - with some delay - influenced the attitude of the administration towards private trade. Given a strong network of socialised trade, private dealing was no longer a threat to the socio-economic system but could frequently fill gaps in the socialised sector. This is why the tax policy was tempered and some facilities were even introduced for persons starting small trading posts. In practice a great deal depended on the attitude of local authorities. Therefore there were districts where private shops developed while elsewhere they remained unpopular with the administration. The attitude towards handicraft workshops also differed.

FOREIGN ECONOMIC RELATIONS

The changing international situation and economic policy in general influenced Polish foreign trade. Centralisation of the planning and management system was accompanied by the concentration of foreign trade organisation in the Ministry of Foreign Trade created in 1949. Within the framework of instructions from the State Commission for Economic Planning the Ministry elaborated plans for exports and imports, as well as exercised control in their own ambit. Industrial enterprises were deprived of the right to deal in foreign trade. Direct foreign trade operations were entrusted to specialised enterprises whose number was limited and which were, apart from six firms, concentrated in Warsaw.

Since 1951 foreign trade turnover diminished, especially in relation to the capitalist countries. More details are found in Table 4.4.

It should be pointed out that the data shown in Table 4.4 were calculated at current prices and since the latter grew the increase of Polish exports in physical terms was less rapid than is shown.

Table 4.4: Polish Foreign Trade, 1950-6

	1950	1951	1952	1953	1954	1955	1956
Imports in $US million	668	924	863	774	903	932	1022
from socialist countries	408	535	563	556	641	605	677
from other countries	260	389	280	218	262	327	344
Exports in $US million	634	762	775	831	869	920	985
to socialist countries	361	434	505	569	602	578	580
to other countries	273	327	270	262	267	341	405

Source: Rocznik Statystyczny Handlu Zagranicznego (Główny Urząd Statystyczny, Warsaw, 1971), p.2.

After 1949 Polish foreign trade relations with the capitalist countries faced growing difficulties. Some Western countries imposed embargoes on the exports of many articles to the socialist bloc. This referred to goods treated as strategic ones. Polish exports faced quota limitations and Poland was accused of dumping. There were cases when Polish vessels were refused unloading facilities. All this led to substantial changes in the direction of Polish foreign trade and to a new commodity structure.

Polish economic policy caused an increased demand for investment goods and raw materials but limited investment in agriculture and light industries, given growing domestic demand, led to a reduction in the range of traditional Polish exports in favour of new commodities. They were mainly supplied to other socialist countries, most frequently under long-term agreements.

However, since investment policy as a whole was similar in most countries of the socialist bloc, foreign trade turnover between individual socialist countries grew less than production. As a result the Polish economy became more and more self-sufficient, though for a medium-size country like Poland this meant limiting the development prospects.

The situation was made more difficult by payment problems, connected with the growing demand for some imported goods and with the necessity to discharge post-war obligations.

Although Poland regained her pre-war gold reserves which were used in payment for the 1950-5 imports, foreign exchange reserves were always limited. The enormous investment demand required purchases of machinery and equipment but export earnings did not cover the cost. Soviet credits proved very helpful. The deficit was also met to a certain extent by the growing surplus of receipts from invisible exports (mainly transport services). Altogether in 1947-57 Poland received about $US1 milliard in Soviet credits, most of which were spent on investments. (30) It was notably due to these credits that the great investment programme of 1950-5 was realised.

Credits also made it possible to cover the 1950-3 trade deficit. But afterwards loans had to be repaid and in this connection imports had to be limited as the increase in exports was too slow for the country's requirements.

The first years of the Six-Year Plan brought a rapid increase in investment imports. In 1946 the share of machinery and equipment out of total imports amounted to a mere 14 per cent, in 1950 it had grown to 32 per cent and in 1953 it reached 42 per cent. Afterwards this share fell to 33 per cent in 1956. Imports of fuels and raw materials remained at stable levels accounting for about half of the total imports (53 per cent in 1950, 48 per cent in 1952, 52 per cent in 1955 and 49 per cent in 1956). As compared with pre-war years the share of foodstuffs decreased considerably (35 per cent in 1946, 7 per cent in 1953 and 12 per cent in 1956). Generally speaking the structure of imports reflected the great investment effort of the Polish economy. The structure of imports from the socialist countries differed from the overall structure. In 1953 machinery and equipment accounted for 47 per cent of the imports from the socialist bloc and only 29 per cent of imports from other countries. In 1955 imports of machinery and equipment from outside the socialist bloc fell to 12 per cent of total imports from non-socialist countries while the share of foodstuffs in these imports grew to reach 23 per cent in 1956.

The structure of exports was constantly changing. In 1950 machinery and equipment accounted for a mere 8 per cent of the total exports, raw materials and fuels for 56 per cent and foodstuffs for 24 per cent. In 1956 these shares amounted, respectively, to 16 per cent, 64 per cent and 12 per cent. (31) But from the geographical point of view the share of machinery and equipment in Polish exports to the capitalist countries increased very slowly (5 per cent in 1956). This resulted not only from cold war restrictions in the West but from the insufficient competitiveness of Polish goods and the scant experience of Polish foreign trade enterprises.

The major trade partners of Poland were the member countries of the Council for Mutual Economic Aid. Co-operation within the CMEA was stable thanks to long-term trade agreements and contracts signed by foreign trade enterprises for many years in close connection with economic plans. Under these circumstances exporters and importers were relatively safe to maintain an exchange of goods without regard to world market trends. At the same time agreements within the CMEA stabilised prices which were only modified in 1954-5.

In relation to other countries prices were fixed according to world market trends. Generally speaking the early 1950s brought an increase in world prices though the increase differed in relation to various commodities. Polish terms of trade were favourable. As compared with 1950 the 1954 terms of trade index improved by 20 per cent and the following years brought further improvement. (32)

Despite promising signs, however, foreign trade development proved too slow for the requirements of the Polish economy. At the end of the Six-Year Plan the major problem was the insufficient increase of exports - at too low a level to repay debts. A partial solution to this problem proved possible thanks to political reasons. The struggle against the so-called 'personality cult' started in the USSR made the Soviet leadership critically analyse previous relations between the socialist countries. The declaration of the Soviet government of 30 October 1956 stipulated:

> Formation of a new system and revolutionary changes in social relations faced many difficulties, unsolved problems and plain mistakes including infringements in the relations between the socialist countries which limited the principle of equality of rights of the socialist countries. The Twentieth Congress of the Communist Party of the Soviet Union has decidedly condemned these infringements and mistakes and put forward the task of a consequent fulfilment of the Leninist principle of equality of nations by the Soviet Union in its relations with other countries. (33)

In this connection Polish-Soviet talks were

started in Moscow which resulted in a reconsideration and settlement of certain matters at issue. They were discussed by Premier Józef Cyrankiewicz at the Seym sitting on 20 November 1956:

> In the course of exchange of views the Soviet comrades were right to call the agreement concerning the unsettled and questioned by our side accounts of the past years as a clearing and paving the way to a further friendly development of relations between our countries. All this, which shadowed our mutual economic relations and was contrary to socialist international co-operation, has been removed. This refers above all to the Polish-Soviet agreement of 16 August 1945 in which Poland was obliged to supply the Soviet Union with a definite quantity of coal at a special price... Remission of debts on the score of credits granted to Poland by the Soviet Union in the past years as on 1 November 1956 releases us from an obligation to repay the amount of more than 2 millard roubles, that is more than 500 million US dollars, in the years 1957-65. This amount should be increased by interest on the remitted part of credits from which we are also released. Financial benefits resulting from remission of debts as on 1 November 1956 entirely cover losses borne by Poland in the years 1946-53 in connection with the coal deliveries stipulated by the agreement of 16 August 1945. (34)

The Polish-Soviet agreement of November 1956 was of great political and economic significance. It released the Polish balance of payments from a serious burden and made possible a more flexible foreign trade policy.

LIVING CONDITIONS

The accelerated industrialisation of Poland brought about a rapid increase in employment. Thus the question of unemployment - one of the major social calamities of inter-war Poland - was solved. Even at the beginning of the Six-Year Plan there appeared a shortage of manpower which made it necessary to recruit workers from the most over-populated rural areas. The recruitment was carried out by industrial enterprises in a hasty and unco-ordinated manner and statistical records concerning this phenomenon are therefore only approximate. It is estimated that 674,000 people were recruited in 1950-5, most of them being employed in building and collective farming. The work of employment agencies in towns was of less importance; in 1950-3 the number of people seeking work through their mediation fluctuated between 4,000 and 10,000 per annum, whereas the number of job vacancies exceeded 100,000. (35) Great efforts were made to increase employment opportunities for women. However, some of the steps which were taken proved unsuitable and women were not encouraged to find employment in trades or occupations requiring heavy physical labour.

The rapid increase in employment was followed by a number of adverse effects which influenced industrial activity. The relative ease with which work could be found led to movements of workers between factories in search of the highest possible earnings which had a tendency to disorganise production. In some factories most workers came from individual farms and found themselves unable to adjust to an entirely different rhythm of work or to a discipline requiring continuous work for a set number of hours. There were cases where some workers, having families in the country, did not turn up at work during harvests which did little to help productivity.

Under these circumstances several legal measures were passed in early 1950 aimed at limiting the free movement of labour and strengthening standards of discipline. The freedom of dissolution of labour contracts was limited in some lines of production, administrative labour orders were introduced for all secondary trade and higher school graduates for a period of three years, new principles of quality control were established (supplemented in 1953) along with penalties for producing poor quality products and, last but not least, the Seym passed a bill concerning the socialist discipline of labour. It stipulated severe punishments for violating work regulations (lateness, etc.) and obliged management to strictly control observation of the law and to bring actions against workers who broke the regulations. On the other hand a system of rewards and privileges was introduced for 'shock-workers'; a propaganda campaign popularised workers who set new records in productivity.

Nevertheless, it must be pointed out that the administrative measures were hardly effective. On the contrary, it raised discontent and bitterness.

A modification of the investment policy after

1953 limited employment opportunities. According to employment agency records in 1953 four working places were available for each person weeking work (for women this ratio was 1.2), whereas in 1956 the index had fallen to 1.2 (0.3 for women). (36) Even if one appreciates the approximate nature of these indices, they undoubtedly show a rapid decrease in the number of job vacancies. Unskilled workers also faced growing competition for work.

The unequal distribution of investments led to the emergence of regions suffering from manpower shortages and areas where it was really difficult to find employment. In 1956 there were even some local unemployment centres. Solutions to the problem were not easy to find as most of those looking for work could not, for family reasons, move to regions where there was a shortage of workers.

Persons starting work outside agriculture usually treated their employment as a kind of social advancement which brought higher earnings and a better standard of living. In urban communities progress consisted largely in reducing unemployment, particularly for those social groups with extremely low incomes. On the other hand real earnings of the more affluent classes were reduced as compared with the inter-war period. Moreover, it is very difficult to evaluate trends of nominal and real wages under the conditions of supply control and the rationing system which included two price levels.

Despite these reservations it is estimated that the Six-Year Plan brought an increase in nominal wages. In 1950 real wages increased by approximately 6 per cent as compared with 1949 but by 1953 diminished by the same rate. Abolishing supply control and the price and wage reform of January 1953 resulted in a further decrease in real wages of about 9 per cent. (37)

At the end of 1953 real wages began to rise slowly. The Six-Year Plan probably brought an increase in average real wages of 10-13 per cent. There were estimates showing a 28 per cent increase but they do not seem likely. (38) Even if one accepts the highest estimate it must be pointed out that the Six-Year Plan targets concerning wage increases were not fulfilled.

One should also mention phenomena which can hardly be expressed numerically. Many workers and other employees were promoted and gained higher earnings thanks to their educational qualifications. Many people, therefore, could have expected a more significant improvement in their situation but after

1953 promotion prospects were limited due to investment cuts.

In these circumstances (especially because of the economic reforms) workers hoped for an improvement in their standard of living. Unfortunate attempts to change norms of work and wages in the middle of 1956 and the disregard of justified workers' demands in other fields became the main reasons for the Poznań riots in June 1956 (see p.224). The Poznań events were a symbolic warning and influenced further changes in the government's economic policy.

The relatively slow increase in real wages was accompanied by a moderate improvement in consumption. At the same time the structure of consumption changed. The most radical improvement was recorded in meat and animal fat consumption which grew from 28.7 kg per capita yearly in 1949 to 39 kg in 1955. Sugar consumption increased from 19.3 kg to 24 kg and fish consumption rose from 1.5 kg to 2.7 kg per capita yearly over the same period, whereas consumption of cereals and eggs grew only marginally. On the other hand consumption of fruits and vegetables diminished. (39)

Extension of the right to paid leave and the development of the system of cheap holidays in rest-houses belonging to trade unions or other institutions was a great success with workers. Immediately after the Second World War few workers could be persuaded to take such holidays since there had been no tradition of this kind. But during the Six-Year Plan holidays in rest-houses became quite popular. Social insurance was extended and included not only hired workers but also pensioners and retired persons. Social benefits were raised. The number of persons served by the social insurance system grew from 22.6 per cent of the total population of Poland in 1946 to 51.7 per cent in 1955, including families. (40) Apart from social insurance a free health service was available to all with regard to a number of preventive measures (for example, prophylactic vaccinations) and the fight against tuberculosis and venereal diseases.

Individual farmers still remained outside the social insurance system. Therefore the undoubted progress made in labour legislation and social insurance also served to heighten the differences between the countryside and towns in favour of the latter.

Large numbers of workers migrating to the towns in search of work underlined the housing shortage. The problem was made worse by the fact that Poland had suffered huge losses in buildings during the Second World War and the housing situation before the war had also been poor for the greater part of society. Enterprises recruiting workers temporarily solved the problem by building various, sometimes very primitive, lodging-houses for their employees. At the same time reconstruction and construction of new housing quarters went on. Data collected during subsequent censuses show a gradual improvement of the situation. In 1946 an average room was inhabited by 2.05 statistical persons, in 1950 by 1.75 and in 1960 by 1.66 persons. The number of households per 100 flats, however, remained very similar - 122 in 1950 to 118 in 1960. (41)

In general, the housing situation in the towns improved very slowly. Nevertheless, considerable progress was made in the field of urban and rural communal facilities. In 1949 only 28.6 per cent of villages had access to electricity while in 1956 this share had risen to 40.9 per cent. The number of urban settlements equipped with water supply systems increased from 399 to 516 between 1953 and 1956.(42)

NOTES

1. If not otherwise stated, statistical data are quoted according to: Ludność Polski w latach 1945-1965 (Główny Urząd Statystyczny, Warsaw, 1966).
2. Rocznik Statystyczny 1970 (Główny Urząd Statystyczny, Warsaw, 1970), p. 36.
3. M. Pohoski, Migracje ze wsi do miast. Studium wychodźstwa w latach 1945-1957 oparte na wynikach ankiety Instytutu Ekonomiki Rolnej (Państwowe Wydawnictwo Ekonomiczne, Warsaw, 1963), p. 56.
4. Rocznik Statystyczny 1957 (Główny Urząd Statystyczny, Warsaw, 1957), p. 316.
5. Plan sześcioletni (Książka i Wiedza, Warsaw, 1950), p. 24.
6. Ibid., pp. 92-3.
7. Uchwały KC PZPR od II do III Zjazdu (Książka i Wiedza, Warsaw, 1959), p. 166.
8. W. Masewicz, Praca w godzinach nadliczbowych w przemyśle polskim w latach 1919-1970. Studium społeczno-prawne (Zakład Narodowy im. Ossolińskich, Wrocław, 1977), p. 173.
9. Pamiętniki pokolenia (Iskry, Warsaw, 1966), p. 277.
10. Rocznik Statystyczny przemysłu 1945-1965, pp. 132-3.

11. A. Karpiński, Zagadnienia socjalistycznej industrializacji Polski (Państwowe Wydawnictwo Ekonomiczne, Warsaw, 1958), p. 213.
12. B. Bierut, 'Zadania partii w walce o szybkie podniesienie stopy życiowej mas pracujących w obecnym okresie budownictwa socjalistycznego', Nowe Drogi, no. 10 (1953), p. 27.
13. J. Beksiak, Zmiany w gospodarce (Państwowe Wydawnictwo Naukowe, Warsaw, 1982), p. 171.
14. Z. Adamowski, J. Lewandowski, Rolnictwo polskie w dwudziestopięcioleciu (Państwowe Wydawnictwo Naukowe, Warsaw, 1970), p. 71.
15. Z. Kozłowski, Obowiązkowe dostawy w planie sześcioletnim (Państwowe Wydawnictwo Naukowe, Warsaw, 1960), p. 89.
16. R. Winiewska, Obciążenia podatkowe gospodarstw chłopskich w Polsce w latach 1944-1955, (Państwowe Wydawnictwa Gospodarcze, Warsaw, 1961), pp. 135-6.
17. O socjalistyczną przebudowę wsi. Uchwały KC PZPR 1949-1952 (publishing house not given, Warsaw, 1953), p. 6.
18. Pamiętniki pokolenia, p. 191.
19. O Budownictwie partyjnym. Uchwały KC PZPR 1949-1953 (Książka i Wiedza, Warsaw, 1954), p. 242.
20. Rocznik Statystyczny 1957, pp. 124, 126, 127, 138.
21. Nowe Drogi, no. 3 (1954), pp. 42, 66.
22. Uchwały KC PZPR od II do III Zjazdu, p. 221.
23. W. Skorupka, Moje morgi i katorgi 1914-1967 (Wydawnictwo Poznańskie, Poznań, 1970), p. 295.
24. J. Kaliński, 'Przeobrażenia i działalność spółdzielczości handlowej' in Gospodarka Polski Ludowej 1944-1955, J. Kaliński, Z. Landau (eds.), vol. 1 (Książka i Wiedza, Warsaw, 1974), pp. 158-9.
25. Rocznik Statystyczny finansów 1945-1967, pp. 251-2.
26. Ibid., pp. 36, 53.
27. W. Jaworski, Zarys rozwoju systemu kredytowego w Polsce Ludowej (Polskie Wydawnictwa Gospodarcze, Warsaw, 1958), p. 182.
28. Rocznik Statystyczny 1957, p. 219.
29. Rocznik Statystyczny 1955, pp. 162, 168; Rocznik Statystyczny 1957, pp. 228, 231.
30. P. Bożyk, B. Wojciechowski, Handel zagraniczny Polski 1945-1969 (Państwowe Wydawnictwo Ekonomiczne, Warsaw, 1971), p. 276.
31. Rocznik Statystyczny Handlu Zagranicznego 1971, pp. 14-17.
32. P. Bożyk, B. Wojciechowski, Handel, pp. 193-6.

33. E. Basiński, T. Walichnowski (eds.), Stosunki polsko-radzieckie w latach 1945-1972. Dokumenty i materiały (Książka i Wiedza, Warsaw, 1974), p. 319.

34. Ibid., pp. 328-9.

35. H. Jędruszczak, Zatrudnienie a przemiany społeczne w Polsce w latach 1944-1960 (Zakład Narodowy im. Ossolińskich, Wrocław, 1972), pp. 154, 156.

36. Ibid., p. 170.

37. S. Jankowski, 'Warunki bytu ludności', in Gospodarka Polski Ludowej 1944-1955, J. Kaliński, Z. Landau (eds.), vol. 2 (Książka i Wiedza, Warsaw, 1976), p. 66; K. Ryć, Spożycie a wzrost gospodarczy Polski 1945-1970 (Książka i Wiedza, Warsaw, 1968), p. 31 ff.

38. J. Meller, Płace a planowanie gospodarcze w Polsce (1950-1970) (Książka i Wiedza, Warsaw, 1977), p. 55.

39. W. Przelaskowski, Spożycie żywności w Polsce Ludowej (publishing house not given, Warsaw, 1968), pp. 86-98.

40. S. Jankowski, Warunki bytu, p. 60.

41. A. Andrzejewski, Sytuacja mieszkaniowa w Polsce w latach 1918-1974 (Państwowe Wydawnictwo Ekonomiczne, Warsaw, 1977), p. 204.

42. Rocznik Statystyczny 1955, p. 180; Rocznik Statystyczny 1958, pp. 175, 282.

IN SEARCH OF EQUILIBRIUM, 1957-70

POPULATION

From the end of 1956 till the end of 1970 the population of Poland increased considerably. In December 1970 it was estimated at 32,658,000 people. (1) The actual increase in population amounted to 4,578,000 persons while the natural increase was higher and amounted to 5,100,000 people. The difference was due to migrations which were much higher than in preceding years. The relatively high natural increase in population was slowing down. In 1957 it amounted to 18.1 per thousand and in 1970 to 8.5 per thousand. However, this phenomenon was only temporary and a repeated rise in the natural increase was expected along with growing up of the generation born soon after the war.

On the other hand the late 1950s brought a rapid increase in the number of children of school age which made the development of schools a high priority (as well as involving higher investment in education). It was not long before the problem arose of providing an adequate number of places for the numerous new generations reaching working age.

External migrations have increased since 1956. In 1956 the Soviet authorities facilitated the repatriation of Poles who could not or would not, for various reasons, return to Poland after the Second World War. A new agreement concerning this question was signed on 25 March 1957. It determined the range of persons entitled to emigrate to Poland (people of Polish and Jewish nationality who had had Polish citizenship on 17 September 1939 and their families) and provided that they could benefit from this right before the end of 1958. In practice some immigrants were still arriving in Poland in 1959. Altogether 255,400 immigrants settled in Poland in 1956-9, most of them coming from the USSR. In 1960 immigration fell to 5,700 and in 1970 to 1,900 people.

At first there was also an increase in emigration. By 1956 21,800 people had left Poland and within the following two years the number of emigrants amounted to 272,700 people. Afterwards emigration diminished; in 1959 it included 37,000, in 1968 19,400 and in 1970 14,100 people. In 1969 there was a temporary increase in the number of emigrants to 22,100 people, this being connected with internal political conflicts and the nationalist proclamations of some politicians after March 1968.

Some emigrants left for the Federal Republic of Germany as a result of the family reunion action, others left for Israel (especially in 1956-9) and the European countries (especially in 1968-9), the latter group consisting mainly of Jews and Poles of Jewish origin.

The total deficit of the migration balance in the years 1957-70 amounted to 303,700 persons. The difference between this balance and data resulting from the comparison of actual and natural growth in the population is due to inaccuracies present in current statistical records.

Although in relation to the total number of the population the size of the migrations may seem negligible, it should be mentioned that it reached a level comparable with the pre-war size of migrations. Apart from formal reasons (family reunion, etc.) many people emigrated because they had heard about the higher standard of living in the West and hoped, sometimes without reason, to find an easy stabilisation or interesting and well paid work abroad.

Professionals and skilled Polish workers were, though on a lesser scale, as specialists taking up contracts abroad - usually for a few years. Doctors, engineers and other highly qualified professionals went to the developed countries. Some Polish enterprises carried on building contracts and employed Polish workers in advanced capitalist countries and in the socialist bloc. Certain Czech factories situated close to the Polish frontier also employed Polish workers. Many of these crossed the border every day (as had been the practice in the border town of Teschen for several dozen years) or once a week.

Internal migrations were decreasing. In 1956 the gross inflow of population to towns was estimated at 694,000 people and at 469,000 in 1970. Altogether about 1,620,000 people moved to towns in 1956-70 excluding those who went to towns but returned to the countryside. The changing size of internal migrations was due to variable government economic policy as well as to changing investment activities.

The internal migration movements resulted in an increase of the share of the urban population from 45.5 per cent in 1957 to 52.3 per cent in 1970. In absolute terms the number of the rural population was rather stable. At the end of 1956 it amounted to 15,486,000 people, in 1960 to 15,395,000 in 1966 to 15,902,000 and in 1970 to 15,570,000 people. It seems that a slow but constant decrease in the number of the rural population began in 1966. Since migration to towns included mainly the younger generation, the age composition of the rural population changed. This is shown in Table 4.5.

Table 4.5: Age Composition of the Rural Population in Poland, 1960-70 (thousands)

Year	Total rural population	Population of working age (a)	pre-working age	post-working age
1960	15,394	8,034	6,062	1,298
1965	15,870	8,035	6,274	1,561
1970	15,570	8,178	5,562	1,830

Note: a. Working age for men:18-64 years; for women: 18-59 years.

Source: Rocznik Demograficzny 1976 (Główny Urząd Statystyczny, Warsaw, 1976), p. 37.

The number of the rural population of working age was relatively stable but the share of people employed outside agriculture increased. On the other hand the number of old people, sometimes hardly able to farm, was growing, the number of young people was diminishing. This led to local shortages of manpower in agriculture.

At the same time the social and occupational composition of Polish society was changing and this was recorded in the 1960 and 1970 censuses. (2) The share of people depending on agriculture fell from 38.4 per cent to 29.8 per cent (in absolute terms it also decreased) whereas the share of people depending on industry grew from 25 per cent to 27.2 per cent. The percentages of those depending on other branches of the economy also increased. The general level of education rose. The share of the population with higher education increased from 2.1 per cent to 2.7 per cent; with secondary education from 10.3 per cent to 12.7 per cent; with primary education from 39.3 per cent to 47.3 per cent and with basic trade education from 3.1 per cent to 10.6 per cent. For 1960 figures refer to people of more than 14 years of age, and for 1970 to those of more than 15 years. However, in 1970 24.5 per cent of the population of Poland more than 14 years old had not graduated, even from primary school. Most of them lived in the country.

Regular progress in education at all levels was made and the compulsory education of children was almost entirely achieved. A growing number of young people continued in higher education. In 1955/6 about 44 per cent of young people between 14 and 17 years of age went to various secondary schools. In 1970/1 the same share among young people between 15 and 18 years amounted to 74 per cent. (3) The number of pupils in secondary trade and agricultural schools was also growing rapidly. The number of students constantly increased reaching 330,800 persons in 1970/1. The growing number of graduates resulted in a relative surplus of some kinds of qualified staff, especially in higher education. Young people were particularly interested in the humanities in which Polish scholars attained an outstanding position (in archaeology, for example) though from the point of view of the country's requirements and possibilities they were of a minor importance. The excess of highly educated professionals appeared in big urban centres, mainly in Warsaw, whereas in many small towns the demand for doctors, teachers, agronomists, engineers, etc. was not satisfied.

INDUSTRY

In July 1956 a much delayed draft plan for the years 1956-60 was passed by the CC PUWP. The Seym adopted the Five-Year Plan Act as late as July 1957. As compared with the previous period the plan stipulated more rapid development in the production of consumer goods. This was aimed at creating the conditions for an increase in the standard of living. Industrial output was to grow by 49 per cent over the whole five years while investments were to increase less than in the early 1950s. Notwithstanding, in March 1958 another plenum of the CC PUWP decided to raise investments again. The modification of the programme resulted from government fears of unemployment. Janusz Beksiak said that 'the development programme started at that time and realised within the following five years had much in common with the 1950-53 programme'. (4)

The repeated increase of investments was realised at the cost of consumption and was accompanied by autarkical tendencies. Contrary to previous years, however, there were attempts to curb the growth of employment.

One of the basic tasks of 1956-60 was to fill gaps in the whole production system through extension of the mining industries and certain processing industries.

At the same time an economic reform was started. In 1957 a central Economic Council was created as a government advisory and consultative body. Many outstanding economists took part in its activities. Oskar Lange became the Council's chairman, while Michał Kalecki and Edward Lipiński were the vice-chairmen. The authority of the central planning and management organs was limited. In November 1956 the State Commission for Economic Planning was substituted by the Planning Commission of the Council of Ministers under Stefan Jędrychowski. In December 1968 his post was taken over by Józef Kulesza. The independence of enterprises was increased and the strengthening of local self-government was pursued. In enterprises

> increasing self-dependence consisted in lessening the role of directive indicators for the formulation of productive targets and in extension of the range of problems solved within the enterprise such as the organisation of production, and changes in applied technology or disposal of development funds. Soon however it proved impossible to change the nature and quality of work in enterprises without changing the character and position of superior units. (5)

The previous organisation had subordinated enterprises to ministries through the so-called central boards created according to a strict branch division. In practice it even came to the division of enterprises which produced articles included in different branch boards. In 1958 all the central boards were abolished and replaced by a smaller number of industrial associations which managed individual lines of produciton in a more flexible way. The associations aimed to create conditions for the development of their lines of production and to control subordinate enterprises but their authority in the field of direct management was limited. On the other hand, associations took over design and construction offices which had been subject to ministries. Apart from that they were to co-ordinate the production of related articles in enterprises belonging to different associations. This new organisation was aimed at reconciling the necessary decentralisation of decisions with co-ordination of the activities of individual enterprises and at a planned development of industry on the national scale. Within enterprises the most radical change was the formation of workers' self-management in the shape of workers' councils.

Subsequent changes in economic policy brought a limitation of workers' self-management. Workers' councils became only one of the three parts of the so-called Conferences of Workers' Self-management, the other two being the factory party committees and trade unions. The role of the Conferences was rapidly brought down to a minimum. The actual importance of the Economic Council was also diminishing and in 1962 it ceased to exist.

In 1957-8 economists and politicians discussed planning and management reforms. Some of the conclusions were introduced and there was a common opinion that further changes in the economic structure and system were inevitable. Various methods were tried out in individual enterprises and local administrative organs. The necessity to reform the price and wage system was stressed. In the contemporary economic situation of Poland this would mean an increase in many prices, especially those of foodstuffs as they should have been adjusted to the costs of production. Political conditions seemed favourable for this. At the beginning of 1957 workers were ready to accept a temporary decrease in real wages in order to facilitate a more radical reform of the Polish economy. Such suggestions, however, were rejected by the party leadership and the government. It was thought that radical reforms ought to be postponed until other methods were tried. Therefore the most favourable socio-political conditions for reform were not utilised.

Gradually the planning and management experiments were given up. Although some of the changes introduced after 1956 proved persistent the reconstruction of the so-called Polish economic model was checked and certain fields even regressed in the 1960s. Above all the degree of workers' influence over management and the actual role of elected administrative bodies decreased in favour of organs appointed by upper levels of administration. The independence of enterprises was also gradually limited.

This kind of policy was most probably due to changes in general economic strategy started in 1958 and to the negative symptoms occurring in the Polish economy since 1959. Emergency measures and decisions to prevent a further deterioration of the market equilibrium were required. According to the view of the Economic Council, the coincidence of several factors led to 'such a deep collapse of the meat market which could threaten the equilibrium of the market for substitute goods and bring about a number of secondary negative effects'. (6)

This resulted from poor harvests, deterioration in Polish terms of trade, overspending investment estimates without achieving any extra benefits and from excessive wage payments.

At the same time Poland faced new tasks. There was enough industry to meet basic requirements; the production of several traditional articles was as a rule sufficient but the supply of many modern products needed by households was still too low. In his report to the Third Congress of the PUWP in March 1959 Władysław Gomułka said:

> Thanks to socialist production relations and the superiority of the planned economy we have made up for a great part of the distance between the backward capitalist economy of pre-war Poland and the most economically advanced countries. Now we are swiftly approaching them in the field of economic development. (7)

This opinion proved to be too optimistic despite all the progress made in the production of many goods. Modernisation of industry was still the number one problem along with that of improving the quality of production and an increased supply of new commodities. All this could not be achieved by former methods. At the same time specific problems arose in the labour market. In 1963 the effects of the post-war population explosion began to appear: thousands more attained working age and had to be provided with work. Investment efforts had to be increased again, at first in education and then in industry, trade, services and housing. The necessity to find employment for all encouraged extensive investments involving low expenses which supplied a large number of new jobs. However, such an investment policy was contrary to the needs of industry: modernisation, quality improvement and reducing the costs of production. There were opinions that a certain margin of unemployment would be good for the economy and that the policy of full employment should be given up along with intensification of industry and the introduction of labour-saving technologies.

Though they were partially justified by economic reasons, these concepts did not become the framework of government policy. Putting an end to unemployment and the universal right of work were the basic social achievements of Poland after 1945. Allowing a certain, if slight, level of unemployment would represent not only a social misfortune but also a denial of basic principles adopted in all socialist countries. Therefore the Third Congress resolved that 'the accelerated growth of investments should provide full employment for the growing up generations'. (8) At the same time the application of new technologies was recommended. In practice two kinds of investments were chosen. Some aimed at modernising and improving the quality of production while others were concerned with the creation of new jobs and preventing the accumulation of local manpower surpluses.

Numerous young people attaining working age were offered a chance to accelerate the development of various services. The latter had been neglected and their importance was growing in the face of industrial development and increased social requirements. This chance, however, was hardly taken up.

All this went to justify accelerating the introduction of a new investment programme determined in the spring of 1958. Another CC PUWP plenum of October 1958 passed the guidelines for Poland's economic development until 1965 stating: 'An analysis of requirements and conditions of economic development in the years 1961-65 shows the necessity to accelerate the growth of investments above the present five-year plan rate.' (9)

This general line of economic policy was maintained in the following five years, given certain detailed modifications and attempts to reform the Polish economic system.

Generally speaking the years 1957-70 brought a further rapid growth in industrial production, as shown in Table 4.6.

In 1957-8 the share of accumulation in the national income was relatively low and production of consumer goods grew more rapidly than that of investment goods. In 1959 a repeated acceleration of growth in industrial investment started together with an increase in the share of capital formation in the national income. The production of capital goods grew more rapidly than average industrial output. At first the rate of increase in employment was rather moderate but in the early 1960s it rose again.

A comparison of the growth in investment and production shows that industrial inputs of the late

Table 4.6: Industrial Development in Poland, 1957-70

	1957	1958	1959	1960	1961	1962
National income (1956=100)	110.7	116.9	122.9	128.3	138.8	141.7
Percentage of accumulation in the national income	22.6	22.7	23.2	24.2	25.0	24.1
Industrial investments (1956=100)	102.2	111.5	131.0	134.6	148.5	171.5
Industrial output (1956=100)	110.4	121.2	132.0	146.0	161.0	174.4
Production of capital goods (1956=100)	107.8	117.3	132.9	151.0	168.6	185.1
Production of consumer goods (1956=100)	112.1	124.3	130.6	141.3	152.9	162.6
Employment (1956=100)	105.1	106.2	107.2	107.8	110.4	114.7

Source: Rocznik Statystyczny 1970, p. 38-39; Rocznik Statystyczny 1977, p. XXX-XXXI, XXXIV-XXXV, XXXVI-XXXVII, 121.

1963	1964	1965	1966	1967	1968	1969	1970
151.5	161.7	173.0	185.3	195.9	213.5	219.7	231.2
25.4	25.4	26.8	27.7	27.1	28.5	27.3	27.9
178.7	184.2	197.2	209.0	233.2	257.2	283.0	285.5
183.7	200.5	218.5	234.9	253.4	277.1	301.5	325.9
199.2	219.2	240.8	260.0	283.1	313.7	345.1	377.5
166.5	179.6	193.7	205.8	217.0	231.6	247.6	267.3
117.4	119.6	125.5	130.1	135.9	141.0	145.9	148.2

1960s were bringing decreasing effects. In 1964-70 average annual growth rates of industrial output ranged from 7.5 per cent to 9.4 per cent while the average annual increase in investment in 1967-9 was at least 10 per cent. This situation made many economists uneasy.

The direction of investments was changed as compared with the Six-Year Plan. In many factories existing machinery was modernised. In metallurgy some old blast-furnaces were replaced by new, more efficient ones. They required less physical strain but higher qualifications. The first fully automated coal mine in the world was started. Consumption of electricity grew; the major railway lines, for example, were electrified. Power and fuels accounted for a particularly high share of investment expense. In 1958-62 both lines received almost one-third of all industrial investment. In 1963, however, power investment began to decrease which led to difficulties in the following years.

Chemical industry grew especially rapidly. Great petrochemical plants were constructed in Płock in co-operation with the USSR. They processed Soviet oil supplied by a newly constructed pipeline. An important sulphur mining region was developed in Tarnobrzeg (with Czechoslovak participation). Production of fertilisers grew as it had to if farming productivity was to be improved. Copper ore mining began along with its processing. Shipbuilding was developed. Investments in the electromechanical industry were at first rather stable but in 1964 they began to increase. A great step forward was made in electronics. As compared with the Six-Year Plan the new investments were usually more technically advanced and production more complicated. Investments aimed at preventing local unemployment were also bringing results, mainly in the shape of a gradual increase in the quantity and quality of articles manufactured in light industry and food processing.

Nevertheless, some of the investments did not produce direct economic results but created conditions for future development. They required large inputs and much time before they could be productive. The diffusion of the investment effort into too many areas led to extra costs and delays in construction time. The deliberate underestimation of investment costs by enterprises or local authorities interested in construction was a serious problem. The initiators wanted to enter the plan ('to catch hold of the plan' was the motto) and to start construction with the reasonable expectation that the central authorities would assign them additional means if the actual costs proved higher than the estimate, so that funds already spent were not wasted. As a result, deliberately exceeding planned estimates became usual practice. It frequently involved giving up accompanying investments having no directly productive importance but necessary from the social point of view. Thus working conditions were bad and environmental protection entirely neglected. Meanwhile rapid industrial development made formerly disregarded problems appear more and more important. River and lake pollution reached alarming levels, reducing available water supplies and raising difficulties for industrial development itself.

The various shortcomings of the industrial investment process were a serious burden for the economy and were frequently discussed in the CC PUWP and the government. These questions were dealt with by CC PUWP plenums in October 1959 and November 1963. Despite the remedial measures taken, the CC PUWP resolved in April 1966:

> There are still serious shortcomings in the investment process despite the improvement of the recent years. We are still building too dearly and too lengthily. Investment estimates are exceeded and the productive effects are achieved too late. Moreover, the planned technical and economic parameters are unfulfilled in structures put into operation. (10)

Improvement of the investment process was also treated as a major task by the April 1969 plenum of the CC PUWP in connection with preparations for the subsequent five-year plan. All kinds of savings were then searched for as temporary solutions to the problems arising. However, a real settlement could not be achieved without further changes in the planning and management system and without improving the functioning of construction enterprises in particular. The existing system in which the income of an enterprise depended on construction costs usually led to expensive materials being used, effectively preventing any economising.

Increasing output was connected with growth in labour productivity. In 1960-70 the industrial productivity of labour grew by 60 per cent, (11) but the share of the increment of productivity in the average growth of the national income was declining. In 1956-60 it accounted for about 68 per cent of the total growth rate but in 1966-70 it had fallen to 54 per cent. (12) On the other hand the growth of employment played an increasing role.

The level of industrial output reached in the 1960s required yet another change in the direction of development. A many-sided investment programme was not possible in a rather small country like Poland. With the foundations for further development being constructed and industry facing more and more serious tasks, it was necessary to choose the most profitable line of economic expansion. There were simply too few means to keep pace with world technological advance in all fields. Further changes in the functioning of the national economy seemed inevitable in order to make the best use of human qualifications and management experience. It was necessary to change the price system and the structure of wages. Partial modifications were, anyway, introduced. In 1960 the selling price system was revised and afterwards retail prices were changed along with passenger tariffs and rents were raised to cover the costs of housing maintenance. In 1961 an unsuccessful attempt was made to introduce incentives for workers and enterprises in order to encourage them to undertake more ambitious plan targets. Some experiments were also aimed at elaborating a system of economic incentives to replace directive indicators in planning.

> All the undertaken reforms and organisation or economic experiments led to a gradual evolution of the economic system bringing positive social and productive effects. This evolution was however too slow and was accompanied by recurrence of old practices and habits. (13)

The second half of the 1960s brought intensive efforts to raise productivity. Yet there were still serious obstacles in the way. Various strains in the economy, insufficient reserves, supply shortages and failure of the steps aimed at improving the investment process led to the intervention of the central administration with a number of improvised measures. Thus, while the economic system required more independent enterprises and a limitation of directive management, current necessities dictated quite opposite policies.

For a certain time reforms could be postponed due to the situation in the labour market: employment increases could still be treated as a leading factor of economic development. On that score Poland differed from other socialist countries which suffered from shortages of manpower. Nevertheless in the early 1970s Poland also faced the approaching 'demographic depression' with falling numbers attaining working age. As a result it seemed impossible to postpone the planning and management reform any longer. Model changes in the economy, it was hoped, would provide for a more effective utilisation of manpower.

Against this background new programmes of development were formulated. In November 1968 Władysław Gomułka told the party's Fifth Congress:

> Premises of industrial development include changes in the branch structure and in proportions of increase of production of means of production and means of consumption. Industries decisive for modernisation of the national economy will develop much more rapidly than the average industrial output. (14)

This principle was called a 'programme of selective development'. It stipulated a far-reaching specialisation of Polish industry and elimination of old-fashioned products and goods whose production had no prospects in Poland. Investment was to be concentrated in selected lines.

> As a result a shift of some existing industries over to other lines of production began. This referred among others to the aircraft industry whose potential was transferred to the production of machine tools and equipment. Nevertheless the scale and methods of these transfers were not too effective and they were given up after a certain time. Therefore it may be concluded that we have not mastered modern methods of control of structural changes on a large scale. (15)

The reconstruction of the economic structure was started by various administrative measures but these faced opposition from lobbies interested in maintaining branches which were to be limited or closed down. Given a general lack of political stability, the execution of central directives appeared impossible and the idea of 'selective development' was realised only partially. The decision of the Council of Ministers to apply efficiency indicators to the evaluation of projected investments could have been significant but its realisation was not feasible because of the faulty price system and the lack of objective calculation methods.

Under these circumstances central decisions frequently had doubtful effects. For instance in 1969-70 brick output diminished due to the great emphasis laid on industrialised building technologies. Production of washing machines, steam turbines, textile and dairy machinery and ploughs was also falling. The output of metal hollow ware ceased to grow. At the same time many of these articles were still in heavy demand and their shortage was to have an adverse influence on farming in following years. On the other hand experiments designed to develop export capacity were quite successful.

The preparations for changes to the management system continued in 1969 together with studies on methods of raising productivity and ways to achieve technical progress. In May 1970 the Politburo member Bolesław Jaszczuk presented the projected reform to the CC PUWP specifying its major principles:

> Actual technical and economic results of 1970 as a constant reference basis for every enterprise;
>
> determination of relations between the increase of average wages and economic progress, as a rule fixed for the forthcoming five years;
>
> determination of a few generally fixed award objectives. (16)

According to this system all enterprises should set objectives whose realisation was to be a prerequisite for any increase in wages. This was aimed at slowing down increasing wage payments. Other minor changes in planning and management methods were also introduced in 1970.

Economic reform was undoubtedly necessary. However, it soon became evident that the steps undertaken in 1970 frustrated common hopes. There was no long-term economic strategy, the changes introduced were not interconnected and sometimes insufficiently worked out. The basic shortcoming of the programme was its neglect of other social implications and probable socio-political consequences. The Gomułka authorities had in effect lost the social confidence they had enjoyed in 1957.

Individual economic decisions were made from the strictly economic point of view disregarding changes in the living conditions of society and with scant respect for public feelings. The new wage principles partially introduced in industry disappointed the workers, since the linking of the wage increases with productivity and financial performance was accompanied by restraints on this increase. Though such a solution was justified by the existing market situation, it clashed with the objectives of the reform - to stimulate production by means of material incentives. The retail price reform carried out in December 1970 (necessary from the point of view of formation of correct relations between prices and costs) badly affected real wages, especially those of lowest paid workers. Changes in the investment structure, forced by the necessity to economise and to concentrate inputs in major lines, brought stagnation to the housing market. Housing production ceased to grow in 1969 and even decreased in 1970, despite growing social needs. Finally, the attempts to economise and cut down investment resulted in fewer resources for social purposes and for environmental protection (baths, cloakrooms, canteens, air conditioning, waste treatment, etc.).

The results of such a policy were disappointing even for strictly economic reasons. The CC PUWP report for the Sixth Congress in December 1971 stated:

> Neglect of working and living conditions in the economic policy which brought about their stagnation or even worse could not create a good climate for the increase of productive activity and social commitment of the working people. General discouragement grew along with mistrust in the social and economic progress achieved by our country and in the prospects of personal promotion and improvement of the material situation. (17)

This was the background to workers' demonstrations in several towns on the Polish coast in December 1970. They turned into scuffles which took a heavy toll of life and material losses. The contemporary leadership of the party and government believed that the riots were only the work of hooligans or even counter-revolutionary forces. This is why they tried to suppress the revolt by force. Many people were killed or seriously injured. This action, however, brought about change in the highest party and government posts.

AGRICULTURE

The CC PUWP resolutions adopted at the end of 1956 caused an immediate dissolution of most co-operative farms. On 30 September 1956 they numbered 10,200 but at the end of 1957 only 1,700 co-operatives remained. (18) The first to be dissolved were co-operatives that had been organised under pressure. But the mass liquidation of co-operatives involved the dissolution of several well-organised and highly productive collective farms whose members were earning relatively high wages. There were cases when some confused local leaders exercised pressure aimed at the dissolution of co-operatives against the prevailing opinions of members.

The suppression of most co-operatives and renouncement of administrative pressures on the collectivisation of farming created a situation calling for new ways of developing the agricultural sector. The basic principle adopted after 1956 was to join a constant increase in agricultural output with a gradual transformation of the existing system. In practice the main emphasis was laid on the growth of production which was necessary from the social and economic point of view. At the same time a system of government influence on private farming was developed. A CC PUWP resolution of May 1957 stipulated that 'the major task of the party in the countryside is to create conditions for a further increase in agricultural output' and then:

> Co-operating with the United Peasant Party [UPP] the party organisations in the country should concentrate attention on the development of various forms of peasant self-management, agricultural associations, machinery collectives, supply and sale co-operatives, dairy, fruit and vegetable co-operatives, credit and savings banks and other forms of simple co-operation... At the same time the party committees should take particular care of co-operative farms. (19)

Above all the government encouraged investment in agriculture. In April 1959 a joint sitting of the CC PUWP and the Chief Committee of the UPP passed a resolution concerning further development of farming in Poland.

> The resolution includes an extensive programme of intensification of agriculture, acceleration of technical reconstruction and socio-economic development of the countryside on the grounds of a mass organisation of peasants - agricultural associations. The resolution foresees a considerable extension of investments in mechanisation and melioration. The resolution stipulates the creation of the Agricultural Development Fund to finance supply to the countryside of tractors, accompanying machinery, threshers and other big machines which will become the collective property of peasants united within agricultural associations.(20)

These decisions led to an increase in the share of investments in agriculture which amounted to 16.1 per cent of the total investment inputs in 1966-70 (during the Six-Year Plan it hardly exceeded 10 per cent). (21) Nevertheless, contrary to all declarations, agriculture was still kept in the background of government economic policy and the increase in farming investments was uneven. In 1960-3 investments in private farms actually decreased. Fluctuations in the inputs in animal husbandry were also distressing as they led to periodical falls in the number of basic stock.

On the other hand there was more investment in industries supplying agriculture with fertilisers, machinery, etc. A general improvement in supplies of industrial goods for the countryside was recorded although at the end of the 1960 several articles were again in short supply. Improvements in these markets made possible the development of rural building and a wider use of machinery, fertilisers, insecticides, etc. The Agricultural Development Fund was established in 1959. It accumulated the difference between prices fixed for compulsory deliveries and purchasing prices. Funds gathered in this manner were then distributed in relation to the degree of fulfilment of the delivery plan by individual villages (75 per cent of the total revenues of the fund) while remaining sums were spent on general farming purposes. The Fund money was used by agricultural associations according to strict regulations. These regulations were designed to ensure that funds were only used for specified investments - such as the purchase of machinery - and gradually proved to be useless to farmers as some indirectly beneficial investments (for example, the construction of a good road) could much more efficiently stimulate production. As the Fund money could not be spent for such purposes, agriculture was unable to make use of considerable sums that had been initially intended for its improvement.

Peasant farms still had to make obligatory deliveries though assessments were reduced in 1957. Obligatory deliveries were continued so as to provide the government with minimum reserves of basic foodstuffs. Besides, they facilitated the accumulation of money in the Agricultural Development Fund. Nevertheless, this system forced farmers to produce a wide variety of foodstuffs which prevented specialisation. As a result there were cases when farmers, who specialised in certain lines of output, had to buy farm products to fulfil obligatory deliveries.

It was also hard to increase production in farms of a lower than average level of technical and economic development. Apart from socio-political measures and the assistance of experts from local administration and agricultural associations, some administrative steps were also taken. In 1966 the government adopted a resolution concerning the protection of arable land, restricting its take-over for non-agricultural purposes and requiring farmers to utilise their holdings properly. The resolution also stipulated that farmers had to purchase a definite minimum quantity of fertilisers, cope with weeds and so on. The system of agrotechnical and zootechnical methods fixed for each village separately and binding on all farmers was called the agrominimum. The government was entitled to take over land from decaying farms. The whole of this programme was summed up by the CC PUWP plenum in September 1967:

> It is necessary to extend gradually the range of the agrominimum. New, raised requirements should be made within this system like proper fertilising, liming, punctual hay harvesting, sowing of aftercrops, etc. They ought to be followed by a systematic social control of fields and farms and the mobilisation of rural public opinion against backwardness, negligence and various forms of waste. In cases of an evident violation of productive discipline, sanctions provided by the laws concerning seed production, plant protection, obligatory fertilising and melioration promotion should be applied against people responsible for that.(22)

All these undertakings resulted from an illusion: that farmers could be stimulated by administrative measures and penalties. Contrary to political declarations, the confidence of peasants in the permanence of their property rights was shaken. At the same time this policy neglected the fact that the best incentive for farmers would be to create favourable conditions for economic activity, remove various obstacles and raise the qualifications required for farming. A farmer from the Hrubieszów region recorded in his diary:

> Very few farmers underestimate the necessity of mineral fertilising. It is right that the land should yield and it must yield but it is not right when judgement concerning colours is passed by the blind. And this is the case with administrative obligation to buy fertilisers while their application is left to its fate. (23)

Professional agrotechnical advisers were too frequently overloaded with administrative functions so that they could not fully co-operate with farmers. The various reasons for the poor state of some farms were not taken into account. Remedial measures to improve the farmers' economy were pursued, but with not enough consequence.

The system of supply contracts was an important part of government farming policy. The diminishing role of obligatory deliveries made the authorities seek new forms of influencing the line of development and to increase the output of private farms, linking them up to the socialised sector. Supply contracts, which had been tested before, were theoretically based on the principle of giving farmers a guarantee of ready sales for their products (at prices slightly higher than those offered outside the system of contracts), and providing them with proper seeds, pedigree animals, fertilisers, feeding stuffs or coal. Co-operative and state-owned purchasing enterprises had simultaneously received an assured supply of farm products. Nevertheless, in practice, the situation differed from the theoretical concept. Insufficient agricultural output led more and more frequently to a somewhat formal treatment of supply contracts. They were usually signed shortly before delivery and became a special form of purchasing. Farmers benefited from the relatively higher prices and the purchasing enterprises were unable to influence the desired direction of development. On the other hand in good harvest years the purchasing enterprises frequently limited the quantity of fruit or vegetables bought,

Table 4.7: Development of Polish Agriculture, 1957-70

	1957	1958	1959	1960	1961	1962
1. Rural population (millions)	15.5	15.5	15.5	15.4	15.5	15.6
2. Gross agricultural output (1950-2 = 100)	122.9	126.5	125.4	132.1	145.8	133.7
3. Market agricultural output (1950-2 = 100)	129.7	142.1	139.1	147.8	164.9	159.3
4. Area under crops (million ha)	15.5	15.3	15.4	15.3	15.3	15.2
5. of which: collectivised farms (%)	15.0	13.7	13.3	13.2	13.5	13.7
6. Wheat yields in q per ha	16.1	15.7	17.3	16.9	19.9	19.4
7. Potato yields in q per ha	127	126	128	132	160	130
8. Cattle (millions)	8.3	8.2	8.4	8.7	9.2	9.6
9. Pigs (millions)	12.3	12.0	11.2	12.6	13.4	13.6
10. Tractors (thousands)	55.7	58.3	57.7	62.8	73.6	87.0
11. Fertiliser use in kg per ha of arable land	30.7	28.3	31.9	36.5	39.1	44.1

Source: Rocznik Statystyczny 1977, pp. XXX-XXXI, XXXVII-XXXIX.

1963	1964	1965	1966	1967	1968	1969	1970
15.7	15.8	15.9	15.9	15.9	15.8	15.9	15.6
139.1	140.8	151.7	159.6	163.4	170.6	162.6	166.1
159.6	168.2	181.9	196.3	202.7	211.3	204.0	210.9
15.3	15.3	15.1	15.1	15.1	15.1	15.0	15.0
13.9	14.3	14.7	14.8	15.0	15.1	15.5	15.9
19.9	18.7	20.6	21.5	22.4	24.8	24.0	23.2
158	169	154	169	176	185	165	184
9.8	9.9	9.9	10.4	10.8	10.9	11.0	10.8
11.7	12.9	13.8	14.3	14.2	13.9	14.4	13.4
101.1	114.8	131.0	145.1	160.6	180.5	202.7	224.5
45.5	49.1	56.4	66.4	80.7	93.4	109.5	123.6

since they were already over-loaded with merchandise they could not promptly sell or process. Farmers felt a lack of stability and as a result the supply contracts only partially connected individual farms with the socialised economy. It was mainly possible as long as the market situation was more or less stable but with increasing market fluctuation the inter connections weakened. The supply contracts functioned relatively well in relation to industrial crops such as sugar beet, tobacco and the like.

Agricultural policy was generally conducive to increased productivity but in 1962 and 1963 unfavourable weather conditions led to a temporary decline in farming production. In 1970 total agricultural output exceeded the 1950-2 level by 66 per cent. Notwithstanding, the increase was lower than expected in the economic plans and resolutions of the party congresses. Moreover, animal husbandry developed very slowly. The Third Congress of the party stipulated that agricultural output should grow by 30 per cent in 1959-65, whereas the actual increase was 21 per cent. At the Fourth Congress it was planned that agricultural output would increase by another 30 per cent in 1966-70 but in practice it grew by only 21 per cent. The Fourth Congress expected the 1966-70 increase in output to be 15-24 per cent higher than that of the early 1960s. Though this task was generally fulfilled, the end of the five-year period brought a decline in production. (24) A rapid increase of fertiliser sales and improved technical equipment, without adequate economic results was quite upsetting. In other words, greater investment was bringing diminishing returns. For all that agricultural output grew more rapidly than in previous years. The market supply increased even faster but social requirements were not satisfied. Animal husbandry faced the problem of feeding stuffs. Their insufficient production led to a growing demand for imported feeding stuffs and the government had to find ways of either decreasing their consumption or improving domestic output. Growing wheat and maize imports from the West was another complication as it diminished foreign exchange funds for the import of investment goods. Basic trends in the development of Polish agriculture in 1957-70 are shown in Table 4.7.

Great importance was attached to the activity of agricultural associations, whose tradition went back to the nineteenth century, and to increasing their share in output. The associations' objectives were to stimulate production through the popularisation of land cultivation methods, collective purchases and utilisation of machinery, etc. Some politicians thought the associations would lead to a revival of collective methods of production. In fact the associations were also involved in other projects - providing, for example, water supply systems or taking over fallow land for collective cultivation, organising animal breeding etc.

However, these associations were gradually subordinated to their superior authorities, which were theoretically supposed to be representing farmers' interests but which in practice became management centres for the associations. This was a serious problem, especially in some parts of Poland. Farmers were losing their influence over the associations' activities. Several factors influencing effects of these organisations were determined by the central authorities (for instance, charges for machinery use) and this contradicted the primary idea of self-management for the associations.

The appearance of manpower shortages in some regions made farmers critical of methods which wasted their time. The methods of purchasing farm products by co-operatives and state-owned processing enterprises lagged behind developments in farming. Suppliers frequently had to wait before their products were accepted; village shops were badly supplied and the settlement of various formalities in offices took a long time as they were usually far away. The necessity to improve this state of affairs was realised by the central party organs (for example, the resolution of the September 1967 plenum of the CC PUWP), but in practice change was very slow and sometimes involved additional investment expense. The Peasant Mutual Aid co-operatives helped a great deal in this respect.

The socialised sector of agriculture included co-operatives (in 1970 they numbered 1,106) and state farms (in 1970 there were 5,356 of them subordinated to the Ministry of Agriculture). Moreover, 3,312 agricultural associations (9.4 per cent of their total number) exercised productive functions. (25) The number of co-operatives and state farms gradually diminished in the late 1960s due to organisation changes. But at the same time their area and employment grew. Growing investment in collectivised agriculture and changes in the system of prices and organisation of the purchasing of farm products stimulated increases in output which were more rapid than in private farms.

The socialised farms worked more and more efficiently. While in the early 1950s their average economic performance was generally worse than that of private farms, the 1960s brought a reversal of this situation. State and co-operative farms achieved higher yields of grain or milking capacity than private holdings. In 1960 socialised farms supplied 11.3 per cent of the total final agricultural output (internal productive consumption deducted), while in 1970 their share grew to 16.3 per cent. (26) Their main shortcoming was high production costs.

Private holdings were undergoing extensive changes. The system of supply contracts, which included a growing number of products, connected small producers with the planned economy. The supply of the rural market was in the hands of co-operatives and state organisations. Despite the maintenance of an open market for farm products, the free market was only a part of the total turnover of these products and prices were mainly determined by government policy. Thus small producers were indirectly absorbed within the system of the planned economy. Although in some specialised lines of production, such as horticulture, private farms survived and developed quite well using hired labour, they accounted for only a small fraction of the whole of private farming. Notwithstanding private ownership of land and domination of private farms, the Polish agriculture was developing into an element of the socialist system, though it developed in specific ways, unknown in other socialist countries.

When agricultural policy was changed in 1956 farmers saw increased earnings. More and more industrial goods entered the rural market but despite technical progress and the spread of modern consumer goods, working conditions in the countryside were still worse than in non-agricultural jobs. Individual farmers had no holidays and did not have the luxury of fixed working hours. Farming as a way of life seemed unattractive to younger generations. Farms belonging to older people, who could neither work efficiently nor give their land to their successors who preferred the towns, were often neglected. The act of 28 June 1962 provided the farmer with the right to make over his land to the state in return for an old-age pension. By the middle of 1968 the number of pensions paid to farmers was a mere 8,000. This lack of interest was due to the paucity of the individual pension and to the attachment Polish peasants felt to their soil. (27) In 1968 the pension act was amended.

Other social benefits given only to hired workers were another problem. Individual farmers could not, with few exceptions, benefit from free medical care or accident and old-age insurances. Their children had more difficult access to education and social advancement which depended on graduating from a higher education institute. The average qualifications of farmers were lower than in other branches of the national economy. In many cases they consisted of practical knowledge acquired from parents. Vocational training was therefore an important factor, one which would determine the future of the Polish countryside.

FINANCE

Note circulation was growing throughout the period in question. At the end of 1957 it amounted to 19,672 million zł, but at the end of 1970 it had reached 58,644 million zł. (28) Retail prices grew relatively slowly. Several foodstuffs had the same fixed price in 1970 as they had had in 1953. The only major price rise, introduced in 1959, was in meat and meat products. Prices of some industrial goods increased whereas others diminished. The free-market prices grew a little more but the increased money supply meant only a slight inflationary pressure.

At the same time savings increased quite rapidly. At the end of 1957 they amounted to 7,291 million zł but at the end of 1970 had risen to 114,797 million zł. (29) To a certain degree this increase was connected with the shortage of some durable goods, like cars or flats, and this is why special forms of saving were introduced to make their purchase possible. It may be presumed that this savings system prevented the appearance of more evident symptoms of inflation in the Polish economy.

Budget revenues and expenses were systematically growing along with increasing government tasks and the expanding production of state-owned enterprises whose payments were the major source of budget revenues. In 1970 the socialised enterprises paid 76 per cent of all budget receipts. In 1957 budget revenues amounted to 157,936 million zł, while in 1970 they amounted to 389,602 million zł. There was a budget surplus throughout this period. (30)

In 1970 defence expenditure accounted for 10.4 per cent of total budget expenses, the national economy for 43.1 per cent. These figures can hardly be compared with the structure of budget expenses in the mid-1950s, since changes in the financial system diminished the share of funds designed for economic purposes in the budget. In 1957-70 the expenditure on education, science and culture rose by 147 per cent and expenses for social welfare, health protection and physical culture grew by 73 per cent.

The changes in the economic policy introduced after 1956 also affected the banking system. In the middle of 1956 the Bank Rolny took over the settlement of co-operative farm accounts from the Narodowy Bank Polski and a year later the accounts of state farms as well. Communal co-operative banks were reformed and named savings and credit co-operatives. The Narodowy Bank Polski Act of December 1958 and the banking law of April 1960 laid down principles of function for the credit system in which the Narodowy Bank Polski had a strong, central position. These principles were modified in 1963 when the authority of the Bank Handlowy w Warszawie SA, concerning foreign trade operations, was extended. In 1966 the latter bank was given the task of settling the accounts of foreign trade enterprises, granting them credits and financial control. Another major change in the banking system came on 1 January 1970. The Bank Inwestycyjny was wound up and its competence was taken over, except for some operations, by the Narodowy Bank Polski. At the same time the financing of foreign trade investment was entrusted to the Bank Handlowy w Warszawie SA.

Most credit activity was related to the socialised economy but credits for the private sector were growing more rapidly. In 1957-70 the total amount of credits for the socialised sector grew from 92,887 million zł to 535,309 million zł, whereas credits for the rural population increased from 3,785 million zł to 43,204 million zł Credits for handicraftsmen and for private housing were also growing. (31)

DOMESTIC TRADE

The trading network was constantly developing; in 1957-70 the number of trading posts grew from 147,300 to 196,200. Socialised trade was predominant. The number of private shops amounted to

25,300 in 1957 and then slightly feel to 18,500 in 1961, to 15,600 in 1963 and afterwards remained at a similar level. (32) These trends were due to repeated restrictions on private trade and some other reasons.

The market situation improved in the late 1950s to deteriorate afterwards. Since 1957 the market supply of industrial goods, formerly produced in insufficient quantities or not manufactured at all, increased. Imports of these commodities played a minor role. But changes in the structure of engineering industries after 1956 were of considerable significance. Making use of reserves resulting from a reduction in the production of capital goods, the engineering industry produced more refrigerators, washing machines, TV-sets and other durable consumer goods. Their supplies increased and became available to a wide range of customers. In 1958 the Economic Council stated: 'For the first time in the recent three years public opinion and the government's attention focused on the market situation are relieved of the formerly constant strain.' (33)

The Council thought the market supply generally sufficient and the situation stable. Nevertheless in the year 1959 a deterioration came, mainly in the field of meat and its products. Their prices were raised but the short supply of meat products was not eased.

On the other hand the supply of durable consumer goods systematically improved. As a result basic requirements in this respect were satisfied and there was a surplus of some of these articles in the late 1960s. This led to the introduction of new models of radios, TVs, refrigerators etc. which were of a higher quality and more up to date.

Import restrictions imposed at the end of this period exacerbated the market situation. The short supply of several imported articles resulted in long queues gathering outside shops. Though these were frequently for goods of a somewhat minor importance (for example, coffee), along with other market shortages it helped to stimulate social discontent.

FOREIGN ECONOMIC RELATIONS

The Polish-Soviet agreement in the autumn of 1956, which reduced Poland's foreign debt, was of essential importance for the economic policy of forthcoming years. Since the Polish balance of payments remained unstable in 1957-60, the USSR granted Poland credits for the purchase of 1.4 million tonnes of grain (payable between 1961 and 1962) and a further 700 million roubles for other goods (payable in 1963-5).(34)

In 1957 some of the financial matters in dispute between Poland and the USA were also settled, for instance those referring to compensation for nationalised American property. Following this the United States granted Poland favourable credits, to be repaid in złotys, which served the purpose of buying grain to fill the gap in the domestic supply. Thanks to these two agreements Poland was given favourable conditions to set her economy in order.

Under these circumstances a deficit in the trade balance could be maintained. In 1959 the rate of growth of foreign trade turnover was raised. The level of industrial development achieved and the tasks designed for the forthcoming years stimulated trade and its new forms. A medium-level advanced country like Poland before the Second World War and in the early post-war years could offer mainly raw materials and foodstuffs and had to import a lot of industrial goods. A rapid development of heavy industry and some processing industries made it possible to extend co-operation with other socialist countries. Moreover, further development in industry required co-operation since it stimulated specialisation in production. Poland could supply several raw materials, their range having grown due to successful geological explorations, but also several kinds of machinery, sea vessels, motor cars, sub-assemblies, etc. On the other hand certain raw materials had to be imported along with machines and other articles not manufactured in Poland. The necessity to modernise Polish industry and to produce large amounts of specialised products seemed obvious. A similar situation was observed in Czechoslovakia and the GDR but other socialist countries were also tending towards specialisation. As a result the whole socialist bloc required a deeper division of labour and an increase in economic co-operation. This was reflected in the programme of the Council for Mutual Economic Aid. In June 1962 a conference of its member countries adopted the principles of the socialist international division of labour and a programme of economic co-operation based on these principles. Joint, international institutions and organisations were established. This process led to formulation of the idea of economic integration of the CMEA countries in 1969. In July 1971 the Twenty-fifth Session of the CMEA in Bucharest passed this programme.

Further economic development in Poland also

required the extension of trade relations with advanced capitalist countries, from where modern technology and equipment were imported, and with the less developed countries. Favourable international conditions facilitated foreign trade turnover between countries of various political systems but it appeared that Polish trade relations with the capitalist world developed too slowly. In 1957 the share of the socialist countries in the total turnover of Polish foreign trade amounted to 61 per cent and in 1970 to 66 per cent. (35) The basic trends of Polish foreign trade are shown in Table 4.8.

Coverage of the considerable trade balance deficit involved growing indebtedness for Poland. In 1957 it amounted to $US232 million, then, after a temporary decrease in 1958, it grew to $US1,752 million in 1960 to fall to $US716 million in 1967 and to increase again to $US1,700 million in 1970. A little more than $US1 milliard were the debts in relation to the capitalist countries. (36) The fear of growing indebtedness forced the government to give up further borrowing in the late 1960s. Investments were checked and a policy of retrenchment introduced.

The commodity structure of Polish foreign trade was gradually changing due to the evolving economic policy and to the changing structure of the national economy. At first the share of machinery and equipment in Polish imports fell to 23.8 per cent in 1957 but then it grew again to reach 36.4 per cent in 1970. The share of fuels and raw materials fell from 53.1 per cent to 47.8 per cent, whereas that of farm products dropped from 17.4 per cent in 1957 to 9.6 per cent in 1970. The share of imports of industrial consumer goods was rather stable and fluctuated between 5.4 per cent and 7 per cent reaching a maximum of 8.4 per cent in 1957. Polish imports were therefore mainly investment-oriented while other goods were bought in view of insufficient domestic supplies. This referred above all to farm products. However in the 1960s non-productive imports were gradually limited.

The structure of Polish exports changed more radically. In 1957 machinery and equipment accounted for 20 per cent of the total exports, fuels and raw materials for 61 per cent, foodstuffs for 18 per cent and industrial consumer goods for 9.3 per cent. In 1970 the respective shares amounted to 38.5 per cent, 32.7 per cent, 13.2 per cent, and 15.6 per cent. In other words, from a country exporting mainly raw materials or roughly processed

Table 4.8: Foreign Trade of Poland, 1957-70

	1957	1958	1959	1960	1961	1962
Imports in million $US	1,252	1,227	1,420	1,495	1,687	1,885
from socialist countries	778	714	923	949	1,054	1,246
from other countries	473	512	497	546	633	639
Exports in million $US	975	1,059	1,145	1,326	1,504	1,646
to socialist countries	578	620	682	830	939	1,034
to other countries	397	439	463	495	564	612

Source: Rocznik Statystyczny Handlu Zagranicznego 1971 (Główny Urząd Statystyczny, Warsaw, 1971), pp. 2-3.

1963	1964	1965	1966	1967	1968	1969	1970
1,979	2,072	2,340	2,494	2,645	2,853	3,210	3,608
1,326	1,306	1,548	1,604	1,737	1,838	2,114	2,473
653	766	793	890	908	1,015	1,096	1,134
1,770	2,096	2,228	2,272	2,527	2,858	3,142	3,548
1,123	1,351	1,409	1,400	1,611	1,878	2,064	2,266
647	746	819	872	915	979	1,078	1,282

goods Poland had become an exporter of industrial commodities.

This trend looked different in relation to various groups of countries. Exports of industrial goods grew mainly in relation to the socialist countries since their co-operative inter connections were strengthening. In 1970 machinery and equipment accounted for 52.7 per cent of the total exports to the socialist bloc, industrial consumer goods for 18.2 per cent. In 1957 both commodity groups accounted for 34.8 per cent of exports to the socialist countries. Though their share in the turnover with other countries was also growing, it remained rather small. In 1957 both commodity groups accounted for 14.1 per cent of exports to the non-socialist advanced and developing countries and in 1970 for 24.5 per cent.

It should be pointed out that Polish terms of trade deteriorated after 1958 causing economic difficulties and an extension of the role of turnover with the socialist countries. Prices adopted within the CMEA differed from the world level and were more stable.

Poland's major trade partner was still the USSR which supplied 37.7 per cent of Polish imports and received 35.3 per cent of Polish exports in 1970. The GDR came second (respectively, 11.1 per cent and 9.3 per cent) and was followed by Czechoslovakia (8.6 per cent and 7.5 per cent). The largest capitalist partners included Great Britain (5.3 per cent and 4.3 per cent), the Federal Republic of Germany (4 per cent and 5.1 per cent), Italy (2 per cent and 3.2 per cent), USA (1.6 per cent and 2.6 per cent) and France (2.4 per cent and 1.7 per cent).

As compared with national income growth and with increasing industrial output, the rate of growth of Polish foreign trade turnover seemed rather slow. Though the turnover increased a little more rapidly than national income, industrial output expanded at a higher rate. Polish turnover could not match the trade development of many other countries. As regards per capita foreign trade turnover, in 1970 Poland was one of the last countries in the European hierarchy.

LIVING CONDITIONS

In 1955 studies on nominal and real wages were resumed in Poland and living conditions may therefore be described more precisely. Generally speaking, real wages grew along with individual farming incomes, though the latter were affected by some fluctuations shown in Table 4.9.

Table 4.9: Real Incomes in Poland, 1956-70

Year	Average nominal wage in socialised economy	Costs of living	Average real wage in socialised economy	Real incomes of farmers
	(preceding year = 100)			
1956	110.9	99.4	111.6	115.1
1957	114.4	105.6	108.3	105.5
1958	105.4	102.0	103.3	101.9
1959	107.8	102.6	105.1	97.6
1960	103.2	104.8	98.5	105.4
1961	104.4	101.7	102.6	111.2
1962	103.6	103.2	100.4	85.2
1963	104.8	102.3	102.4	110.7
1964	103.1	101.0	102.1	102.0
1965	102.6	102.6	100.0	108.6
1966	104.5	101.2	103.3	103.7
1967	104.0	101.5	102.5	99.7
1968	103.8	102.5	101.3	108.3
1969	103.2	101.5	101.7	84.2
1970	102.9	101.2	101.7	102.2

Source: Rocznik Statystyczny 1977, pp. XXXII-XXXIII, XXXVIII-XXXIX.

The average monthly wage in the socialised economy was 1,118 zł in 1956 and 2,235 zł in 1970, the latter sum being due to increasing nominal rates. At the same time the average pension grew from 226 zł to 1,144 zł. Pensions remained at a very low level so their radical increase in 1957-9 was an obvious necessity. Nevertheless in the course of time pensions, calculated on the grounds of wages of the retirement year, were gradually losing their value. Though the average nominal pension grew, it was only a result of the increasing number of persons who retired much later on, when their wages had increased proportionately. As there was a constant increase in prices, the problem of insufficient pensions arose again and was not solved.

A considerable growth in real wages was recorded in 1956/7. In 1958-9 the increase was already lower and the 1960 drop was a result of the price rise of late 1959. Afterwards real wages grew very slowly and their improvement was hardly noticed by workers. Since nominal wage rises only applied to some categories of workers, others often faced a temporary fall in real wages. Moreover, a short market supply, appearing repeatedly in the 1960s, made many people feel that living conditions were getting worse in some periods instead of improving.

Public feelings did not always correspond with reality. Some economists, however, criticised the methods of data collection applied by the Central Statistical Office (Głowny Urząd Statystyczny) and questioned the accuracy of figures illustrating the increase in real wages.

One of the basic reasons for the over-optimistic image resulting from the statistical data concerned various concealed price rises. Many producers only slightly changed the composition of their articles or simply changed the name and packaging of the product and demanded a higher price. Though the goods formerly produced were still manufactured, fewer supplies of them were available and customers had to buy new commodities at higher prices; for statistical purposes, however, the old price was adopted, though in practice the old article could not be bought. Journalists quoted several examples; in 1962, for example, one of the weeklies stated:

> Whereas in March last year 841 tonnes of cheap beef was sold in Warsaw along with 159 tonnes of the 'extra' beef, in the current year the ratio changed in favour of the 'extra' beef: 531 tonnes of old beef was accompanied by 337 tonnes of the 'extra' beef. (37)

This kind of situation raised social discontent since it mainly affected the poorest people.

The price reform announced on 13 December 1970 had similar consequences. Price reductions referred to 40 groups of industrial goods and varied from 8.6 per cent (toilet soap) to 40.5 per cent (nylon stockings). They also included radio and TV-sets, tape recorders, refrigerators, washing machines, bulbs, paints, matches, roofing paper, etc. At the same time prices of 45 groups of articles, mainly foodstuffs, went up. The price of meat and its products grew on average by 17.6 per cent, flour by 16.6 per cent, fish and its products by 11.7 per cent, jam by 36.2 per cent, spaghetti by 15.3 per cent, coal by 10 per cent and coke by 20 per cent. Building materials, textiles and other industrial goods also became dearer. (38) In practice these changes mainly affected the worst-off groups in society for whom food expenses played a major role. This led to the already mentioned protests by workers, social indignation being stimulated by unfortunate propaganda which tried to hide the consequences of the price increases. Since the price rises came in December 1970, the consequences do not appear in the above-quoted indices of real wages.

Considerable fluctuations were recorded in the real incomes of farmers. They were due both to changing weather conditions and the volume of products sold, as well as to changing purchasing prices fixed by the government. Generally purchasing prices showed an upward trend, this being aimed at counterbalancing the price growth of industrial goods bought by farmers. Nevertheless the proportions between various prices changed. It must be pointed out that the increase in purchasing prices was not as a rule accompanied by adequate rises in retail prices of foodstuffs. As a result the budget constantly subsidised sales of some consumer goods whose prices were lower than their costs of production. The list of such goods was gradually extended.

As compared with the inter-war period the average level of real wages largely increased but the improvement referred mainly to workers. According to an estimate by the distinguished economist, Michał Kalecki, the average real incomes in 1960 of all workers, clerks and officials (including the unemployed) outside agriculture were 73 per cent higher compared with 1937, while for those actively employed the increase was only 36 per cent. For manual workers only the increases were 130 per cent for all workers (employed and unemployed) and 75 per cent for those employed. For clerks and officials they decreased by 15 and 26 per cent respectively. These differences give some indication of the influence of unemployment. (39)

The above-quoted data show a certain averaging out of incomes as compared with the inter-war period. Salaries became more in line with wages. So, the average standard of living being undoubtedly higher, the social groups which had been privileged before the war faced a deterioration in their financial status. The quoted figures also show how important the ending of unemployment had been, since before the war it had seriously lowered the average standard of living of the urban population.

Even more significant changes were recorded in the real income of farmers. According to estimates by Leszek Zienkowski, the average per capita consumption of the peasantry in 1960 was about 2.5 times higher than in 1937. (40) Even if a relatively wide margin of error is accepted for methodological reasons and because of a shortage of precise statistical evidence, the improvement cannot be questioned. But in this case as well the rate of improvement differed in relation to various groups of the rural population and to individual regions. The largest advance was recorded where post-war land reform brought an end to agrarian over-population.

The growth in average incomes was accompanied by a changing consumption structure. The consumption of meat had grown from 42.5 kg per capita in 1960 to 53 kg in 1970. Nevertheless demand was growing rapidly and it was mainly the short supply of meat that limited its consumption. The meat supply had become a major economic and political problem. Evolution of the market showed that subsequent nominal wage rises were mainly spent on buying more meat and its products. The consumption of sugar rose from 27.9 kg to 39.2 kg over the same period, whereas that of fish went up from 4.5 kg to 5 kg. Consumption of milk, dairy products and eggs was also growing but cereals consumption was decreasing. A rapid increase in alcohol and tobacco consumption was disturbing. Though there were attempts to prevent this happening with price increases, the effect was short-lived. What is more, excessively high prices for vodka led to illegal distilling which could not be stopped even with high penalties. (41)

Political changes and modification of the planning system also influenced working conditions. The practical role of collective labour contracts increased which regulated certain relations within enterprises not determined by labour legislation. Several repressive measures were abolished. There was a trend to limit overtime. In 1955 an average industrial worker worked 138 overtime hours per annum (the evidence being probably incomplete) and 96 hours in 1960; the law stipulating a limit of 120 hours. The average number of overtime hours diminished again after 1964. In 1970 it amounted to 66 hours per worker per annum. (42) However, there were individual cases where workers took little notice of labour legislation, disregarding the overtime limit.

A gradual but very slow and inconsistent improvement in housing conditions was an important change. The years 1955-8 brought an acceleration of housing development but investment was soon limited. In 1956-60 the share of housing in the total investment was 19.1 per cent but in 1966-70 it fell to 14 per cent. (43) One of the main sources of finance for housing came from savings. Housing co-operatives developed after 1956. Individual house-building was also facilitated. The situation in the villages looked worse as after 1960 the government gave preferential treatment to economic investments and limited funds for residential building.

Despite these reservations it should be stated that housing production increased. In 1956-60 an average of 4.3 flats were built per 1,000 inhabitants and in 1966-70 this ratio grew to 5.8. In relation to each 1,000 new marriages the number of flats built in 1956-60 was 482 and 740 in 1966-70. Urban areas were more privileged, since 1,023 flats were built in 1961-70, whereas in the country only 375 flats per 1,000 new marriages were constructed. Nevertheless it should be pointed out that the large demand for flats in towns was partially due to migrations from the country to towns.

At the end of the 1960s the rate of housing development decreased. The number of new flats diminished compared with the growing number of marriages. In 1970 only 693 flats were completed per 1,000 new marriages.

Newly-built flats were also of poor quality. The industrial investment requirements of 1962-4 forced the government to limit investments in housing. As a result the number of flats put to use diminished, their average area fell due to an official decrease in the dwelling standards and their equipment deteriorated. Tenants, for example, received flats without baths which they had to install themselves. Government investments in housing decreased and more and more flats were built from co-operative resources.

Despite these unfavourable symptoms, criticised by economists and architects, the decade between 1960 and 1970 brought an increase in the number of flats per 1,000 inhabitants from 228 to 229, the average number of rooms in a flat rose from 2.42 to 3, and the average number of persons per room fell from 1.80 to 1.44, the number of households per 100 flats from 118 to 116.

Particularly rapid improvement was recorded for

various installations. New houses were equipped with water supply and sewage systems, power, central heating and sometimes with gas points. Old houses were modernised and repaired and essential facilities were installed. Even in the relatively poorer provinces of Białystok and Kielce the number of flats with electric light grew from 60 per cent to 90 per cent between 1960 and 1970. At the same time the number of flats with a water supply increased throughout Poland, from 29.2 per cent to 47.3 per cent (from 55.4 per cent to 75.2 per cent in towns and from 3.7 per cent to 12.1 per cent in the country). It must be mentioned that housing conditions varied enormously in different regions of Poland and the average equipment of flats in the countryside was still much worse than in towns.

NOTES

1. Unless otherwise stated the population data are quoted according to: Rocznik Demograficzny 1976.
2. Rocznik Statystyczny 1977, p. 32.
3. Rocznik Statystyczny 1970, p. 402; Rocznik Statystyczny 1977, p. 360.
4. J. Beksiak, Zmiany w gospodarce, p. 171.
5. B. Gliński, System funkcjonowania gospodarki. Logika zmian (Państwowe Wydawnictwo Ekonomiczne, Warsaw, 1977), p. 18.
6. Sytuacja gospodarcza kraju w roku 1959, (Polskie Wydawnictwa Gospodarcze, Warsaw, 1960), p. 4.
7. Nowe Drogi, no. 4 (1959), p. 33.
8. Ibid., p. 676.
9. Uchwały KC PZPR od II do III Zjazdu, p. 287.
10. Uchwały KC PZPR od IV do V Zjazdu (Książka i Wiedza, Warsaw, 1968), p. 93.
11. M. Nasiłowski, Analiza czynników rozwoju gospodarczego PRL, (Państwowe Wydawnictwo Ekonomiczne, Warsaw, 1974), p. 46.
12. Ibid., p. 27.
13. J. Pajestka, K. Secomski, Doskonalenie planowania i funkcjonowania gospodarki w Polsce Ludowej (Państwowe Wydawnictwo Ekonomiczne, Warsaw, 1968), p. 23.
14. W. Gomułka, Przemówienia 1968 (Książka i Wiedza, Warsaw, 1969), p. 225.
15. B. Gliński, Zarządzanie gospodarką socjalistyczną. Logika postępu (Państwowe Wydawnictwo Ekonomiczne, Warsaw, 1980), p. 188.
16. V plenum KC PZPR 19-20 maja 1970. Podstawowe materiały i dokumenty (Książka i Wiedza,

Warsaw, 1972), p. 11.

17. VI Zjazd PZPR 6-11 grudnia 1971 r. Podstawowe materiały i dokumenty (Książa i Wiedza, Warsaw, 1972), p. 28.

18. Rocznik Statystyczny 1969, p. 249.

19. Uchwały KC PZPR od II do III Zjazdu, p. 221.

20. Uchwały KC PZPR od III do IV Zjazdu (Książka i Wiedza, Warsaw, 1964), p. 466.

21. Mały Rocznik Statystyczny 1972 (Główny Urząd Statystyczny, Warsaw, 1972), p. 69.

22. Uchwały KC PZPR od IV do V Zjazdu, p. 136.

23. W. Daruk, Bez głaskania po głowie. Wspomnienia (Ludowa Spółdzielnia Wydawnicza, Warsaw, 1973), pp. 246-7.

24. IV Zjazd PZPR. Stenogram (Książka i Wiedza, Warsaw, 1964), pp. 21, 884; Rocznik Statystyczny 1977, p. XXXIX.

25. Ibid., pp. 213, 217, 221, 244.

26. Rocznik Statystyczny 1971, p. 267.

27. E. Spirydowicz, M. Rutkowski, W. Kostkiewicz, Nowe ustawy rolne (Ludowa Spółdzielnia Wydawnicza, Warsaw, 1975), p. 155.

28. Rocznik Statystyczny 1970, p. 543; Rocznik Statystyczny 1977, p. 419.

29. Rocznik Statystyczny Finansów 1945-1967, p. 252; Rocznik Statystyczny 1981, p. 595.

30. Rocznik Statystyczny Finansów 1945-1967, pp. 36, 53; Rocznik Statystyczny 1977, pp. 413-5.

31. Rocznik Statystyczny Finansów 1945-1967, pp. 230-1; Rocznik Statystyczny 1977, pp. 420-1.

32. Rocznik Statystyczny 1977, pp. XLII-XLIII.

33. Sytuacja gospodarcza kraju w roku 1958. Materiały II posiedzenia plenarnego Rady Ekonomicznej w roku 1959 (Państwowe Wydawnictwo Ekonomiczne, Warsaw, 1959), p. 144.

34. E. Basiński, T. Walichnowski (eds.), Stosunki polsko-radzieckie, pp. 329-30.

35. Unless otherwise stated the foreign trade data are quoted according to: Rocznik Statystyczny Handlu Zagranicznego 1971.

36. Rocznik Statystyczny Finansów 1945-67, p. 60; Rocznik Statystyczny 1981, p. 590.

37. B.W. Olszewska, J. Rolicki, 'Plaga', Polityka no. 22 (1962).

38. M.F. Rakowski, Przesilenie grudniowe. Przyczynek do dziejów najnowszych (Państwowy Instytut Wydawniczy, Warsaw, 1981), p. 22.

39. M. Kalecki, Z zagadnień gospodarczo-społecznych Polski Ludowej (Państwowe Wydawnictwo Naukowe, Warsaw, 1964), pp. 97-8.

40. L. Zienkowski, Dochód narodowy Polski

1937-1960 (Państwowe Wydawnictwo Ekonomiczne, Warsaw, 1963), p. 198.

41. Rocznik Statystyczny 1977, p. 73.

42. W. Masewicz, Praca w godzinach nadliczbowych w przemyśle polskim w latach 1919-1970. Studium społeczno-prawne (Zakład Narodowy im. Ossolińskich, Wrocław, 1977), pp. 173-5.

43. Data concerning the housing situation are quoted according to: A. Andrzejewski, Sytuacja mieszkaniowa w Polsce, p. 178 ff.

ATTEMPTS TO ACCELERATE DEVELOPMENT, 1971-80

POPULATION

By the end of 1980 the population of Poland had reached 35,735,000 people. (1) The total increment of the 1970-80 decade amounted to 3,077,000 persons, whereas the natural increase in population reached 3,366,000 people. According to current records the external migration balance showed a deficit of 210,000 people. Emigration figures were far greater than immigration - which was insignificant, fluctuating between 1,400 and 1,800 people.

The natural increase in population began to grow again. In 1971 it amounted to 8.5 per thousand, in 1979 to 10.3 per thousand; in 1980 it fell slightly to 9.6 per thousand. On the grounds of previous trends and the changing number of contracted marriages it may be presumed that in the 1970s Poland reached the culminating point of the demographic trend and that forthcoming years will bring a slowdown in population growth. It seems the current cycle is less differentiated than the previous one. This points to an evening out of the demographic effects of the Second World War. Poland is still one of the most demographically dynamic countries in Europe.

A new phenomenon, not so widely recorded before, was the increasing number of old people. In 1970 this group numbered 3,559,000 people and in 1980 had reached 4,227,000. On the other hand the number of the population of pre-working age amounted to 10,775,000 in 1970 and to 10,297,000 people in 1980. This tendency was due to the post-war lengthening of the average human life. Thanks to an improvement in living conditions and better medical care more and more old people reached an advanced age. As a result increasing sums had to be assigned for pensions and for new forms of medical and social care.

Emigration, which reached 30,200 people in 1971, gradually fell until 1975 when it amounted to 9,600 people. Afterwards it grew again to reach 34,200 people in 1979. In 1980 the number of people leaving Poland decreased to 22,700. It may be presumed that the emigration boom of the early 1970s was mainly due to the agreement signed with the Federal Republic of Germany concerning facilitation of family reunion, though in many cases it was only a cover for emigration due to material reasons. Some emigrants also left because of inconsistent agricultural policies, additionally exacerbated by local authorities. The economic development and evident improvement in standards of living recorded in following years checked emigration which had increased in the late 1960s, mainly due to worsening political and material prospects for the younger generation.

Nowadays it is very difficult to estimate just what are the circumstances and the range of emigration aimed at finding a job abroad. The only data available refer to trips based on official agreements signed by enterprises and institutions. According to these data in 1981 there were 84,600 Polish citizens working abroad, mainly in connection with contracts concerning construction, repairs, etc. (55,800 people). (2) Many young people also went to work abroad during their summer holidays.

Internal migrations were gradually growing. In 1971 about 171,000 people moved from the country to towns and in 1979 some 211,000 people moved in this way. In 1980 the number fell to 192,000. It seems likely that this trend will continue. As a result of migration the urban population grew to 58.7 per cent in 1980. In absolute terms the rural population diminished reaching 14,756,000 people in 1980. As compared with 1970 the number of the rural population of working age fell slightly to 8,096,000 people, while the number of people of pre-working age decreased to 4,646,000 and the number of old people of post-working age increased to 2,014,000. According to the 1978 census the share of the population depending on agriculture decreased to 23.4 per cent, whereas that of people depending on industry increased to 26.7 per cent. At the same time the share of persons living on non-pay sources, such as pensions, etc. grew to 14.8 per cent (10.4 per cent in 1960), on trade to 5.6 per cent (4.9 per cent in 1960) and on some other services as well.

In the early 1970s numerous age groups of the post-war demographic explosion reached working age. As a result employment grew, especially in the socialised economy. In 1970 average employment in the socialised sector amounted to 10,325,000 people and in 1975 to 12,202,000 - an increase of 1,877,000 people. The following five years brought an increment of a mere 516,000 people and the 1980 employment of the socialised sector amounted to 12,718,000 people.

The 1976-80 increase in employment was much lower than that expected by demographers. According to Krzysztof Górski, director of a department in the Ministry of Labour, Pay and Social Affairs, this was due to a number of reasons:

> A relatively large increase was recorded in the private sector. This was not only an increase recorded by statistics, but also an unregistered, temporary or illegal employment. Another factor consisted of the decisions made by the government in the field of social policy and mainly of the possibility to retire ahead of time for several groups of employees, of favourable pensions and of regulations entitling young mothers to benefit from three-year unpaid leaves... There is still another clear and increasing, though hardly measurable, phenomenon. I mean a growing number of young people who terminated education and are fit for work but do not start it. (3)

We do not think that illegal employment (and the number of people refusing to work) was growing to an extent noticeable in the national economy but the difference between the increase in employment and demographic forecasts was also due to emigration. As a result the late 1970s brought a growing manpower deficit to some branches of the economy, while other lines revealed an excess of it. There was a severe shortage of unskilled workers in jobs requiring intense physical strain. On the other hand a number of graduates of higher schools could not find work consistent with their qualifications.

The manpower deficit seemed sometimes to be only an apparent one. A large part of the growth in industrial output was still achieved thanks to increasing employment, but labour productivity remained poor. Many factories had concealed manpower reserves but their disclosure and utilisation required a consequent reform of the planning and management system.

The shortage of unskilled workers was largely due to a rapid increase in the share of vocationally qualified people. According to the 1978 census 4.5 per cent of the population of more than 15 years had received higher education (19.9 per cent secondary; 17.4 per cent basic trade and 45.7 per cent primary education). Only 12.5 per cent of these people had not graduated from primary schools. More than half of this population were people of 50 years and over living in the country.

The growth in the level of education was a permanent feature and is shown by the growing number of pupils and students. In 1980/1 the number of students reached 453,700. At the same time 80.7 per cent of youth between 15 and 18 years of age were still receiving education.

INDUSTRY

Demonstrations and scuffles in the towns of the Polish Baltic coast in December 1970 led to essential changes in party and government leadership. At the end of December 1970 the Seym recalled Marian Spychalski from the office of the Chairman of the Council of State (appointed in April 1968) and several other top leaders were removed in the following months. Józef Cyrankiewicz, who quit the office of prime minister, became a new Chairman but was substituted by the well-known historian, Henryk Jabłoński, at the beginning of 1972. At the end of December 1970 the Seym also recalled several ministers and the office of prime minister was entrusted to Piotr Jaroszewicz. Further ministers were replaced in February 1971.

On 20 December 1970 Władysław Gomułka and some other top leaders were forced to give up their posts. The position of the First Secretary of the party was taken over by Edward Gierek, the former leader of the Katowice party organisation.

Modification of political activities and the changing social climate were even more important. These changes, which started in late December 1970, also had a considerable impact on the economy. Workers usually appreciated direct party and government consultations with large factory staffs concerning suggested decisions. Remarks gathered in this way were to serve as one of the conditions of selection of economic policies. Before long, however, these consultations lost their practical value. In February 1976 they were introduced into the amended constitution as a form of citizens' influence on government policy but in practice this institution decayed and was not supplemented by executive regulations.

At the beginning of 1971 the announced price rise was withdrawn and preparations for a new five-year plan were resumed along with studies on the reform of the planning and management system. In mid-February 1971 the new premier Piotr Jaroszewicz told the Seym:

> Above all we have started repairing the damage due to the policy of neglecting the necessity of a close connection between politics and the economy, between economic and social planning

> and between the increase of production and investments and the improvement of living conditions. (4)

He also announced further work concerning economic plans as well as improvements in planning and organisation.

The basic targets of the new five-year plan for the years 1971-5 were considered at the Politburo sitting in mid-May 1971. In this connection the deputy chairman of the Planning Commission, the well-known economist, Kazimierz Secomski, said: 'It is necessary to restore correct proportions of development and to eliminate serious negligence in the field of living conditions, giving these problems preferential treatment in the forthcoming five-year plan.' (5)

The increase in real wages by 18-20 per cent resulting from an accelerated rate of growth of the whole economy was, in his opinion, the crucial issue of the new plan. The plan targets were to take into account the possibility of bad harvests or unfavourable foreign trade conditions which meant making an allowance for reserves.

The key problems of the new five-year plan were carefully analysed by the CC PUWP in June 1971 and afterwards by the party's Sixth Congress in December 1971. The Congress passed the main guidelines of the plan which included targets slightly more moderate than those considered in the spring. This was due to a more realistic evaluation of the economic situation and to the maintenance of a high rate of investment. The resolution of the Sixth Congress read as follows:

> In the years 1971-5 it is necessary to assure, given full employment, an increase of the average real wage in the socialised economy by 17-18%. This increase will differ in relation to various occupational groups since it is necessary to eliminate disproportions infringing the principle of just pay and checking the increase of the social productivity of labour. The total increase of consumption should amount to 38-39% over the current five-year period, whereas the per capita consumption should amount to about 33%.

The resolution went on to say:

> Apart from the real wage increase, the major

> socio-economic targets include assurance of employment for young people entering working age. In the current five-year period they will number about 3.5 million persons. The entry of especially numerous age groups of young people to working age means extending national productive forces. (6)

The guidelines determined the increase of national income at 38-9 per cent. Industrial output was to grow by 48-50 per cent and agricultural production by 18-21 per cent.

Realisation of full employment and the growth of production required a considerable increase in investment effort. Investments were expected to grow by 42 per cent as compared with the previous five-year plan. Since investments were to increase more rapidly than national income, their share had to grow at the cost of consumption.

The fulfilment of the plan was subject to investment expansion. In practice about 1,900 milliard zł were spent on investments within the whole five-year period, that is about 31 per cent more than had been planned. (7) This resulted above all from an extension to the range of undertakings due to pressure from local authorities and various industrial lobbies as well as to the current requirements of the national economy. A number of decisions concerning new investment undertakings were not adjusted to the real possibilities of the Polish economy and to other parameters of economic plans. Cost estimates were systematically still overrun.

New investments extended the fuel and raw material basis of the national economy. For instance, a new coal mining region was developed in Lublin province, although results were expected only during the 1980s. The transportation network was extended by the construction of new roads to satisfy growing motor-car traffic. Important investments were made which facilitated the development of foreign trade, like the Gdańsk Northern Port or the container terminal in Gdynia. A railway line of a wide gauge adjusted to the Soviet transportation system was built to simplify the supply of Silesian steel mills with Soviet iron ore and some exports eastward. Despite the extension of the railway system it failed to meet the requirements of the whole economy. It proved that the development of railways lagged behind these requirements and at the end of the 1970s irregularity of railway traffic became an everyday phenomenon.

Large investments were undertaken in metallurgy. The growing demand for iron and steel meant that the government had to modernise existing plants and start the construction of a huge Huta Katowice steel mill near Sosnowiec in Upper Silesia. It was expected not only radically to increase the output of metallurgy but also make it possible to close old and inefficient plants. However, it soon turned out that the decision concerning the location of the Huta Katowice and some other problems involved was made without regard to existing conditions. Criticism was suppressed by administrative measures. Moreover, economies in iron and steel consumption were neglected, though Polish economists frequently showed such consumption to be excessive.

At the same time large-scale production of industrial goods was started, some of which had been until recently treated as luxury items. The most impressive undertakings of this kind included the development of the motor-car industry. For instance, a low capacity motor-car factory was constructed in Bielsko-Biała under Fiat licence.

The utilisation of numerous licences and imported machinery and equipment was another typical feature of the investment programme of the early 1970s. The number of imported licences grew from 18 in 1970 to 87 in 1973 to decrease to 30 in 1978 and to 6 in 1980. Altogether in 1971-80 Poland bought 452 licences including 416 licences imported from the capitalist countries. Most of them were bought in the Federal Republic of Germany, France and the USA. The decreasing number of licences actually put to use was criticised. In 1970 only 112 out of 142 licences were applied in practice, and in 1976 only 238 out of 385, though in later years there was some slight improvement. (8)

For instance, the Fiat licence and equipment for the production of motor cars were bought in Italy, the Berliet bus licence in France and the Massey-Ferguson tractors in Great Britain. Many licence agreements were based on the principle that the credits involved would be discharged by means of supplies of licensed products. In practice it turned out that the construction of several factories extended over too long a period and tied up capital to an unreasonable degree. Moreover, some licence decisions proved unfortunate. The bus licence, for example, was strongly criticised but in this case any public discussion was made impossible either. There were cases when people making decisions concerning licence imports had not examined domestic designs. The achievements of Polish tractor designers were thereby entirely neglected. Last but not least, there were examples of licences being bought which were of no economic importance, even useless.

The general policy of industrial modernisation was undoubtedly rational and purchases of foreign technologies could stimulate economic development. A medium-sized country like Poland was unlikely to develop various lines of production and keep pace with world technological progress. The decrease in investment productivity recorded in preceding years seemed to justify the import of modern technology.

Waldemar Kuczyński noticed that 'Technical reconstruction was to reverse this trend which in the long run led to stagnation or to a conflict between the government and society due to an excessive share of accumulation in the national income.' (9)

In the early 1970s most licensed production was of export quality which would help with the discharge of credits. However, in the course of time the range of investments connected with licence imports exceeded Poland's capacity and capability - which led to the cancellation of some investments and to huge waste. Many licences were related to more imports which were sometimes irrational from the point of view of the whole economy. As a result the policy helped to bring about Poland's immense indebtedness abroad.

The investment policy of the 1970s also consisted of joint ventures. Within the CMEA co-operation programme Poland supplied her partners with motor-car and aircraft sub-assemblies in exchange for other goods. Poland's allies participated in several Polish investment programmes in return for future supplies of raw materials. Poland, in turn, took part in similar undertakings realised in other socialist countries and in the USSR in particular. The extension of co-operation links with some capitalist countries was an exciting innovation.

Large investment programmes precluded government interest in small enterprises which manufactured small quantities of products but whose production was necessary for the market. As a result the production of many articles declined and some of the smaller factories were closed down. The effects were especially felt in the chemical industry. The reorganisation of this industry led to the merging of small, sometimes co-operative enterprises with large factories. Theoretically this was aimed at improving the quality of products and co-ordinating production programmes. But large factories were not interested in small lots of diverse articles and, despite previous promises, gave up their production. The market began to lack many simple but necessary reagents, formerly produced from domestic raw materials, or medicines. The growing shortage had to be filled by imports which additionally charged the balance of trade. At the end of the 1970s the lack of domestic output of these articles badly affected the functioning of many large factories.

Housing was another important part of the investment programme. The housing question was to be solved by introducing industrialised methods of house-building and the production of prefabricated elements in the so-called 'housing factories'. At the same time traditional building materials were neglected. Production of brick, roofing-tiles and the like radically diminished and their quality worsened. In the late 1970s the output of roofing paper and gypsum decreased. This had an unfavourable impact on building, especially in the countryside.

Some economists warned against excessive investments and the danger of engaging in projects beyond the means of the Polish economy. They pointed to the damage caused by the neglect or even stoppage of production of traditional articles in small enterprises and to the concentration of effort in modern industrial giants. The coupling of accelerated investments with a considerable increase in real wages was a particularly risky part of the economic programme. To a certain extent this risk seemed justified since increasing real wages stimulated motivation. However, it soon appeared that these possibilities were not to be realised. Satisfactory economic performance in 1971, partially due to changes in government policy but also to a good harvest, made the politicians - responsible for economic development - complacent. The experience of one year led to the groundless conclusion that the previous success would continue and that investments would continue to grow.

After a few years it was clear that this kind of policy inevitably produced negative, if predictable, effects.

> It appeared more and more frequently that the constructed structures would cost more than had been estimated and that to make them function it was necessary to supplement them by means of formerly unplanned projects. Disproportions in

> the developed productive potential were gradually disclosed checking utilisation of this potential. A whole wave of investment demands faced by the political and economic leadership, demands hard to refuse, since a refusal would mean freezing or a loss of the already engaged funds, had led to a situation in which it was necessary to invest more than was desired and to run into debts higher than had been planned. For various reasons, and mainly for the maintenance of social peace and quiet, financing of the investment increase, induced by extraordinary circumstances, at the cost of wages was out of question. (10)

Under these circumstances alarming symptoms augmented in the late 1970s, aggravated by unfavourable conditions independent of government economic policy. The general trends of industrial output and investment in 1971-80 are shown in Table 4.10.

Data presented in Table 4.10 call for explanation. Above all it must be pointed out that total industrial output includes the production of private firms, whereas data concerning this output in relation to capital goods and consumer goods refer to the socialised sector only. In 1971-80 private industry was characterised by a higher rate of growth than that of state-owned enterprises. Though in absolute terms it did not mean much (in 1980 private industry supplied about 2 per cent of the total industrial output), the respective indices slightly differ. The industrial output of the socialised sector showed a decline in 1980. Another reservation refers to accuracy of the presented data. The late 1970s brought a tendency in many industrial enterprises to show results better than they actually were. This procedure was aimed at receiving benefits resulting from an over-fulfilment of the plan targets. Falsification of statistical records was punished if disclosed but there is no evidence showing how common this procedure was. Nevertheless it may be presumed that the actual performance of Polish industry at the end of the 1970s was slightly worse than is shown in Table 4.10.

A very high share of capital formation in the national income, unprecedented in the whole previous history of People's Poland after 1944, was especially worth attention. Such an immense investment effort, impossible without foreign credits, brought evident effects in many fields. The economic boom of the early 1970s made the party and government

Table 4.10: Industrial Development in Poland, 1971-80

	1971	1972	1973	1974	1975	1976	1977	1978	1979	1980
National income (1970=100)	108.1	119.5	132.5	146.3	159.4	170.3	178.8	184.1	179.9	169.1
Percentage of accumulation in the national income	28.5	30.6	34.1	36.7	35.7	34.3	31.4	30.6	25.7	19.3
Industrial investments (1970=100)	110.6	149.1	190.5	232.8	259.6	238.2	232.5	221.6	187.5	161.4
Industrial output (1970=100)	107.9	119.4	132.8	148.0	164.1	179.4	191.7	188.1	184.2	184.2
Production of capital goods (1970=100)	108.3	119.8	133.7	149.7	165.8	181.8	193.4	202.0	207.2	206.6
Production of consumer goods (1970=100)	108.2	120.1	133.1	147.2	164.0	178.4	191.4	201.6	206.0	206.0
Employment (1970=100)	103.2	107.3	110.4	113.1	116.3	116.8	117.8	117.8	117.6	117.2

Source: Rocznik Statystyczny 1981, pp. XXXII-XXXIX, 228.

leadership feel optimistic despite the repeated warnings of economists and unfavourable symptoms which occurred both in the world economic situation and in Poland from 1974. Under these circumstances in December 1975 the Seventh Congress of the party decided to continue the previous economic strategy. The Congress resolution stipulated the 1975-80 increase in real wages to amount to 16-18 per cent, the national income increment to 40-2 per cent and the industrial output increase to 48-50 per cent. In 1976-80 total investments were to grow by 37-40 per cent as compared with 1971-5, while the share of capital formation in the national income was to decrease but only slightly. (11) Therefore the government's desire was still to force large investments and to maintain a simultaneous, rapid increase in the standard of living.

In 1976 it appeared that to continue with the previous economic policy without radical change was impossible. One of the reasons for that failure was the world economic recession which influenced the situation in Poland through foreign trade and credits. This influence was accompanied by the effects of the excessive investment effort and by insufficient agricultural development.

In the summer of 1976 the government tried to restore market equilibrium and proper relations between the costs of production and prices by means of a considerable rise in prices of basic foodstuffs. This referred above all to meat and its products whose prices grew by about 50 per cent. On 24 June 1976 premier Piotr Jaroszewicz presented the Seym with a draft project of the price rise and promised to hold consultations with large factory staffs. The urgency of the matter made these consultations only a rhetorical phrase. And though the project included compensation to keep up the standard of living, public opinion felt that these measures were insufficient. As a result workers protested again, the largest demonstrations being recorded in Radom and Ursus, with the government giving up the price rise project.

At the end of 1976 economic policy was changed again. It was called an 'economic manoeuvre' which consisted of attempts to curb imports, a slowdown in the rate of investment and a change of investment structure. This programme was similar to that announced in 1954 and it did not bring satisfactory effects either. The consequences of the 'manoeuvre' were summed up by Janusz Beksiak as follows: 'As a result an economic collapse came with a check of economic growth, decline of the national income and consumption and the derangement of the whole economic system. The country entered a social and political crisis.' (12)

The effects of disproportional development and investment delays became evident. There was a shortage of raw materials, semi-manufactures and power.

The failure of partial reforms made the party and government leadership give up previously planned projects and seek new solutions after the political crisis of December 1970. In February 1971 a commission was created by the party's Politburo and the Presidium of the Council of Ministers to elaborate principles for economic reform. Withdrawal of the unfortunate 1969-70 policies did not solve the problem but only meant its postponement. The commission decided on a new programme of reforms. (13)

> The projected decentralisation included a considerable limitation of the authority of the central power and an increase in the independence of enterprises. Economic organisations were to be relieved of most of the directives cramping their initiative, like employment limits, wage funds or investment and foreign exchange funds. These factors of production were to be regulated by synthetic measures like profits and the value added and parameters centrally fixed for several years. It was assumed that economic organisations would determine their productive programme entering into adequate relations with other organisations. Productive directives were to be limited only to extraordinary cases. (14)

This reform was to be based on Large Economic Organisations (Wielka Organizacja Gospodarcza - hence the name of the 'WOG reform') or associations of enterprises. The success of the reform, however, was subject to a general price reform and to adjustment of prices to the costs of production.

It should be pointed out that the projected reform was based on the Polish experience of 1957-8 as well as on reforms introduced in the USSR, Hungary and the GDR.

The practical application of the WOG reform started at the end of 1972 and was developed in 1973-5. In 1975 organisations functioning on the grounds of new principles supplied more than 60 per cent of the total industrial output of the socialised sector. In the meantime, however, the economic situation deteriorated. Factors, which at first stimulated accelerated growth, began to disappear while the world market suffered from a recession. In Poland inflationary pressure began to disorganise the financial system of large organisations, especially those producing for exports. Several factors were conducive to an increase in wages without productive effects.

All this made the government modify the WOG system in 1975. Directive management was partially restored. This did not mean a return to the former system, since the large organisations maintained some of their independence, but the latter was temporarily limited by the central power.

Finally, the announced reform of the Polish economic system, thought inevitable by economists, was washed away. The changes introduced were only partial and the system resulting from them was inconsistent. The worsening economic situation of the late 1970s caused the practical abandonment of reforms, although they were inevitable to overcome the crisis. In the course of time economic strains increased, the whole system was more and more disorganised and the unavoidable social costs of reforms grew.

AGRICULTURE

Acceleration in the growth of real incomes, considered one of the basic objectives of economic policy, required a rapid increase of agricultural production and especially animal husbandry. To achieve this objective it was necessary to create favourable conditions for farming and encourage farmers to raise productivity.

In 1971 the purchasing prices of cattle for slaughter and milk were raised. The following years brought further purchasing price rises concerning foodstuffs. They substantially improved the remunerativeness of agricultural production. Yet they aggravated the problem the government had faced for many years: a growing imbalance between the purchasing prices paid to farmers and the retail prices fixed by the administration. As a result of unfortunate attempts to change prices made in preceding years, the government feared the political effects of a more radical price reform and decided to stabilise the retail prices of foodstuffs, advertising this decision as essential social policy. In this connection budget subsidies for foodstuffs were rapidly growing. In many cases purchasing prices became higher than retail prices. For instance, in 1975-80 the retail price of milk was 2.90 zł per litre, whereas the purchasing price increased from 3.69 to 6.53 zł per litre. (15) The difference was covered from the budget.

Under these circumstances, and given the gradual growth of foodstuffs' prices in the world market, the Polish economy faced the more and more urgent question of how to adjust retail prices to the costs of production and purchasing prices of foodstuffs. The problem was additionally complicated by the fact that demand, which grew more than supply in the socialised trading network, led to an increase in free-market prices. Thus, for example, the average purchasing price of wheat rose from 396 zł per 100 kg to 513 zł between 1970 and 1980, whereas the average free-market price increased from 461 to 897 zł per 100 kg.

The share of investment in farming in total investments fell at first (from 16.2 per cent in 1970 to 13.4 per cent in 1975), this being connected with a very high rate of industrial investment, but afterwards it grew to 16.1 per cent in 1980. (16) The socialised farms were explicitly privileged. For instance, the development of farm machinery production was aimed at supplying state farms with large machines unfit for small peasant holdings. On the other hand, the production of small tractors and tools needed by individual farmers was entirely neglected. Such a policy was connected with government hopes that within a short time small peasant holdings would decline in favour of large state and co-operative farms. Paradoxically, despite the growing output of tractors, amateurish makes manufactured by hand in some villages were often more suited to peasant requirements.

At the same time the government gradually removed the formal fetters preventing individual farmers from choosing the most rational line of production and strengthened the social status of peasants. In 1972 obligatory deliveries were entirely repealed. The relationship between individual producers and the state or co-operative purchasing organisations was based on supply contracts only. This system facilitated specialisation in farming. The taxation system was also changed. After the repeal of obligatory deliveries the land-value tax included previous charges for the Agricultural Development Fund. Apart from that progressive taxation was moderated and some tax reductions were introduced. The new policy favoured well-qualified farmers who were ready to intensify their production. In 1972 farmers were included in the free medical care system on the same principles as employees in other branches of the national economy. The take-over of farms belonging to old people was pursued in return for pensions. This procedure was logically supplemented by including individual farmers in the old-age benefit system in 1978. Though it was criticised (for example, as being constructed with a view to stimulating the purchase of farm products) the 1978 act meant a change in government attitude towards individual farmers.

These changes illustrate the government's desire to assist in the development of individual farming in close connection with the socialised economy. Polish farmers were finally considered independent owners who, acting within the socialist economic system, could make their own decisions regarding development, investments, etc.

Yet many top managers of the Polish economy remained distrustful towards individual farming and tended to seek methods to accelerate the socialisation of agriculture regardless of economic efficiency. Some of them even thought it inevitable to abolish individual farms in the indefinite future. As a result the government's current agricultural policy lacked consistency.

On the one hand the government tended towards a full utilisation of arable land even if it meant giving land to individual farmers warranting good economic results. This was due to the disquieting diminution of the arable land area, mostly due to the development of industry and towns. The standing regulations did not safeguard reasonable utilisation of land. In October 1971 a new law was passed which embodied protection of all arable land, irrespective of the form of ownership. The law laid down a number of obstacles to the take-over of land for non-agricultural purposes and methods preventing the deterioration of soil fertility, as well as the owners' duty to utilise their land properly. It was stipulated that owners of agricultural farms should be professionally qualified, either as a result of graduating from adequate schools or having gained appropriate practice. Qualified individual farmers received the right to buy land belonging to the state administration (within the so-called State Land Fund). The area of land in government hands grew due to the take-over of farms of old peasants in return for pensions. But the question was how to utilise this land most economically. In this connection the Minister of

Agriculture, Kazimierz Barcikowski, told the CC PUWP plenum in January 1977:

> We have encouraged the take-over of land by farmers who want to extend their farms and raise production. These farmers can lease or buy land from the State Land Fund. The question is to make possible a rational utilisation of land for everybody who can increase market production, so necessary for the country. The question is also to create stable conditions for the development of farming, to encourage young people to stay in the countryside and to attract the most qualified and ambitious people to farming. (17)

On the other hand, however, opposing principles were also formulated. The Politburo programmatic report for the October 1974 plenum of the CC PUWP read as follows:

> The government will promote the transition of land from owners mismanaging their farms to good and efficient farms. By taking over land in return for pensions, the government is able to influence directly the utilisation of this land. The State Land Fund should be treated as an important instrument of structural changes in agriculture. Its land should be in the first place given to socialised farms: the state farms, productive co-operatives, agricultural associations and their co-operative organisations. This land may also be taken over by collectives of farmers. The basic form of individual use of the State Land Fund land should consist of a long-term leasing by efficient farmers. The principles of leasing should be aimed at the most intensive use and ought to provide a stable basis for development of production. (18)

As a result agricultural policy was variously interpreted by lower administrative organs which were frequently hostile towards individual farmers. There was an opinion that the transfer of land to the State Land Fund and then to state farms would ultimately lead to collective farming; that officials would not worry about the declining agricultural population but spend their time trying to prevent the transition of land to private hands. The standing regulations were used to expropriate poorly managed farms, mainly those of old peasants. Some economists tried to find a theoretical justification for such a policy, neglecting the fact that smallholdings taken over from old farmers were usually in poor shape and could not be properly cultivated by machinery from large state farms. They also neglected the fact that more and more individual farmers felt uncertain about the future.

Journalists were alarmed that, contrary to CC PUWP and government decisions, individual farmers faced growing obstacles. In October 1977, for example, the weekly Polityka quoted news reported by the daily press:

> Heads of communes unwillingly sell land to individual farmers, even if the latter have cards of specialised farms, and to productive collectives as well. They delay handling problems already settled, withdraw from promised contracts and raise various formal or legal difficulties... Private sales are quite limited. According to a popular opinion, administrative mediation does not help, but, on the contrary, checks settlement of problems. In many provinces not a single hectare was sold to individual farmers. (19)

Though at the end of the 1970s the situation slightly improved, government inconsistency as well as the hesitation and arbitrariness of local authorities strengthened farmers' distrust in the government's intentions - which had a negative influence on production. Paradoxically, yet quite understandably, farmers began to enter into informal, almost secret co-operation. They feared that the introduction of organisational changes promoted by the authorities would lead to more bureaucracy and that the overwhelming interference of this bureaucracy would cramp their economic activity.

At the end of the 1970s other negative factors also influenced Polish farming. The growing strains in the national economy, supply difficulties and foreign trade problems brought about a deterioration in supplies to farming of several necessary goods including coal. The latter was above all provided for industry, exports and urban households and only afterwards to the rural areas.

The necessity to improve the market supply of farm products compelled the government to start the construction of large animal farms. Chicken, pig or cattle farms adjusted to mass production required large quantities of fodder concentrates. All these investments caused an increase in production but the

Table 4.11: Development of Polish Agriculture, 1971-80

	1971	1972	1973	1974	1975	1976	1977	1978	1979	1980
Rural population (millions)	15.5	15.6	15.4	15.3	15.2	15.0	14.9	14.9	14.8	14.7
Gross agricultural output (1950-2 = 100)	172.0	186.4	200.0	203.1	198.9	196.7	199.5	207.7	204.6	182.7
Market agricultural output (1950-2 = 100)	220.6	242.8	266.2	280.2	283.7	284.8	291.4	313.3	312.4	293.7
Area under crops (million ha)	14.9	14.7	14.7	14.7	14.7	14.7	14.7	14.6	14.6	14.5
- of which: socialised farms (%)	16.4	17.1	17.5	17.9	19.0	20.5	21.9	22.8	23.6	24.2
Wheat yields in q per ha	26.5	25.1	29.6	31.7	28.3	31.4	28.9	32.6	27.0	26.0
Potato yields in q per ha	149.0	183.0	194.0	181.0	180.0	203.0	169.0	198.0	203.0	113.0
Cattle (millions)	11.1	11.5	12.2	13.0	13.3	12.9	13.0	13.1	13.0	12.6
Pigs (millions)	15.2	17.3	19.8	21.5	21.3	18.8	20.1	21.7	21.2	21.3
Tractors (thousands)	248.4	278.8	319.2	364.8	401.2	434.0	472.6	514.5	573.1	619.4
Fertiliser use in kg per ha of arable land	131.8	149.1	157.6	173.6	181.9	193.3	189.0	190.3	188.9	192.9

Source: <u>Rocznik Statystyczny 1981</u>, pp. XXXII, XLI and XLIII.

effects were bought at very high costs (including rapidly growing imports). Applied technology were also imported (mainly from the USA) along with feeding stuffs not produced in Poland for climatic reasons. The development of feeding technologies based on domestic resources was neglected. The moment that costly feeding stuffs imports had to be limited, the first to bear the consequences of this policy were individual farmers. As compared with 1975 the socialised farms in 1976 received more feeding stuffs, whereas individual farms had much less, although they were more economical and supplied most of the marketable meat. As a result livestock production by peasants collapsed. The general trends in agricultural production in 1971-80 are shown in Table 4.11.

The failure to fulfil the plan targets aimed at increasing agricultural production was also due to unfavourable weather conditions whose effects proved to be much worse than those allowed for.

The government's inconsistent policy towards individual farms led to a gradual decrease in their number and role in the national economy. In 1970 there were 3,224,000 individual farms in Poland and 2,897,000 in 1980. Their structure also changed. While in 1970 farms of more than 10 ha accounted for 12.6 per cent of the total number, in 1980 their share grew to 14.7 per cent. At the same time the share of the smallest holdings between 0.5 and 2 ha increased from 26.9 per cent to 30 per cent. (20) The smallest farms usually belonged to people having additional sources of income outside agriculture. The number of these farms grew, mainly due to the more and more frequent combination of industrial employment and farming.

The number of socialised farms diminished due to organisational changes. At the same time the area cultivated by these farms extended. In 1970 their share in the total area of land amounted to 19 per cent, in 1980 to 25.5 per cent, while the share in total agricultural production increased from 14.3 per cent to 23.3 per cent. (21)

The productivity of socialised farms, except for some agricultural associations, was usually better than that of individual farms. However, it must be pointed out that the latter utilised their arable land more efficiently with much lower production costs. Since individual farms were more and more handicapped by lack of supplies (coal, fertilisers, etc.), it should be concluded that the private sector had large, unexploited reserves.

FINANCE

The economic policy started in 1971 involved a rapid increase in the money supply. In 1970 it amounted to 58,644 million zł, in 1975 to 141,197 million and in 1980 to 296,684 million zł (an increase of 406 per cent). The growth of savings deposits was only slightly slower - from 114,797 million to 492,909 million zł (an increase of 330 per cent). (22) At the same time retail prices in socialised trade were relatively stable and the market supply was growing less than earnings. According to an estimate by Czesław Bobrowski, the market supply in 1970 was worth about 95 per cent of all earnings which made possible a normal increase in savings, but in 1980 the market supply of goods and services accounted for 87 per cent of earnings. (23) As a result huge monetary reserves were accumulated, threatening the market. Since many prices were fixed, the buying up of goods increased along with speculation. Simultaneously, prices of goods and services in the private sector, not controlled by the government, began to grow rapidly. The free-market price-level of 1980 was 181 per cent higher than in 1970, the most rapid increase having been recorded after 1975. (24)

Budget revenues and expenses were also growing. In 1970 revenues amounted to 209,487 million zł and expenses to 200,115 million zł, but in 1980 these were 1,215,188 and 1,246,275 million zł, respectively. (25) In 1980 a budget deficit was recorded for the first time since the Second World War.

Budget revenues included increasing payments from state-owned enterprises, while the share of taxation diminished. The tax burden of individual farmers did not change. In 1971 the taxation of handicraft workshops was raised along with that of private industrial and trade enterprises. As a result some of them were closed which made the government lower taxes again.

Growing expenses included subsidies for enterprises which sold their products below the costs of production. Data referring to this problem differ in various publications. According to the official statistical records the total sum of these subsidies rose from 25,309 million zł (including 7,459 million for the food complex) to 272,259 million (including 163,938 million zł for the food complex) between 1970 and 1980. (26)

The banking system was reorganised. The banking law of 12 June 1975 incorporated the Powszechna Kasa Oszczędności (a savings bank) into the Narodowy Bank

Polski, though it meant little change for customers who were still served by branch offices under the former name. A more important change was the creation of the Bank Gospodarki Żywnościowej (instead of the Bank Rolny) as a mixed, co-operative and government institution granting credits for agriculture, forestry and the food-processing industry. It also became a financial centre for the rural credit co-operatives. The extension of credits to the private sector and individuals was also important. The increase in the total sum of credits granted for economic purposes was connected with changes in the functioning of the whole national economy which implied a growing role for banks.

On the other hand credits for agriculture were rather limited, despite repeated opinions stressing the need to accelerate the development of farming.

A systematic moderation of the foreign exchange regulations was a real novelty in financial policy. In 1971 foreign exchange quotas for Polish tourists going abroad were raised. Afterwards they were adjusted to the current balance of payments situation. Private persons were allowed to establish foreign exchange bank accounts and to dispose of these savings. In 1970-8 foreign exchange deposits, mainly in the Bank PeKaO, grew from $US5 million to $US406 million. (27) This contributed to an increase in foreign exchange reserves available to government banks. In view of growing economic difficulties, at the end of the 1970s the freedom of disposal of private foreign exchange accounts was limited.

DOMESTIC TRADE

In 1970-80 the number of trading posts grew much more slowly than before: from 196,200 to 203,500. This meant an increase in the average number of buyers in every shop. It must be mentioned that the increase in the number of state and co-operative shops was markedly slow: from 180,600 to 182,400, while private shops developed more dynamically, their number having grown from 15,700 to 21,200. (28)

The early 1970s brought a concentration of state-owned trading enterprises by creating specialised associations including wholesale and retail enterprises organised according to the administrative division of Poland. This reform was the result of the introduction of a new management system which was aimed at increasing the independence of enterprises. The new administrative division of Poland introduced in 1975 (abolition of districts and establishment of

49 provinces) caused another reform in the organisation of domestic trade. In 1976 rural trade turnover was entrusted solely to the Samopomoc Chłopska (Peasant Mutual Aid) co-operatives. The state-owned and co-operative trading enterprises in towns kept on working but their competence was strictly separated. The State Domestic Trade Head Office controlled the trade in textiles, clothing, furniture and recreation articles. The Head Office of Consumer Co-operatives Społem managed the trade in foodstuffs (as well as some of the food-processing industries), articles of daily use (soap etc.), restaurants and services.

The co-operative trading network extended at the cost of state-owned trade enterprises. Small shops, mainly those employing one man, were frequently leased on an agency contract basis. Nevertheless the growing market shortages of the late 1970s limited the development of the agency trade because many agents could not bear the risk without adequate profits.

Investments undertaken in state and co-operative trade consisted mainly in shop equipment. The number of various cooling facilities, cash-registers, etc. was gradually growing. But organisational solutions still lagged behind technical progress.

The delay of investments in new residential quarters was a serious shortcoming of the trading network. Building enterprises were mainly interested in putting flats to use and, despite directives, postponed the construction of other buildings such as shops or department stores. As a result those living in new quarters suffered shopping difficulties.

The market supply was improved at first, especially with regard to modern domestic appliances and imported articles. Some goods were manufactured under foreign licences (for example, motor cars), while others were the result of Polish designs. The supply of foodstuffs grew less than demand so it became necessary to import some of these. At the beginning of the 1970s a number of newly imported commodities appeared, extending the range of goods available, particularly in large towns. In the late 1970s these imports were gradually limited along with the decreasing supply of domestic products. For instance, the supply of clothing and footwear diminished. Further deterioration in the market supply came in 1980 as a result of reduced imports and the general decrease in domestic production.

A very complicated situation existed in the foodstuffs market. After a certain increase in supply in the early 1970s, the following years brought a check (except for chicken) or even a slight decrease in supply (sugar, chocolate products). After the unfortunate attempt to raise prices in the summer of 1976, sugar rationing was introduced at the previous price of 10.50 zł per kg, while additional quantities could be bought at a much higher price (26 zł per kg). This system of double prices was also introduced for meat and its products. The so-called 'commercial shops' were established. They sold articles of a higher quality but at much higher prices. Long queues became a real hazard for customers at meat shops. People gathered in crowds waiting several hours for a delivery. Queues were also common practice with 'commercial shops'.

There were serious problems when buying other goods. Furniture, especially when inexpensive or for small flats, was constantly in short supply. Motor cars were sold within a system of prepayments and special savings accounts or on the grounds of coupons distributed in enterprises and offices. Since the free-market prices of cars were much higher than official ones, speculation on these coupons began. Modern radio and TV-sets, tape recorders and gramophones were in short supply. Along with increasing inflationary pressure the position of consumers was gradually worsening. This had a negative impact on the quality of products, because producers knew very well that even goods of a lower standard would find a ready market. Thus the seller's market was strengthened.

FOREIGN ECONOMIC RELATIONS

The growing investment effort connected with modernisation of industry required a revised foreign trade policy. In the second half of 1971 the concept of borrowing in the West crystallised. Soon it appeared that the recession in the most economically advanced capitalist countries, connected with dramatic rises in the price of oil, would assist in the realisation of this economic strategy. Faced with the necessity of cutting back on production many Western businessmen saw in the Polish investment programme a chance to counteract the effects of the recession. Apart from that the increasing price of coal raised Polish import capacity. As a result, after 1970, Polish foreign trade turnover rapidly grew, especially in relation to the capitalist countries. Credit operations made it possible to increase imports without a similar increase in exports. Exports were to grow, but afterwards, when new productive plants were completed. Export expansion was to include co-operation with foreign partners. The general trends in Polish foreign trade are shown in Table 4.12.

The data presented in Table 4.12 reveal several characteristic facts. First of all, Polish foreign trade relations with the socialist countries fluctuated but until 1979 were relatively balanced. The year 1980 brought a serious deficit in these relations. As regards other countries the trade balance deficit appeared in 1972 and rapidly increased until 1976. Since 1977 the deficit had slowly decreased but it still remained quite considerable. The whole decade of 1971-80 brought a trade deficit with the capitalist countries amounting to $US15,956 million, of which as much as 70 per cent accumulated in 1973-7. The effects of such an accumulation of debts, whose dates of payments were not co-ordinated, inevitably meant an accumulation of repayments within a relatively short time. This phenomenon increased in the late 1970s, though its effects were at first moderated by the relative easiness of contracting new loans.

Such a policy led to a constant increase of the foreign debt burden in 1970-80. In relation to the socialist countries this indebtedness (outstanding sums deducted) increased from $US400 million to $US589 million and in relation to other countries - from $US800 million to $US21,746 million. (29) The Polish balance of payments was seriously burdened. In 1971 debt service costs accounted for about 17 per cent of the total export receipts, in 1973 for 14 per cent, in 1976 for 34 per cent and in 1980 for 82 per cent. (30)

Credits contracted for investment purposes seemed quite justified and provided a chance to accelerate economic development. The success of such a policy was subject, however, to the achievement of an adequate increase in production and exports in order to repay the accumulating debts. This could not be done without the most rational utilisation of the loans contracted. But the hasty contracting of foreign credits adversely affected their economic utilisation. Soon the range of foreign loans exceeded all reasonable limits. According to Stefan Jędrychowski, even at the beginning of 1973 some economists had emphasised the dangerous symptoms of this policy at a conference in the Ministry of Finance.

> Too ambitious plans of imports of machinery and equipment from the capitalist countries made the ministries hastily sign contracts without regard to optimisation of the price and credit terms. It was pointed out that the number of machines

Table 4.12: Foreign Trade of Poland, 1971-80

	1971	1972	1973	1974	1975	1976	1977	1978	1979	1980
Imports ($US millions)	4038	5334	7857	10482	12537	13867	14616	16096	17598	19064
- from socialist countries	2721	3265	4059	4656	5745	6498	7587	8715	9554	10598
- from other countries	1317	2069	3798	5826	6792	7369	7029	7381	8044	8466
Exports ($US millions)	3872	4932	6428	8315	10282	11017	12265	14120	16262	16974
- to socialist countries	2442	3136	3901	4634	6162	6578	7390	8630	9907	9489
- to other countries	1430	1796	2527	3681	4120	4439	4875	5490	6355	7485
Balance: socialist countries	-279	-129	-158	-22	+417	+80	-197	-85	+353	-1109
Balance: other countries	+113	-273	-1271	-2145	-2672	-2930	-2217	-1891	-1689	-981

Source: Rocznik Statystyczny 1981, p. XLV.

> waiting to be assembled had grown as a result of acceleration of deliveries of imported machinery ordered for 1973 in December 1972. (31)

Economists also warned of other dangers and especially of the insufficient growth of exports. Nevertheless, it is evident from the quoted data that these warnings did not cause any change in foreign trade policy.

Further problems resulting from foreign trade difficulties were connected with the unwelcome, though predictable effects of some contracts. Industrial expansion required a further increase in imports of certain raw materials, semi-manufactures or components. Despite considerable efforts, Polish industry could not replace imports by products made at home. Domestic semi-manufactures were often of a lower quality than those required by foreign customers, so in order to export it was necessary to import first.

In the late 1970s the government put a growing emphasis on the increase of export production and on the limitation of imports. The effects of this policy were quite insignificant - due also to the internal economic situation. Given a growing shortage of goods in the home market, the quality requirements of Polish customers had to diminish and producers could easily sell articles of a rather poor quality. Foreign customers could not be so easily satisfied and export benefits for enterprises were rather limited. The whole of foreign trade turnover was concentrated in the hands of specialised state-owned firms, whereas direct producers only executed their orders. Thus some economic journalists formulated an idea which has never been put into effect:

> A *sine qua non* condition of the export orientation of our industry consists of a radical change in the economic planning system aimed at the creation of motivation and incentives to direct producers in order to stimulate their initiative and to raise export production. This is the only principle which will make possible the future export specialisation of our economy.(32)

The commodity structure of foreign trade turnover considerably changed due to the policy of accelerated investments and consumption. Above all the share of imports of fuels and power grew from 6.7 per cent in 1970 to 18.1 per cent in 1980, mainly as a result of rising oil prices. The share of the electromechanical industry rose from 38.5 per cent to

40.3 per cent between 1970 and 1975 to fall to 34.6 per cent in 1980. Imports of foodstuffs accounted for 7 per cent in 1970 and 9.1 per cent in 1980. Imports from the socialist countries were dominated by electromechanical products, fuels and power, as well as metallurgical goods (altogether 63.4 per cent in 1980). Imports from other countries included above all the electromechanical products (20.8 per cent), chemicals (18.3 per cent), farm products (18.7 per cent), power and fuels (11.9 per cent).

In Polish exports the major commodity group were the electromechanical products whose share had grown from 40.6 per cent to 43.3 per cent over the years 1970-80. They prevailed in exports to the socialist countries, whereas in relation to other countries their share was growing but had reached only 24 per cent in 1980. The second largest group was coal (9.2 per cent in 1980) whose share grew until 1975 but then diminished. Coal exports were especially important in Polish relations with the European capitalist countries. The share of foodstuffs decreased. In relation to the capitalist countries their share decreased from 23.3 per cent to 10 per cent of total exports. (33)

The changing commodity structure of Polish foreign trade was partially due to the effects of economic development but the second half of the 1970s brought growing limitations connected with the increasing domestic, economic and social strains and with feverish attempts to raise exports to the capitalist countries in order to secure money to repay debts. It should be pointed out that Polish terms of trade were generally favourable, except for a slight deterioration after 1976. Yet the promotion of Polish products in the advanced capitalist markets proved to be a very difficult task and the export effects of industrial development were relatively small. The costs of obtaining one US dollar in złoty terms was still very high. Co-operation with some large concerns, connected with licence purchases, was of some help since well-known partners could promote Polish makes in Western markets.

A real novelty in the Polish economy consisted of regulations allowing the so-called polonijne enterprises to be established in Poland by foreign citizens of Polish origin. They could benefit from import licences to buy raw materials and semi-manufactures abroad. The costs of such imports were covered by exports of their finished products, some of which were also sold in the Polish market.

The major Polish trade partner was still the

USSR which supplied 33.1 per cent of the total Polish imports and brought 31.2 per cent of Polish exports in 1980. The next largest socialist partners were Czechoslovakia (5.7 per cent of imports and 6.9 per cent of exports) and the GDR (6.6 per cent and 6.9 per cent, respectively). From among the capitalist countries the major role was played by the Federal Republic of Germany (6.7 per cent and 8.1 per cent respectively), France (4.2 per cent and 2.9 per cent) and Great Britain (3.5 per cent and 3.2 per cent). The largest overseas partner was the USA (4 per cent of imports and 2.5 per cent of exports). In 1970-5 the share of the socialist countries in Polish imports decreased from 68.6 per cent to 45.8 per cent to grow again to 55.6 per cent in 1980. (34)

The importance of relations with the CMEA countries consisted mainly in the stability of terms. In 1971-5 mutual trade relations were based on average world prices for the years 1965-9 which were only slightly modified. Then the CMEA countries adopted a system of average prices for the five-year periods preceding delivery dates. This system eliminated the somewhat unpredictable and violent fluctuations in world prices, and proved especially valuable in view of the rapid growth of oil prices. Long-term agreements were a stable basis of CMEA co-operation. As a result Poland's participation in the Council made it possible to avoid some effects of the variations in the capitalist markets. Nevertheless, it could not solve all the economic problems of Poland.

LIVING CONDITIONS

The new economic strategy started in 1971 at first stimulated rapid growth in real wages. This tendency is shown in Table 4.13.

The data presented in Table 4.13 should be treated with a certain amount of scepticism. We are of the opinion that only in the first half of the 1970s did the official indices reflect what could judiciously be termed as realistic figures. However, in 1976-80 the costs of living seemed to be underestimated, whereas the increase in real wages was overestimated. Of course, all estimates were very difficult since there were several price levels. Apart from the basic, state-controlled low prices there were 'commercial' prices and some customers bought the necessary articles in the free market. Moreover, cheap goods were gradually superseded by more expensive but not always higher quality ones. Finally, the accuracy of the records, on which the official

Table 4.13: Real Incomes of the Population, 1971-80

Year	Average nominal wage in socialised economy	Costs of living	Average real wage in socialised economy	Real incomes of farmers
	(preceding year = 100)			
1971	105.5	99.8	105.6	115.2
1972	106.4	100.0	106.4	114.9
1973	111.5	102.6	108.7	103.4
1974	113.8	106.8	106.5	93.4
1975	118.8	103.0	108.7	93.8
1976	108.8	104.7	103.9	108.0
1977	107.6	104.9	102.3	110.1
1978	105.8	108.7	97.3	105.6
1979	108.8	106.7	102.1	95.0
1980	113.5	109.1	104.0	92.0

Source: Rocznik Statystyczny 1981, pp. XXXV, XLI.

statistics were based, is doubtful.

Even if these doubts are ignored, the appraisal of living conditions must take into account growing market shortages which appeared at the end of the period under consideration causing an immense loss of time for people waiting in queues or looking for necessary articles.

The agricultural population, which made up for the 1969 decrease in real incomes in the favourable years of 1971 to 1973, faced a deteriorating situation. Their average real incomes reached the 1973 level as late as 1977 but the improvement was only temporary.

On the other hand the late 1970s brought a certain increase in pensions whose dynamism in preceding years was very slow. In the spring of 1977 a general increase in pensions was introduced. It referred to pensions granted before 1975 but further rises were also foreseen. Therefore in 1980 average nominal pensions were twice as high as those of 1973, though it must not be forgotten that most pensions were still very low when compared with the cost of living. Moreover, this action proved to be temporary and was not followed by further steps preventing a gradual depreciation of pensions. As a result of all rises the average nominal wage in the socialised economy reached 5,789 zł in 1980, while the average nominal pension was 2,681 zł monthly.

Despite all the economic troubles and unfavourable trends contrary to social aspirations, the average level of consumption was relatively high. In 1980 an average inhabitant of Poland consumed 127 kg of cereals, 74 kg of meat, 8.1 kg of fish, 21 kg of fat, 262 litres of milk, 223 eggs or 41.4 kg of sugar per annum. (35)

The average indicators covered the growing differentiation in incomes of various groups of the population. They were connected with the programme of accelerating the growth in the standard of living formulated in 1971. This programme was to a certain extent forced by the circumstances of the December 1970 political crisis. The new party and government leadership took over responsibility for the economy in a situation in which it was necessary to restore public confidence in the authorities. The leadership did not decide carrying out further changes in the political system which would have normalised relations between the various organs of political power and individual social groups. The consultations mentioned above were the only step taken in this direction and though they somehow impressed some social circles, their practical importance proved quite limited. What is more, they were soon abandoned. The leadership's disinclination to attempt further reform resulted most probably from the opinion that socialist social relations required the maintenance of the predominant position of the state in the economy and politics. This opinion limited initiatives for social participation, for the determination of the direction of development which would, inter alia, have allowed for the sharing of responsibility regarding the policies undertaken. As a result social interests were mainly directed towards the growth of consumption, which was encouraged by the government. The planned advance of the national economy was based on such an attitude.

This kind of an approach was logically followed by investments aimed at making available more motor cars, TV-sets, refrigerators or washing machines and foreign trips for as large a part of society as possible.

Under these circumstances material incentives were playing a decisive role. Apart from official incomes there appeared various forms of unofficial benefits. It became an accepted principle that people holding some managerial positions were allowed to take personal advantage of their privileged situation. This included coupons for motor cars, facilities for buying houses or building plots and materials, a special system of high pensions for the ruling elite, etc.

The great investment programme of the 1970s was sometimes compared with the economic efforts made in the first years of People's Poland which was accompanied by real social enthusiasm and productive initiatives. 'Construction of a second Poland' was the press motto. But the similarities were only formal. In the post-war years the basic objective was deliverance from the disastrous effects of war; and to create the conditions for the development of an independent state. The investment programme and the huge effort of the whole society were therefore aimed at the solution of national problems. In the 1970s the efforts promoted by the government were more or less aimed at the improvement of the individual standard of living, while the social objectives were all too frequently treated only as propaganda slogans.

At the same time certain social groups were on the verge of poverty: pensioners without families, for example, and young people who had to wait for an independent flat for a very long time after having gathered a large sum of money. The disparities were less perceptible in the early 1970s, when real wages generally grew and new hopes were aroused for a solution to the housing problem. Nevertheless in the mid-1970s these favourable changes came to an abrupt end - and the housing programme proved to be unrealistic.

At the end of the 1970s the differentiation of real income appeared to the full extent. According to the Central Statistical Office in 1980 the per capita real income decreased, as compared with the preceding year, in 68.9 per cent of pensioners' households, in 54.5 per cent of peasants' households and in 45.5 per cent of households with employees in the socialised economy. (36)

The workers' discontent was additionally raised by an extension of working hours. The requirements of the national economy, and exports in particular, made the government force the growth of coal output. This increasing output was partially due to extended working hours and to work on Sundays. At first this was only exceptional, but then the exception became the rule. According to data, most probably underestimated, the average overtime per worker amounted to 131 hours in 1979. In industry the figure was 91 hours, in building 138 hours and in transportation 309 hours. In 1980 overtime working slightly decreased. A simultaneous increase in the number of hours wasted for various reasons proved the incompetent organisation of management. (37)

Housing was one of the basic elements of the socio-economic programme formulated in 1971-2. The early 1970s brought considerable progress in this field, though the improvement of the housing situation was less than initially announced. In 1971-4 the number of dwelling units constructed grew from 643,000 to 895,000 per annum. This progress was made after several years of stagnation. In 1970-5 the number of new flats per 1,000 newly contracted marriages increased from 693 to 750, which was still insufficient. However, soon afterwards the rate of growth in housing production diminished and in 1979 it even began to fall. Although the number of newly contracted marriages diminished as well, in 1980 only 706 flats were built per 1,000 new marriages. (37) The quality of flats at first improved but then deteriorated. In all likelihood the quoted indicators are still too optimistic, as building statistics were in some cases falsified.

Despite the failure of the accelerated housing development programme, living conditions were gradually improved. In 1980 one room was on average inhabited by 1.11 statistical persons, though this average covered the growing differentiation of conditions of various social groups. (38)

CONSEQUENCES OF WRONG ECONOMIC POLICY

The economic crisis which began in Poland in 1979, and which became the direct reason for the strikes in the summer of 1980 and the essential political changes involved, was of a specific nature. Contrary to the Great Depression of 1929-35 and to other economic recessions, the Polish crisis was not the result of a typical business cycle.

After the Second World War Poland faced periods of economic troubles and socio-political conflicts, but for the first time industrial output seemed about to collapse. It would be wrong to ascribe the decline only to the strikes of the second half of 1980, since the fall in industrial output began much earlier.

Likewise it would be difficult to attribute the Polish crisis to the unfavourable market situation in the capitalist world. As already mentioned, terms of trade were rather favourable for Poland in the 1970s. This is why Józef Pajestka seems to be right when he says:

> Our crisis has not been 'imported'; it is a product of our own policies and attitudes. In my opinion this thesis is of a fundamental significance for understanding the present situation and for finding the way out of it... It is only us who can improve this situation by means of our own work and activity. (39)

The economic collapse was above all the result of post-1970 economic policies, which were at first successful but were then continued against the warnings of many economists - with disastrous consequences.

Public distrust towards the Gierek regime, which increased in the late 1970s, did not help to find a solution. Waldemar Kuczyński was right to write:

> Before August 1980 there was no chance that the authorities could stop the economic collapse themselves, by means of some arbitrary steps. There was no possibility to introduce interventionist counter-depression measures and to maintain public law and order. (40)

Political changes were inevitable if a real reconstruction of the economic and management system - which would temporarily decrease the standard of living - was to be undertaken.

In fact the Polish crisis means a crisis of certain methods of rule. An outstanding Polish economist Józef Pajestka has drawn the following conclusions from the experience of recent years:

1. It is unthinkable in the future to pursue a policy without its social approval. This requires democratisation of the decision-making process with all the necessary consequences in the system of institutions and information.
2. It is inevitable to extend largely the 'economic constraint' resulting from economic mechanisms. The point is not automatically to introduce unemployment, bankruptcy, etc. But the economic necessities must be realised much more strongly than before. It is especially important in this connection to introduce self-financing of investments, an increase in wages as well as the elimination of easy budgetary subsidies. (41)

In the post-war years Poland developed considerably her economic potential. Fundamental social transformations were accompanied by a general increase in the standard of professional qualifications. All this means a stepping-stone for overcoming the present crisis, on the condition that its real reasons are removed.

NOTES

1. Data concerning population are quoted according to: Rocznik Statystyczny 1981, pp. 36, 37, 43, 45, 47, 54, 64, 516 and 518; Rocznik Demograficzny 1980, pp. XVIII-XXI, 147.
2. Rzeczpospolita, 4 May 1982.
3. 'Gdzie są ludzie?', Kultura, no. 25 (1980).
4. Trybuna Ludu, 14 February 1971.
5. Ibid., 19 May 1971.
6. VI Zjazd PZPR 6-11 grudnia 1971. Podstawowe materiały i dokumenty (Książka i Wiedza, Warsaw, 1972), p. 553.
7. VII Zjazd Polskiej Zjednoczonej Partii Robotniczej 6-11 grudnia 1971 r. (Książka i Wiedza, Warsaw, 1972), p. 514.
8. Rocznik Statystyczny 1981, p. 514.
9. W. Kuczyński, Po wielkim skoku (Państwowe Wydawnictwo Ekonomiczne, Warsaw, 1981), p. 78.
10. Ibid., pp. 92-3.
11. VII Zjazd Polskiej Zjednoczonej Partii Robotniczej. Stenogram. Warszawa, 8-12 grudnia 1975 r. (Książka i Wiedza, Warsaw, 1976), p. 723 ff.
12. J. Beksiak, Zmiany w gospodarce, pp. 177-8.
13. W. Kuczyński, Po wielkim skoku, pp. 27-8.
14. B. Gliński, Zarządzanie gospodarką socjalistyczną, p. 317.
15. Rocznik Statystyczny 1981, pp. 457, 468.
16. Ibid., p. 184.
17. VI plenum KC PZPR 21 stycznia 1977 r. Podstawowe dokumenty i materiały (Książka i Wiedza, Warsaw, 1977), p. 45.
18. XV plenum KC PZPR 22-23 października 1974 r. Podstawowe dokumenty i materiały (Książka i Wiedza, Warsaw, 1974), pp. 54-5.
19. J. Maziarski, 'Nie słyszeli o plenum?', Polityka, no. 44 (1977).
20. Mały Rocznik Statystyczny 1977, p. 167; Rocznik Statystyczny 1981, p. 342.
21. Rocznik Statystyczny 1981, p. 299.
22. Ibid., pp. 590, 595.
23. Z Czesławem Bobrowskim o gospodarce rozmawia Maciej Wierzyński. Wywiady telewizyjne przeprowadzone od końca grudnia 1980 do początków marca 1981 (Książka i Wiedza, Warsaw, 1981), pp. 20-1.
24. Rocznik Statystyczny 1981, p. 454.

25. Ibid., p. 583 ff.

26. Ibid., p. 585. On the other hand Henryk Kisiel said the subsidies for the food complex had grown from 50,200 million zł to 287,000 million zł over the years 1970-9. Cf.: 35 lat gospodarki Polski Ludowej (Państwowe Wydawnictwo Ekonomiczne, Warsaw, 1979), p. 241.

27. 35 lat gospodarki Polski Ludowej, p. 247.

28. Rocznik Statystyczny 1981, p. 436.

29. Ibid., p. 590.

30. S. Jędrychowski, Zadłużenie Polski w krajach kapitalistycznych (Książka i Wiedza, Warsaw, 1982), p. 154.

31. Ibid., p. 35.

32. S. Grużewski, 'Specjalizacyjne niekonsekwencje', Polityka, no. 50 (1979).

33. Rocznik Statystyczny 1981, pp. 410, 419.

34. Ibid., pp. 415-17.

35. Warunki życia ludności 1980 (Główny Urząd Statystyczny, Warsaw, 1982), p. 103.

36. Ibid., p. 26.

37. Rocznik Statystyczny 1981, p. 76.

38. Ibid., pp. 54, 489.

39. J. Pajestka, Polski kryzys lat 1980-1981. Jak do niego doszło i co rokuje (Państwowe Wydawnictwo Ekonomiczne, Warsaw. 1981), p. 18.

40. W. Kuczyński, Po wielkim skoku, p. 161.

41. J. Pajestka, Polski kryzys, pp. 59-60.

BIBLIOGRAPHY

There are many books and articles in the Polish language concerning the economic development of Poland. Those that are quoted here will give an overall view of the most important questions, topics or periods. The literature in other languages - including English - is not so rich. We have tried to list here books and articles in English and to some degree in French, German and Italian which will provide the Reader with additional information or different views of the questions discussed in this book. We have tried, at the same time, to present the achievements of Polish historiography if published in the above languages. It is, however, not a complete bibliography of Polish economic history.

BIBLIOGRAPHIES AND REVIEWS

Davies, N. (1977) Poland, Past and Present. A Selected Bibliography of Works in English, Oriental Research Partners, Newtonville.

Janowska, H. (1973) 'Research on Economic Emigration', Acta Poloniae Historica, 27, 187-208.

Landau, Z. (1962) 'Polish Economy of the Years 1918-1939 in Polish Postwar Publications', Acta Poloniae Historica, 5, 141-63.

Landau, Z. (1973) 'Review of Works on the Economic History of the Second Republic Published in the Years 1962-1971', Acta Poloniae Historica, 28, 137-67.

La Pologne au XIIIe Congrès International des Sciences Historiques à Moscou (1970) 1-ère partie. La recherche historique en Pologne 1945-1968, rédigée par A. Wyczański, Państwowe Wydawnictwo Naukowe, Warszawa.

La Pologne au XIIIe Congrès International des Sciences Historiques à Moscou (1970) IIème partie,

Bibliographie sélective des travaux des historiens polonais parus dans les années 1945-1968, rèdigée par J. Tazbir, Państwowe Wydawnictwo Naukowe, Warszawa.

Tomaszewski, J. (1975) 'Historische Forschungen über die Struktur der Bevölkerung Polens im 19. und 20. Jahrhundert', _Jahrbuch für Wirtschaftsgeschichte_, _3_, 217-41.

STATISTICAL SOURCES

Basic Data on Socioeconomic Development of Poland (1961) Główny Urząd Statystyczny, Warszawa.

Concise Statistical Year-Book of Poland (1930-8) Główny Urząd Statystyczny, Warszawa.

Concise Statistical Year-Book of Poland (1941) Polish Ministry of Information, London.

Concise Statistical Year-Book of the Polish People's Republic (1959) Główny Urząd Statystyczny, Warszawa.

Ernst, M.C. (1965) _Indexes of Polish Industrial Production, 1937-1960_, Columbia University Press, New York.

Statistical Yearbook of Poland (1947-9) Główny Urząd Statystyczny, Warszawa.

STUDIES OF GENERAL CHARACTER OR CONCERNING LONG PERIODS

Bagiński, H. (1942) _Poland and the Baltic_, Oliver and Boyd, London.

Bobińska C. and Pilch, A. (eds.) (1975) _Employment-seeking Emigrations of the Poles World-wide, XIX and XX_, Universitas Iagellonica, Kraków.

The Cambridge History of Poland. From Augustus II to Piłsudski (1967-1935), the University Press, Cambridge, vol. 2, 1951.

Davies, N. (1982) _God's Playground. A History of Poland_. Vol. I _The Origins to 1795_. Vol. II _1795 to the Present_, Clarendon Press, Oxford.

Drozdowski, M.M. (1974) 'Urbanization in Poland in the Years 1870-1970', _Studia Historiae Oeconomicae_, _9_, 222-44.

Jędruszczak, H. (1968) 'Employment in Poland in 1930-1960. Dynamics and Structure', _Acta Poloniae Historica_, _18_, 250-63.

Gieysztor, A., Kieniewicz, S., Rostworowski, E. and Wereszycki, H., (1979) _History of Poland_, 2nd edn, Państwowe Wydawnictwo Naukowe, Warszawa.

Landau, Z. (1974) 'Comparative Research on the Long-Range Economic Growth of Poland (A Proposal Con-

cerning the Selection of States for Comparison)', Acta Poloniae Historica, 29, 111-36.
Landau, Z., Tomaszewski, J., (1970) Bank Handlowy w Warszawie S.A. History and Development 1870-1970, Bank Handlowy w Warszawie SA, Warszawa.
Leslie, R.F., Polonsky, A., Ciechanowski, J. M. and Pełczyński, Z.A. (1980) The History of Poland since 1863, Cambridge University Press, Cambridge.
Meyer, H. (1980) Standortverteilung der Produktion und regionale Wirtschaftsstrukturen in Polen vor 1945. Zur Vorgeschichte und zum Verlauf der 'verspäteten kapitalistischen Industrialisierung' mittel- und südeuropäischer Länder, Peter D. Lang, Frankfurt a. M./Bern/Cirencester.
Misztal, S. (1970) 'Changes in Distribution of Industry in the Area of Poland in the Years 1860-1965', Studia Historiae Oeconomicae, 5, 231-41.
Rose, W.J. (1948) Poland Old and New, G. Bell and Sons, London.
Taylor, J. (1952) The Economic Development of Poland 1919-1950, Cornell University Press, Ithaca, NY.
Tomaszewski, J. (1977) 'Some Problems of Capital Formation and Investments in the Capitalist Societies of East-Central Europe', Acta Poloniae Historica, 35, 145-69.
Zieliński, H. (1970) 'The Role of Silesia in Central Europe in the 19th and 20th Centuries', Acta Poloniae Historica, 22, 108-22.

1918-39

Carbone, M. (1976) La questione agraria in Polonia (1918-1939), Giannini Editore, Napoli.
Dewey, Ch. (1930) Combined Reprint of the Quarterly Reports of the Financial Adviser to the Polish Government, Bank Polski SA, Warsaw.
Drozdowski, M. (1963) Polityka gospodarcza rządu polskiego 1936-1939, Państwowe Wydawnictwo Naukowe, Warszawa.
Drozdowski, M.M. and Żarnowski, J. (1969) 'Die Sozialstrukturellen Veränderungen in der II Republik Polen', Studia Historiae Oeconomicae, 4, 47-79.
Górecki, R. (1935) Poland and Her Economic Development, Allen and Unwin, London.
Kagan, G. (1943) 'Agrarian Régime of Pre-War Poland', Journal of Central European Affairs, 3(3), 241-69.
Kofman, J. (1978) 'Das polnische Grosskapital und die allgemeinen Grundsätze der staatlichen Wirtschaftspolitik in den Jahren 1929 bis 1939. Konvergenzen und Divergenzen', Jahrbuch für

Wirtschaftsgeschichte, 3, 49-76.
Kruszewski, Ch. (1943) 'The German-Polish Tariff War (1925-34) and Its Aftermath', Journal of Central European Affairs, 3(3), 294-315.
Landau, Z. (1979) 'An Appraisal of Poland's Economic Development in 1918-1939', Oeconomica Polona, 3, 383-400.
- (1967) 'The Basic Trends of the Labour Market and Wages in Poland in the Years of Inflation (1918-1923)', Studia Historiae Oeconomicae, 2, 185-200.
- (1976) 'Le developpement de la legislation sur les cartels pendant la IIe Republique et la politique du Gouvernement vis-à-vis de ces associations', Studia Historiae Oeconomicae, 11, 119-40.
- (1978) 'The Extent of Cartelization of Industries in Poland, 1918-1939', Acta Poloniae Historica, 38, 147-70.
- (1974) 'The Foreign Loans of the Polish State in the Years 1918-1939', Studia Historiae Oeconomicae, 9, 281-97.
- (1973) 'The Great Depression in Poland (1929-1935) and Its Consequences', Studia Historiae Oeconomicae, 8, 337-54.
- (1977) 'Impact of the May 1926 Coup on the State of Polish Economy', Acta Poloniae Historica, 35, 169-87.
- (1981) 'Industrial Recession in Poland 1924-1925', Acta Poloniae Historica, 43, 171-94.
- (1982) 'The Inflow of Foreign Capital into Poland after the Coup d'État of May 1926', Acta Poloniae Historica, 46, 159-77.
- (1965) 'The Influence of Foreign Capital upon the Polish Economy of 1918-1939' in La Pologne au XIIe Congrès International des Sciences Historiques a Vienne, Państwowe Wydawnictwo Naukowe, Warszawa, pp. 133-45.
- (1983) 'Inflation in Poland after World War I' in Schmukler, N. and Marcus, E. (eds), Inflation through the Ages: Economic, Social, Psychological and Historical Aspects, Brooklyn College Press, New York, pp. 510-23.
- (1976) 'National Income in Historical Research On Material from the Period of Interwar Poland', Acta Poloniae Historica, 33, 93-119.
- (1939) 'Poland and America: The Economic Connection 1918-1939', Polish-American Studies, 2, 36-50.
- (1969) 'Poland's Economy Against the Background of World Economy; 1913-1938 (General Remarks)', Acta Poloniae Historica, 20, 75-93.
- (1963) 'Polish Countryside in the Years 1929-1935', Acta Poloniae Historica, 9, 28-47.

- (1973) 'Polish Village as a Market for Industry in the Period of the Great Depression', Studia Historiae Oeconomicae, 7, 171-88.
- (1966) 'Quelques problémes économiques des relations polono-américaines en 1918-1920', Studia Historiae Oeconomicae, 3, 201-20.
- (1968) 'The Reconstruction of Polish Industry after World War I', Acta Poloniae Historica, 18, 238-49.

Landau, Z.and Tomaszewski, J. (1977) Druga Rzeczpospolita. Gospodarka, społeczeństwo, miejsce w świecie (sporne problemy badań), Książka i Wiedza, Warszawa.
- (1982) Gospodarka Polski międzywojennej 1918-1939 w czterech tomach. I, W dobie inflacji 1918-1923, Książka i Wiedza, Warszawa, 1967. II, Od Grabskiego do Piłsudskiego. Okres kryzysu poinflacyjnego i ożywienia koniunktury 1924-1929, Książka i Wiedza, Warszawa, 1971. III, Wielki kryzys 1930-1935, Książka i Wiedza, Warszawa, 1982. IV, Lata interwencjonizmu państwowego 1936-1939 (in preparation).
- (1964) Kapitały obce w Polsce 1918-1939. Materiały i dokumenty, Książka i Wiedza, Warszawa.
- (1981) 'The International Movement of Capital in Central and South-East Europe before the Second World War' in Assorodobraj-Kula, N., Bobrowski, C., Hagemejer, H., Kula, W. and Łoś, J., Studies in Economic Theory and Practice. Essays in Honor of Edward Lipiński, North-Holland Publishing Company, Amsterdam/New York/Oxford, pp. 20-37.
- (1971) Robotnicy przemysłowi w Polsce. Materialne warunki bytu 1918-1939, Książka i Wiedza, Warszawa.
- (1981) Zarys historii gospodarczej Polski 1918-1939, 4th edn, Książka i Wiedza, Warszawa.

Mieszczankowski, M. (1960) Struktura agrarna Polski międzywojennej, Państwowe Wydawnictwo Naukowe, Warszawa.

Orczyk, J. (1969) 'The Main Features of the Agricultural Crisis in Poland in the Years 1929-1935', Studia Historiae Oeconomicae, 3, 221-41.
- (1972) 'Profitability of Agricultural Farms in the Years 1929-1937', Studia Historiae Oeconomicae, 7, 141-58.

Pologne 1918-1939, vol. 1, Vie politique et sociale, vol. 2, Vie économique, Éditions de la Baconnière, Neuchatel (1946).

Puchert, B. (1963) Der Wirtschaftskrieg des deutschen Imperialismus gegen Polen 1925-1934, Akademie-Verlag, Berlin.

Rakowski, J. (1938) The Polish Central Industrial Zone Scheme, The Baltic Institute, Gdynia.
Tomaszewski, J. (1968) 'The National Structure of the Working Class in the South-Eastern Part of Poland (1918-1939)', Acta Poloniae Historica, 19, 89-111.
- (1970) 'Die polnisch-sowjetische Handelsbeziehungen in den Jahren 1920-1929', Studia Historiae Oeconomicae, 5, 266-86.
Wellisz, L. (1938) Foreign Capital in Poland, Allen and Unwin, London.
Zweig, F. (1944) Poland Between Two Wars. A Critical Study on Social and Economic Change, Secker and Warburg, London.
Żarnowski, J. (1973) Społeczeństwo Drugiej Rzeczypospolitej 1918-1939, Państwowe Wydawnictwo Naukowe, Warszawa.

1939-45

Jastrzębowski, W. (1946) Gospodarka niemiecka w Polsce 1939-1944, Czytelnik, Warszawa.
Łuczak, Cz. (1978) 'Die Ansiedlung der deutschen Bevölkerung im besetzten Polen (1939-1945)', Studia Historiae Oeconomicae, 13, 193-203.
- (1976) 'Basic Assumptions of the Economic Policies of Nazi Germany and their Implementation in the Occupied Poland', Studia Historiae Oeconomicae, 11, 193-213.
- (1968) 'The Deportation of the Polish Population by the Occupation Nazi Authorities in the Years 1939-1945', Studia Historiae Oeconomicae, 3, 243-54.
- (1970) 'Mobilisierung und Ausnutzung der polnischen Arbeitskraft für den Krieg', Studia Historiae Oeconomicae, 5, 303-13.
- (1977) 'Nazi Spatial Plans in Occupied Poland (1939-1945), Studia Historiae Oeconomicae, 12, 153-9.
- (1969) 'Plunder of Polish Property in the Polish Territories Occupied by Germany and 'Incorporated into the Reich' (1939-1945)', Studia Historiae Oeconomicae, 4, 171-9.
- (1972) 'La politique agraire des autorités hitlériennes dans le 'Pays de la Warta' au cours de la seconde guerre mondiale', Studia Historiae Oeconomicae, 7, 189-98.
- (1979) Polityka ludnościowa i ekonomiczna hitlerowskich Niemiec w okupowanej Polsce, Wydawnictwo Poznańskie, Poznań.
- (1974) 'Recrutement d'ouvriers sur les territoires Polonais pour les travaux forcés dans le Reich

au temps de l'occupation hitlérinenne', Studia Historiae Oeconomicae, 9, 299-311.
- (1979) 'Die Wirtschaftspolitik des Drittes Reiches im besetzten Polen', Studia Historiae Oeconomicae, 14, 87-103.
Madajczyk, Cz. (1970) Polityka III Rzeszy w okupowanej Polsce, vols. 1, 2, Państwowe Wydawnictwo Naukowe, Warszawa.
- (1973) 'Principes généraux et caractère des transferts de population opérés par les nazis', Studia Historiae Oeconomicae, 8, 3-34.
Mańkowski, Z. (1973) 'L'action nazie d'expulsion et de colonisation dans la région de Zamość (modèle ou improvisation)', Studia Historiae Oeconomicae, 8, 169-86.
Seeber, E. (1964) Zwangsarbeiter in der faschistischen Kriegswirtschaft, VEB Verlag der Wissenschaften, Berlin.
Sobczak, J. (1973) 'Transfert au Reich des Allemands pendant la deuxième guerre mondiale et son rapport avec la déportation de la population polonaise', Studia Historiae Oeconomicae, 8, 187-212.
Tillmann, H. (1969) 'Zu einigen wirtschaftlichen, politischen und kulturellen Aspekten der "Deutschtum" - Politik des deutschen Imperialismus gegenüber Polen', Studia Historiae Oeconomicae, 4, 123-40.

1945-80

Alton, Th. P. (1955) Polish Postwar Economy, Columbia University Press, New York.
Beksiak, J. (1982) Zmiany w gospodarce, Państwowe Wydawnictwo Naukowe, Warszawa.
Bromke, A. and Strong, J.W. (eds.) (1973) Gierek's Poland, Frederick A. Praeger Publishers, New York.
Drewnowski, J. (ed.) (1982) Crisis in the East European Economy. The Spread of the Polish Disease, Croom Helm, London and Canberra, St Martin's Press, New York.
Fallenbuchl, Z.M. (1977) 'The Polish Economy in the 1970s' in Hardt, J.P. (ed.), East European Economies Post-Helsinki, Joint Economic Committee of the US Congress, Washington.
- (1973) 'Industrial Structure and the Intensive Pattern of Development Poland', Jahrbuch der Wirtschaft Osteuropa, 4, 27-45.
Feiwel, G.R. (1971) Poland's Industrialisation Policy: A Current Analysis, Praeger, New York.
- (1971) Problems in Polish Economic Planning: Continuity, Change and Prospects, Praeger, New York.

Flakierski, H. (1973) 'The Polish Economic Reform of 1970', Canadian Journal of Economics, 6(1), 1-15.
Gołębiowski, J.W. (1967) 'Nationalization of Industry in Poland', Studia Historiae Oeconomicae, 2, 209-32.
Jezierski, A. (1980) 'The Stages of Economic Development in Post-war Poland. The Problems of Investment Oscillations', Studia Historiae Oeconomicae, 15, 49-54.
Jezierski, A. and Landau, Z. (1970) 'The Directions of the Economic Development of People's Poland in the Years 1944-1969', Studia Historiae Oeconomicae, 5, s.329-49.
Jezierski, A. and Petz, B. (1980) Historia gospodarcza Polski ludowej 1944-1975, Państwowe Wydawnictwo Naukowe, Warszawa.
Jędruszczak, H. (1972) 'Land Reform and Economic Development in the People's Democracies of Europe', Studia Historiae Oeconomicae, 7, 199-211.
- (1974)'Die soziale Struktur der Stadtbevölkerung in der VR Polen (1944-1970)', Studia Historiae Oeconomicae, 9, 313-28.
- (1970) 'Der Wiederaufbau der Industrie in Polen nach dem 2. Weltkrieg', Studia Historiae Oeconomicae, 5, 315-28.
Karpiński, A. (1964) Twenty Years of Poland's Economic Development 1944-1964, Polonia Publishing House, Warsaw.
- (1968) Zarys rozwoju gospodarczego Polski ludowej. Fazy rozwoju, 2nd edn, Książka i Wiedza, Warszawa.
Kersten, K. (1968) 'International Migrations in Poland after World War II', Acta Poloniae Historica, 19, 49-68.
- (1975) 'The New Territorial Shape of the Polish State and Evolution of Political Attitudes of Polish Society (1944-1948)', Acta Poloniae Historica, 31, 119-50.
- (1964) 'The Transfer of German Population from Poland in 1945-1947 (on the Example of West Pomerania)', Acta Poloniae Historica, 10, 27-47.
Korboński, A. (1960) Politics of Socialist Agriculture in Poland, 1945-1960, Columbia University Press, New York.
Kostrowicka, I. (1974) 'Stages of the Development of Agriculture in People's Poland', Studia Historiae Oeconomicae, 9, 329-41.
Landau, Z. (1977) 'Monetary Reforms in the Polish Territories in 1945', Studia Historiae Oeconomicae, 12, 175-90.
- (1965)'Le politique monétaire du Comité Polonais

de Liberation Nationale (juillet 1944-janvier 1945)', Acta Poloniae Historica, 12, 66-86.
- (1970) 'The Rate of Growth of the Economy in People's Poland', Acta Poloniae Historica, 21, 5-24.
- (1979) 'Were Banks Nationalized in People's Poland?', Acta Poloniae Historica, 40, 153-74.
Landau, Z. and Tomaszewski J., (1978) 'Stages of the Economic Growth of Poland after 1944', Studia Historiae Oeconomicae, 13, 207-20.
Lane, D. and G. Kolankiewicz (eds.) (1973) Social Groups in Polish Society, Macmillan, London.
Lipiński, E. (1955) Development of Agriculture and Industry, 'Polonia' Foreign Languages Publishing House, Warsaw.
Markiewicz, Wł. (1965) 'L'aménagement des territoires occidentaux de la Pologne 1945-1965' in La Pologne au XIIe Congrès International des Sciences Historiques á Vienna, Państwowe Wydawnictwo Naukowe, Warszawa, pp. 147-62
Montias, J.H. (1962) Central Planning in Poland, Yale University Press, New Haven.
Nasiłowski, M. (1973) 'Le développement économique de la Pologne au cours des années 1950-1970. Essai d'analyse globale', Revue de l'Est, 4(3), 27-47.
Orczyk, J. (1974) 'Factors Affecting Differences of Agricultural Productivity (in Particular Voivodships) in People's Poland in the Years 1945-1970', Studia Historiae Oeconomicae, 9, 343-62.
Pawlak, W. (1972) 'La formation de la structure agraire en Pologne Populaire (1944-1970)', Studia Historiae Oeconomicae, 7, 213-28.
Piesowicz, K. (1975) 'Les facteurs sociaux dans l'evolution démographique de la Pologne dans les années 1945-1970', Acta Poloniae Historica, 31, 87-118.
- (1983) 'Social and Demographic Consequences of World War II and the German Occupation in Poland', Oeconomica Polona, 1, 65-94.
Rosset, E. (1967) 'Demography of the New Poland', Acta Poloniae Historica, 16, 109-37.
Turowski, J. and Szwengrub, L. (eds.) (1976) Rural Social Change in Poland, Zakład Narodowy im. Ossolińskich Wydawnictwo, Wrocław.
Schechtman, J.B. (1949) 'The Polish-Soviet Exchange of Population', Journal of Central European Affairs, 9(3), 289-314.
Słabek, H. (1976) 'At the Origins of the Social Structure of Rural Areas in the Western and Northern Territories of People's Poland', Acta Poloniae Historica, 33, 121-39.
- (1966) 'Grundsätze der Agrarreformen in den

sozialistischen Ländern (1944-1948)', Studia Historiae Oeconomicae, 1, 187-209.
- (1970) 'Les transformations sociales en Pologne Populaire', Acta Poloniae Historica, 21, 25-41.
Szarota, T. (1970) 'Les problèmes du peuplement et de l'taménagemen des territoires recouvrés', Acta Poloniae Historica, 21, 42-52.
Szczepański, J.V. (1970) Polish Society, Random House, New York.
Yakowicz, J.V. (1979) Poland's Postwar Recovery. Economic Reconstruction, Nationalization and Agrarian Reform in Poland After World War II, Exposition Press, Hickville, NY.
Zieliński, J.G. (1973) Economic Reforms in Polish Industry, Oxford University Press, London.
Zyzniewski, S.J. (1959) 'Coal in Poland's Economy and Foreign Trade', Journal of Central European Affairs, 19(3), 260-75.

INDEX